Kyiv, Ukraine

Kyiv, Ukraine

The City of Domes and Demons from the Collapse of Socialism to the Mass Uprising of 2013-2014

Roman Adrian Cybriwsky

Amsterdam University Press

Cover illustration: Evelina Beketova

Cover design: Coördesign, Leiden
Layout: Crius Group, Hulshout

Amsterdam University Press English-language titles are distributed in the US and Canada by the University of Chicago Press.

ISBN   978 90 8964 664 4
e-ISBN   978 90 4852 340 5 (pdf)
e-ISBN   978 90 4852 341 2 (ePub)
NUR   906

To my parents Dr. Alex Cybriwsky (1914-1996) and Myroslava (Baczynska) Cybriwsky (1914-2014). They were the first to teach me about Ukraine. Also in fond memory of Wilbur Zelinsky (1921-2013), the most cultured of cultural geographers. He taught me about doing fieldwork up close and about social conscience in geography. In honor as well of the heroic Nebesna Sotnya, the "Hundred in Heaven" who paid the ultimate sacrifice for Ukraine in February, 2014, during the Euromaidan protests in Kyiv. Their memory will live forever.

Table of Contents

List of Illustrations and Tables

List of Illustrations

List of Tables

A Note about Transliteration

The transliteration of the Ukrainian language to the Roman alphabet follows the Ukrainian national system that was codified in 1996. The exceptions are in cases where people's names are spelled differently because that is how they themselves write them. Thus, I write names that had already been transliterated in the manner in which they appeared in my sources, which in some cases originate with the individuals themselves, and transliterated or transcribed names that I encountered only in Ukrainian or Russian according to the official Ukrainian system. With the exception of "Ukraine," which is not normally transliterated as Ukraina or Ukrayina, I follow the Ukrainian national system for geographical names. Thus, we have Kyiv instead of the Russian-based Kiev, and Dnipro for Kyiv's river instead of Dnieper or Dnepr. To the extent that I am capable, I use the same system as well for transliteration of book titles, etc., in the bibliography, and for transliteration and transcription of direct quotations and Ukrainian words in the text.

For those who might be interested, my own family name is Ukrainian and is spelled Tsybrivskyi according to the official system. That is how relatives in Ukraine on my father's side romanize it. However, I use only Cybriwsky, the way the name was spelled on documents when my parents were registered as "displaced persons" in the wake of World War II and became immigrants to the United States with me and a sister in tow.

Preface and Acknowledgements

My final edits for this book are being prepared during an extraordinarily tumultuous time in Ukrainian history. After nearly three months of mass protests that began in November, 2013, the spectacularly corrupt and highly unpopular president of the country, Viktor Fedorovych Yanukovych, a major character in this book, was chased from office and is in hiding, probably in Russia. He is reported to have sailed there from Crimea on his personal yacht, which has the ironic name *Bandido*. His closest cronies in the Party of Regions that he headed are gone too, probably also to Russia and other countries, because of corruption and other criminal charges that they face. A new provisional government made up of Euromaidan (the name of the protest movement) activists is in charge until nationwide elections can take place. However, the victory for Euromaidan was at great cost, as more than 100 civilians were killed when the government stormed their encampment. The largest number of deaths occurred during February 18-20, 2014, in fires that were started by Berkut forces (an elite anti-riot unit), and from fire by government snipers positioned atop tall buildings and hillocks around Independence Square, the main protest venue. The victims of Euromaidan are referred to collectively as Nebesna Sotnya, the "Hundred in Heaven" or "Heaven's Battalion," and are regarded by most Ukrainians as heroes.

No sooner were these victims buried when, in the wake of the closing ceremonies of the 2014 winter Olympics in Sochi, Russia, armed Russian forces seized control of the Crimean Peninsula, sovereign Ukrainian territory with a large Russian-speaking population. The ostensible purpose, as explained by Russian President Vladimir Putin without supporting evidence, was to protect Russians from hostile Ukrainians. There are ongoing Russian incursions at this time as well in Donetsk, Kharkiv, and other cities near the international border, and casualties among Ukrainian civilians. As a result, there is the threat of war between Ukraine and Russia, and a rekindling of the Cold War between Russia and the democracies of the West. Atop all that is a serious financial crisis in Ukraine, as well as continued stoking by both sides of religious, ethnic, and language tensions between Ukraine's Ukrainian and Russian-speaking citizens, and an unfortunate shortage of good leadership with a clear and popular vision for the country. And so, no one knows what the future will bring, disaster is entirely possible, and the country is on edge.

Regardless of what eventually happens, I think that this book will help the reader understand why Ukrainians became so angry. I saw during my research in Kyiv and on my travels through Ukraine that there is too much poverty in a country that is rich with resources and superb farmland, and that too many good people are truly hurting. Furthermore, where there was once at least a semblance of equality under socialism, there is now glaring inequality, as the wealth of the nation has been appropriated by a new class of oligarch billionaires and exported to offshore banks and luxury offshore residences and yachts. Instead of my own anger, I have strived to convey that of Ukraine with my writing, and if you sense it in this book, then I will have succeeded as a reporter. A great many citizens for whom Kyiv is home shared their pains with me, and many of those who knew that I was working on a book urged me to write swiftly, before it was too late, and to explain what was going on. I was urged to not hold back. *"V Ukraini nemaye poryadku!"* summarizes what people say now, 23 years after independence: "In Ukraine there is no order" or "Ukraine is in disarray." The same holds for Kyiv. Some informants even begged with tears for me to tell the city's story. I strive to be their voice, as I also strive to be fair and balanced, and to back up what I say with data, specific examples, and my own close-up observations.

Thus, this book is both reportage and ethnography, at least in many parts, and tells what I saw and heard during fieldwork in the city. If I seem overly strident at times, it is because I convey the stridency of many informants from all levels of society and all walks of life. To a man or woman, without a single exception other than those closely and officially affiliated with the Party of Regions, the political party that held power in Ukraine until the latest events, Kyiv's citizens were extraordinarily critical about where they see Ukraine headed and skeptical about her prospects. Many professed great fondness for Kyiv despite the problem and see it as tragically emblematic of the country's mess. Public opinions poll in the country support my assessment. I came to understand the cause that many Kyivans share, which is to save a great city, and became a believer. It is for them that I strive to write a book. I hope to accurately reflect their concerns and to write something that is interesting and credible for readers who do not know Kyiv (or Ukraine) and who do not have a direct stake in its future.

This book was written during the administration of President Viktor Fedorovych Yanukovych, the fourth president of independent Ukraine. He assumed office on February 25, 2010, after winning an election that almost certainly had a fair share of vote rigging in his favor. The bulk of my research was done during his administration as well. Therefore, Yanukovych comes under particular scrutiny in this book, as does his political party, the Party of Regions. Because in Ukraine the president has (taken) very great powers, including considerable influence over the administration of the city of Kyiv and, in turn, over city planning and land development even though he himself is not a Kyivan, Yanukovych figures especially heavily in this book, much more so than would, say, a president of the United States in a book about an American city, even about Washington, DC. Necessarily, I look at Yanukovych not just with respect to his policies for Kyiv and Ukraine, but also personally. He has chosen to consume a disproportionate amount of space in the city, even in comparison to his three predecessors, and has implemented questionable personal construction projects that impact the fundamental geography of Kyiv and its iconic urban image. After reflection, I agree with informants that there is much to criticize about Yanukovych's treatment of Kyiv, and do so in the pages ahead based on what I was told and shown, what I read about in both the free and controlled press, and most especially, what I saw with my own eyes. Even though the criticisms are harsh and include a separate section that I have called "A Geography of the President," I am convinced that they are accurate and are deserved. Had I written this book earlier during another presidential administration, then I would have been critical of either Leonid Makarovych Kravchuk, the first president (in office December 5, 1991, to July 19, 1994), his successor, Leonid Danylovych Kuchma (July 19, 1994, to January 23, 2005), or the third president, the Orange Revolution's Viktor Andriyovych Yushchenko (January 23, 2005, to February 25, 2010), all of whom also raised the ire of Ukrainians for how they conducted their responsibilities and for what they allowed to take place in Kyiv. Good government has not been one of Ukraine's strengths.

This is not my first book about urban change. I have been around a few years, have grey hair, and have worked in the past in various parts of the world. I've investigated gentrification and related urban transition in Philadelphia and other cities in the United States, in Vancouver in Canada, and then, with considerable production, in Tokyo, the fascinating and dynamic capital of Japan where I lived for many years. I have worked as well in Southeast Asia in Singapore, Jakarta, and Phnom Penh. This project in Kyiv is my first professional venture into Europe and into the worlds of socialist society, Soviet control, and centralized planning, and then the emergence of newly independent countries, turns to capitalism, and the uncertain paths of postsocialist urban restructuring. I apply my earlier experience at studying cities to this project, plus a good knowledge of Ukrainian, which is the language my parents taught me, and Russian, which I studied a long time ago in college and then learned much better more recently, ironically, in Japan from a Russian-speaking Ukrainian resident who now lives in Ukraine again. Her name is Ilona Arkhangelska, and she is the first person I acknowledge by name because she has continued to provide me with insights into her country. I had been aware of Ukraine since childhood, since my immigrant parents made it a point to teach me as much as they could, and I had maintained an interest in the country all through my life. I chose not to focus my career on Ukraine because I had sensed as a young man that my Ukrainian-American ethnic community, as well as my family, would have expectations of me that I did not want to face, so I became a geographer of cities in other parts of the world instead. It is only now after many years of doing other things that I turn to the subjects that my parents had always wanted me to write about.

Although I had been to Kyiv several times before and have since been to the city several times more, often staying weeks at a time, the center of this project is the full year that I spent in the city as a Fulbright scholar. That was academic year 2010-2011, when I had a sabbatical from my long-time faculty position at Temple University in Philadelphia in order to write this book. During that time I was attached to the National University of Kyiv Mohyla Academy, one of Ukraine's best universities, and taught undergraduates and graduate students in the Department of Sociology. My classes became sounding boards for my ideas. For most of that time, I lived in a comfortable apartment in the very center of the city on a beautiful historic street named Horodetskoho after a famous architect. The street had previously been named Vulytsya Karla Marksa (Karl Marx Street) after an architect of different sorts. From that vantage point I had easy access to all directions in Kyiv and was at the doorstep of the city center, most notably Maidan Nezalezhnosti (Independence Square), where there were often concerts, demonstrations, political protests, and other events that helped me understand Ukraine. A building on my block had an exclusive shop on the ground floor that sold diamond jewelry, but above the door there was still a prominent stone relief of a crossed hammers symbol of communism and the Soviet Union. That combination was a constant reminder that I was studying a society in transition.

Later, on a longer return visit, I stayed for a while with a friend in a typical apartment in the far reaches of Troyeshchyna, a huge residential complex on the Left Bank that is famously far from any subway line, and then for a longer time in the very comfortable Art Hotel Baccara, a floating hotel that is moored on one of the banks of the Dnipro River. From the latter vantage, I was able to enjoy Kyiv's famous beaches and other recreation in

Hidropark (a large public park), and see Kyivans at play during a prolonged heat wave. I also met Kyivans who lived in the park out of necessity – poor people who had found for themselves a hideaway in the forest or in some old, abandoned facility from the Soviet period, much like the homeless who sleep on street-side benches or in derelict old buildings in the city center. It was during that time, too, that I gained a better appreciation for the natural environment of Kyiv, and for the famous bluffs of the city that stretched along the opposite bank of the river from my hotel room deck for nearly as far upstream and as far downstream as I could see. Several of the city's major landmarks, glorious in the day and beautifully lit at night, were my landscape neighbors, as were several new buildings on the bluffs that Kyivans refer to as "monsters" because they so poorly punctuate the historical profile of the city.

The methodology is straightforward. I spent as much time in Kyiv as I could, explored the city daily, walked endlessly, and talked to as many people as I could. I also read what I could in English, Ukrainian, and Russian, attended public forums and lectures about the city (and spoke at several myself), attended political events and public protests, visited museums, libraries, and art galleries, went to concerts, opera, and ballet, and sampled some of the ample (but clean) nightlife that Kyiv offers. I suppose that such activity qualifies the research as participant-observation. Even more than I did in Tokyo when writing my book about a controversial nightclub district, I avoided all places where I would not want to be with my adult children. Except for reporting on it from a distance, the famous sex-oriented nightlife of Kyiv did not interest me. My explorations of the city were supplemented by various interviews that I scheduled with key informants; mapping projects of my own such as of buildings in the city center by land use and visible condition, distributions of billboards by content, and the distribution of construction sites in fast-changing Podil; statistical data from the government of the city of Kyiv and other sources; examination of hundreds of historical maps and photos; and views of the city and its neighborhoods as provided via satellite images from above. In short, preparation of this book involved a range of methodologies and a sustained immersion in the city as I think good social geography requires.

There are quite a few footnotes and references in my text to news sources from Ukraine, especially those that publish in English (*Kyiv Post, Ukrainian Week*). I have included these not only to acknowledge the sources of some of my information, but even more so to provide a service to readers who might want to look for more information on a given topic. As this book is based mostly on field work, I include these various citations also to provide back-up to what I have observed myself. This is because some of what is described in *Kyiv, Ukraine* might look too weird to be true, and I want to document that others have also seen what I have seen.

After various permutations and numerous drafts (this file is version number 13 on my hard drive), I finally settled on a book with 12 chapters plus this preface and an epilogue. Each chapter is divided into 3 to 8 sections, with the total number of sections being 72. That means that some sections are quite short – no more than two or three pages in length. I choose to write this way because I personally prefer books that open many topics, even if briefly, and find that such reading is easier because one can opt to read about topics that interest one more and dismiss those that do not. The essays are also short because, in some cases, only so much can be said about a given topic. This is especially so for a city like Kyiv – a recently Soviet city for which the kinds of data about socioeconomic conditions, land use and development, and goings-on in local and national government that exist for urban areas in other parts of the world are simply not available. I would like to think that everyone who picks up this book will find something of interest from among the 72 relatively short essays. As much as is possible without continually redefining terms, I tried to make individual sections stand on their own so that they could be read in any order. Nevertheless, there is a broad flow to all 12 chapters, too, from topics that are general and provide background to those later that focus more on particular issues or problems, and from historical and geographical orientation to the city at the start to individual districts, individual construction projects, and individual people later on. I conclude the book with examples of activists who defend Kyiv and some of the remarkable fights that they have taken on. There is no "conclusion," because Kyiv after socialism is a work actively in progress, and is itself not concluded. Instead, I offer "reflections." I imagine that a writer about the reshaping of space and society in postsocialist Kharkiv, Odesa, Moscow, St. Petersburg, Irkutsk, Tbilisi, Baku, or Tashkent, to mention some other examples of former Soviet cities, might also say something similar. Finally, I want to say that I aim to be reader-friendly and to avoid the worst academic jargon, pretentious or invented words, unnecessary kowtows to writers of dense theory, and other annoying trappings of the academy today. I simply want to tell you about Kyiv.

* * *

I now turn to my acknowledgements, which by happy coincidence I am composing on an appropriate American holiday – Thanksgiving Day. In addition to the aforementioned Ilona, many people helped me with this book, enormously so, and I am deeply indebted. I begin with the 27 students I taught in an urban sociology class in Spring 2011 at the National University of Kyiv Mohyla Academy (NaUKMA). It was my first class at this venerable institution, and an experience that stands out as the most memorable and pleasant teaching experience in my career of more than 40 years. We spoke much about Kyiv during our seminars, and I learned a lot from these intelligent and eager young men and women. I can't name them all here, but note that the group was comprised of two male students (a Eugene and another Roman), and five Katyas, four Marias, and three Yulias among the 25 women. Roman Driamov, Maria Anchishkina, Maria Kuts, Yulia Mantrova, Dasha Pankratova, and Lily Chulitska deserve special thanks for going out of their way to be helpful. All 27 of them were wonderful, and I am happy to have my photo with them in this book. They, plus the one student who was absent on the day the photograph was taken, represent the future of Ukraine.

Likewise, I thank NaUKMA for hosting me during my Fulbright fellowship year in Kyiv, and especially the Sociology Department and its acting chair that year Olena Bogdanova, my faculty colleagues in Sociology, Volodymyr Ishchenko and Tamara Martsenyuk, Vice President for Foreign Cooperation Larysa Chovnyuk, and the very capable president of the university, Dr. Sergiy Kvit. I also benefited from being a frequent guest at the Visual Culture Research Center, where I attended many events and met numerous fascinating students, scholars, authors, and artists, including Olga Bryukhovetska, Oleksiy Radynski, Vasyl Cherepanyn, Nadia Parfan, and Anastasia Ryabchuk. Even though VCRC is no longer affiliated with NaUKMA, it remains a leading center of intellectual activity in Kyiv. I also benefited enormously from regular attendance at various conferences and workshops about Kyiv that were sponsored by the Heinrich Böll Foundation of Germany. For this, I am especially thankful to the foundation's officers in Kyiv, especially Dr. Kyryl Savin and Andrij Makarenko.

I also want to acknowledge the US Fulbright Commission for the research and lecturing fellowship that I was awarded, and the Fulbright director in Ukraine at the time, Dr. Myron Stachiw, an expert in architectural history with whom I shared many conversations about Kyiv. Myron's staff in the city, including Natalia Zalutska, Inna Barysh, Oksana Parafeniuk, and Anna Pasenko, was also very kind and helpful. I also thank Temple University for the sabbatical year from my faculty position, the Department of Geography and Urban Studies where I am based, and the department chair at the time, Dr. Sanjoy Chakravorty, who signed on the dotted line when it was needed. Sanjoy has been especially supportive of this book project from the beginning to the end, and is a close professional colleague about cities, book writing, and the politics of university life. Drs. David Ley (University of British Columbia) and John C. Western (Syracuse University) have also been greatly supportive, especially at times when I felt discouraged. Finally, also from the North American side of the Atlantic, I offer special thanks to two Ukraine-expert Americans who were kind enough to offer insightful criticisms and superb suggestions from an earlier version of this book: Dr. Alexander Motyl of Rutgers University in Newark, NJ, and author of the widely read blog "Ukraine's Orange Blues," and Dr. Blair Ruble, Director of the Woodrow Wilson Center's Program on Global Sustainability and Resilience, and author of books about Kyiv, Leningrad, and Yaroslavl. They, along with John Western and Sanjoy Chakravorty, helped me through the process of selecting a publisher. From Amsterdam University Press, I single out Saskia Gieling, my editor Marjolijn Voogel, Magdalena Hernas, Valeria Mecozzi, Atie Vogelenzang-De Jong, Daniela Pinnone, and my sharp-eyed copy editor, Jaap Wagenaar, for special thanks. It has been a pleasure to work with such a highly professional team.

The list of people who helped me in Kyiv is especially long, and it includes fellow academics, architects, city planners, and others who work on the problems of the city, civic activists, and numerous life-long and short-term residents of Kyiv of various ages, ethnicities, occupations, and social standing. It is not possible to name them all, but I can start the list with super thanks to super friends Tamara Martsenyuk, Svitalana Slipchenko, and Natalia Moussienko for their special support, professional advice, and intelligent insights, and then continue in alphabetical order with thanks to Anna Andrievska, Müge Atala, Iryna Bondarenko, Kateryna Botanova, Sasha Burlaka, Olena Dmytryk, Oksana Dutchak, Marta Dyczok, Ilko Gladshtein, Oleksandr Glukhov, Oleksandr Hudyma, Mykola Ilchuk, Rev. Mykola Ilnytskyi, Anna Khvyl, Iryna Koshulap, Vitaliy Kovalinskiy, Ihor Lutsenko, Andrew Mac, Alla Marchenko, Maria Mayerchyk, Taras Myronyuk, Varvara Podnos, Raphi Rechitsky, Olena Reshetnyak, Yulia Soroka, Inna Sovsun, Catherine Stecyk, Lou Urenek, Andrea Wenglowskyj, Viktor Zagreba, Zenon Zawada, and Maxym Zayika. Furthermore, I am indebted to Evelina Beketova for generous permission to use one of her bright and happy paintings of Kyiv for the design of the cover of this book. In addition to that work, I am fortunate to own two other of her urban portraits and recommend that readers who are interested should look her up by name on the Internet. All the other photographs in this book are my own except for Figure 2.1, which is reproduced via the graces of Vitaliy Kovalinskiy, Figure 3.3 for which I am indebted to Alexander J. Motyl, Figures 6.4 and 11.3 (right), were provided to me by Vladyslava Osmak, and Figure 11.4, which Viktor Kruk kindly allowed me to use. I thank these individuals for their additions to this book.

Three Kyivans merit the most special recognition. Dr. Lyudmyla Males, a sociologist at the Kyiv National Taras Shevchenko University, guided me personally through unfamiliar parts of Kyiv, introduced me to Ukrainian literature and websites about the city, and put me in touch with many individuals who became key informants, new sources of information, and new personal friends. I am deeply indebted to her and am proud to have her as a close professional associate and friend. The same is true for Nadia Parfan. A native of Ivano-Frankivsk, she is a PhD student in Cultural Studies at NaUKMA and was actually the first person in Kyiv with whom I had contact about this project. She, too, was a local guide and door opener for me, and a great friend. I was especially blessed to have her nearby in Philadelphia when she was a Fulbright scholar in my department during the year that I was writing and revising this manuscript. Not only did she help me with Kyiv, she learned Philadelphia at lightning speed and inspired me with original insights to my own home city that form a basis for a possible next book project. Finally, there is Vladyslava Osmak. She is also affiliated with NaUKMA, is a talented historian of Kyiv and professional tour guide, and a dedicated activist in support of Kyiv. She helped me immensely with answers to my questions, access to information and photographs, and unfailing support for this project. Without such friends, there can be no book.

Lyudmyla, Nadia, and Vladyslava are forever within a warm circle of other close friends and family that I want to acknowledge as well: Anna-Maria Yanchak, Olya Yanchak, my brother Zenon Cybriwsky and sisters Anna Skubiak and Christina Jermihov, George Baran, Ekaterina Korobova, Elena Shpak, Elena Rodin, Rickie Sanders, Robert Mason, Anne Shlay, Yulia Mosiakina, Ruslana Havrylyshyn, Rev. Myron Myronyuk, Rachel Wandless, Anastasia Aleksiayuk, my daughter Mary Cybriwsky, Chad Koch, my sons Adrian and Alex Cybriwsky, and my daughter-in-law Natalia Vibla. They have all taken care of this old widower and his health, and despite my ways have been kind, loving, and sensible, and believers in this project. Finally, I thank the people of Kyiv, too. Theirs is a great city. I applaud them for standing up to the demons who would destroy it and their country, and I pray for their success in building a just and prosperous society.

Figure 0.1　The author and 26 of his 27 students at Kyiv Mohyla Academy, May 2011, plus Peter

1   Far from Heaven

1.1   A Curious Face

When Kyiv is stripped of its roads, buildings, bridges, and other man-made features and is seen from up high in satellite view, it is said to resemble the face of God in profile. At least that is the central argument of a somewhat wacky but surprisingly interesting 2010 book entitled *Kyiv: Sviaschennyi Prostir* (Kyiv: Sacred Space) by two environmentalists/landscape architects: V.V. Kolin'ko and H.K. Kurovskyi. The photograph at the start of the book is quite striking in this regard: we see very clearly the face of a handsome man faithfully outlined by the combination of the right bank of the Dnipro River where Kyiv was founded, the contours of high bluffs that face the river, the other hills of the city, and its various deep ravines and stream valleys. When we add place-names to the photograph, we see that the district called Pechersk and its ancient monastery, Pecherska Lavra, form the forehead, Stare Misto (Old City) shapes the left eye and eyebrow, while the centuries-old church of St. Sophia, still the central-most historical landmark in Kyiv, is the iris. St. Michael's Church, also a prominent architectural landmark, is between the bridge of the nose and the forehead. We also see that the nose itself is the storied river-flat neighborhood of Podil, that the highlands of Sirets form the contours of the chin, and that the contours of the ear are shaped by the uplifted topography of Sovki and the network of small ponds that are located between Sovki's hills. It's bizarre, and anyone who knows Kyiv should be awed.

   On the other hand, we have to remember that stripping a satellite photograph of man-made features means manipulating that photograph so that only selected natural features are shown. Who knows what other enhancements were made in the process? Some strategic selection of orientation with respect to cardinal directions and colors for the photo at the outset, a dash of extra shading here, a deeper ravine there, and an inconvenient highland or stream course subdued or removed from some other place, and we have a human face. With more manipulation, we could perhaps present the city as a *kolach* (traditional Ukrainian braided ring-shaped bread) or as the face of a healthy Ukrainian sunflower. Incredibly, there is no explanation about how the book's key photograph was created. Also, there are no references of any kind whatsoever in the book, so we have to take it on faith from Kolin'ko and Kurovskyi that the face that we see is that of God and not, say, that of Peter the Great, famous czar of Russia, or one of

Ukraine's two world boxing champions, the brothers Vitalyi and Vladimir Klitschko. We also would need to accept the authors' assumption that God is male and has European features.

Why bother mentioning such a book? Because the rest of it is brilliant. Even if we dismiss completely the authors' premise that Kyiv is sacred space because it the face of God on earth, we can agree with them about what follows: it is wrong to wantonly destroy natural environments; urban development and construction based on greed and selfish motives are immoral; and urban planning and modernization efforts should always respect both nature and the historical heritage of a city. Today's Kyiv is badly wanting on all these counts, the authors argue, and needs a gentler, greener, and more sustainable approach for growth, expansion, and redevelopment to avoid environmental and cultural disaster. For example, the poor construction practices that are now underway near the city's center will hasten the erosion of the high bluffs along the river and will eventually cause ancient churches and other landmarks to tumble, while the filling in of streams and ponds for highways, new shopping malls, and upscale condominium towers provides a weak foundation for urban development and invites subsidence and collapse. These are warnings worth heeding, I think, because Kyiv is indeed being recklessly developed. We will see countless examples of the city's construction demons in action in the chapters ahead, as well as examples of the demons of increasing inequality and injustice in contemporary Kyiv society. Whether these offenses are actually against the face of God is another matter.

Whether one considers the mangling of Kyiv to be offenses against the very face of God or not, anyone who has experienced the charms of the city should be angry about what is going on. Put simply, a great city with enormous potential to be one of the greatest capitals of Europe, in a country that is itself rich with potential, is, in many ways, being destroyed. The demons at work are a new, post-Soviet breed of corrupt business interests and politicians that care nothing for the city or Ukraine and who use their positions only to line their pockets. Meanwhile, the great majority of the Ukrainian people struggle with daily life; many are desperately poor. The city's proud history, which goes back to the glorious 10th-13th-century princely state of Kyivan Rus and even earlier, is being taken away as real estate developers hack away at historical architecture and sacred sites, and museums and cultural institutions are evicted from their premises by "raiders" (as they are called) who want their buildings. There is also significant environmental spoilage in a city that has been known for its beauty, and brazen takeover by those with connections of land in parks and at the riverfront, as well as of buildings, institutions, and workplaces all over the city that had once belonged to the people. Corruption is rampant, even if there have been marginal improvements, and there is still too little rule of law in a city with thugs with open palms in high office. Foreign investment is stifled because opening a business in Ukraine means that you will be asked for bribes. Many of the smartest people have emigrated. Such a mess defines this particular stage of urban transition in Kyiv from "socialist city" to "postsocialist" and is the focus of this book.

1.2   Graffito

We turn to a graffito. Like other cities, much of Kyiv is littered with wall writings (Parfan, 2010). Most of it is trash, but there are also occasional gems of skilled artistry, sharp social or political commentary, and unexpected canvases. An example of the latter is found near where I lived in the center of the city, deep below the surface under Independence Square, on the vertical risers of steps on Section 27 of one of the longest escalators in the world, one connecting the subway platforms of Khreshchatyk Station with the world outdoors. The message is on an up escalator, and the words are distributed neatly top to bottom on three adjacent risers: "UKRAINE IS FAR FROM HEAVEN" (Figure 1.1). Provided that no passengers are standing just there to block the message, riders who board the escalator below Section 27 can read and ponder these words for the full 2 minutes and 26 seconds that they and the graffito jointly ascend heavenward. The words are in English. I asked my students at the National University of Kyiv Mohyla Academy, one of Ukraine's most prestigious universities, why they think that the writer chose English. Instantly, there was a consensus reply: "To tell the world. Ukrainians already know what a mess the country is." As we spoke further, we agreed that Kyiv is a mess as well, both on its own account and as a mirror of the country that it capitals.

1.3   A New American

Ukraine is a mess and its future is emigrating. Its citizens go abroad for short-term labor opportunities and as permanent migrants, and the nation's population is dropping. It had peaked at just over 52 million soon after Ukraine's independence in 1991, and then in combination with the impact of low birth rates, has been declining unswervingly year by year since 1994

Figure 1.1   "Ukraine Is Far from Heaven" graffito

to a total now of less than 46 million – a net loss of 12 percent in less than two decades. Remittances from abroad prop up not just individual families or villages in poor regions, but the economy as a whole, as at least 7 percent of the nation's workforce is employed beyond Ukraine. Neighboring Russia and Poland rank first and second in this regard, but Ukrainian workers are also very prominent in the Czech Republic, Portugal, Italy, and Spain, as well as in other EU countries, in North America, and in parts of Africa and the Middle East, notably Libya (medical personnel), Nigeria (oil and construction engineering), and Dubai (tourism economy). I met immigrants from Ukraine during my years living and working in Japan. As a whole, the emigration is both a brain drain and a labor drain, involving many of the best and brightest of the country, as well as many of the hardest-working individuals. The result is not only smaller population totals for Ukraine (peak in 1993 at 52.2 million; 2012 population at 45.6 million), but also a country that is poorer and more vulnerable to the demons who feed off what is left. In fact, there is so much emigration that black humor speaks of the need to turn off the lights at Kyiv's Boryspil Airport when the last Ukrainian departs.

My young friend "Nina" thinks that Ukraine is far from heaven, too. She was 17 when I met her in a Kyiv café where she worked and is now

20. Despite her youth, or perhaps precisely because of it, she was able to drive home for me precisely where the problems lie. She could be one of Ukraine's bratty spoiled rich kids, as her stepfather is a *narodnyi deputat,* one of 450 "national deputies" or members of Ukraine's notoriously inept and punch-happy parliament (see Chapter 3), and has all sorts of lucrative connections for a privileged life. I saw this to be true when I met Nina's mother and visited their spacious apartment on a high floor in Kyiv's tallest residential building. But Nina worked as a waitress when I met her; she did not want her stepfather's money and had a personal goal to break away. "My step-dad steals for a living," she explained to me, and then in the language of an angry teenager added this: "Sorry to say this, but he is a total piece of shit." She is completely disenchanted with the man her mother married and is looking to move abroad. She would like to study in the United States and then stay. And indeed, less than four months after that conversation, not long after she turned of age, I found Nina to be living and working in the geographic shadow of New York City. We have resumed our conversations. She is amazingly resourceful for a person her age, and managed to find a way to enter the country legally, expressed no desire to return home, and is exploring options for how to stay. I have no doubts that she will succeed in every endeavor. A collection of photographs on her Facebook site under the title "New Life" shows her as a new American. She no longer wants to speak to me in Ukrainian. Her English is excellent and that is what she uses. Her Russian remains strong because that was her first language and is the language of ties to her family, but Ukrainian, which she learned in school in her postindependence country, is being forgotten.

1.4   Domes and Demons

This is a book about Kyiv (formerly Kiev), the capital of Ukraine, the largest country that is wholly within the boundaries of Europe. According to official data, the city's population is 2,797,533 (2010), up about 8 percent from the year of independence (1991) total of 2,593,400, while that of the metropolitan area is about 3,648,000. However, everyone knows that counts based on residency permits and officially recorded addresses are way off, and that Kyiv is chock full of unregistered new migrants, circular migrants, temporary workers, sublet renters, and other newcomers who have arrived under the radar of the government's people counters, much like in a typical capital city in a developing country. Therefore, we have unofficial estimates that the true total is several hundred thousands more and that Kyiv may have as many 3.5 million inhabitants and the metropolitan area well over 4 million. Even at the lower total of 2.8 million, Kyiv is Europe's seventh-largest city (after Istanbul, Moscow, London, St. Petersburg, Berlin, and Madrid), larger than Rome and Paris (numbers 8 and 9, respectively), and would rank fifth at the higher estimate of 3.5 million. It would certainly be the city to name if asked which European city, whether it is a national capital or not, is the largest city about which least is written and about which least is known. That makes Kyiv Europe's biggest urban secret.

This book is not a history text, although that is also needed about Kyiv, but is rooted in an understanding of the past in order to take stock of what is going on in the city currently: an aggressive remaking of urban space for Ukraine's new elites at the expense of Kyiv's ordinary people and rich cultural and historic fabric. There is grossly inequitable appropriation of both private and public spaces such as parks for construction for the rich, the destruction of cultural and environmental heritage, and the debasement of normal urban life by an emerging layer of post-Soviet society that is self-obsessed, automobile-oriented, sexist, classist, and racist. Although trappings of success and urban progress are also prominent in the landscape and many citizens have, in fact, succeeded upwards, the reality for far too many others is that gaps between rich and poor in Kyiv have widened into chasms, and that most people struggle to make a living. Uncertainty looms large, and old ladies resort to selling radishes and flowers on the street to supplement their income. Kyiv, once a proud and beautiful city known for its ancient golden church domes and rich intellectual and cultural life, is now a city being devoured by the hard edge of capitalism and greed.

The subtitle "City of Domes and Demons" captures the essence of what is taking place, i.e., that in Kyiv we have (1) a beautiful city with a rich and proud history that can be symbolized by iconic golden church domes; and (2) a city that once again is being devoured by demons. This time, however, instead of armies of Mongols or Tatars on horseback, invading Nazis, or the murderous Joseph Stalin, all of whom had brought their distinctive combinations of death and destruction to the city, we now have demons of destructive urban development and "monster construction," demons of social injustice, and demons of sexism and sex tourism, among others. As opposed to invasions or colonialism from abroad, there are now domestic demons aplenty, some of whom are in the highest positions of government. That includes President Viktor Yanukovych and his *banda* (gang) of Party of Regions associates, as they are called by their many critics. We will meet some of these people in power personally in later chapters, as well as those who oppose them. The new destroyers have been running rampant since the fall of the communist state (and even earlier), and continue to mangle a great city and the lives of its people. It was even worse in the old Soviet Union and, indeed, most citizens do not miss that regime in the slightest as there are so many new freedoms – the freedom to pray, to choose among political parties, to speak out, and to emigrate, among others. However, the inexcusable inequalities of life after socialism, the disorder and corruption of today's Ukraine, the chaotic free-for-all that now mars urban growth and development in Ukraine's beautiful and historic capital city, as well as concomitant erosions of some of the new freedoms, are all aspects of a deep, post-Soviet downside that need to be explicated.

What we have, then, is a case study of unhappy urbanism in a struggling country after the fall of the Soviet Union. A similar social geography is evolving simultaneously in Moscow, St. Petersburg, Odesa (formerly Odessa), Dnipropetrovsk, and other cities in Russia and Ukraine, as well as in Minsk, Riga, Tbilisi, Baku, and Tashkent in other post-Soviet countries. The only variable is the degree of blatant social inequality and heritage destruction in these cities. The Kyiv story also stands in, at least in part, for Sofia, Bucharest, Budapest, and the east of Berlin, all cities of the former Soviet bloc countries in the heart of Europe. Wherever we go in this part of the world where the Communist Party once reigned, we see that now "money sings." This is a term taken from the title of a book about the Russian city of Yaroslavl by Blair Ruble, which in turn is a translation of the expression *den'gi poiut* that an informant that Ruble described as a "shady New Russian" used to describe the brash culture of post-Soviet times. "That explains it all," he added. Informed by Ruble that in America the expression is "money talks," the informant responded "Well, we Russians have always been more extravagant" (Ruble, 1995, p. 1). In our treatment of contemporary Kyiv, we add that "money stings" as well.

1.5   A Changing City

"It was not all that long ago that you could always find a seat on the Metro," a Kyiv-resident friend recently told me, referring to the crowds of commuters that are now routinely jammed on the city's three color-coded subway lines (Red Line, Blue Line, Green Line) during busy parts of the day and evening. It was her way to make a point about Kyiv's recent boom in population growth, especially beginning in 2003 as she remembers it, and the changes to city life that have come as a result. In a country that has been losing population to 45.6 million, Kyiv has been gaining, and it is ever more the nation's main metropolis as well as capital city. The jump in population is all the more remarkable because Kyiv, like Ukraine as a whole, is a city of low birth rates, rising death rates, and high rates of emigration abroad.

And so, Kyiv has a half a million or so additional residents since 1991 and the subway is much more crowded indeed. Many of the extra passengers are newcomers to the city, and with them come changes in how people dress, how they conduct themselves during the ride, and where they are going and what they will do when they get there. During Soviet times, cities had their familiar rhythms as determined by the working hours of a centralized economy, a population with internal passports and residence permits, and times and places for recreation, shopping, and other activities that were generally set by centralized authority. But without Soviet government, a new order – or perhaps more precisely, a disorder – has set in and we have new people, new activities, and new rhythms of time and place that give Kyiv and other postsocialist cities a perceptibly different feel. The changes are felt as well on the city's enormous and growing fleet of minibuses (*marshrutkas*) that are indispensable for carrying people where subways do not go; in the numbers of private automobiles that now often barely inch along city streets, intersections, and approaches to bridges across the river; the invasion of open space everywhere for parking those vehicles; and in the profusion of billboards and other advertising that has taken over the landscape seemingly everywhere in numbers much, much larger than Soviet communist propaganda signs ever reached in the past.

Furthermore, there is a rising skyline of glass-skinned office buildings and upscale condominium towers, and a landscape of busy shopping malls, new restaurants and nightclubs with bright neon lights, and, along busy highways, the golden arches of McDonald's on poles reaching to the sky. In the center of the city there are beautiful people in beautiful fashions. But we also see that there are poor people, too, plenty of them, as well as anxious migrants who have come in search of work. Some are buskers on the subway where they sing or play music from car to car for tips or sell inexpensive novelty products on commission for a boss who hires them, while others work the streets and sidewalks of the city as vendors or buskers, or walk back and forth as human sandwich boards that advertise pawn shops, English-language classes, or marriage agencies that help foreign men take home Ukrainian brides. Others gather early in the morning at Vokzal, the city's central train station, in hopes that labor agents might select them for a job in either construction or old-building destruction in the changing city. Unfortunately, there are also many long-term Kyivans who are poor, newly so in the newly competitive economy, including old people who could otherwise be enjoying a well-earned retirement. These people also struggle in the informal economy to make a living, and they are plainly evident in the harsh cultural landscape that is Kyiv today.

The iconography of the city has changed, too. Instead of the flags of the USSR and the Ukrainian SSR, we have hanging atop government buildings and in the center of the city at Independence Square, the blue and yellow flag of an independent nation. The colors are also on the license plates of motor vehicles, on public service billboards that remind people to love Ukraine, and on various advertising designed to appeal to feelings of patriotism. In Soviet times, as well as earlier during the czarist and Polish rule of different parts of Ukraine, that flag and those colors were forbidden. Likewise, there are now monuments to heroes of Ukraine, as opposed to Soviet heroes, and even to Ukrainians who had openly and bravely opposed Soviet rule such as the dissident Viacheslav Chornovil (1937-1999). There are monuments as well to the victims of Soviet crimes, most notably the artificial famine of 1932-1933 that took millions of lives. The city even has a small museum called the Museum of Soviet Occupation. Furthermore, we see and hear the Ukrainian language more. In the time of the USSR, Russian dominated the city, especially in the media, on street signage, on the names of buildings and stores, and so on in the landscape. Ukrainian was even banned for a time, as it was earlier during times of Imperial Russian rule. Now, *ridna mova* (the native language of the country) is the official language of government and is common.

A small example from the prestigious street in the center of Kyiv where I was lucky enough to live encapsulates the changes. There is a shop down the block that is in a building that was once one of the many branch offices of the communist government. It is in a grand, historic structure from very early in the 20th century that was rehabilitated, at least in terms of the façade, from the devastation of battle in World War II. Above the door, the Soviets had installed a handsome plaster relief of two crossed hammers. That emblem is still there even though the government ministry that it represents is gone, and the door now opens not to an office for bureaucrats, but to an exclusive store selling expensive jewelry. The shoppers are new elites in Ukraine, and the tone is very upscale. The sign out front reads "Royal Diamonds" in English. To round out the scene with a bit more detail, I add that, as on many older buildings in Kyiv, a strong wire-mesh net stretches across the façade above the emblem in order to protect pedestrians from falling mortar and plaster. At night, there are old lady flower sellers who walk up and down the street hoping to entice customers from among the many young couples who are out on dates, as well as a bevy of leggy young women in short skirts and the highest of spike heels who are clearing looking to entice dates. In the small square across the street, near a popular sushi restaurant and a fancy confectionary, the benches around the well water pump are packed at night in good weather with amorous couples, groups of friends enjoying cheap beer, and an assortment of the poor, the homeless, and the hopelessly inebriated.

That is what this book is about: the new social geography of Kyiv after the Soviet period ended. It is a case study of what is taking place simultaneously in many other cities of the once-Soviet realm as well – places like Moscow, St. Petersburg, and Kazan in the Russian Federation; Kharkiv, Odesa, L'viv, and Dnipropetrovsk in other parts of Ukraine;[1] Minsk, Riga, Tbilisi, Yerevan, and Tashkent in other countries of the former Soviet realm, and in Sofia, Bucharest, Budapest, and the east of Berlin in the formerly Soviet bloc countries in the heart of Europe. The change was "unexpected" as in the title of a book about Ukraine by Andrew Wilson (2000), and was, therefore, not planned for. Consequently, the emerging social geography of Kyiv is one of excessive chaos in place of a strict order, and one of an emerging new order that does not yet have a name other than "postsocialist city" or "post-Soviet city," overlapping terms that we use interchangeably because both apply in this region. What comes next is not yet fully shaped, as Kyiv after socialism is a work in progress, as is new Moscow, new Odesa, new St. Petersburg, and new Baku. What is certain is that "money sings" in all of these new landscapes (Ruble, 1995), and that raw capitalism deepens the divide between those who score in the new society and the much larger number of others who find themselves far behind.

1.6   Angry Citizens

I was on a little walking and photography excursion one spring Saturday morning near the Pechersk subway station, knowing that there would be the weekly farmers' market to explore as well as one or two other places in the neighborhood that I had been looking for the opportunity to photograph in good light. I was taking the most innocent of photographs – that of a tall statue of the famous Ukrainian poet and social activist Lesya Ukrainka (1871-1913) – when a stranger who later gave his name as Oleksandr Bo-

---

1   Formerly Kharkov, Odessa, L'vov, and Dnepropetrovsk as they are transliterated from the Russian language.

rysovych approached from seemingly nowhere and began to shout from some distance that I need to send those photographs to the president of Ukraine and to the members of Verkhovna Rada (the parliament). "Why?" I asked as he came near, thinking of possible answers from what I knew about the biography of Ukraine's most famous woman writer. He pointed to the surroundings, including the nonfunctioning fountains at Lesya's feet and the litter and graffiti where there were once pools of water, and expounded with great agitation about what a disgrace it was to have such a fine monument in such a miserable setting. I agreed, but thought that it was bit strange to make such a deal about what was, quite frankly, not unusual for Kyiv: neglect of public spaces. I told him so, adding that I had seen far worse landscapes around Kyiv. He was pleased that I was on board about the physical condition of the city, and asked about my photography and accent. I told him about this book and he figuratively leaped at the chance to make sure that I was aware of all the demons in Kyiv that he believed needed to be exposed.

He asked me where in the United States I live, expressed recognition about Philadelphia when I replied, and then pointed down the block at the Bentley and Lamborghini automobile dealership, which ironically was the one thing that I most wanted to photograph on that particular excursion, and asked how often I see a Bentley on the streets of Philadelphia. "I don't know, maybe once a year," I estimated with an uncertain shrug of the shoulders. He then compared the relative wealth of the United States and Ukraine, and asked rhetorically where I see more such automobiles. I pleased him again when I mentioned the short street in central Kyiv on which I was living and told him that, at minimum, there are often four Bentleys parked there every day. "We have a government of thieves. Not one of them is honest. Not one of these cars was earned via honest work," he gushed, and then swept his right arm against the backdrop panorama of rapid redevelopment along Lesya Ukrainka Boulevard and added: "and this is where they live, our *narodnyi deputaty*, in these new buildings, in their enormous, marble apartments." He pointed to the windows of a 17-room residence (his count) of someone whose name I did not recognize, mentioned the numbers of millions of dollars that this apartment and that one cost, and railed on and on about corruption and inequities until I finally excused myself. He shouted back as I left to make sure that I put it all in the book.

Next, we meet four Ukrainian women. Perhaps the whole world now knows of FEMEN, the Kyiv-based protest group comprised of attractive young Ukrainian women who call attention to social and political problems by baring their breasts at public rallies. They always attract a crowd and observant media coverage, and photos of photographers' favorites of the protesters are all over the Internet. I had my first personal encounter with the group when they gathered once in Independence Square in the center of Kyiv for a racy (but not topless) and creative (believe me) protest against, of all things, the anti-feminist president of neighboring Belarus, Alexander Lukashenko. Trust me: I introduce this topic not to capitalize on FEMEN, but to tell what happened next. As the slinging of tomatoes and eggs at a large hand-drawn portrait of Lukashenko from erotic FEMEN-leg slingshots wound down, and a FEMEN spokesperson finished her interview session in front of a crowd of eager news microphones, a Kyivan woman in her 50s, very obviously blue-collar and not FEMEN-like in appearance, took advantage of the media presence and spoke her piece. Some of the news photographers and mike handlers turned away, others laughed, but many heard her out. For people such as herself, she said in so many words, Ukraine is a mess: prices are rising; there are new taxes to pay and stupid bureaucratic forms to fill out; pensioners are struggling; young people are emigrating; and the oligarchs are stealing everything that is still left. This litany of complaints one hears daily; what struck me on this particular day was the boldness of "Valentina Ivanova" to steal mike time from FEMEN and her desperation to be heard. "We are losing our freedoms," she said with punctuation, "and if we don't speak up now, we won't be able to speak later." I liked that FEMEN members stood beside her, like feminists should, perhaps assuring as a result that a good number of cameras and microphones would stay in place until their not-so-glamorous fellow citizen had finished.

There is also Olena Zhelesko, an older woman born the year the Great Patriotic War ended (making her exactly my age) who broadcasts her messages about Ukraine's mess not by microphone but by megaphone (Figure 1.2). I met her at Independence Square, too, but months earlier, when I first heard her reciting verse to passersby near stairs for the subway. She spoke in unusually rapid-fire Russian, so I had trouble understanding, although I knew it was about politics and could tell it was witty. When she took a break I asked her if the verse was her own, and what she was all about. In response to my Ukrainian, which she recognized correctly as "Diaspora Ukrainian," she switched to Ukrainian, her own first language, and explained with impromptu verse: bards have long told the story of Ukraine's people, and that is exactly what she was doing, not with song and a *bandura*, the national stringed instrument, but with her own poetry and a megaphone. She continued with verse to explain that she was speaking about the sorry state of life in Ukraine and that people need to stand up and not be afraid. "Is this how you make a living? Is this for tips?" were my crude questions.

Figure 1.2   Olena Zhelesko with megaphone

She followed with more impromptu rhymes: the duties of citizenship center on support for fellow citizens and free flow of information. "Today's Ukraine is not free," she versed, and "people need to speak up before they are driven down even more." I told her that a headline in that morning's Ukrainian newspaper, *Moloda Ukraina* (Young Ukraine), an article about a former political prisoner, was this: "God's Eleventh Commandment: Do Not Be Afraid." She liked that and a good conversation ensued.

I told her about this book that I was writing and she told me what she thought was important for me to know. It was her choice to focus on the specific topic of Ukrainian people in Kyiv; I did not steer her in that direction. The capital was never a Ukrainian city until recently, she explained; it was always Russian, Jewish, and Polish, and Ukrainians never formed more than a tiny minority. Now there are many Ukrainians in the city, but the city is still not fully theirs. They are disproportionately at the bottom of society. To see Ukrainians, she urged, I should go to the open-air markets where Ukrainians work for bosses as low-paid vendors, or where they make meager livings selling farm products from the nearby villages that they come from. Go, too, to the central rail station in the morning when the passenger trains come in and see Ukrainians arriving from around the countryside to begin looking for work and a place to live. Also, see those who would exploit them waiting for them at the station, and watch the action. To see Kyiv's Ukrainians, I should talk to the beggars, the small-scale flower sellers, and other vendors who are found everywhere in the center of the city and at every pedestrian underpass. Speak to them in Ukrainian. They will be happy to tell you about their lives and their difficulties. Fully 50 percent of the people in this city are struggling, truly struggling, and I should get to know them, she urged. I told her that I was doing just that – that I have been at the rail station many times already and have photographed the amazing early morning scene of modern-day peasants encountering the big city. I told her that I talk to people all the time, and that that was why I was speaking with her. She liked that and told me that my book is much needed.

I never did tell Olena that I do not fully agree with her presentation of inequality in Ukrainian society or Kyiv social history. I chose not to challenge her viewpoints and debate, but to be a listener only. However, I know that in Kyiv, and indeed throughout Ukraine, there are a great many Ukrainians who are successful economically and in positions of power, and that increasingly they make up the country's middle and privileged classes. She knows that, too, I am sure, but for my benefit kept emphasizing the truth that historically Ukrainians have had it hard in the territory that is now their country because of foreign rule, and that there are still strong vestiges of discrimination and belittlement against Ukrainians. I assume that she is aware as well that in Russian-speaking parts of Ukraine there are many ethnic Russians living in poverty, although she never said anything about that. In the largely Russian, gritty industrial zones of Donetsk, for instance, one sees as much poverty and poor living conditions as anywhere in Ukraine. It is from this region that Ukraine's president, Viktor Yanukovych, hails. In Donetsk, Kyiv, and elsewhere in the country, poverty is primarily a class issue, and maybe partly ethnic, but nationalistic ethnic Ukrainians like Olena do not always make that distinction.

I have seen Olena Zhelesko several times since that first meeting, always at protest rallies about one or another aspect of the country's mess. She typically finds a perch for herself and her megaphone somewhere near the center of the action, and before the main speakers start, entertains the arriving crowds with fresh verse about the specific subjects of the protest. She speaks mainly in Ukrainian, and I never did understand why it was Russian that she was speaking when I first heard her. She seems to be widely known and generally appreciated by the activist-citizens who turn out again and again when political and environmentalist websites announce a time, place, and specific issue for the next *aktsia* (action), although there are those who refer to her as "that crazy nationalist woman with the megaphone." Most people, however, regardless of where they stand on Ukrainian nationalism, seem to especially enjoy her lampooning of the country's incompetent, corrupt, larcenous and not-for-Ukraine government political leaders, such as those in the Verkhovna Rada (parliament) where Nina's stepfather is 1/450th part, who are said to be responsible for the mess in the country.

Let me introduce you as well to a third woman, 17-year-old Daria Stepanenko, a freshman student at Kyiv Mohyla Academy who publicly took on Ukraine's controversial Minister of Education and Science, Dmytro Volodymyrovych Tabachnyk. The context is this: Tabachnyk is a prominent member of the ruling Party of Regions, and was twice deputy prime minister when his sponsor, today's president, Viktor Yanukovych, was prime minister and the head of presidential administration. In his present post, the Education Minister has supported pushes to establish Russian once again as Ukraine's official language (this time along with Ukrainian as opposed to in place of Ukrainian) with the goal of changing not only how government conducts its business, but also the fundamental character of schooling in Ukraine. The result of such a change would mean that Russian-speaking children would be much less likely to ever learn Ukrainian well enough to function in that language, and therefore assure over the long haul that Russian remains in the forefront of Ukrainian life. Thus, had Tabachnyk had his way when Nina was in school, she never would have learned Ukrainian in the first place.

Tabachnyk is controversial not just because of such beliefs, but also because he often advocates his positions with venom and in pit bull fashion. Also, his past is clouded with accusations of influence-peddling, falsification of personal credentials, and other sins. He was appointed to his current post on March 11, 2010, over the vocal objections of Ukrainian-oriented Ukrainians in the country, and there have been calls ever since to remove him from office. For example, within a week of his start as education and science minister, the administration of the highly respected Ukrainian Catholic University in the western city of L'viv went public with this opinion: "Tabachnyk has been openly and publicly humiliating the Ukrainian intelligentsia, as well as Ukrainian language and culture, kindling hostility among the various regions of Ukraine, vindicating the human-hating Stalinist regime" (Ukrainian Catholic University, 2010).

Enter Daria Stepanenko. On September 22, 2011, she earned 15 minutes of nationwide fame (and fame in Russia, too) when, dressed nicely in an unassuming black dress and matching grey jacket, she walked into the hall in the center of Kyiv where Minister Tabachnyk was participating along with delegates from the European Union in an international conference about education and approached him at the head table with a long bouquet of flowers. She extended the bouquet and smiled, he came closer, and then she used the flowers to slap him in the face. Immediately, she was led away, quietly without resistance, most audience members pretended to not notice, and the proceedings of the conference apparently went on as if nothing happened. This is all on YouTube. She was charged with petty hooliganism and quickly released because of her age. Afterwards she held a press conference, also seen on YouTube, in which she explained her motivations. Tabachnyk, she said in the purest of Ukrainian language, deserved to be slapped because of his many anti-Ukrainian actions and because "he is a person who, quite simply, hates Ukraine and everything that is associated with the country." She urged Ukrainians to clamor for his dismissal. Her particular protest may have been inappropriate and is unlikely to hasten Tabachnyk's departure. Her actions may also have brought her some trouble at her university atop the trouble she faces with the law. The university was quick to publicly distance itself from her action, so much so that some fellow students have suggested that she may have been a paid provocateur hired by unspecified russophilic forces in order to discredit her unequivocally pro-Ukraine university. But for us, even if we are to regard her as just a misguided teenager, Daria Stepanenko is emphatically a "Ukrainian voice" who reflects the palpable anger of a great many Ukrainian people about the mess that is their country.

Finally, meet a fourth Ukrainian woman, Lyudmyla Savchenko, a famous voice in Ukraine as reader of weather forecasts on public radio. I don't know her personally, but read in the press and heard on tape what transpired on her live broadcast just three days before this writing. I introduce her so that you know that I am not making these people up; everything I write about her is verifiable in the media. The context is perfect May weather this year for day after day, not just in Kyiv, but all over Ukraine. There were no storm fronts to report and no cold snaps, only bright, beautiful, sunny spring days. As translated and reported by the *Kyiv Post* on May 18, 2011, Savchenko unexpectedly stepped out of line and volunteered the following after forecasting a continuation of perfect weather:

> One cannot remain indifferent to this beauty which shows in the
> tender scent of lilac and lily of the valley and the melodious trilling of

the birds. ... At times it seems that such miraculous days are a gift from nature to compensate us for the chaos, lawlessness and injustice which reigns in our country. It is simply incomprehensible that anyone can dislike this paradise on earth, this country, [and] the Ukrainian people so much that they [the current Party of Regions government and its associates] treat it so badly. (Kyiv Post, May 18, 2011)

That may have been Ukraine's last live weather report. As reported by Kyiv's Associated Press office on May 20, Savchenko was quickly taken off the air. Opposition politicians expressed protest, but the office of President Yanukovych and has remained silent.

1.7   Linking to the Literature

There is a strong undercurrent of "before and after" in this book, as we are concerned with how Kyiv has been changing from the characteristic urban form that was very imposed by Soviet urban planning. While the city may not have been the quintessential Soviet city, as in the case of Magnitogorsk (Kotkin, 1992, 1995) or Minsk (Belarus) as it was rebuilt after World War II, the Soviet impact on Kyiv was enormous nonetheless for at least three reasons: (1) like Minsk, which was greatly destroyed in the war, the Soviets needed to rebuild much of Kyiv, too, and did so according to their template; (2) the city was strategic in terms of industry, the military, and scientific research, well as the capital of a major republic, so construction according to Soviet form was appropriate; and (3) the city grew rapidly during the decades after World War II, so many new districts needed to be added, which was done in the Soviet way. Instead of a discreet section about Soviet Kyiv, which could easily be a book in itself, this book recalls characteristics of the Soviet city throughout as it discusses what is new. The authoritative text about what the Soviet city was like in general is the now classic book by Bater (1980). It makes many references to Kyiv throughout. Other key works include the collection of essays about socialist cities edited by French and Hamilton (1979), and reflections about the Soviet urban heritage by French (1984; 1995) with Moscow as a prime example, and Grava (1993), who has studied primarily Riga.

Now, as a complement to these and other studies about Soviet urbanism, a considerable literature is emerging about the postsocialist city as a generic urban type. The new studies are mostly articles in academic journals and chapters in edited books on the subject. With the exception of the aforementioned *Money Sings* about Yaroslavl, Russia, which was published in the early post-Soviet year 1995, this book about Kyiv is the lone book-length case study of a postsocialist city. It is also worth noting that Kyiv has been especially understudied. There are some fine histories of the city, both in English and in local languages (e.g., Bakanov, 2011; Boychenko et al., 1968; Byelomyesyatsev et al., 2012; Hamm, 1986, 1993; Kudrytsky, ed., 1982; Malakov, 2009, 2010, 2011, 2013; Meir, 2010; Nasyrova, Nevzorov, and Kruchynin, eds., 2008; Shulkevych and Dmytrenko, 1982), but there is virtually nothing in English about the city today except for the occasional piece of journalism, some of which seems to focus disproportionately on the antics of the topless women's protest group FEMEN, or short travel articles. There is not much either in Ukrainian or Russian, and certainly no book such as this. However, the local literature is growing rapidly. Key sources that relate to the subjects covered here are a topical issue of the Ukrainian sociological journal *Spilne: Zhurnal Sotsialnoi Krytyky* (Commons: A Journal of Social Criticism), volume 2 (2010); a collection of papers about city planning in Kyiv edited by Ksenia Dmytrenko (2011); a collection of essays about social and landscape change in Kyiv edited by Makarenko et al. (2012); a detailed study about Troyeshchyna, a blue-collar residential neighborhood at the margins of Kyiv, by Blair Ruble (2003); and various other papers, including at least two by Natalia Moussienko about historical preservation in the city and citizens' struggles against irresponsible construction projects (2009a and b).

A recent article by Sýkora and Bouzarovski (2012) outlines a conceptual framework for analysis of the socialist to postsocialist urban transition and offers a helpful bibliography. Because the subject is compelling, and because the socialist world in Eurasia covered a huge territory and many countries and cultures, the literature ranges widely geographically. Examples run from the former Soviet satellite states of Balkan Europe (e.g., Hirt, 2006, 2007, 2010, Nae and Turnock, 2011; Pojani, 2009 and 2010; Staddon and Mollov, 2000) and Poland (e.g., Michlic, 2009; Musekamp, 2009; Thum, 2009; Tölle, 2008), into the heart of Russia (e.g., Argenbright, 1999; Kalfus, 1996; Makhrova and Molodikova, 2007; Medvedkov and Medvedkov, 2007; Molodikova and Makhrova, 2007; Pagonis and Thornley, 2000), to the distant "blue cities" of Russia (Engel, 2007) and the far reaches of Buryat Siberia (e.g., Baldayeva, 2007; Humphrey, 2007; Hürelbaatar, 2007; and Manzanova, 2007), and perhaps beyond.

At least with respect to the issues that are emphasized in this book, the central contribution to the literature is the edited book *Cities after the Fall of Communism* (Czaplicka, Gelazis, and Ruble, eds., 2009). Like in our own approach to Kyiv, each of the book's 11 case studies "focuses on a postcommunist city with a particularly interesting story to tell" (p. 2). There are 4 cases from Ukraine: Odesa ("Odessa" in the text), Sevastopol, Kharkiv, and L'viv; as well as chapters about cities in countries nearby: Vilnius in Lithuania, Novgorod and Kaliningrad in Russia, Tallinn in Estonia; and Wrocław, Łódź, and Szczecin in Poland. A "deceptively simple" initial question runs through the case studies: "What time is this place?" This question was first posed in 1961 by Anselm Strauss in his analysis of the changing American urban landscape, and it is one that the editors of this book see correctly as "central for those reimagining and remaking the cities of the former Soviet Union and postcommunist Central and Eastern Europe" (p. 1). As each city moves forward into the new era, it also reflects on its past and reworks history in ways that the communists did not allow. Often, there is wholesale renaming of streets and city districts in order to substitute one set of memories for another, replacements of old monuments and hero statues with those that are new and different, and a return of historical foundation for cities to past times of urban glory and national strength. In Ukraine, the city of L'viv especially has broken with its Soviet past, as this was always a rabidly anti-communist and anti-Russian city, and has reinvigorated its Ukrainianism in the landscape, as well as erected monuments to both honor and acknowledge its Polish and Jewish pasts (Hentosh and Tscherkes, 2009, pp. 255-280).

A second important collection of essays is the book edited by Alexander, Buchli, and Humphrey (2007). It focuses on urban life in post-Soviet Central Asia and includes among other essays those cited above for Buryat Siberia. It describes a distant and different world from that of Kyiv, but a world nonetheless that the Soviets had transformed with the same mold that had reshaped Kyiv and other cities in the Slavic heartland. A third collection of essays, edited by Kiril Stanilov and also published in the same year (Stanilov, 2007a), focuses more on European Russia (e.g., the Russia chapters cited above), as well as on the Baltic countries and key capital cities in the former Eastern Bloc such as Prague, Sofia, Budapest, and Bucharest. Chapters about the changing geography of office development and other commercial uses in a mix of East European cities by Stanilov (2007b) and about the emerging geography of commercial real estate in postsocialist Moscow by Makhrova and Molodikova (2007) link especially well with my own observations in Kyiv, as does a superbly detailed chapter by Yuri Medvedkov and Olga Medvedkov about the changing geography of elite residential areas in Moscow and its surroundings (2007). A fourth edited book, *The Post-Socialist City*, looks at the impact of social-political change in East Europe and the former USSR on the form of public squares, monuments, and other elements of urban form as seen in Bucharest, Prague, Warsaw, and Prishtina, among other cities (Kliems and Dmitrieva, eds., 2010). One chapter, by Wilfried Jilge, discusses the form of Kyiv's Maidan Nezalezhnosti (Independence Square), a subject that we will take up in Chapter 6 (Jilge, 2003; 2010). Finally, a fifth edited volume is by anthropologists and looks at changes to everyday life since the end of socialism in various countries in East Europe, in Armenia, and in Russia. Its wide-ranging chapters cover the rebuilding of synagogues in East Europe, rock music in Budapest, and gay tourism to Prague, among other topics (Berdahl, Bunzl, and Lampland, eds., 2000).

There has been significant in-depth research about one city in particular, Tbilisi, the capital of Georgia (Van Assche, Salukvadze, and Shavishvili, eds., 2009; Van Assche and Salukvadze, 2012). This ancient city that itself had contributed to the shaping of earliest Kyiv, had been reworked considerably by Soviet planners and city-builders during the 70 years (1921-1991) that it was part of the USSR, but has since experienced what is perhaps a leading edge of post-Soviet reconstruction. The new era is one of a return to both national themes and religiosity in the landscape, and of redevelopment in all parts of the metropolis by a profit-minded real estate industry. These "new actors" on the urban scene in Tbilisi area atuned to Western architectural forms and development practices, and are, in a sense, "reinventing" the city, as the author's title for their article suggests (Van Assche and Salukvadze, 2012). Tbilisi is an especially pertinent case study to consider alongside Kyiv because the city is also deeply historic and rich in religious architecture. And, like Kyiv, the city suffered the destruction of old churches and wreckage of history during the Stalinist years. A little more solidly than Kyiv and Ukraine, Tbilisi and Georgia have embraced democracy, perhaps providing a model for democracy advocates in Ukraine; and much more than Kyiv, but certainly akin to the nationalistic feelings that dominate L'viv and other parts of the west of Ukraine, Tbilisi and Georgia have said no to Russia and aspire to a future with the West.

Moscow is another key city for comparison with Kyiv. For a long period, it was the Soviet "big brother" of the Ukrainian capital, and is now a city that perhaps more than any other is being remade by rich capitalists and the "New Russian" consumer class. Among the many sources to read about this city are the following: Adams (2008); Badina and Golubchikov (2005); Kolossov, Vendina, and O'Loughlin (2002); Kolossov and O'Loughlin (2004); Pagonis and Thornley (2000); and three articles in a recent issue of the journal *Slavic Review* (Stella, 2013; Griffiths, 2013; and Rossman, 2013). The publications of R. Anthony French are key, too, although they are a bit older and predate some of Moscow's most dramatic transformations (French,

1984; 1995). The most central case study is probably the ethnography of everyday life in the years following the demise of Soviet order by Williams College sociologist Olga Shevchenko (2009). The book is recent and richly detailed, and it focuses on ordinary people as opposed to the smaller group of nouveaux riches who have gotten disproportionate attention in other literature. The first chapter is entitled "Living on a Volcano." This is a metaphor that Shevchenko said she heard often in her interviews as Moscow's rank-and-file continually faces social and political instability, and lives with uncertainty about what the next day might bring (Shevchenko, 2009, p. 8). We read that people have had to come up with home-grown ways to protect themselves from the hazards of everyday life in postsocialist Moscow's perpetual "state of emergency." One example, set in the context of rising crime rates, concerns the proliferation of super-strong steel doors for apartments and metal garages in residential areas, even if there was very little of value in the apartment or the garage to protect. One informant, Andrei, laughingly told Shevchenko, "I believe that our apartment door is our most expensive possession," while another, Sergei Mikhailovich, explained that alternative forms of protection such as vigilant neighbors or alert police were no longer available in his post-Soviet neighborhood, and added that "although police are needed, one is afraid of the police these days" (Shevchenko, 2009, p. 113.) These comments, too, ring familiar for the Kyiv I have observed, and they could just as easily have been framed by Shevchenko via my metaphor of urban demons (her city also happens to have spectacular church domes) as by her chosen one of tectonic volatility.

The distinguished Cambridge University anthropologist Caroline Humphrey has also addressed changes in society after socialism, and has written about various aspects of Moscow and other locations in the former USSR and Mongolia in her descriptively titled collection of ten of her own essays: *The Unmaking of Soviet Life* (2002). She, too, gives more attention to ordinary people than the rich, including those living in far-off rural and small-town Siberia, but one chapter in particular is about the rich in Moscow and other cities and relates to topics that we will discuss for Kyiv. This is Chapter 9, the "Villas of the 'New Russians,'" which describes the geography and architecture of the lavish homes that are being built by suddenly moneyed citizens of emerging post-Soviet society. These new homes represent the first boom in construction of large, individually owned houses for single families since the Revolution of 1917 (p. 175). She interprets the new landscapes as emblems of a rising culture of consumption and new symbols of status and individual independence. In comparison to the traditional dacha, "the villa has a quite different appearance," Humphrey writes,

> for the owners do not see themselves as engaged in creating domestic-
> ity in the face of state-dictated homogeneity. ... The purchaser of a villa
> is a master who signals the social position of an independent operator.
> His walls and gates connote withdrawal from the mass of the people,
> and his turrets evoke an "I'll look after myself" defiance. (p. 188)

In the chapters ahead in this book, we will see many examples of opulent construction for personal use by the "New Russians" of Kyiv (yes, the term is used
in the Ukrainian capital), as that is indeed one of the principal dimensions
of the city's current remaking, and will recall Humphrey's highlighting of
consumption culture and self-centeredness as factors in their construction.

A case study of a different sort, more directly focused on the impact on
urban space of a city's structural economic transformation after socialism,
is the more quantitative analysis of Russia's second city, St. Petersburg,
by Axenov, Brade, and Bondarchuk (2006). The findings of this study also
parallel what I have observed, at least in bits and pieces, in Kyiv. The authors
have compiled considerable data about changing economic enterprise in
post-Soviet St. Petersburg, and they have documented both the extremely
rapid increases over a short period in numbers and variety of business in
the city and the spatial distributions of new businesses. Apropos to the
example above about strongly locked doors, I note the example of private
security companies: their numbers in St. Petersburg increased from 1 in
1988 to 80 in 1996, to 390 in 2002. Other data concern the changing numbers
and geographic distributions of food stores, automobile service enterprises,
tourism agencies, and hypermarkets, and the distributions of various kinds
of business such as very small kiosks around busy Metro stations, and along
particular streets, and in specific squares.

Still another pertinent case study is the research about Kazan by Liliya
Nigmatullina (2010). The city is the capital of the Republic of Tatarstan, an
oil-rich district within the Russian Federation located on the Volga River
to the southeast of Moscow, and is sometimes referred to as "Russia's Third
Capital." Both Kazan and the small-town and rural areas of Tatarstan have
changed tremendously since the loosening of Moscow's hegemonic rule after
Soviet times, as the republic has been able to exchange its vast oil resources
for additional autonomy within the Russian Federation. That autonomy has
taken on strong cultural expression and is reflected in an emphatic post-
Soviet revival of ethnic Tatar and religious Islamic life. Nigmatullina's work,
which was written as a master's thesis signed by yours truly, documented
with considerable original data the return of her native Kazan to ethnic and
religious roots that had been suppressed since the Russian conquest of the

city by Ivan Grozny (Ivan the Terrible) in 1552. The most symbolic event was the reconstruction in 2005 of the spectacularly beautiful Qolşärif mosque in the Kazan Kremlin (I was there and saw it with my own eyes), a sacred and historic structure that was demolished during Ivan's murderous siege of the city. It is now the largest mosque in Russia and the largest in Europe outside Istanbul. At the same time, dozens of other mosques have been constructed, reconstructed, or converted back to religious use from secular uses during Soviet (or even czarist) times in Kazan and its surroundings. There are also many new Islamic schools, renewed instruction of and in the Tatar language, and new retailing of halal food, Tatar and Islamic religious reading material, and Tatar and Islamic clothing, both for ceremonial and everyday use. All of this was either banned or suppressed during the many years of Russian and Soviet rule. Nigmatullina also documented the revival of ethnic Tatar vernacular architecture in and near Kazan as seen in single homes, the fences that bound property lines, and ethnic-oriented businesses and cultural centers, among other examples.

Such expressions of ethnic and linguistic identity, national past, and religiosity are seen commonly in historically non-Russian areas of the former Soviet Union because much of this was taken away during Soviet communism (or even earlier in the cases of territories such as Tatarstan that had been annexed by the Russian Empire). In addition to Kazan and L'viv (annexed after World War II), which I singled out above, there are other examples from Ukraine (e.g., Gubar and Herlihy, 2009; Kravchenko, 2009; Richardson, 2008), as well as those for the capital cities of the three newly independent countries of the Caucuses (e.g., Tbilisi as presented in the recent volume edited by Van Assche, Salukvadze, and Shavishvili, 2009; and in Bouzarovski, Salukvadze, and Gentile, 2011), and the capitals and other cities in the three Baltic Republics that are equally happy to no longer be Russia's (e.g., the chapters about Estonia's Tallinn by Jörg Hackmann and Lithuania's Vilnius by Irena Vaisvilaite in *Cities after the Fall of Communism*; and the article by Aleksandravičis about both Vilnius and Kaunas). There is also an emerging literature about post-Soviet urban Central Asia, e.g., the essay about Tashkent by Marfua Tokhtakhodzhaeva in the book *Urban Life in Post-Soviet Asia* edited by Alexander, Buchli, and Humphrey (2007). This study traces this ancient city from the 19th century when it was the capital of Turkestan, through those years of the 20th century when it was the administrative center of Soviet Uzbekistan, to its substantial transformation in the present century into its postsocialist form as a thriving capital city of an independent Uzbekistan (pp. 102-124). The same text also has case studies about Astana and Almaty in Kazakhstan. All of these cases bear in one way or another on Kyiv, because, as we will see, this city, too, has undergone a post-Soviet burst of national (i.e., Ukrainian) ethnic and linguistic expression (even as the Russian language continues to be widely used), as well as a revival of religions and places of worship, including various flavors of Orthodox, Catholic, Jewish, and Muslim faiths, and evangelical Christianity.

In our presentation of Ukraine's capital, we will consider not only the sequence of historical periods that make up the landscape of the city, but more importantly the choices that confront the metropolis about precisely what to preserve from the past and how, what to memorialize with new construction and how, and which paths of urban development should be followed for the future. These choices are often complicated for cities like Kyiv because of the dark histories of the communist past, particularly during the terror of Joseph Stalin, and the equally hard years of Nazi occupation and murder, and the extraordinarily painful memories that they engender. While citizens may rejoice with the fall of the Soviet Union and its repressions and the coming of independence, they know also that they will need to confront the bloody secrets of the Soviet apparatus and bring uncomfortable truths from government archives and people's memories to light. In Ukraine, the most critical such history is that of the Holodomor, the Stalin-induced famine in 1932-1933 that took several million lives. It was a forbidden topic under the Soviet regime, but after independence it became a responsibility to uncover the truth and to memorialize and teach it. A recent case study of a post-Soviet city that bears on such issues is that by the historian Cathy A. Frierson about the northern Russian city of Vologda and the torments that citizens faced on account of detailed revelations after the Soviet period that their city had been a key part of the apparatus of the Gulag and the repeated site of gruesome, government-committed mass murders (Frierson, 2010). Likewise, we have an excellent case study from Minsk, Belarus, the nearest national capital to Kyiv, that discusses conflicts in that city about (1) construction of the "Nemiga 99" monument to 53 young people who were killed in 1999 in a tragic stampede at a rock music concert; and (2) the Stalinist character of the city's Oktiabrsky Square as a reflection of the anachronistic ideology of the present government of Belarus (Barykina, 2008).

1.8   Postsocialist Urbanism

We now turn to a short summary of the changes that are taking place as "postsocialist" and "post-Soviet" urban transitions (Table 1.1). The changes are wide-ranging and include not just fundamental shifts in political and economic systems occasioned by the fall of communism and the Soviet Union, but also major transformations in culture and society, as well as in urban form. Writing specifically about Russia, but I think also having equal application to the cities of Ukraine, Graybill and Dixon have observed that "the built environment has changed so dramatically since 1991 that many cities are nearly unrecognizable to those accustomed to quiet, somber Soviet landscapes" (2012, p. 239). Generalizations can be risky because, as we have seen, the former Soviet/socialist realm of Eurasia is an enormous region with a full range of indigenous cultural and geographic variety, and various countries have taken different roads in the postcommunist world. Nevertheless, we do collect our thoughts on the matter because they will be a basis for the examination of Kyiv that follows and for understanding the city's new dimensions of urban process and conflict. We see one of many possible snapshots of Soviet/socialist to postsocialist transition in Kyiv in Figure 1.3. Taken from a viewpoint atop a bluff on the right bank, the photo looks across the Dnipro River at Hidropark, a large Soviet-era park in the center of the city, and its wonderful beaches, and then beyond at left-bank Kyiv where the Soviets had built many of their expansive housing estates. We also see post-Soviet geography: e.g., incursions to the park by private businesses (a floating restaurant and floating hotel, from left to right); the dome of a small chapel peeking from among trees in the park; a large new church on the far bank (the Patriarchal Ukrainian Catholic

Figure 1.3   A view of Kyiv across the Dnipro River

Cathedral of the Resurrection of Christ); a business-oriented convention and exposition center nearby; new, taller apartment and condominium towers for the new middle class rising above Soviet constructions; and a wide road with cars and new shopping malls along the right edge.

The key points are organized below in a "before" and "after" format, the break being the end of the USSR and birth of post-Soviet independent nations. The characteristics that I list for postsocialist cities are gleaned from the literature that we have just reviewed (colored, I am sure, by my own experiences in the postsocialist landscape), while the parallel list of "before" characteristics during socialism comes from (1) that same literature; and (2) from what are widely considered to be the definitive studies about Soviet and socialist cities specifically (e.g., Bater, 1980). Many of the boxes below include interrelated, overlapping information; hence, it was not possible to group them into neat categories. However, the flow of the table tends to run from "economic transformations" near the top, through "urban physical change" near the middle, and "social and cultural change" toward the end.

Table 1.1   Socialist and Postsocialist Cities Compared

BEFORE: Key Characteristics of Soviet/ Socialist Cities	AFTER: Parallel Characteristics of Postsocialist Cities
The economy is centralized and controlled by government. Government is essentially everyone's employer and there is officially no unemployment. There is limited private enterprise.	Much of the economy is decentralized and privatized. Private enterprise expands, sometimes with little control. Some enterprises fail and there is unemployment.
The government owns the land and what is built on it.	Land ownership is privatized. The number of landowners is large.
Government buildings dominate the urban center.	Office buildings, international hotels, and upscale shopping are appearing fast.
The architecture of government authority marks the skylines of cities.	The skyline is increasing postmodern and commercial.
Central public squares are for rallies to support government and/or for the government's monuments.	Increasingly, public squares are sites for new business (e.g., kiosks) and in some cases support divergent political discourse.
Within the USSR, nationalism is subdued except for the Soviet state as a whole.	National identity emerges as an important element of landscape. Independence monuments are found in all post-Soviet countries but Russia.
The practice of religion is forbidden or restricted; churches and other places of worship are few and under close watch; many places of worship have been either destroyed or converted to new uses.	Energetic rebuilding of important places of worship that were destroyed under communism; energetic construction of new places of worship; religious holidays become part of the national calendar.

BEFORE: Key Characteristics of Soviet/Socialist Cities	AFTER: Parallel Characteristics of Postsocialist Cities
Most people live in fairly homogenous and crowded developments of government-built apartment blocks with few amenities within buildings.	There is private ownership of apartments and more personalization of spaces behind an apartment unit's closed doors. Often, public spaces in residential areas are neglected because mechanisms for maintenance and social control have weakened.
Better housing for privileged people such as party members is found in the center, but with little fanfare.	Exclusive neighborhoods for the wealthy are developed in various parts of the city. Wealth is conspicuously displayed.
Although there is social inequality, most citizens are more or less on the same footing. People in major urban centers live better than in isolated countryside locations.	The urban–rural divide is exacerbated. Within cities, there is much greater social-economic inequality, with huge gaps in income between the few who are extraordinarily rich and most other citizens. Happily, a middle class emerges, albeit perhaps too slowly.
Many cities have large industrial districts, many industrial workers, and pollution problems that come with heavy industry.	Some industries are no longer competitive and close.
Large parks serve as the lungs for cities and as places of day-off getaway for city residents.	Parts of popular parks are appropriated by government or well-connected private enterprises for nonpark use. Other options for leisure compete with parks.
There is a reliance on mass transit.	There is more usage of private automobiles, and there are more traffic jams and shortages of parking.
Shopping is done in a central department store, and in government stores for food, bread, meat, etc. Sometimes there are shortages of goods. There are small-scale vendors, too.	Supermarkets appear, as do chain stores from abroad, fashion boutiques, and shopping malls. There are larger numbers of small-scale vendors along sidewalks and at other public spaces.
Personal wealth is not displayed openly.	Many people chase money openly and aggressively, and make a point of showing their wealth by how they dress, the cars they drive, and how they spend it.
With the exception of university students from developing countries, there are comparatively few foreigners. Those who are there have restrictions on their activities.	There are many more foreigners and many opportunities for foreigners.
Foreign travel is restricted and is available mainly to those who are well-connected.	The borders are open for trips abroad and even emigration. Many people leave.
Social controls are tight, although alcoholism is common.	Disorder replaces social control. Alcoholism, crime, prostitution, etc. all increase. There is said to be a decline in moral standards.

2 The Missing Museum of the History of the City of Kyiv

2.1 Life in Limbo

We begin with a tangled story about a wonderful museum that had the misfortune of becoming homeless. It is the Museum of the History of the City of Kyiv. I began to learn its story soon after I arrived in Kyiv for this project and ventured on a first outing. I had been there years earlier during a short visit to the city with my late father, and now I wanted to study the museum in detail as I began to immerse myself in any- and everything that I could learn about Kyiv. A handsome English-language guidebook that sells well in the city had reminded me where to go: 8 Orlyka Street in what was described as the "aristocratic Lypki" district, in a beautiful two-story baroque building from 1753-1755 that was once called the Klovskyi Palace, a residence for VIP guests to Pecherska Lavra, the Monastery of the Caves, the ancient golden-domed Orthodox religious complex that is Kyiv's leading visitor attraction. For a time later, the building housed the first Kyiv Gymnasium (a school) and then the Women's Theological Seminary. It became the city's official history museum in 1981. The guidebook promised that the museum's "carefully assembled collection gives a detailed picture of the past and the present of the Ukrainian capital" and that "the museum has been recognized as a center of knowledge about Kiev."[2] I did not doubt these claims, but I remembered the museum as somewhat of a clutter of thousands of old objects in glass cases. As it turned out, I was going to learn a lot more about the present from the museum than about the past.

There was no museum at 8 Orlyka; the guidebook was outdated. Instead, I was confronted with the new location of the Supreme Court of Ukraine, a guarded gate, and a security guard who told me that the museum had moved, but that he did not know where. I found out the next day that Kyiv's history was even closer to home, at 2 Khreshchatyk, in "Ukrainian House," a newer, Soviet-style building on a low hill overlooking European Square. The building had been Kyiv's Lenin Museum for the several years between its construction in 1982 and the fall of Lenin's statue. Lenin, I already knew had never been to Kyiv, and the Lenin Museum, I learned later, never became

---

2   Quotations from Malikenaite, ed. (2002), p. 76.   The text of the guidebook refers to "Kiev," but itself has "Kyiv" on the cover page. So it goes with this city.

a local favorite. According to a current Ukrainian guidebook, the museum amounted to nothing more than a "communistic agitation-propaganda center" (Kurus et al., eds., 2010, p. 171). And so once again, still new to the city, I set out for a day of learning at the Museum of the History of City of Kyiv, and once again the lesson would be about the city today more than about history. I climbed the broad stone stairs from European Square and entered through the one door among several that was marked open. A guard asked me what I wanted. There was an empty rotunda before me, a nice stylized map of Ukraine above that decorated the empty space, and dead stillness except for the guard whom I seem to have disturbed. I asked him about the museum of Kyiv's history. "It's on the fourth floor," he told me, and pointed the roundabout way around the rotunda to my choice of stairs or elevator. I asked if I could shoot a photo of the rotunda and the map but he said no. I was puzzled but took him at his word, and went upstairs. From the fourth floor balcony, I looked down at where I had just been and photographed the same guard with his head down on his desk.

A sign on a partly opened door said in Ukrainian "Museum of the History of the City of Kyiv." I peered in and a startled woman at a mostly bare desk inside welcomed me in. I asked for the museum and she said that this was it. The only exhibit was in the next room, she said. There was a nominal cost, and I was welcome to see it. The room, it turned out, was about the size of my bedroom and the exhibit was made of about 20 or so watercolors and oil paintings of Kyiv scenes from various times during the Soviet years. I enjoyed the show, although it was hard to linger for longer than about ten minutes, and I signed the register as the first visitor of the day. Before I left, I explained that I was hoping to see more, and that I had come from the United States to learn about Kyiv. The woman at the desk explained that for the time being there is no more, although exhibits in the adjoining room will rotate and I was welcome to come back. I said that I had been to 8 Orlyka Street in the past, and had been anxious to see the exhibits again. As I asked what was going on and told her something about my professional credentials and a plan to write about Kyiv, she said that perhaps I should meet the head of the museum, and that he would explain it all to me.

And so it is that after a few minutes I was taken to another room and entered the office of Vitaliy Vasylovych Kovalinskiy, aged 70, famous Kyiv historian, prolific author of Kyiv history, editor of the journal *Kupola* (Dome, as in Kyiv's iconic church domes), and head of the barely visible Museum of the History of the City of Kyiv. The room was the size of my modest office at the university, but there were many, many more books piled everywhere, posters, Kyiv maps, and mementoes on the walls, a desk with higher piles of paper than on my messy desk, and a desktop computer that was not exactly yesterday's but more from the day before yesterday. He welcomed me warmly, heard me out about my interests, and then did indeed explain it all as promised. He said a lot more, too, as we met quite a few more times, often because I had a list of questions from reading homework that he "assigned" me. As soon as I raised my first questions about history, he turned me to selections from his nine volumes of *Kyivski miniatury* (Kyiv Thumbnails), fun essays about all sorts of Kyiv topics that he had published between 2002 and 2011. I began to buy the books as soon as I left the first meeting in the old Soviet-style bookstore on the other side of European Square, and forevermore thereafter walked Kyiv's streets with insights from what I had read. In this way, Vitaliy Vasylovych became for me an early and key informant. In subsequent meetings, he railed against ill-conceived proposals to erect super skyscrapers in historic districts and about the neglect of aging infrastructure and historic monuments. Once, he walked me to the landmark statue of Prince Volodymyr the Great, the 988 baptizer of the Kyivan population, to show me its wear and to discuss efforts to arrest corrosion. On another occasion, we went through his computer files

Figure 2.1   Exhibits from the Museum of the History of the City of Kyiv being packed up for moving to limbo (Courtesy of V. Kovalynskyi)

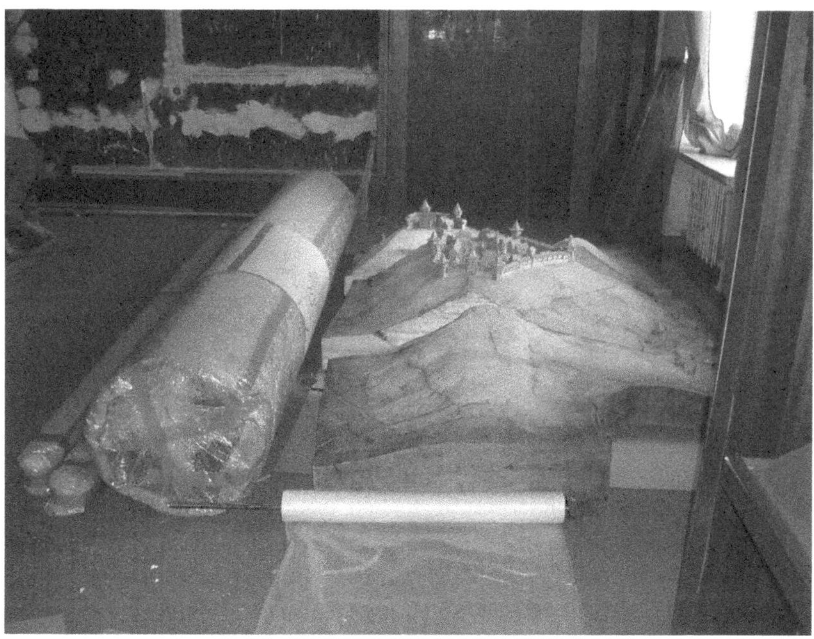

and slid electronic copies of documents, photographs, news clippings, and other information about the now-invisible museum from his hard drive to my jump drive (Figure 2.1).

Our conversations started as soon as we exchanged business cards at the start of the first meeting. I noted that his *vyzitivka* (business card) had only phone numbers and an email address as contact information, and no street address for the museum that he directed. His response to my question opened the door to learning how land use politics works in Ukraine and proved invaluable. As he explained the situation, he spoke in the deliberate and professional tone of a senior and respected museum head. Yet, I could also see that Vitaliy Vasylovych was angry. The museum had been kicked out of its quarters on April 24, 2003 (the date of the official notice), simply because the Supreme Court liked the building and had more pull. Now, more than eight years later, a skeleton staff was trying to keep busy in a far corner of the former Lenin Museum, while the museum's 40,000 exhibits were locked away in crates in the building's bowels. Promises swirled about a new location, first this one and then another one, and then another one still, but none had come to fruition despite Vitaliy Vasylovych's best lobbying efforts, despite considerable support for the museum's cause from Kyiv's cultural community, and even despite a strong letter of support from the head of Ukraine's parliament. The Supreme Court is fully entrenched in Klovskyi Palace, and one after another plans for replacement quarters fall through. And so, Kovalinskiy and the other employees found themselves to be exiled for an indeterminate term to a Ukrainian limbo, a silent place called Ukrainian House that used to be a museum about Lenin.

2.2   An Imperium of Raiders

The fate of the Museum of the History of the City of Kyiv is the result of what Ukrainians call *reyderstvo* (raiding; the same word appears in Russian). I later learned about dozens of other examples where people or institutions with superior connections to power were able to displace those without, and I saw that this was a fundamental element of the way that Kyiv works today. Cultural institutions such as museums, art galleries, libraries, and bookstores were disproportionate victims, but raiders also took places of business, residential buildings, schools, at least one medical clinic, and many, many plots of ground that had served neighborhoods as public squares, children's playgrounds, or green spaces that Soviet city planners had once carefully allocated. If someone wanted your site or even the business that you had worked hard to grow, they simply pulled strings to have you investigated for tax fraud, building code violations, unpaid customs levies, or any of a number of other trumped up charges, and you were gone. The courts would rarely help, because there, too, raiders bought influence. And if need be, thugs would be hired to hasten your departure. In the new Kyiv, instead of the wisdom of planning professionals, the voices of citizens, and even the laws of the state, the only forces that mattered in what land was used for by whom were connections to power. In many cases, those connections were rooted in family ties, as a father might be a member of parliament and a son or son-in-law might be a developer-entrepreneur, but more often it was money that did the singing. I witnessed dozens of protests about the situation at City Hall and other venues, read honest reporting by journalists, saw citizens' petitions for redress, and even attended some hearings in court, but almost always the result was the same – money sings loudest and opens doors to power and property.

Sadly, Ukraine has become an imperium of raiders. Even during communist times, there were elites and politically connected thugs who lived above the law and profited from the wealth of the others and the nation as a whole, but now since the blunt force of capitalism has been unleashed the actions of raiders run central. As expressed by Kyiv architectural historian Mykhailo Kalnytskyi, "[in the past] the Bolsheviks destroyed many things for the communist belief, and today people will destroy anything for money" (Kozmina, 2000). In addition to the countless cases of heartache, misery, and injustice that are brought on, the net result is (1) an enormous concentration of wealth into relatively few hands; (2) *more* concentration of *more* wealth into fewer hands as the most adept raiders raid raider-competitors; (3) enormous gaps in incomes and levels of living between the most adept raider class and the rest of Ukraine; and (4) the general impoverishment of the country as a whole. What is more, the very realistic threat that raiders will take over any successful business has hampered foreign investment into Ukraine and chased away potential investors. Furthermore, even humanitarian aid for the poor or victims of a disaster such as a flood, be that aid from within Ukraine or a form of foreign aid, is subject to hijack, as raiders have routinely helped themselves to shipments of food, medical supplies, and other necessities which they then put on the market for their own profit.

That is only half the story. Although we will never be able to quantify it, the other half is that a very large share of the profits from raiding leaves the country. Some raiders are Russians and work as if there were no boundaries between the two countries, so the money goes to Moscow and other cities to the north, but most are citizens of Ukraine who invest, spend, and squirrel away what they have taken in other countries. There are Swiss banks and banks in Cyprus among other places where transparency is hampered, yachts in the Mediterranean, and villas in the south of France, in Spain, and elsewhere. There are ski chalets in Switzerland, expensive apartments in London or in the United States, beachfront property in Thailand, and second homes in Israel. The money goes also for shopping sprees in Paris and London, and for expensive private schools and universities in the United Kingdom, the United States, Switzerland, and other countries for the children of the rich. Details come from anecdotal evidence, investigative reporting, and "outing" by political opponents, but proof is scarce and a total picture, including knowing the total monetary amount that has gone offshore, is not possible.

2.3   Theater at Teatralna

Having said all this about *reyderstvo*, there is more to add about the saga of the Museum of the History of the City of Kyiv. Fast-forward two years and Kovalinskiy is now retired, his staff has dispersed, and there is no longer a trace of the museum in Ukrainian House. Lenin's place is now a venue for rotating displays for things to buy from abroad: high-end automobiles, wedding dresses, Japanese electronics, and popular fashions in clothing and accessories. From time to time, the airy rotunda where the revolution's leader had once stood provides a floodlit runway for leggy models. The museum, meanwhile, was reorganized (more than once) under new leadership, was renamed the Museum of the City of Kyiv, and was assigned a new location. It was opened to the public near the end of 2013. I know the new building well, and I have visited the museum. The staff was extremely courteous and I felt very welcome. I was even able to get in at the discounted rate for senior citizens of 15 hryvnia as opposed to the normal price of 30 hryvnia (US$2 as opposed to US$4 in round numbers), even though I offered to pay full fare as I am not a Ukrainian citizen. The nice woman at the ticket desk insisted that as long as I am a senior citizen and speak Ukrainian, I should get in as a Ukrainian. The rest of the story about the new museum continues with tales about demons. This part of the story can be called "Theater at Teatralna."

Teatralna is the name of a busy Metro station in the center of Kyiv that is near various popular theaters, including the Theater of Russian Drama at the very intersection where the Metro exits and Kyiv's beautiful Opera

Theater just up the street. On weekend evenings there is also an interesting "theater" played out belowground near the entry to the subway system – a dance party for pensioners to live accordion music. The oldsters dance with one another as couples, as well as in groups stepping together around a perimeter, and there are always plenty of onlookers clapping in time to the music. But the "Theater at Teatralna" that I describe here is neither one of the theater buildings nor the oldsters' dance party beneath the street intersection, but the singular "theater" that has accompanied the illegal construction of a multilevel commercial building on the site of a small public square at the Teatralna Street intersection. This construction project was frequently and vociferously protested by "Save Kyiv" activists. I went to these protests regularly, developed good sources about the situation, and saw it as an excellent case study of Kyiv's mess in microcosm. You can think ahead about how this new building figures into the story of the museum.

The address is 7 Vulytsya Bohdana Khmelnytskoho (Bohdan Khmelnytskyi Street). Perhaps because it is a central street-corner location that is much desired, the site has changed often in character. In the mid-19th century, it was the residence of an educator named Klymovych. It was then sold in 1871 to the noted Ukrainian political figure Hryhoriy Halahan who made Number 7 his own residence and turned Numbers 9-11 next door, a total of five buildings, into a private educational institution named for his father Pavlo Halahan. In 1919, after the Revolution, Number 7 became a medical clinic, then for a short while a theatrical school, and then from 1928 it was an institute for writers. The much-used building was finally taken down in 1981 when the subway was put through and Teatralna Station constructed. From that time until 2003, the site was a "square" – a small, green open space where passersby and local residents alike could take a break in a busy city center. The space must have been much beloved because when it was taken away in 2003 for development, all hell broke loose. The conflicts have not stopped since.

What happened is this. In November 2003, the Kyiv City Council announced that it had entered into negotiations with a company called Alliance-Center, Ltd., a construction and development company owned by two companies registered in Kyiv that wanted to build a multilevel commercial complex on the site. Neighbors began to protest that the city was taking away their square, and then after initially signing off on the proposal, the Kyiv Metropolitan System (the subway company) voiced objections, too, saying that the construction would imperil the rotunda above the entrance to Teatralna Station directly below. Even more, concerns were voiced that a collapse could occur just where people passed through turnstiles into and out of the station and lined up to purchase tokens and passes. Other complaints came later with the start of construction from neighbors who complained about noise. The Theater of Russian Drama across the street protested that noise and vibrations were interfering with performances and rehearsals. Critics also argued that a new commercial center was not needed, because there were already too many shopping areas in the center of Kyiv that lacked customers and a surfeit of empty office space. As a result, in July 2006 the city withdrew its authorization to continue construction, attaching the site to a "zone of protection" around local theaters, but about 18 months later, after who knows what transpired, the land was sold by the Kyiv government to Alliance-Center, Ltd., with the understanding that construction would continue.

Protests stepped up. At the end of 2009, opponents of the project had gathered more than 3,000 signatures of citizens against the project. There were frequent gatherings across the street from the construction site, speakers, placards, and clever programming by protest organizers. One event involved a theater-like performance by costumed characters who passed bribes from builders to city officials, who in turn produced documents that the builders need to start construction. The press was always present, as protest leaders made sure to inform journalists in advance about their activities. Police were always there, too. On February 2, 2011, the Cabinet of Ministers of the government of Ukraine proclaimed that the construction needed to stop, but it did not. On February 2 of that year, the head of Kyiv city administration Oleksandr Popov ordered that construction had to be halted by February 9, but it continued. On February 10, the chief architect of the City of Kyiv, Serhiy Tselovalnyk, said that the crane that supported construction would be taken down on February 17, but it was not taken down. On March 28, 2011, an appellate court upheld an earlier court decision that the construction was illegal, but construction continued. On April 7 it was announced in the press that demolition of the building was started, but on April 8 it was reported in the same sources that construction was continuing. In May 2011, the Kyiv City Council declared that such construction could not be permitted, because 7 Vulytsya Bohdana Khmelnytskoho fell within the historic preservation zone centered on the St. Sophia Cathedral complex, but constriction continued.

Informants explained that builders were able to continue building despite orders to cease because they faced no risk. If they ever actually had to stop and were ordered to dismantle what they had erected, they would be paid for their trouble, i.e., for the cost of construction *and* for the cost of demolition and clean-up. Apparently, such is the close relationship in Kyiv between well-placed builders and their sponsors in key positions of government. As a result, one of the protest leaders, Natalia Moussienko, a neighbor of the project, proposed tongue-in-cheek that if the building were allowed to stand, it should be not a commercial center but Kyiv's Museum of Corruption.

2.4   A Dubious Home

Natalia was close, but not quite accurate. As hinted above, this building, now completed, is the new Museum of the City of Kyiv. This is because of a "Solomonic" compromise that the well-meaning Oleksandr Popov announced with great satisfaction on August 26, 2011: the public would get back space that it had lost to the developers, and the museum would at long last get its new home. When the museum's directors protested that the site was way too small for the 40,000 exhibits that they had boxed into crates, and that they did not want to be in an illegal building, and that they did not want to fall through the subway station's rotunda onto the Metro tracks below, they were replaced. The government of Kyiv and the government of Ukraine had had enough of the bickering and here was the solution, no matter what. Besides, Euro 2012, a major football tournament that Ukraine and Poland were cohosting, was fast approaching and was going to occupy everyone's attention, so this matter had to be put to rest. Plus, it would look good to have a museum for visitors to see. There was not enough time, of course, to actually open the museum in time for summer 2012 visitors, but signs were put up high and low that this was the Museum of the History of Kyiv, along with a brass plaque that is so shiny that it can function as a mirror. It reads that this building is a "gift to the people of Kyiv" from Alliance-Center, Ltd. There was a "grand opening" of the museum on May 26, 2012 (just before the start of the football tournament), complete with blue and yellow balloons (the colors of Ukraine's flag). It was scheduled for 3:00 p.m., but just in case there were protestors who intended to disrupt the event, it was held earlier, as the Soviets would have done, at 1:00 p.m.

No one really believes that Alliance-Center, Ltd., actually gave its building away. Conventional wisdom is that in these kinds of "scandalous" situations (from the word *skandalnyi/skandalna* that is applied often to construction by raiders), the taxpayers keep paying, in this case for a building that they did not want on a piece of land that was illegally taken from them. And what a structure they got! Not only is the building said to be unsafe with respect to the Metro below, the architects gave it an eleventh hour "museum look" by sticking six cheap-looking statues of medieval knights and Cossacks in a row on the roof line (they have hooks on the back for hoisting), and above the doors are female caryatids with their backs against the building. They look silly as could be holding up nothing more than thin pieces of clear Plexiglas that provide a sliver of shelter from rain. Other than the nice staff, what is inside is goofy, too. There are two floors of displays in cases from a catalogue. While it is refreshing to not have the usual clutter of thousands of objects, the displays as a whole are very thin and represent only a tiny fraction of the old museum's wealth. Also, the exhibits are not especially well chosen and not always well explained, although most key times in the city's history from when Kyiv was the glorious capital of an impressive princely state called Rus to independence in 1991 are touched on at least a little. However, some display cases are curiously empty. While the first floor has a wonderful model of ancient Kyiv as a centerpiece that I remembered seeing a long time ago when I visited 8 Orlyka years ago with my late father, the second floor centers on something entirely unexpected – a beautiful silk Japanese kimono accented with gold thread. The sign says that it was a gift from the city of Kyoto. In fact, we might close this discussion by saying that everything about the museum, from the creepy statues with hooks on their backs on the roof to the inexpensive display cases with hastily assembled displays inside, says that Kyiv's history resides in this building only temporarily. The museum, we conclude, is still in limbo, its collections, if they have not been raided, are still in crates, and the man who (among others) lovingly cared for them, Vitaliy Vasylovych Kovalinskiy, is out of the picture.

Alexander Motyl, a specialist on Ukrainian politics and Professor of Political Science at Rutgers University in Newark, NJ, minced no words in a *Kyiv Post* article entitled "Misrepresenting History at the Kyiv Museum" (2013).[3] He begins with the question "Does Kyiv have a history" and concludes that based on the weak exhibits, visitors to the museum would answer the question with a resounding "No." "The bottom line," Motyl writes, "is that this is unlike any exhibit of history I've ever seen. There are no narratives, no stories, no highlights, no themes – just a bunch of almost randomly collected stuff. Stuff, needless to say, may make for a great flea market, but it does not amount to a museum exhibit." I agree. I agree also with Motyl's assessment of why such a poor museum exists:

3   The article is also available on Motyl's blog in the online journal *World Affairs*: http://www. worldaffairsjournal.org/blog/alexander-j-motyl/misrepresenting-history-kyiv-museum.

> So who is to blame for this disaster? … The Yanukovych regime. The
> ministries of culture and education are run by Regionnaires [members
> of the Party of Regions] committed to emptying Ukrainian history,
> culture, and language of all content and reducing them to footnotes of
> some grand Soviet/Russian narrative. The last thing the Regionnaires
> want is a capital city with a genuine history: that might suggest that
> Ukraine has a history and that – heaven forbid – Ukrainians have an
> identity.

I am glad that Motyl wrote what he did because it both opens the door
and offers independent support for arguments that emerge in the pages
ahead – that Yanukovych and his fellow Regionnaires are to be counted as
central demons in Kyiv's present traumas.

3   Sketches from the Capital

3.1   Castle Hill

It is good to get high, so we climb Zamkova Hora (Castle Hill), a high promontory in the center of Kyiv, to reflect on a city rich with history and promise, and on the predicaments of today. The hill is also known as "Lysa Hora," ("Bald Mountain"). From there we gain a panorama of the city and various places that we will discuss in the pages ahead, as well as have a close-up look at the hill itself and its peculiarities. An entire book can be written about this place. Indeed, the hill has inspired many: Nikolai Gogol (1819-1898) used Castle Hill as the setting for his haunting short story "The Eve of Ivana Kupala" (1830); which in turn was the inspiration for the classic symphonic poem called "Night on Bald Mountain" (1867) by Modest Mussorgsky (1839-1881); which in turn was presented in a new arrangement in 1886 by Nikolay Rimsky-Korsakov (1844-1908) as a "fantasy for the orchestra" called "Night on Bare Mountain"; which in turn was incorporated by Walt Disney (1901-1966) as a scene in his popular animation film *Fantasia* (1940). Nowadays, the Rimsky-Korsakov rendition of the original piece by Mussorgsky is heard widely as "Halloween music."

The panorama is indeed a representation of Kyiv. We are on the city's Right Bank, beside the hills where the walled city of Prince Volodymyr the Great stood and where his son Yaroslav the Wise enlarged Kyiv and built additional walls of his own. Those ramparts are gone, but we can still imagine their courses along the ridges that we see across the deep ravines 100 to 200 yards (91 to 183 meters) away in the directions of Kyiv's historic core. We also see the domes of churches and high bell towers beyond, some dating from the city's early years and others the recent work of Kyiv's postsocialist "rebuilding of religion." The distinctive green-and-gold domes of St. Andrew's Church are the closest. These various churches, however, do not rise alone and are being increasingly crowded by the high-rise office buildings and apartments of New Kyiv. Some of them, in turn, are capped with domelike shapes of their own – the "oligarch domes" of postsocialist urban-architectural fashion. There are also stretches of greenery. One of them, an area nearby just beside the National Museum of Ukrainian History, is called Peyzazhna Aleya (Landscape Alley) and represents an important victory by a coalition of Kyiv's green-minded citizens against greed-minded development. In the other direction, we look down to see historic Podil at the level of river below, and we can pick out its various conflicts between history and new construction. Across the river to the horizon are the plains of the Left Bank. This is where the famous steppes of Ukraine come to Kyiv's door and where, especially in Soviet times, countless districts of standardized apartment blocks were constructed. In the direction of Troyeshchyna in Kyiv's northwest, this residential landscape merges with the horizon. The river itself is an imposing sight: wide, edged here with greenery or sandy beaches and there with highways, concrete, and industry. In all directions are tall buildings, many of them of an invasive type that Kyivans call "monsters." Construction cranes signal more tall buildings to come and a large city in transition.

For a period of months recently, St. Andrew's Church was surrounded by scaffolding and construction equipment. That was because the church had been listing and was in danger of sliding down its own slope, and the city government had initiated a project to save the structure. It seems that the hill the church stands on has been made unstable because of new construction activity and tree-cutting nearby, and it can no longer carry the heavenly weight without the pilings and concrete reinforcements that needed to be installed. A cobblestone lane winds downhill along the bottom of a ravine that begins just beneath the church for more about a kilometer (0.6 of a mile) into the heart of Podil below. This is Andriyivskyi Uzviz or Andriyivskyi Spusk (St. Andrew's Descent), the funky street filled with art galleries and studios, cafés, small museums, and vendors of handicrafts and trinkets for tourists that we will look at in Chapter 6. From our hilltop perch we see the roofs of landmarks such as the Castle of Richard the Lionhearted (as it is called), and look down at the controversial destruction, construction, and reconstruction that has turned *uzviz* (the slope) into one of Kyiv's main battlegrounds between preservationists of history and builders of what critics call "monsters."

Looking down from our hill in the opposite direction, between us and the undulating ridges where the walls of Kyiv once ran, is an even deeper ravine. Here, one fork that is called Honchari was once an old stream-course lane populated by potters and other artisans, while another, called Kozhumyaki, was an historic district of tanneries and leather workers. Now, the whole area has been freshly redeveloped and goes by still another historic name, Vozdvyzhenka. As described in Chapter 7, it is one of the craziest-looking urban districts that I have ever seen.

In addition to the view in various directions, there are lessons about Kyiv from Castle Hill itself. By some accounts, the promontory is linked to the very beginnings of the city and was the supposed home of Kyi himself, the person after whom the city is named. He was the city's legendary founder in the 6th or 7th century along with his younger brothers, Shchek and Khoriv, and his sister, Lybid. While the founding story of Kyiv is dubious, we do know that the hill was once named Kyevytsia, again after Kyi, a person who may or may not have actually existed. The hill takes its present name from two castles that stood on the heights much later, the first built by a Lithuanian ruler in the 14th century when Kyiv was part of the Grand Duchy of Lithuania, and the second, a 16th-century rebuilding of the first, that came to be occupied by rulers from the Kingdom of Poland. The first castle was destroyed in 1482 by Crimean Tatars, while its reincarnation came down in 1651 in the war against the Polish nobility by Ukrainian Cossacks led by Bohdan Khmelnytskyi. There has been no castle since, but the name "Castle Hill" has survived. In the early 19th century, part of the hill was used as a cemetery for citizens of Podil, and in 1854, the hill (or part of it) was assigned to Podil's Florivsky Monastery, which built a hilltop chapel and opened a cemetery of its own. In Soviet times, a communications tower stood on Castle Hill. Except for decrepit foundations and piles of old bricks from the chapel, and turned over and a vandalized gravestones amid underbrush, there is not much at all on the hill today. Part of it is thickly forested, hiding whatever relics there are from the 19th century from public exposure, while another part is curiously barren, alternating between grassy fields and stretches of bare ground. It is perhaps that aspect that gave Castle Hill that other of its many names, Lysa Hora (Bald Mountain).[4]

Indeed, perhaps the most overwhelming feeling that one gets on the bald Castle Hill is that something is missing – that here, in the very center of Kyiv, in a spot surrounded by so much visible history and so much urban variety, energy, dynamism, and change, is a wild emptiness. I have been to the top dozens of times, often as the only person in sight. The first time I went, I was unprepared for the scene and was actually afraid. What if something happens to me? What if there are robbers or killers? Or packs of wild dogs? As it turned out, nothing bad ever happened because most of the time, there was simply no one there. I observed that even dogs did not roam the heights, presumably because for them, too, Castle Hill was a void. Instead, they concentrated at the lower slopes nearer the neighborhoods where they could get food. On Sundays and holidays with good weather there were other visitors: urban explorers like myself, photographers, and

---

4   Other names for Castle Hill have been Khorevytsia after Khoriv, the brother of Kyi; Kysilivka after the 17th-century Ukrainian political figure Adam Kysil; and Florivaska Hora (or Frolivska Hora) after the 16th-century monastery and convent in Podil. There are other hills in Kyiv that are also "bald" and are also referred to as Bald Hill or Bald Mountain.

couples and small groups of friends who wanted to get away. Sometimes there were picnickers. But mostly, there was a palpable emptiness and quiet, the kind of stillness in which a chirping bird or a flying insect causes a disturbance. Almost two centuries ago, Nikolai Gogol may have had similar eerie feelings when he visited the hill.

One ascends Castle Hill from one of two places, one in Podil, and the other along St. Andrew's Slope, where there are stairs. In Soviet times, for a while at least, the hill was counted as parkland and was presumably appropriately maintained, but now even the stairs are decrepit. Where the landings and handrails were made of decorative cast iron or other metal, many pieces have been taken away by collectors and scrap metal thieves. On the other way up, where flat stepping stones were placed into cuts on the slope, we now have at least two decades of erosion by the elements and destruction by vandals. When it has rained, the way up or way down is nigh impossible because of slippery mud. Along both stairs and at the summit, there is trash – lots of it. Clearly, there are people who have been here in times past, but not necessarily so many, as the trash looks to have been accumulating for a long period, perhaps even for the two full decades that the Soviet Union and its trash-cleaning services have been out of business. Forays into "garbology," reveal vodka bottles, beer bottles, and more vodka bottles, as well as other drink containers, empty cigarette packages, picnic refuse, and the occasional spent condom. There are graffiti, too, although surfaces for writing are few. Nevertheless, we see the signatures of visitors who came before us on the stairways and on gravestones, and even on the trunks of some of the trees.

This is indeed a strange landscape to encounter, given that we are in the center of a large capital city of a large European country. We feel that we have slipped off the radar screen and stepped into a void. The space appears to be under no one's control or responsibility and is left to the elements as it was before Kyiv was settled. Human visitors are few, although once there were more as the broken stairways and architectural fragments on the summit attest, but now the space is left for drunks and vandals, for lovers under blue skies, and for occasional urban adventurers. The nights of May 1 (Walpurgis Night, a Central and Northern European witches' festival) and July 6 (the feast of Ivana Kupala [St. John the Baptist], formerly a day associated with a pagan fertility rite) seem to be different and attract party crowds around bonfires. I have also seen students shooting a film with characters dressed in costumes from the Middle Ages, a model shoot, and an excursion group with a guide speaking Russian, but on the summit I am almost always alone. Even the dogs stay away.

One last point: the dogs might know something. There are rumors that the hill is haunted, which might be one of the reasons why Kyivans choose to stay away and why this otherwise prime piece of real estate is neither a fine park nor, as yet, a development site. There are stories about headless riders on horses, flying witches, and bloodstains that won't wash away, as well as reports that in the evenings after rains and during windy weather, one can hear the crackling sounds of a castle burning and the crashing of its timbers, pierced by the desperate cries of the dying who were trapped inside. Some think that the screams are those of the young wife and children of the last Lithuanian prince to have resided in a castle, a man named Lelkovych who is said to have locked his family inside a burning tower in 1608. It is also said that one often sees the ghost of a nun dressed in black kneeling in prayer beside the ruins of the old chapel. I have never had any of these experiences, and I even managed to sneak home a souvenir brick with the brickmaker's logo and the date 1857 from those same ruins without having my hand slapped by a nun, whether real or apparent.

Other mystical aspects of Castle Hill can be seen be any visitor: the hill is a sacred place for believers in ancient Ukrainian pagan faiths and has amid the trees and on a specific "bald spot" at the summit ritual places of worship and sacrifice. There are places where large rocks have been arranged in symbolic geometries across the terrain, a stone altar with charred embers in the center from some sort of ritual fires, mysterious ribbons tied to tree branches, and various other signs of communion among people who are true believers that this particular hill, which they prefer to call Khorevytsya, has a sacred place in the distant history of Ukraine. I find the entire scene, from stairways to ghost stories and witches to be fascinating, and almost did not want to tell you about it to help keep it private. I have the greatly uncomfortable feeling that before long this neglected parkland on a hill will become the haunt of the rich. The monsters of Vozdvyzhenka can rise from the depths of their ravine and overtake the slopes and summit. From the top, the moneyed princes who rule today will have their showy castles with modern-day gates, and the rest of Kyiv can look up from below.

3.2   Notes from Euro 2012

We continue with a tidbit from recent news that, I think, reflects well on Kyiv and speaks to the city's potential to be one of Europe's leading urban centers. So much that I will report on later is negative or irregular, so a start with good news might be welcome. The story is a bit odd, but there are others below about real people and real events in Kyiv that are odder, so something offbeat might help set a tone, too. To wit, Kyiv, it seems, will soon put up a monument to honor the thousands of football (soccer) fans from Sweden who came to the city in summer 2012 to enjoy themselves as they supported their national squad in the UEFA Euro 2012 tournament. The games were hosted jointly by Poland and Ukraine and were held in four cities in each of the two countries. The opening match was in Warsaw on June 8 and the championship match, won by Spain over Italy, was in Olympic Stadium in Kyiv on July 1. By draw, Sweden, one of the 16 European countries that had qualified for the tournament, had its games scheduled in Kyiv, so Swedish fans came to the city in large numbers and stayed the longest. Their first match was against Ukraine, which the Ukrainian squad won 2-1. Later, Sweden lost to eventual Group D winner England and then defeated the team from France, but it was eliminated in the quarterfinals.

The games worked out well in the end for both host countries, but there were many worries and controversies beforehand. In Kyiv, for instance, there were enormous cost overruns on renovations to Olympic Stadium and concerns in the period before the games that the facility might not be ready on time. There were almost certainly considerable levels of corruption in this project, as well as in other aspects related to games facilities and preparations, including the costly expansion and renovations at the city's main airport. Moreover, there were not unfounded allegations by critics within Ukraine that only the rich and politically connected would benefit financially. Other worries were that Kyiv and the other host cities (in Ukraine they were Dontesk, Kharkiv, and L'viv) would be overrun by soccer hooligans, drunks, and sex tourists. Kyiv has unfortunately become a global-scale haven for the latter since the fall of the Soviet order (see Chapter 10), and there was every reason to believe that those who promote the sex industry in Kyiv and other games cities, and those who work in the industry on the front lines, would seize the opportunity for a huge jump in business. Outside Ukraine and Poland, there were concerns about price-gouging by taxis, hotels, airlines, and other vendors, and about the safety of foreign players and fans alike. It was said that players of African origin and other people of color would be subjected to racist taunts from the stands, and that foreign visitors to the host nations, be they of color or not, would be subjected to violent attacks by neo-Nazi skinheads. Such predictions came especially from England and were fanned by a BBC documentary (*Euro 2012: Stadiums of Hate*) that showed film footage of anti-Semitism and white power slogans and salutes by young toughs in both Poland and Ukraine. A well-known Scottish footballer, Ian Campbell, urged British fans to stay away from the host countries because of the supposed dangers. Also, Western European political leaders – most notably those in France, Britain, and Germany – announced boycotts of the games in the Ukrainian host cities because of Ukraine's recent lapses in human rights and the imprisonment of opposition leader and former Ukrainian Prime Minister Yulia Tymoshenko on charges of corruption and malfeasance in office that are said to be selective.

This is not the place to fully assess all of what took place with Euro 2012 or to account for the distribution costs and benefits of the project. An in-depth study would be fascinating, but in Ukraine, a truly detailed study could possibly be dangerous for the researcher. Relevant data are not easy to find and asking too many questions in a setting of rampant corruption would invite serious trouble. I can say instead about the games that the worst did not happen. Tymoshenko, however, continues to be imprisoned despite attempts by European leaders to use the football tournament as leverage on the Ukrainian government; and it is almost certainly true that the Ukrainian public as a whole paid for hosting their share of the games while the largest share of profits by far went into relatively few hands. But my main point is about Swedish fans. They apparently had a great time in Kyiv, with no major negative incidents, and left with mainly good memories except perhaps for the lack of their team's success on the field. They showed their gratitude to Kyiv with "Thank you" signs that they held up at the final match, and with handshakes and personal thanks to the nearest Ukrainian locals in their last days in the city. I was thanked myself multiple times by happy Swedes, although I had nothing to do with hosting them.

During the course of the tournament, the Swedes had their own zone within the larger "Fan Zone" that had been set up for the duration along Khreshchatyk, the main street though central Kyiv. There, they drank enormous quantities of beer, sang songs, waved Swedish flags, and enjoyed the music and other entertainment that they had arranged for themselves on a "Swedish stage." They were boisterous, had fun, and behaved themselves as much as or more than one could expect from football fans away from home. On the day of their first match, they held a loud and happy march through Kyiv and past the city's major landmarks on the way to the stadium, all without incident. The only sour note to report from my own observations was a British stand-up comic whose performance on the Swedish stage centered on tasteless jokes about Ukrainian culture and on Ukraine as a preferred destination for inexpensive sex. Ukrainian passersby who understood English looked on silently and perhaps wondered as did I about just where this lout thought he was; we all felt relieved when some of the partying Swedes began to jeer his act.

A great many of the Swedes, at least 5,000, camped in tents in the city. "Camp Sweden" was set up with official permission in Trukhaniv Park, an area of Dnipro River beaches that was walking distance to the center of Kyiv (but up a steep incline along the bluffs). They were able to party long into the night amid the trees, and on hot days to enjoy the beach. There were initial worries that not everything would be ready in time, but soon enough fresh water, portable toilets, and trash-removal services were provided by the city of Kyiv. Also, there was police security, electricity, and access to Wi-Fi. Taxis served the park, too, to help with luggage and camping gear. Shops were set up as well, offering souvenirs, snacks, and drinks. Mostly though, the Swedes ate and drank in the city, or purchased food, beer, and vodka in the same stores in the city where Ukrainians shopped. Therefore, they avoided much of the price gouging that may have been aimed at foreign visitors. They certainly avoided high hotel prices. In fact, the presence of this camp may have contributed to a reduction in the prices that hotels had originally intended to charge during the games, as it came clear to hoteliers that the marketplace was not in a mood for high prices in multistar hotels, and many rooms remained empty. I myself wound up paying a very fair price in a fine hotel not far from Camp Sweden during that summer.

The Swedes left happy, and Kyiv was impressed with the Swedes. There are exceptions on both sides, I am sure, but in general the relationship tilts heavily toward mutual admiration. And so now, months later, we read an announcement that in gratitude to the Swedes for their graciousness and good behavior, a monument would be set up on the site of Camp Sweden. How nice is that! A monument to tourists who have come through the city! Details about the form of the proposed monument are not set yet except for the beginnings of a competition among artists for a winning design.[5] A part of the context for understanding this plan is that Kyiv is part of a wider culture from Soviet times and even earlier that routinely builds monuments, erects historical markers and plaques, and awards certificates and elaborate medals for various categories of achievement. Another interpretation, also with merit, is that such a monument validates Ukraine's hosting the games and puts aside any criticisms that one might have about the games such as those about the ultimate distribution of financial benefits. However, the overall lesson is that Kyiv is proud to have hosted the games successfully, sees itself as all the more "European," is thankful to the Swedes for having been if not model visitors, then "better than expected" visitors, and is

5   The monument to the Swedes was unveiled June 8, 2013, exactly one year after the start of Euro 2012, and it sits where they camped. It has horns like a Viking.

eager to show to doubters and critics alike that the city and Ukraine as a whole are fine places with good people. That last point is a reminder for us, too, because in the pages below we will be discussing some of the serious problems that Ukrainians and Kyivans now face.

3.3   Monumental Woes

Almost directly across the river from where the Swedes camped and high atop a bluff is another beautiful park, this one named Khreschatyi Park. It is part of a much larger complex of parks along the Dnipro, and is scenic, romantic, historic, and everything else that one could ask of a park in the urban core. It was established in the mid-19th century by Kyiv's merchant elite and has long been known for summer concerts and other cultural events, notable statues and other monuments, and ornate cast-iron fountains. There are tall chestnut trees, steep slopes and deep ravines, peaceful winding paths, and comfortable benches for young lovers, old pensioners, and everyone else alike just meters away from the bustle of Kyiv's main streets. From promontories, we see the wide river itself, its beaches, islands, and other parks, including Trukhaniv Park, the historic district of Podil below, the spectacular statue of St. Volodymyr the Great and his brightly illuminated cross on a neighboring promontory, and kilometer after kilometer of newer residential districts across the Dnipro in Kyiv's Left Bank in the distance. Views are spectacular. So, too, is the enjoyment of nature – in all four seasons. It is a place in which to love Kyiv.

The main landmark in Khreschatyi Park is the People's Friendship Arch. It is positioned at the top of the hill that rises from the foot of Khreshchatyk, the city's main street, and it is here where we find insight into the tribulations of the city after the demise of the USSR and encounter a telling example of what I call Kyiv's "monumental uncertainty." The monument is an enormous (50 meter diameter; 164 feet) titanium rainbow arc that was constructed in the late Soviet year of 1982, and is one of the best-known and most recognizable symbols of the city. It is found on every map and in every guidebook, and it was erected to celebrate what at the time were presented as inseparable bonds between Ukraine and Russia. At night it is ablaze with rainbow colors that can be seen for quite a distance. It can be seen as well from along Khreshchatyk, as the monument rises from high above Evropeyska Ploshcha (European Square) where Khreshchatyk begins. From up close, we see that in addition to the arc there are two clusters of sculptures that complete the assemblage: tall bronze sculptures directly beneath the rainbow of two muscular male workers, one Russian and the other Ukrainian (which is which is neither evident nor important), who together and triumphantly hold aloft a characteristically Soviet, oversized "Soviet Order of Friendship of Peoples" medallion (Figure 3.1); while off to the side are granite sculptures of Ukrainian Cossack leader Bohdan Khmelnytskyi and other solemn principals at the 1654 Treaty of Pereyaslav that formally bound Ukraine to Russia.

Figure 3.1   Under the People's Friendship Arch

The monument is superb socialist-constructivist art but its message does not fit postindependence Ukraine. What to do? It could be taken down like a passé Lenin statue and replaced with something more patriotically Ukrainian, or it could stand because it is well-executed and because, even after the divorce, Ukraine and Russia can still be friends. Besides, the monument is new and it was expensive. So, for the time being, we see a mid-course solution: the rainbow and the statues stay but the bronze caption that had accompanied the two healthy comrades of socialist labor on the pediment beneath them has been removed. That action took place, I am told, very quickly after independence during a period of "No more Russia" euphoria. However, the message can still be read because every letter of every word has left a legible shadow: It still reads (first in Russian and then in Ukrainian translation below it), "In recognition of the union of Ukraine and Russia." The drill holes for every letter are still there, too, and I wonder if the bolts and letters are in storage somewhere in case of remarriage, but I was not able to find an answer to that question. So, what we have is a little of post-Soviet Ukraine's confused international politics in microcosm: we are separate from Russia but we are not.

Even more interesting is what has become of the space immediately around the titanium elephant. The high promontory continues to attract visitors both day and night for its great views, summer breezes, and peaceful setting just minutes from the hub of urban bustle. It also continues its twin after-dark roles as a place for young people to drink beer and for young lovers to get to know one another better. Rich kids with status-symbol cars sometimes drive to the very top for these purposes, using a service drive and the pedestrian access to get there, knowing that there is impunity against traffic violations simply because of the kinds of cars they drive. I have a photograph of a Mercedes CL55 with a telling license plate that begins with AA 7777 (the more As and 7s on a plate, the more you can be certain that the driver is well-connected) parked under the arch. Also, there is now a carnival for kids beside the uncertain monument – a thoroughly cheap-looking carnival complete with pony rides, bumper cars, and shooting galleries for useless prizes. Other new attractions are a trampoline jump, blaring US pop music (e.g., Michael Jackson), and an assortment of brightly painted mechanical contraptions that flash lights, make noise, and carry screaming passengers on two-minute rides up and down, or this way and that in looping circles and other configurations. A blue-and-yellow tent (Ukraine's colors) for administration of this new zone is identified with the ironic name Tsentralnyi Park Kultury (Central Park of Culture). Moreover, you can now climb from the backside of the arch and walk atop the hard heads of the signatories of the Treaty of Pereyaslav, as my adult children did when they visited me in Kyiv. No one cares; no one monitors. From there, the view of Kyiv is even better. You also get to study the stern bronze faces of the strapping Russian and Ukrainian chums up close, and can see a leaping Keanu Reeves (the American movie actor) on a poster plagiarized from the film *The Matrix* as the backdrop. Just before the Euro 2012 fans began to arrive, still another attraction was added to the array: a long ropeway along which paying passengers could descend individually in a thrill ride from high atop the viewpoint in Khreschatyi Park across the Dnipro to the sands of Trukhaniv Beach below. For daring Swedish campers, this was doubtlessly a fast way home from the city.

3.4   Demons at Desiatynna

Desiatynna (meaning "one-tenth") was the name of the first great church that was built in Kyiv after Prince Volodymyr the Great had his subjects baptized into the Christian faith in 988. It was completed in 996 and stood prominently within the original walled city on a high promontory overlooking the Dnipro River. Its formal name was the Church of the Dormition of the Virgin, but it came to be known popularly as Desiatynna because its cost was covered by a one-tenth portion of Volodymyr's wealth. Thus, in English the historic church is often referred to as the Church of the Tithes. By the end of the long (1019-1054) reign of Volodymyr's supremely enlightened son Prince Yaroslav I, known with great respect as Yaroslav the Wise, more than 400 churches studded much enlarged Kyiv. The city was called the "New Jerusalem" because it was envisioned as both a rival to the Abrahamic holy city and as an alternative religious capital to Muslim-controlled Jerusalem.

We no longer know much for sure about the dimensions and the form of the original Desiatynna, but it was certainly built in the Byzantine architectural tradition and was the first exemplar of Kyiv's domes. There is a cathedral in Chernihiv, a Ukrainian city to the north of Kyiv, that was built in the 1030s that is said to resemble Volodymyr's church, but even that is not known for sure. What we do know is that after his death in 1015, Volodymyr was buried in Desiatynna alongside his wife, Anna, and that after a reburial ceremony while Volodymyr was still ruler, the church had also become the final resting place for his grandmother, the brilliant Princess Olha (Olga), the first Christian ruler of Rus (945-963).

The church is long gone. It was destroyed along with the rest of Kyiv in the Mongol invasion of 1237-1240. Hundreds of Kyivans had taken shelter in the church during the onslaught and perished when the burning structure collapsed. In the 17th and 18th centuries there were botched attempts at reconstruction that disturbed the architectural integrity of the ruins, and now even those latter-day churches are gone. There is just bare earth at the site, beneath which are fragments of foundation, although they are more from the reconstructions than from the original church. The site was an active archeological dig until recently, but now whatever the specialists were looking at has been covered again with earth and the premises are enclosed by a high wooden fence painted green, just like the fences all over the city that surround construction sites and sites where old buildings await demolition.

Despite the fact that there is no longer anything to see there, the vacant ground is held sacred by all flavors of Orthodox and Ukrainian Catholic believers as a place of origin of their Christian faith. It is also held holy because it links them to the proud history of Kyivan Rus. However, there are differences in historical interpretation between nationalistic Ukrainians on the one hand and nationalistic Russians on the other about which nation is more directly descendant from Rus, and whether Ukrainians are truly a national population. Consequently, the Desiatynna site has enormous emotional meaning for both Ukrainians and Russians, and has occasionally been the locus of conflict between hardliners on both sides. This has held back decisions about what, if anything, should be built. The choices seem to be some combination of a church, a museum, or a prominent monument, or perhaps nothing at all except an historical marker. Instead of Solomonic compromises or civil discourse between competing interests, what we have instead at the summit of Prince Volodymyr's hill is more of the incessant chaos and conflict that have marked Ukraine since independence. The story is ugly, pure and simple, and factions on all sides behave like demons. Let me tell you what happened at Desiatynna on Saturday, May 28, 2011, a day that I describe as one for the notebooks.

Beside the wooden fence that surrounds the site of the old church is the Ukrainian National Museum of History on one side, the city's oldest tree, a 370-year-old linden, near the fence on another side, and the beautiful baroque St. Andrew's Church in a third direction. Just there, Andriyivskyi Uzviz (Andrew's Slope), the popular street for arts and crafts and tourist souvenirs, begins its winding descent to the elevation of the river below. Also just outside the fence, on the grounds between the imposing history museum and a forbidding green fence, and amid various relic stones that had been unearthed from other chapters of history on this very plateau, is a small and low-slung Orthodox church. It is about eight years old, has an

Figure 3.2   The small and controversial Church of the Nativity of the Blessed Virgin. In the background is the historic, baroque St. Andrew's Church, while to the right is a fence that demarcates the site of Desiatynna Church. The signboard announces that a museum is slated to be built. The photograph is from March, 2014.

ornate iron front gate and low iron fence of its own, a lot of loud bells to ring the faithful to services, and an attractive, modern-style Orthodox cross on the roof. Until recently it was made of timber and resembled a log cabin, but now it is larger and is finished with masonry (Figure 3.2). It also has great ambitions: depending on the source, it plans either to rebuild Desiatynna, to build a great new church on the Desiatynna site, or to build a new church beside the Desiatynna site in a way that would preserve and celebrate the sanctity of Desiatynna. Regardless of which path is true, the small structure that stands now is temporary and the plan is to erect a grand new church.

The small church is the Ukrainian Orthodox parish of the Nativity of the Blessed Virgin. It is actually a Russian Orthodox Church that answers to Volodymyr, the Moscow-appointed Metropolitan of Kyiv and of All Ukraine, who comes to visit regularly in his black Mercedes, and in turn to his ecclesiastical superior, the controversial Kirill, a man whose title is Patriarch of Moscow and All Rus and Primate of the Russian Orthodox Church. The controversies about the Patriarch swirl because of his alleged past as a KGB agent codenamed Mikhailov; his close relations with President Putin of Russia, also from the KGB; his running a business importing cigarettes into Russia by exploiting the duty-free status that was given to the church; and his apparent wealth. In addition to expensive tastes in automobiles, we have seen Kirill on a photo on the church website wearing a pricy Breguet brand Swiss watch. However, it has since been airbrushed out, probably because the original photo became an Internet hit. If the parishioners and their priests succeed in building a huge shrine either atop or beside the Desiatynna site, they will symbolically claim the religious and historic center of Kyiv for the capital city of Russia. Such a possibility infuriates those Ukrainians who identify with the two rival, Ukraine-based Orthodox confessions, Ukrainian Catholics, and millions of other Ukrainians with strong nationalistic, anti-colonial, and anti-Russian sentiments. Thus, when newspapers and other media reported on the morning of May 25, 2011, that trucks with construction equipment had arrived during the postmidnight hours and were admitted within the locked enclosure of the Desiatynna archeological site by Russian Orthodox priests with keys for the gates, all hell broke loose. Who gave them, a religious faction, the keys to important national property? Did they also receive authority to build? What did the archeologists know about this?

For now, these are unanswered questions in no-transparency Ukraine. Thinking nothing but the worst, by May 28 the picketing by "Moscow-phobic" Ukrainians was fast and furious. I was there that day as an observer, and I saw Ukraine depressingly deeply riven by national identity, language, and flavor of faith. There was profound hatred on all sides. Among the protestors, some of whom may have been provocateur-plants (you never know), I heard the ugliest of chanting and saw the most vile messages on picket signs (for example, that Russian Orthodox "priest-pigs" should be carved up to make sausages). Meanwhile, the lineup of priests and monks who faced the angry masses from behind a protective barricade of police at the gate of their little log church were positively disgusting with their smirks and eye-daggers on this day when they held the cards. "Their" president, Yanukovych, nominally himself a member of the Moscow church and, clearly from much evidence, a great fan of Kirill, had allegedly authorized the start of construction, and on that day the protestors could do no more than vent their frustrations.

Jerusalem, Constantinople, Ayodhya, and Kyiv, I thought, all ancient cities fraught with both domes of religion and demons of hatred. The Soviets had kept such factionalism suppressed, but when the weight of their authority lifted unexpectedly in 1991, Ukrainians became free to debate their allegiances and to behave against one another just like the country's notoriously pugilistic parliamentarians who are discussed in the next section. The police impressed me with their professionalism. They had managed to keep the peace such that despite all the anger, by the end of the day no one had hit anyone and no one was hurt. Months later, as I write this, the log cabin church still stands and is guarded round the clock by a hired private security service. I also see Kyiv police on the site quite often and young Russian Orthodox priests who look like boxers. I note that the holy men drive Mercedes automobiles and I always look to see what kind of watches are on their wrists. The church stopped dumping its trash behind the green fence, because protestors had made a big deal about the fact that they had found cards where the Orthodox faithful had written out their intentions for prayers by the priests (for which they had paid) among the refuse. Protestors show up from time to time and write graffiti on the fence, which is then repainted after they leave. The conflict wears on and on.

3.5   The Ukrainian Fight Club

Not surprisingly, the coming of independence was greeted with great joy by many Ukrainians as the start of a new era. For them, the old demons of communist rule and Russian cultural imperialism were dead or about to die, and there were great promises for a bright future. The break wasn't all serendipitous, of course, as many brave citizens had been clamoring for human rights and challenged Soviet authority for decades before independence finally arrived, and some dissidents such as Alla Horska, Vasyl Stus, Oksana Meshko, Oleksa Hirnyk, and Oleksa Tykhyi had given their lives for these causes. In Ukraine, as well as in other former republics that had once been part of Moscow's "prison of nations" or "family of nations," depending on one's stance about the Soviet Union, exuberant citizens toppled or otherwise dismantled the huge statues of Lenin that had stood in the centers of capital cities, removed other symbols of Soviet rule, and celebrated in the streets as the good news unfolded. It was only later that the reality began to sink in that there was work ahead to build a new order, and that there would be new demons along the way that would dash dreams of easy freedoms and a smooth ride to democracy and prosperity. In Ukraine especially, more so than in some of the other non-Russian republics (especially the Baltics), a "Wild West" ensued in which there was more disorder than anyone had imagined in the place of the order that, for better or worse, had been imposed by Soviet authority.

Now, more than 20 years later, there is still no clear recipe for Ukraine's future nor consensus about what the post-Soviet world should be like. That is one of the main reasons for the mess. Perhaps more so than in the other former republics other than the Russian Federation itself, a free-for-all for opportunists ensued: former communists refashioned themselves as democrats and capitalists and scrambled for political power under new constitutions and for entire industries for personal gain. They took over metallurgy, mass media, agribusiness, natural gas, chemicals, the airlines, banking, and even sports teams, among other branches of the economy that had once been the property of the state, and joined the ranks of the richest people in the world. People were killed in the scramble, including political rivals and business competitors, as well as journalists and other citizens who complained about the widespread theft of national wealth and endemic corruption. Instead of a country run by privileged members of the Communist Party, power shifted to well-connected, new-billionaire oligarchs and the politicians they supported, while true democracy and an open, civil society took a back seat. For 20 years since independence, it has been two steps forward and one step back, followed by one step forward and two steps back in Ukraine, depending who is in power or how you view that particular political party. Ukraine is still in many ways as disorganized as it was in 1991. Indeed, as we will see, under President Viktor Fedorovych Yanukovych (in office since February 25, 2010) and his Party of Regions Ukraine is taking many more than two steps back. The European Union has become highly critical of this situation, and it seems that Ukraine is now further from being allowed to join rather than closer. Moreover, the country is deeply and complexly divided both geographically and ethnically/linguistically, and according to many observers, hardly functions as a single state with a common goal. Yanukovych is said to have worsened the divisions, such that the very basics of what Ukraine is and what kind of place it should be are, for better or worse, still up in the air.

Incredibly, one often hears in Ukraine that the country is run by Ukraine-haters. Even more, Ukraine's citizens in significant proportions apparently genuinely believe that the politicians in charge actually despise the country that elected them and work instead for foreign powers! Critics of former "Orange Revolution" president Viktor Yushchenko said that about his turning of Ukraine between 2005 and early 2010 to the West and in particular the United States, where his wife is from; while critics of Yanukovych, the president who succeeded him, argue with equal conviction that he and his *"kirilivska-donetska banda"* (his Party of Regions gang from his hometown, Donetsk, in the east of Ukraine and his close ties to Kirill, the patriarch of the heavily political Russian Orthodox church based in Moscow) are actually working for Russia. The more billboards that Viktor II erects to tell the nation to love Ukraine, the more millions and millions of citizen-critics say that the message is a front and that under Yanukovych the nation is being nudged back to its neighbor to the north. For example, in an action that was both symbolic and would have practical implications, the Verkhovna Rada voted early 2011 to return the country to the same time zone as Russia by abolishing the use of daylight savings time, which had been adopted in 1992 specifically to bring Ukraine one hour closer to the rhythms of Europe. Until it was reversed in response to the popular outcry, the decision put Ukraine once again on Moscow time, like it was during Soviet winters, and back two hours from the clocks of Europe. Could there be another such country on the planet where the top-most leaders, one election after the other in succession, are routinely accused of being agents of foreign powers?

The court of world opinion is also negative about today's Ukraine. At the time of the Orange Revolution, the country was the darling of post-Soviet nations in Western eyes, with tangible prospects for democracy, an open society, and free-market prosperity, but more recently Amnesty International, Freedom House, and other international human rights bodies (e.g., Reporters without Borders, Human Rights Watch, and the United Nations Human Rights Committee) have all flagged Ukraine as a disturbingly regressive state. They and other independent observers sound alarms about everything from endemic corruption to dubious election processes and documented worrisome declines in Ukraine in basic freedoms and government transparency from soon after Yanukovych took office. So, too, Europe is ever more wary of Ukraine as a potential EU member, citing recent slippage in freedoms for the press, economic freedoms (164th of 183 nations as reported by the US–Ukraine Business Council), and academic freedoms and policies that would integrate the country's higher education system with practices in other countries. There are also concerns about selective prosecutions of political opponents, most famously those against former Prime Minister Yulia Tymoshenko, whose circuslike trial for abuse of powers began in 2011 the day after Ukrainian Constitution Day (June 28) and concluded with a guilty verdict and a seven-year prison sentence that she is now serving. There were also dubious charges brought against former Interior Minister Yuryi Lutsenko, who for a time was on a hunger strike in protest of accusations against him, and against former Finance Minister Bohdan Danylyshyn, another member of Tymoshenko's inner circle, who has been granted political asylum in the Czech Republic.

I wonder if there is another country in the world that tolerates tacky commercial advertising just outside its capitol building. Amazingly, that is the case on Capitol Hill in Kyiv, outside the Verkhovna Rada building, the building of the national parliament and formerly a seat of Soviet Ukrainian bureaucracy. The building itself is an elegant and inspiring structure with classical columns and a large glass dome (designed by V. Zabolotny; erected in the harsh Stalinist years of 1936-1939), and one of the main national landmarks in the city. The street immediately outside the building is Vulytsya Hrushevskoho (Hrushevskyi Street), named after the famous Ukrainian historian Mykhailo Hrushevskyi (1866-1934) who was president of the short-lived 1917-1918 Ukrainian National Republic. The street was previously named Kirov Street after the prominent Bolshevik leader Sergei Kirov (1886-1934) after whom so much else was also named in the Soviet Union (Kirovograd, the Kirov Ballet, etc.), and it was once lined with red Soviet flags and communist symbols and slogans. However, in today's Kyiv it is advertisements for the products and services of capitalism that adorn the street. There are commercial billboards large and small, and banners positioned one after the other along the full length of Vulytsya Hrushevskoho that span the street overhead from one side to the other. On the summer day that I made a full photographic inventory in 2012, the advertisement closest to the capitol building of Ukraine was for a business enterprise 100 meters away that offered Thai massages, while the banner that followed advertised *"Kvantova Epilatsiya"* in large font between suggestive silhouettes of two curvy female figures. The words mean "Quantum Epilation," apparently the proper name for the hair-removal salon that paid for the ad. Other text on this banner explains that the hair-removal process is new, painless, and lasts forever.

Finally, in case there is still doubt that Ukraine is a mess, we visit Ukraine's parliament to see *narodni deputati* (national deputies; members of parliament) in action. It might be that they are all relaxed from massages and well-groomed in their nether regions, and it might also be that some *nardeps* are wonderful human beings with genuine agendas for building a strong country, but as a whole the 450 members are nothing short of being an embarrassment to the nation. For one thing, the group is highly inbred, with many father-son, uncle-nephew, husband-wife, and sibling pairings, proving that either superior talent for politics runs in gene pools or that nepotism (*kumivstvo*) runs rampant. Second, it seems that the Verkhovna Rada is known globally as the parliament that fights: an assemblage with too many hot-headed and immature middle-aged men who throw furniture and microphones at one another (e.g., December 16, 2010); release smoke grenades and throw eggs and tomatoes in the hallowed chambers where they meet (April 27, 2010; the date when the speaker of the parliament, Volodymyr Lytvyn, tried to preside over the assemblage from under an umbrella held by aides); and shout in the foulest of language and call each other street-language names (too many incidents to enumerate; hardly news any more). More recently (on May 21, 2011), the vice-speaker of parliament, Adam Martynyuk of the Party of Regions, grabbed fellow *nardep* Oleh Lyashko, an opposition politician affiliated with the bloc headed by Tymoshenko, by the neck in a choke hold. That incident, too, is on film all over the Internet, and the world laughs at Ukraine, the name pun, and the "choke" that is Ukraine's leadership. Lyashko has since tried to capitalize on the incident by posting billboards showing a photo of the attack and the caption "And this is how they choke Ukraine," but in response the blogosphere laughs at the idea that he is somehow a sympathetic symbol of the nation. And then more recently still (March 20, 2013) is proof that assaulting one another is simply business as usual. On that day, 20 or more *nardeps* of opposing parties went after each other when Oleksandr Yefremov, the leader of the Party of Regions in parliament, spoke in Russian and members of the Ukrainian-nationalist Svoboda (Freedom) Party began to jeer him. That brawl is recorded on YouTube as well.

If only the Ukrainian Fight Club was always about issues of national importance, then we could at least say that this was democracy in action, albeit crudely. It sometimes is, as was in the case on smoke-and-eggs day on April 27, 2010, when the dispute was about the national administration's decision to renew for 30 more years a lease by Russia for a naval base on Ukrainian territory in Sevastopol, a naval port city in Crimea. But just as often, what is at stake in the fights is not national policy but lawmakers' personal access to the nation's wealth. Unlike many other countries in the world where government service is an honorable calling to work for the good of the nation, in Ukraine it is seen as a position from which one can enrich himself. That is why people run for office in Ukraine and cheat in elections to win. That is also why Ukrainian government service attracts crooks. President Yanukovych himself, for example, used to steal hats from passersby he could outrun when he was a young man, and he served two jail terms before becoming a politician, one for 18 months after a 1967 conviction for theft, and the other for 3 years for assault in 1969 soon after his return from behind bars. Sadly, Ukraine is a kleptocracy and corruption is among the worst in the world, be it in national government or at local levels, including as we will see, in Kyiv. According to data for 2009, Ukraine as a whole was 146th out of 180 countries on the Transparency International Corruption Perception Index (CPI), the worst score in Europe except for Russia, another "Wild West" nation, with which Ukraine was tied (Timor-Leste and Zimbabwe were also 146th).

3.6   A Missing Mayor

The situation is not necessarily better at the local, municipal level. Consider the example of the city's most recent elected mayor, Leonid (Lonya) Mykhaylovych Chernovetskiy,[6] a man who has also been called Lonya Kosmos, i.e., "Cosmos" in English as in "Lonya the Space Cadet." The nickname is intentionally derisive and stems from but one of many odd statements and eccentric actions that he had made while in office, this one a public announcement of a plan to fly into space with his cat. He also gained attention for recording a compact disc in 2009 of "very tragic songs" of the 1980s that he said he sings better than anyone but God, for impromptu performances at rallies and political appearances, and for unexplained attempts to auction off his own kisses. When city officials called for a medical examination of Chernovetskiy's mental health, he responded by posing for photographs in tight swimming trunks to show that he was indeed qualified for the mayor's job. There are rumors that he has problems with alcohol or drugs, although there is no evidence of either. However, his wife, Alina Aivazova, told an interviewer from the news magazine *Segodnia* (August 11, 2011) that were it not for her, "Lonya" would be an alcoholic in a gutter (*"Yesli bi ne ya, Lonya bi stal alkoholikom i valialsia v kanave"*).[7] In 2008, Chernovetskiy showed himself to be a fighter like his chums in parliament when he emerged bloodied in the face after sparring with the aforementioned Yuryi Lutsenko at a meeting of Ukraine's National Security and Defense Council.

Eccentricity is not a sin, and even addiction, if true, can often be dealt with as a person continues to work. Much more damning are credible allegations that Chernovetskiy had been dishonest in office, and the undisputable fact that for nearly two years until shortly before he resigned in mid-2012 just before his term was set to end, he was absent from the job without explanation. There were only guesses about his whereabouts. Chernovetskiy was elected to the mayor's office in 2006 as a member of a small Christian Liberal party. He won with only 32 percent of the vote in a contest with multiple candidates, and he was then reelected in a snap election in 2008 with a mere 38 percent of the vote. He was on the job, such as it were, until the middle of 2010 after which he was seen only sporadically and ever less. Then, after some weeks of unexplained absence, he turned up unexpectedly

6   The usual way to transliterate the surname would be Chernovetskyi, but he himself uses Chernovetskiy.

7   http://www.segodnya.ua/life/interview/alina-ajvazova-ecli-by-ne-ja-lenja-by-ctal-alkoholikom-i-valjalcja-v-kanave.html

on February 24, 2011, to attend a routine meeting of the city council (*miska rada*). He disappeared immediately afterwards and was AWOL until the summer of 2012, when he finally turned up and resigned. In the meantime, President Yanukovych had appointed Oleksandr Popov, the popular former mayor of the small town of Komsomolsk in Poltava oblast, to be the head of the Kyiv city administration and cover for Chernovetskiy's absence. In the nearly year and half that he was gone, the mayor was apparently seen in Switzerland and Georgia, as well as in Tel Aviv. Although he is an active member in a fundamentalist Christian sect that some think of as a cult, he has a Jewish background and is rumored to hold dual Ukrainian and Israeli citizenship.

The best explanation for why Chernovetskiy vanished seems to be that whether high or low on the totem pole, the people of Kyiv wanted to speak with him – perhaps even to cuff him. There are many questions to ask, including about the sale during his administration of 90 historic buildings in the center of the city – mostly once-beautiful "sugar boom" mansions from the turn of the 20th century – to private buyers at a tiny fraction of their true value. There might be questions as well about the origin of €4.5 million (US$5.7 million) worth of jewels that Chernovetskiy's daughter Khrystyna Chernovetska said were stolen from her Paris hotel room on February 15, 2010. Ironically, Chernovetskiy's 1984 doctoral dissertation at Kharkiv Law School was about how prosecutors investigate corruption by public officials.

As a result of all these machinations, Kyiv does not have an elected mayor as it is supposed to have: there is only the presidential appointee Oleksandr Popov. He has been assigned the duties of mayor from his post of head of city administration. An election is overdue but has not been scheduled by the president because it is not certain that his candidate, Popov, would win. Kyivans are not great fans of the president or the Party of Regions, and they could well decide to cast their lot with someone else. Moreover, there is at least one, literally, very strong potential candidate who could not only win the election but also use the post of mayor as a springboard for challenging Yanukovych for the presidency because he is popular across the country. That person is Vitayi Klitschko, PhD (a real doctorate), philanthropist (mostly schools, churches, and children's causes), and the reigning World Boxing Council heavyweight champion. He came in second to Chernovetskiy in the 2006 election. He is already a member of parliament, where he heads the growing political party that he founded, Udar (a striking blow as in a punch). However, he has not joined in the parliamentary fisticuffs, and is not likely to do so, as he presents himself differently from the colleagues who are thugs.[8] There are also other possible candidates for the mayoral vacancy, so Popov and Yanukovych could have a fight on their hands if there were an election. Even though the acting mayor is a man of talent and reasonably popular, at least in comparison to his presidential mentor, Kyivans seem to be increasingly impatient and have begun clamoring for an election. As I write this, there is a four-page leaflet being handed out widely in Kyiv under the banner *Vladu Kyianam!* (Power to Kyivans!) that agitates for an election.[9] It is in Ukrainian, but a recent issue (#3), features the Russian-language headline *POPOV! Davay, do svidaniya!* (POPOV! Let's Go, Good-bye!).[10] The text refers to the city administrator as a puppet of Donetsk (*donetska marionetka*; the president's home base) and begins as follows:

> In Kyiv there is no mayor. Instead, the city is being run by the head of city administration. The difference is that a mayor is elected by the citizens of Kyiv, while the head of city administration is appointed by the president … Kyivans need a mayor who will protect their interests and address the problems of the city. The government knows very well that Kyivans will never elect a Donetsk person [*donetskoho*] for this post. But the Regionnaires will do anything to ensure that today's head of city administration Oleksandr Popov will occupy the coveted seat of mayor of Kyiv.

3.7   A Geography of the President

President Viktor Fedorovych Yanukovych is a good choice for special attention because he is a raider at the top of his class and because his personal life history is so quintessentially dishonest. Born in 1950 in Yenakiyevo (now Yenakiyeve), a small city near Stalino (now Donetsk) in the eastern part of the Ukrainian SSR, his story has been a trajectory from childhood

---

8   Klitschko's nickname in the ring is Dr. Ironfist. His professional boxing record is 45 wins against 2 losses that came on days of an aggravated shoulder injury, and his knockout percentage rate is an astonishing 87.23 percent, just a hair under the world heavyweight record for all time of 87.76 percent. At his mother's request, he has never boxed against his younger brother Volodymyr, the reigning World Boxing Association heavyweight champion. Volodymyr is called Dr. Steelhammer and has a ring record of 60 wins against 3 losses. Once, in New York City, I challenged Vitalyi Klitschko to a fight but he declined.

9   It is authored by Kyiv activist Mykola Katerynchuk.

10   Popov speaks Ukrainian well. The choice of Russian for the headline is for effect.

poverty in the gritty coal-mining region called Donbas, to teenage years and young adulthood as a tough street punk with richly deserved prison records for hat-raiding (stealing hats off the heads of passersby) and for assault, and eventually to the top position of political power in Ukraine in 2010. Along the way, he studied mechanical engineering and worked in the transportation sector in Donbas, and then turned to Donetsk oblast politics, first as a communist and then as an ascending star in the Party of Regions. He was appointed vice-head of Donetsk oblast administration in 1996, and then less than a year later he was made governor. His official biography claims that he was a professor on the Faculty of Automotive Transport at the Donetsk State Academy of Administration in 1999, although it seems doubtful that such a department ever existed at the institution. His biography also states that he earned a doctorate degree in Economics in 2000 from the Academy of Economic Sciences of Ukraine, although there is no record on file of the required dissertation nor records of his having fulfilled any other requirements for that credential. He misspelled the occupational title "Proffesor" among a dozen mistakes on a Central Election Commission form in which he declared his candidacy for the presidency of Ukraine in 2004. He lost that run to Orange Revolution candidate Viktor Yushchenko, but then he narrowly won the post in 2010 in an election that is widely considered to have been fraudulent in his favor.

After becoming president, the tough guy from Donbas wrote a book for the apparent purpose of building Ukraine's profile abroad and attracting foreign investment. It was put together in Russian, the language that he speaks best, but was published in English, a language he does not know. It is called *Opportunity Ukraine* (Yanukovych, 2011), and describes itself on the jacket as "a practical guide for prospective investors." A main item of advice is that "naturally, those who come to Ukraine first will reap the most benefits." Because Yanukovych has no grace with words in any language, this book, like books by other celebrities, was put together by ghostwriters. In this case, however, the writers may have been thieves, as reviewers immediately flagged parts of the text for egregious plagiarism. Not only was it reported that there are word-for-word passages from previously published material (i.e., from the weekly news magazine *Korrespondent*), but incredibly and crudely, also from a Russian essay-sharing website, *referat.ru*, that cheating college students use to buy papers for classes (Associated Press, 2011). Can anything be more embarrassing? Yet, in Ukraine, as with so many other scandals in the country, news about the plagiarism disappeared from the press just as suddenly as it appeared. People are used to malfeasance, have been acculturated to look the other way, and go about their own business instead. In the meantime, the book itself has quietly vanished from store shelves and libraries as if it had never existed, and inquiries about its whereabouts are met with blank stares or the reply, "I don't know." In one bookstore where I asked just for fun, the clerk laughed uproariously at my question. The book is not available on Amazon or on eBay, but it does indeed

Figure 3.3   President Yanukovych's notorious book *Opportunity Ukraine* (Courtesy of Alexander J. Motyl)

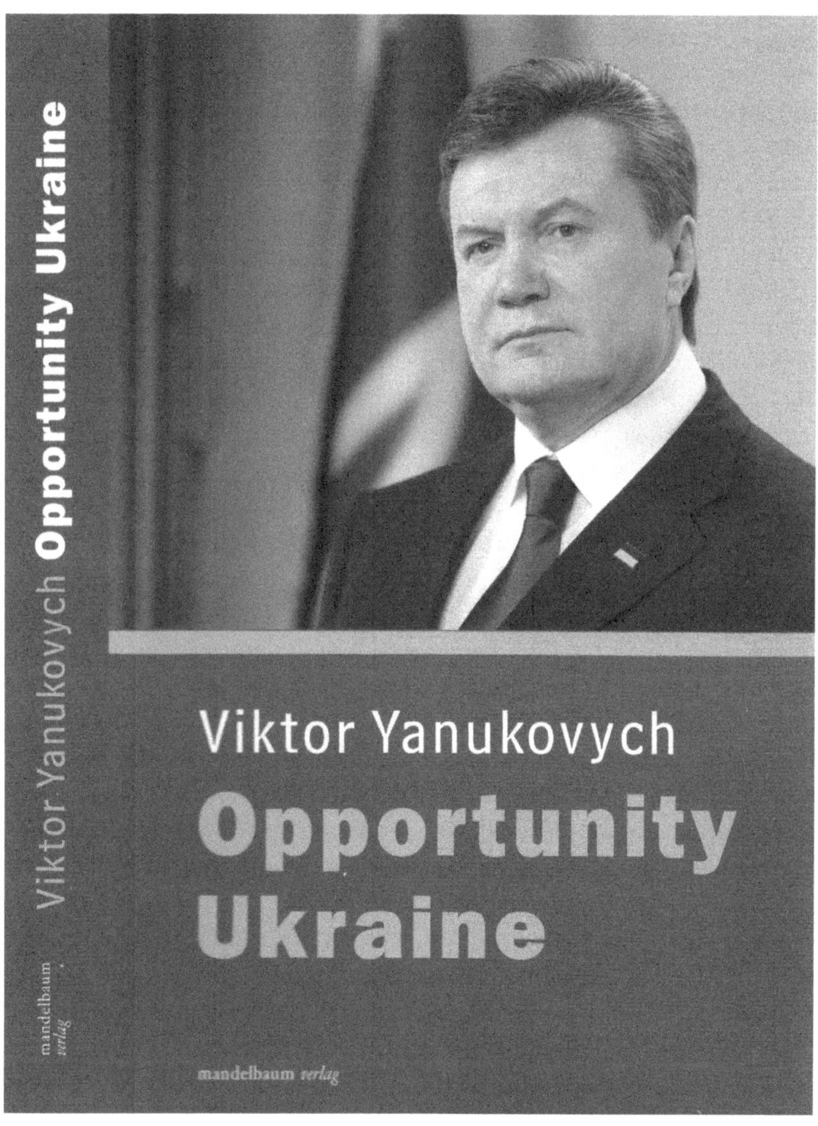

exist (Figure 3.3). Ironically, the back cover explains that "the author is honest and sincere with his readers in offering them deep insider analysis … and in offering his advice," and promises that "readers will be enticed by the author's genuine and straightforward manner, his sharing his dreams for his country, and [confusingly or inexplicably, as in 'where did this come from and what does it mean?'] his opposition to populism" (Motyl, 2011a).[11]

As president, Viktor Yanukovych is proving to be especially costly for the citizens of the country to support. He lives far beyond the means of not just the vast majority of fellow citizens, which is normal for a head of state, but also, it seems, in comparison to most European presidents and prime ministers, as well as most leaders elsewhere around the world. The latter comparison is especially out of whack given Ukraine's relative poverty. If there are spending similarities with leaders in other countries, then they would probably be with unfavorable people in poverty-bound countries where high-level corruption is the rule. Specific details are, of course, hard to come by, but the muckraking Internet magazine *Ukrayinska Pravda* (Ukrainian Truth), the news source that was established by murder victim Heorhiy Gongadze (see Chapter 4), reported that going into his second year in office Yanukovych has been by far the most expensive of Ukraine's presidents to maintain, with budgets for housing, transportation, upkeep of his properties, and presidential administration that approach the budgets of entire Ukraine oblasts (provinces).

Yanukovych lives in Mezhihirya, a 138-hectare estate located in the village of Nova Petrivka on the west bank of the Dnipro River about 22 kilometers to the north of Kyiv's center. The land traces back to a monastery that was founded there in the 16th century and that the Soviets had destroyed in 1921. Later, the tract became home for top Communist Party officials, including Nikita Khrushchev (1894-1971), the former leader of the Soviet Union. Yanukovych moved there in 2002 when he left his native Donetsk to serve as prime minister under the former president, Leonid Kuchma, and he has remained there on a tract of 1.7 hectares that he somehow managed to lease for personal use even though it was government land. Virtually everything else about Yanukovych's relationship to Mezhihirya is shrouded in secrecy thicker than the forests that abut the tract, although it is also public record that the rest of Mezhihirya has since been leased out as well without tenders – 7.6 hectares to a Donetsk-based foundation affiliated with Party of Regions and Yanukovych's elder son Oleksandr called Renaissance of Ukraine, and 129 acres to a Donetsk company, Tanalit,

---

11   I am thankful to Professor Motyl for sharing his copy of the book with me.

also with close personal ties to the president. Investigative journalists for *Ukrayinska Pravda* have followed the labyrinthine trail of front men and proxy companies related to these leases, and they have reported that since 2007, when Yanukovych was in his second term as prime minister, the entire Mezhihirya property had come under his personal control. They also report expenditures in the multiple millions of dollars for his family residence, and many millions of dollars more for other construction on the site: a golf course and clubhouse, a boat house and yacht club, tennis courts, a bowling alley, swimming pool, sauna, horse stables and equestrian club, a parking garage for 70 automobiles, and a dedicated highway between the estate and the main road to Kyiv. There are also reportedly ostriches, llamas, and kangaroos on the grounds, although they do not seem to be visible from satellite photographs. Some of what we know about how Yanukovych has personalized Mezhihirya comes from journalist Tetyana Chornovil (also written as Tetiana Chornovol), who scaled the 5-meter (16.5 feet) wall "James Bond style" with a tow rope and plank and spent three hours inside the grounds with her camera before she was betrayed by barking dogs.

Whatever there is and is not on these grounds north of Kyiv, it all seems to be paid for by the citizens of Ukraine. Yet, from the beginning to the present there has been virtually no transparency about anything regarding Yanukovych's relationship to the estate, including leases, land transfers, construction costs, capital improvements, and payments to contractors and suppliers. The result is lots and lots of suspicion and nasty questions about financial conflicts of interests regarding bills for maintenance and capital improvements, and a conclusion on the part of just about anyone who has an interest in the topic that Mezhihirya has become Yanukovych's by sleight of hand (Tuchynska, 2013). In what was perhaps an empty offer made during an unguarded moment, Yanukovych once issued an invitation to journalists to see his house, but when a preannounced group arrived at the gates with notebooks and cameras on June 6, 2011, the Day of Journalists holiday in Ukraine, they saw instead the president's motorcade whiz past them without stopping on its way out of the property. The visitors were greeted, instead, by Yanukovych's press secretary, who offered flowers and cake as consolation. A different group of journalists did manage to tour the president's home more recently, but judging from the official film record of the event and the softball questions that the participants asked, the visitors were carefully prescreened and preselected. Indeed, the event appears to be so carefully stage-managed that the president's house did not even look lived in. More recent information about that tour shows it to have been yet another Yanukovych sleight of hand and a boldfaced lie: the house that the visitors saw was in fact the guest house, a much smaller and more modest structure than the president's true residence through the trees nearby. Small wonder that it did not look lived in! The actual residence is truly enormous: three stories high as seen from one direction and five stories high from the other because it is built into an excavated slope, and has a footprint that appears to be three or four times larger than the house that the compliant journalists were shown.

The president's commute to work from Mezhihirya is a show. Every head of state needs expert security to guard him from possible wrongdoers, and I have no intention of compromising any procedures to protect President Yanukovych, but within a year after he took office, his travels by motorcade from his gated residence to Kyiv's center and back, as well as his travels around the city as he conducts his work, started to become legend. I lived just two blocks from his executive office building on Bankova (Bank Street) on a steep hill at the top of my street, so I was able to see the routine many times. It begins with sound, or more precisely the absence of it, when the city's constant background rumble of automobile tires on cobblestone streets is suddenly stilled. Here, at Evropeyska Ploshcha (European Square) and its connector Hrushevskyi Street, which lie between Mezhihirya and Bankova, there are no longer any vehicles on the roads as they have been blocked from entry at side streets, and there are police on foot all along the route making sure that the president's way is clear. Anyone who is interested looks north, in the direction of Mezhihirya, in anticipation. It can take as long as ten minutes before he finally arrives, enough time for hundreds and hundreds of drivers who are also in a hurry to have safely passed, but traffic in this whole section of the city is now hopelessly backed up until the president has finished his trip. Occasionally you can hear a frustrated driver's horn blowing from a side street, but that seems to be the case less and less, as drivers generally know that the traffic stoppage is official and that it does not help to complain.

Then, finally it happens. First, one speeding police car passes by, then, another, then a third, then a pair of cars side by side, and then finally an entire fleet of police cars with blue lights and identical black SUVs, also with blue lights, speeding up the hill of Hrushevskyi Street toward Bankova. The SUVs drive in zigzags and trade places seemingly randomly across all four traffic lanes so as to not offer a target for any potential harm-doer, even if one was to know which vehicle the president was actually in. The shuffling of the vehicles reminds me of a fast and dishonest game of three-card monte. The last vehicle of the motorcade is a Yanukovych trademark: his private yellow VW ambulance/field hospital bus in case harm does come to him. I've seen this scene again and again and it never ceases to amaze. Interestingly, that ambulance was recently involved in an accident while trailing behind the president (it has trouble keeping up with the high speed of the front vehicles) and a taxi driver was killed and his two passengers injured. That happened on a highway near the airport when the presidential motorcade was at full throttle. Recently on a stretch of that highway within city limits, I saw that members of the city's police force were standing at attention, one after another every few feet apart, in anticipation of the motorcade and then snapping smart salutes one after the other as the speeding SUVs passed. This, I am told, is a new procedure in response to a presidential directive that he be shown more respect.

At the conclusion of President Yanukovych's end-of-the year press conference on December 21, 2011, Mustafa Nayem, a journalist for TVi, an opposition television channel, asked what was described as an "inconvenient" question. It was worded in Russian and was translated into English as follows:

> I will ask you the following question. You have spoken of the poor situation of [the] economy in Ukraine and how many people do not feel the improvement in the standard of living and how there is no money in the budget neither for Chernobyl cleanup veterans, nor for Afghanistan war veterans. Yet, every day we observe how your personal life improves. We see you rent a helicopter for one million dollars from the company, which, according to *Ukrainian Truth* [an opposition news source], belongs to your son or at least is controlled by him. We know that the construction work in Mizhhirya [Mezhihirya] is performed by the companies under your son's control. Could you tell us where this disproportion comes from and what is the secret of your success? Why is our country doing so bad [sic] and you so well? Thank you.

As seen on YouTube,[12] the president tried to present a relaxed face in response, but then he lost a little of his cool and gave an answer that ended with what was widely interpreted as a personal threat to Nayem. Although Ukrainian is the official language of the country and he sat between Ukrainian flags and in front of a backdrop with words in Ukrainian reading "Press Conference of the President of Ukraine," Yanukovych spoke in Russian. As translated into English, his exact words were as follows (Nieczypor, 2011):

> I will say that what you are so emotionally describing does not interest me at all. I will tell you why. Because ... I have little time for pleasure.

---

12   https://www.youtube.com/watch?v=gCxcRqFIkKo&list=PL4oEGvvioYoDhPaHh2tMdXGp
yDdHhd-GM

> Scarcely any. Yesterday, for example, I came home at three in the morning and got up at six. The day before yesterday, it was even earlier. This goes on and on. That is why I do not know the sweet life you are talking about, neither do I know why you constantly discuss my family. I would like to tell you that I do not envy you.

At the point when he said "I don't envy you" ("*Ya vam ne zaviduyu*"), Yanukovych looked his adversary in the eye and then began to laugh. After a pause, Nayem laughed back and nodded that he understood what the president had just said. Yanukovych nodded in return and added:

> We know each other well and understand each other. ... The rest you can guess.

3.8   Helipad from Hell

Thanks to President Viktor Yanukovych, Kyiv now has a new centerpiece-landmark to complement the golden domes of old churches and monasteries that have long been its principal icons. It is a helipad located smack in the middle of middle-most parkland, i.e., amid the greenery that rises from the level of the Dnipro River to the bluff-top heights of historic Kyiv (Figure 3.4). It is near the nation's government buildings as well as the spectacular architectural treasure of Pecherska Lavra, the centuries-old Monastery of the Caves that is a UNESCO world heritage site. Conveniently, the helipad is several blocks from the president's office on Bankova Street, even closer to the parliament building, and almost immediately adjacent to Mariyinsky Palace, the beautiful baroque palace built by the czars in 1744 that is now the official ceremonial residence of Ukraine's president. A new road with a bridge connects the whirlybird site with all this. The plaza in front of Mariyinsky Palace has a lookout point that has long been popular for its panorama of Kyiv's parks, the river below, and the flat expanses to the horizon of the city's Left Bank steppes across the river, but now the foremost feature is a large-footprint, multilevel, reinforced concrete structure with a two-H helipad on its roof and the road-bridge connection directly to the government district. Although details are murky about just how this construction came about, it seems certain that, yes indeed, the president of Ukraine has ordered a wide, blocky, and tall concrete structure to be erected just there, in the center of the view of Kyiv from the river and the Left Bank, and that its roof will be his private heliport.

Figure 3.4   The helipad from hell

The construction of this monstrosity was started soon after Yanukovych took office. We learned more than a year after it happened that on December 28, 2010, Kyiv City Council had transferred 2.18 hectares of public park to a private company named Amadeus that is registered in faraway Belize and that was authorized to move forward with construction. There was no announcement that work was to begin or even what was to be built: workers simply started cutting trees in the park, clearing a site the size of a football field. Then, construction equipment and construction workers began to arrive. I witnessed all this. Once the workers started pouring concrete, I wandered by and asked what they were building. They said that they did not know, and then a security guard came to warn me away. That the structure had to do with helicopters was an open secret and conventional wisdom in Kyiv, as the president has been known to be a whirlybird fan since at least as far back as his campaign for office in 2004, and he could quite easily travel between work in Kyiv and his residence in Mezhihirya by flying above the river. Moreover, his 38-year-old son Oleksandr Yanukovych is in the helicopter business (allegedly among other concerns that profit from government contracts), and is widely believed to be renting a helicopter to his father for the US$1 million fee to which Nayem referred above.

It is not unusual, of course, for a head of state to have a helicopter and landing spaces at his disposal. The point here is that the president is a raider and the whole structure is rooted in lies: a central slice of the public's land was taken with no or very limited due process and no transparency whatsoever. Furthermore, the view of Kyiv from the river and the opposite bank, once a spectacular and iconic view of golden church domes, now has front and center among the remaining domes a tall, blocky concrete structure to support the president's travels. Even though it became known in due course that the main purpose of the structure is a landing place for helicopters, it is still not known what the rest of the structure is – that is, the two levels below the rooftop. There had been various media reports that this large space would be a casino, a discotheque, a bowling alley, a restaurant, or a "cigar hall" among other possibilities related to leisure and entertainment. In response to reporters' questions, even the appointed mayor of Kyiv, Oleksandr Popov, could not say what was to be in the building. The most that he could offer was that the project was funded by a "private investor" who expected a return on the investment. A more recent source confirmed that the chief architect for the city of Kyiv, Serhiy Tselovalnyk, was also in the dark, at least initially, as to what the structure would be, but subsequent to that, Tselovalnyk was able to tell reporters that the structure below the landing level on the roof would be a "business and entertainment center." The city's chief architect is also on record as defending the helicopter landing place by stating that this particular helicopter base was not built for the president, but for dignitaries who would be arriving for the Euro 2012 football tournament. That did not happen, however, as the helipad was not ready in time. In any event, Tselovalnyk never explained why such an intrusive structure would be built for an event that will last for only a short while. The city's chief architect then added that this was to be the first of 19 helicopter pads that were being planned for Kyiv so that people in need of emergency medical attention could be more quickly transported to hospitals. However, he said nothing about the fact that this particular landing pad is not near any hospital.

Not long ago, I stood for a long time on a bright and cold winter day at the famous lookout point beside the Mariyinsky Palace and took in the changing panorama as construction workers kept busy just below. As much as the view, I was transfixed by the behavior of Kyivans at the lookout point that day, and I managed to engage some in conversation. As opposed to the reactions that one would expect from people when they come upon a beautiful viewpoint on a sparklingly clear day, here was a somber crowd. They were looking at a familiar view that had been spoiled. They stood quietly, almost motionless, and simply stared. When they did speak to companions, it was in whispers, as if they were afraid of being overheard, or as if they were standing together at the casket of a loved one and were sharing a memory. One pair was reluctant to speak with me until they noted that I was a foreigner, and they then explained that it was the president's helipad under construction that they came to see, because they had recently heard about it in the media. There was disbelief at the violence to the panorama and sadness that something fundamentally Kyiv had been lost. That's what they told me straight on, and I was sad for them. No one stayed long. When visitors finally walked away from the scene, they shook their heads.

More recently (summer 2013), I stood again at the same spot looking at what was then the completed building. I had returned to Kyiv for a visit and wanted to see helicopters coming and going. There were none and I wondered why. The two big H symbols in a circle were big as daylight below me, but there was only stillness. A man ambled over beside me and started a conversation. He stood incredibly close, with his hand holding me near to him by the shoulder or bicep, and his face so close that his saliva splattered my cheeks. I would have escaped except that he was interesting. He was Nikolai (Kolya), aged 65, and told me that he was a retired air force officer. He spoke in Russian. He had approached me to commiserate about Kyiv's loss and the stupidity of the helipad before us. When he learned that I was a foreigner, he wanted to be sure that I understood what we were looking at: "We [the citizens of Ukraine] did not ask for this building. No one asked us. They just took parkland and built on it. It happens all the time. The president does anything that he wants. He knows no laws."

I asked what the glass-sheathed levels below the roof contain.

"Only God knows," he replied. "They never tell us. I don't even know if it is finished, or if there will be something in the future [that will become known to us]. Whatever is there, it is not for us. Look at all the security. Ask a security guard, and they will say that they do not know what they are guarding. They will tell you to scram."

He then squeezed my bicep extra firmly and turned up the saliva shower as he explained why there were no helicopters.

"Romashka, listen to me," he said, using a diminutive form of my name. "The president changed his mind about helicopters. Someone told him that there is no trick to shooting one down. Look at all that forest land below, one side of the river and the other. They cannot patrol it all. This president is famous for his paranoia. The nation's military forces have gotten smaller over his term, but his personal security apparatus has grown by an even greater amount. We [Ukrainian citizens] pay for all that. No, he has become afraid to fly up and down the river by helicopter. So instead, he is improving the road between here and Mezhihirya. And this building before us? No one needs it at all. It has spoiled our bluffs. And the bluffs will destroy *it*. The bluffs are unstable and will erode. The building will crack. It is not a safe structure.

I cannot vouch for the accuracy of all that Nikolai chose to tell me, but I see all the more clearly that, yes indeed, Ukraine is far from heaven and the story of Kyiv today is, sadly but verily, a tragicomedy.

4   Soviet Ways, Post-Soviet Days

4.1   Looking after Lenin

During Soviet times, there was a likeness of Vladimir Ilyich Lenin (1870-1924), Russian revolutionary and founder of the Russian Communist Party and the USSR, in the center of virtually every city and town from the border with Poland and other East Europe satellite states in the west to the Pacific reaches of Siberia in the east. Many communities had multiple Lenins, as statues of him were also erected in front of schools, libraries, and other public buildings, and at factories, rail stations, and virtually everywhere else where there were Soviet citizens to pay homage. Vladimir Ilyich was a ubiquitous icon as well on Soviet political posters and banners, lapel medals and other awards to Soviet heroes, and on postage stamps and currency of various denominations. For a time, the leader's presence was rivaled by that of Joseph Stalin (1878-1953), but de-Stalinization after the dictator's death returned Lenin to sole position at the top of Soviet iconography until the Soviet Union itself crashed in 1991. That ushered in a time of choice for citizens of the vast territory, with the result that a great many statues of Lenin were opportunistically toppled or dismantled, often to great cheers from crowds in anticipation of better days. The first such event in Ukraine apparently took place in L'viv on September 14, 1990. After that, Lenin removals spread or were repeated almost instantly in many other areas of Ukraine and in other collapsing Soviet republics, and they have continued sporadically ever since in the post-USSR era, sometimes via dead-of-night vandalism (Wanner, 1998, pp. 172-199).

In Kyiv, we have a story of Lenins removed, Lenins that never were, and one prominent Lenin who still stands. Its history with the statues is, therefore, probably somewhat typical of the former USSR, although as a bigger urban place and strategically important because of military research and industrial production, there were probably more Lenin statues in the city than in most other Soviet cities. With respect to removal of Lenins after the end of the Soviet Union, Kyiv is probably somewhat in the middle for Ukraine. In the west of the country, Lenin statues were taken down with glee as soon as it was possible to do so, starting with the toppling of the statue in front of the Opera Theater in L'viv. Instead, monuments to icons of Ukrainian nationalism were erected in these cities. In the east and south of the country, by contrast, where the Russian language dominated and the Communist Party was stronger, most cities tended to retain their Lenin statues. Kyiv's middle path reflects its geographic centrality and perhaps that, as capital, it reflects all regions of the country. A young student in Kharkiv, Varvara Podnos, daughter of a prominent sociologist who coaches her on the topic, has undertaken a large project to inventory the principal monuments and statues that stand in the centers of all the hundreds of cities and towns across Ukraine, and to prepare a map of the nation that shows who stands where in post-Soviet Ukraine.

We have already touched on one of the Lenin statues that was removed after independence, the one that stood in the rotunda of what is now Ukrainian House, formerly the Lenin Museum, and for a number of years, a place of limbo for the Museum of the History of the City of Kyiv (Chapter 2). That statue did not stay long, as the museum's lifespan was only 1982-1993. Now, as I write this, fully half of the façade of the structure is a banner advertising Audi automobiles from Germany, and at the top of the stairs is a fiberglass swimming pool on its side with a sign inviting pool shoppers to see the displays. A much larger statue of Lenin stood just down the street in October Revolution Square. It was erected in 1977 in connection with the celebration of the 60th anniversary of the Russian Revolution, when the square was renamed from Kalinin Square, and was a huge cubist monument carved from granite. This is today's Independence Square and the site is where the Independence Monument now stands. This granite Lenin was neither toppled by joyous crowds nor quickly disassembled, because at some 1,000 tons the figure was one of the largest monuments in the Soviet Union and removal would take weeks. The head alone weighed 15 tons. Moreover, the sculpture's removal had implications for the integrity of the subway concourse that was beneath the plaza and required expert engineering. Nevertheless, it was only two weeks or so after the proclamation of Ukrainian independence that the task of separating the sculpture's pieces was started (on September 9, 1991) on orders of Kyiv's mayor and the Cabinet of Ministers. Happy crowds witnessed the process. Eventually, the monument was trucked off in 84 pieces for storage on the grounds of 8 Pylypa Orlyka, at the time the site of the Museum of the History of the City of Kyiv, and then seven years later, after the museum was evicted in favor of the Supreme Court of Ukraine, the components were taken to a place called A.T. Ukrrestavratsiya to be recycled for new needs. Perhaps that was to guarantee that this Lenin would never return.

Even after this changeover, there were still as many as 18 statues of Lenin left in Kyiv as late after independence as 2008, as well as monuments to other Soviet leaders. A particular case in point was the much-hated statue of the much-hated Hryhoriy Ivanovych Petrovsky (1878-1958) that stood on

European Square across the way from the Lenin Museum. He had been a close ally of both Lenin and Stalin, was a former top official of the Soviet secret police, and was a fully complicit prime minister of Ukraine during the great famine (Holodomor) during which millions of Ukrainian peasants perished. Yet his stony likeness remained in place until late 2009. There had been attacks by vandals for years and episodes of graffiti ("To Petrovsky, executioner of the Ukrainian people"), but it was not until an order by President Viktor Yushchenko just before a memorial celebration of the Holodomor that this particular monument was removed. Some of the 18 Lenins were removed, too, to popular calls demanding *Lenina na smitkyk!"* (Lenin for the trash heap!), but perhaps as many as half still survive. For most citizens, the "minor Lenins" are not a bother and simply reflect history, and not many people give them much thought. Some Ukrainians, however, object strenuously to any monuments to Soviet leaders and occasionally respond with vandalism. It was this that did in Kyiv's statue of Nadezhda Krupsakaya (1898-1939), the wife of Vladimir Lenin and also a revolutionary activist. She lost her nose on June 16, 2010.

There is one very non-minor monument to Vladimir Lenin that still stands in the city, nearly seven decades after its erection.[13] He is also on Khreshchatyk. This is "Bessarabian Lenin," so called because across the street is the Bessarabian Market, a fresh-food bazaar named after an historic region in the south of Ukraine. Unveiled in 1946, it is a full-length statue of the revolutionary leader made of red granite. It stands 3.45 meters high atop a black granite pediment that is almost twice as tall. This particular monument was spared demolition perhaps because it is a part of postwar reconstruction history, or because it has more artistic merit than run-of-the-mill Lenins. It may also have been an appeasement to that fraction of Ukraine's and (Kyiv's) population that venerates the man. Whatever the reason for its longevity, "Bessarabian Lenin" has been a flash point between opposing sides in Ukraine's politics ever since independence and in recent years has come to be the target of deliberate vandalism. Lenin's nose and a part of his left hand were smashed with a sledgehammer on June 30, 2009, by a small group of nationalistic Ukrainians, and then red paint was thrown at the statue (it actually landed on the base) on November 27 of that year just as members of the Communist Party were cheering its unveiling after restoration.

---

13   In a later development, this statue was toppled by Euromaidan protestors on December 8, 2013, and smashed to bits.

Fearing more attacks, members of the Communist Party take shifts in a round-the-clock watch over the statue. According to a *Kyiv Post* article entitled "Lenin Stands Tall and Guarded" (Oleshko, 2010), there are reportedly eight sentries who take turns at 12-hour day and night shifts. They do this not for the small amount of money that they are paid by the party, but reportedly because of ideological conviction. A red tent at the statue's base provides shelter in bad weather and a place to rest. There is also a police vehicle on site with two police officers in case of a confrontation. On days when a Ukrainian nationalist group (such as the Svoboda Party) holds a rally in central Kyiv, the communists turn up at the Lenin monument in greater numbers to keep a close watch over their hero, and on days when the communists rally, they often start or finish their marches at this statue. On April 22, 2010, while communists were laying flowers at the statue on the occasion of the 140th anniversary of Lenin's birth, other Ukrainians had made an effigy and had Lenin kneel at a monument to the Holodomor to ask for forgiveness. To them, it mattered not that Lenin had died some eight years before the Stalin-imposed famine.

There is also the story of the giant Lenin that never was. It was part of a plan that was put forward in 1935 to make Kyiv into an architecturally complete and truly socialistic center of Soviet Ukraine, and to build a monumental center for Soviet Ukrainian government on the high hill where the capital of historic Rus once stood. Two ancient churches, the Monastery of St. Michael of the Golden Domes and the Church of St. Basil, were dynamited to make way for the project, and a grand boulevard/ parade ground to be lined with imposing office buildings for government ministries was planned from the promontory where they had stood to the sprawling complex of religious structures that centered on St. Sophia Cathedral, which itself would be converted into a government museum of history and architecture. A statue of Lenin would rise from one part of the once-religious promontory above the river. The problem was this: which way should Lenin face? If he faced the river, which made sense given the bluff-top perch, then his back would be to the parade ground, which made no sense. Alternatively, if he faced the parade ground, then he would also be extending his arm, as seems to be his favorite pose, not just to the parades but also to St. Sophia. That would definitely be a no-no. Even worse, if he faced the parade ground, and even if Sophia were to be removed from the scene altogether, as was also an option, his butt would be aimed at Moscow. In the Great Terror, that would have invited a ticket to Siberia or worse for any- and everyone involved. As far as I know, no one dared to suggest a revolving pedestal as a solution, i.e., a uniquely "revolutionary Lenin."

Thus, the discussions about plans wore on, architects showed blueprints to commissions of experts, but nothing was built. Incredibly, for a time there was a volleyball court on the site. Then the Germans arrived without an invitation, and that was that.

4.2   Red Army Birthday

The Soviet Union collapsed in 1991, but there are still many vestiges of Soviet life in Ukraine. Some citizens have an unapologetic nostalgia for the Soviet past and are determined to keep alive the traditions and celebrations that they hold dear. Historian Catherine Wanner has written about this subject and Ukraine specifically (1998). As we move forward to concentrate on the great changes that have swept across the country since independence, we pause here at a bridge between the two worlds to reflect on a particular day and a particular event that both recalls the routines of citizens' life in the recent past and, I think, shows hesitancy by some citizens to move the clock forward to today's time. The story is all the more interesting because it takes place on Independence Square, which is commonly called simply Maidan (Public Square), precisely where a hulking granite memorial to Vladimir Lenin had stood until 1991, and where there is now the tall column that is the Independence Monument. I write from my notes from February 23, 2011, a day that factions in Ukraine revere as the anniversary date for the founding of the Soviet Red Army and that is known in Ukraine, Russia, and other parts of the former USSR as the Day of the Defenders of the Homeland. I could also have been writing about October 7, the anniversary of the October Revolution, another holiday that, for some, is a day of nostalgia for communist rule. I have heard fervent participants in such events referred to uncharitably as "people from the past."

For more than two weeks, Independence Square had been closed off with a high wooden wall, and its perimeter was patrolled in twos and threes by roving guards. Why? The official reason was to repair damage to stone pavement tiles that occurred during a period of mass protest near the end of the previous year. These were protests about tax issues by shop owners and other small business entrepreneurs that went on for day after day in November and December 2010. On some days there were 10,000 or more people present. They were energized and boisterous, angry about the financial squeeze that they were in, and chanted slogans against the president and the Party of Regions, and about revolution. It was said that tent stakes that had been driven between tiles had caused damage, but I saw with my own eyes that there was really nothing significantly wrong, and that no repairs were being made. Clearly, damage to the pavement was not the reason to wall off the square. Broken pavements elsewhere in the city are usually left as they are to become even worse, and if repairs are made, it is never done by closing off an entire area. This wall around the square existed to keep protestors away. They never had their issues satisfactorily settled, and those in power feared that once good weather returned, there might be another Orange Revolution. There were small groups of protestors who gathered from time to time outside the walled perimeter, clearly in a mood to pick up where they had left off some two months earlier. All of us agreed that the fence was there simply to prevent a new wave of mass gatherings, and that the security patrols were simply guarding the fence to make sure that no one knocked it down.

During the night from Saturday to Sunday, February 19 to 20, the walls came down and Maidan was opened for the first time since the protesters were scattered in December. Why? Trucks arrived with workers and equipment, along with the equipment needed to set up an enormous sound system, and then by Wednesday the 23rd the answer was obvious: there would be a celebration of the anniversary of the birth of the Soviet Red Army. This day had been a traditional holiday in the USSR, and some people in Ukraine, Russia, and Belarus still celebrate it. They do so now with official Party of Regions sponsorship. I was new to this, not having personally experienced the Soviet Union and found what transpired during the evening of the celebration to be fascinating.

As it happens I was on the street at 6 p.m. on that day, just in time to see a crowd emerging from a subway entry on my block. They kept coming, dozens of them, hundreds, all going in the same direction, down the street toward Maidan. Within 10 minutes, out of nothing, there was a mass of several hundred individuals at the end of my street, near Maidan but not in it, standing in discrete groups – a hundred here, another hundred or so there, still another hundred a few feet away… Some were older people, older than me, men and women in leather coats or in furs. Gold teeth glistened. There were also young people – college student types. They were in their own groups of about a hundred. I already had a good idea about what was going on, but decided to play the role of the puzzled foreigner so that I could ask questions. I asked some passersby what was going on, but they said that they had never seen such a thing before and were wondering the same thing. I now conclude that such nonanswers were probably an echo of Soviet Kyiv: the less you claim to know and the less you say, the better off you will be.

I started questioning the people in the organized groups. Some of them had carried canvas bags of collapsible flag poles and flags, and they began distributing these items to their charges as they lined them up row by row, 5 across and about 20 deep. The flags were Ukrainian blue and yellow, and the blue and white "map flags" of the ruling party of Ukraine, Yanukovych's Party of Regions. The most anyone would tell me was that it was a *praznik* (holiday) and they had come to celebrate. There would be a concert, they said. They would not answer when I commented about how organized they seemed, how they all appeared all of the sudden from nowhere, and why they were so neatly lined up. Maidan was empty and the stage was set: it was marked "February 23, Party of Regions, Glory to the Defenders of the Homeland." I asked why they weren't going into Maidan for the concert, why they remained standing at the side of the square, and all I got was the reply that "we will go in soon." Someone managed to tell me that the groups were organized by *raion* (region of the city). At precisely 6:30, all of them moved at once the 150 to 200 feet to the open plaza and took their places in orderly groups in front of the stage. Before they left their staging area, I took some photographs and observed people turning their faces away from the camera. I kept trying to talk to people, and I was continually told, "No comment" or "I will not answer your question." "Why do you bother us?" they asked me. "It's a holiday. February 23. We came here for a concert."

I also photographed the attendance-takers. Yes, I said attendance-takers. Each group had at least one person with a book in which were handwritten names. They were checking off people as present. The books were identical from group to group in size and shape. When I started asking why attendance was being taken, some book-handlers got angry. When I asked if the people were being paid to attend the *praznik* and hear the concert, some laughed me off as ridiculous, others got angry, and others turned away and tried to hide. Even though I knew full well that what I was witnessing was a carryover from the Soviet period of compulsory participation in official events, I kept up the role of disoriented foreigner and asked why they were afraid: "You can tell by how I speak that I am not from here. I can't do anything to you. Why are you afraid of me?" The response: "We are not afraid of you. This is a democracy. We just do not want to talk with you." By the way, any responses that I was given, as well as verbal brush-offs, were consistently in Russian, even if it was Ukrainian that I was using.

The concert began precisely at 7:00 p.m. I had tried to get on stage before then, as I often manage to do in this country where if you are brazen enough, uncertain security guards will fear you as probably being one of their superiors. However, this time I was stopped. The guards and I had a big laugh that a foreigner was so disoriented that he did not know better. I asked with feigned bewilderment why there was the sudden appearance of so many hundreds of people in such precision and who was behind this, and they laughed again and said, laughing, that this is a democracy and people are here for a holiday concert. I asked if the crowd is being paid and they said, while laughing, that all they know is that they are security guards and that they are being paid themselves for their work, but that this is a democracy and people can come to a concert if they want to. "No, no one is forced to be here; they are here because this a *praznik*, and they came for the concert," one of the guards said while laughing.

The concert opened with a military officers men's chorus (Figure 4.1). They performed patriotic, military anthems in Ukrainian and Russian. There were politicians from the Party of Regions in dark suits and conservative neckties. The one first spoke in Ukrainian, the second in Russian. They offered platitudes about defending the Ukrainian homeland, about the bravery of war veterans, and about the glorious Party of Regions and its love for democracy. There was a good-looking female MC and a handsome male co-MC. She spoke in Ukrainian; he alternated with her in Russian – not one translating the other, just intertwining the languages. Then came more acts. A much be-medaled (20 to 30 medals on one chest) veteran of the Afghanistan War sang songs to heroism in Afghanistan. He was followed by rock singers who performed in Russian, Ukrainian, and English as the

Figure 4.1   **A scene from the Soviet-like February 22 (2011) "Defenders of the Homeland" celebration. The words read "Party of Regions Ukraine."**

song required. Then the stage was given to a bevy of dancing babes in fur coats. Oh yes, it was about 12 degrees F (-11 degrees C).

After that, there were still more acts and still more speeches. I took pictures. I managed to sneak up on stage, at the side, and took crowd shots. I tried talking with people. They shooed me away. Occasionally, someone would approach me and ask where I was from. Sometimes I would say that I am Ukrainian. "No, where are you *from*?" they would press. "Over there, on Horodetskoho Street," I would answer. At other times my reply was like this: "I am Ukrainian. I am here in the capital of Ukraine, speaking to you in *ridna mova* (the native tongue), the official language of the government of Ukraine. You ask me in Russian where I am from? I should ask you where you are from?" They walked away at that point and you could hear the mumbling: "Provocateur." I suppose they were right.

It was damned cold but the concert wore on and on. There was a front line of people who paid attention and were engaged with the music. But most people paid no mind to what was on stage. They milled about, spoke among themselves, ducked belowground to subway level for warmth and tea. They looked incredibly bored and incredibly cold. There was no answer to the question, "Why are you still here in this miserable cold if you are not enjoying the show?" As the music went on, the front line got thinner, and the "I can't wait to get out of here" crowds in the back kept growing. I concluded that the old people knew the meaning of the event. More than one told me that they were veterans or widows of veterans. The young people had no idea what this was about. I concluded that they were students on a part-time earning opportunity.

A very fat old lady (my age) was leaving early. She could barely walk, she was so fat, it was so cold, and there were slippery stairs. I offered her my hand. She hesitated for a moment but took it. For the next few minutes, I escorted her to the subway entrance and we talked. She was amazed by my courtesy. "Oh, you are an American!" And she asked some questions about my background and where in America I was from. I asked her if she enjoyed the concert. She said, "They told me to come, so I came."

4.3   One Day in the Life of the Ukrainian Language

The day is June 5, 2012, graduation day for my students from a year earlier at the National University of Kyiv Mohyla Academy, and simultaneously a momentous day at the Verkhovna Rada where Ukraine's fight-club law-makers were set to vote on a the first reading of a proposed new law that would change the language of the country. Instead of Ukrainian as the sole official language of Ukraine as stipulated in the country's postindependence constitution of 1996, the proposal by Yanukovych's Party of Regions would add their language, Russian, as a second official language in parts of Ukraine that wanted that option. It also opens the door for Romanian near the western border and possibly other languages, although it is really a question of Ukrainian, Russian, or both. The topic is immensely hot in Ukraine, especially at times of political electioneering, and is seen by many citizens as vitally important for how Ukraine evolves in the future. The issue inspires enormous passion on both sides, Ukrainian-only or Ukrainian and Russian. I juggled both venues that day, graduation on campus and the protests that were taking place outside Verkhovna Rada, as did many of the graduates, their teachers, and university administrators. Supporters of the Ukrainian-only side speak Russian as well and many use it daily. However, their argument is that in a country with a history of long domination by a much larger and characteristically acquisitive Russian neighbor, there can be no true independence without critical breaks in the public sphere from the Russian past. "Without our language there can be no nation," is a translation of one of the slogans of the pro-Ukrainian side, while I read another, "No Language – No Ukraine," splashed across the cover of an English-language edition of a major news magazine that also took a stand on the question (*The Ukrainian Week*, 9 (32), June 2012). I want to tell the story of what transpired that day at Verkhovna Rada in order to bring more focus on the issues involved, to introduce Kyiv more closely as the capital nation where two major languages are in use, and also to say something about Kyiv as a diverse city in which the linguistic divisions of Ukraine matter little on a daily basis.

The roots of the language conflict in Ukraine lie in the long history of the country as a part of the Russian and then Russian-Soviet Empires, during which times Russian was imposed on the local population, many Russians were resettled onto Ukrainian lands and into Ukrainian cities, and the Ukrainian language was, as a rule, denigrated both by the state and in ordinary social relations. During these times, Ukrainian remained strong in the small towns and countryside of the west and center of the country, while in the industrial cities of eastern and southern Ukraine, Russian came to be the dominant language. Russian was also the state language across much of Ukrainian territory, and the language into which many ethnic Ukrainians and other non-Russians in the country were acculturated. Furthermore, to be more precise, much of the west and center of Ukraine was Polish as well, with the Polish language being seen by many ethnic Ukrainians as a colonial tongue just like Russian was in other parts of the country. There was also a large population that communicated in Yiddish. An outcome of this geography was that Ukrainian became identified as a peasants' or farmers' tongue, while Russian (or Polish in the West) was thought of as the language of industry, modernity, and urban-intellectual life. Writers who bucked this pattern by creating beautiful and sophisticated literary works in "the language of peasants" such as Taras Shevchenko (1814-1861), Lesya Ukrainka (1871-1913), Panas Myrny (1849-1920), Mykhailo Kotsiubynsky (1864-1913), and Ivan Franko (1856-1916), instilled Ukrainian national pride in the face of neighbors and are still regarded as great national heroes.

The 20th century removed Poles to across newly drawn international borders and, in the worst of all crimes, destroyed the country's Jewish communities altogether, eventually leaving the country as a territory with essentially just two main languages, Ukrainian and Russian. When independence came to the country in 1991, much of the Ukrainian language faction of the country (which constitutes about 42.8 percent of the population as defined by those who speak the language at home) typically rejoiced in the rebirth of the Ukrainian language, while much of the slightly smaller Russian-speaking population (38.6 percent),[14] which is concentrated mainly in the east and south, felt put upon and had to either learn a new language or start kicking. When their man Viktor Fedorovych Yanukovych, a Russian speaker and bumbler in Ukrainian, was elected president in 2010, the swing back to Russian commenced in earnest, leading to what took place on June 5.

Yanukovych's Party of Regions had been kicking about language for some time, particularly through its chief ideologue on the issue, the aforementioned Dmytro Tabachnyk, whom Yanukovych appointed to the nation's Minister of Science and Education and the person whom the young Daria Stepanenko slapped in the face with flowers (Chapter 1). Both Yanukovych and Tabachnyk have seen themselves as being on a mission to undo much of what the pro-Ukrainian Orange Revolution had accomplished before 2010, particularly with respect to what they see as the forcing of Ukrainian down the throats of Russian speakers; their party, therefore, introduced the legislation in question. We have already seen the Ukrainian Fight Club (Verkhovna Rada) in action. During an evening session in parliament on May 24, 2012, when the language proposal was placed on the docket, yet

---

14   These numbers are for 2011 and are from survey data maintained by the Institute of Sociology of the National Academy of Sciences of Ukraine as quoted in Kramar (2012). Some 17.1 percent of respondents answered that they speak both Russian and Ukrainian at home. Also see Duda (2012).

another fistfight erupted. I don't know who started it or who landed blows on whom, but regardless of who was more at fault, the two sides went at it for quite some time. During the peak of the melee, a score or more lawmakers pummeled one another with their fists, threw burly bodies over podiums and other furniture, and ripped one another's clothes. This continued for at least 5 minutes and 11 seconds as was seen in an action-packed video shown on YouTube.[15] Two weeks later, on June 5, a vote on the first reading was rushed into action by the Party of Regions majority.

Word spreads fast in Kyiv when there is a big issue at hand and a protest is being organized. Many activists are on the Internet daily and follow news from like-minded people and organizations about upcoming events, including calls to action. I personally learned about the protest by the pro-Ukrainian side the day before by different means: a stranger on the street in the city's downtown handed me a newspaper from which fell a printed flyer about the planned protest. "Be there at Verkhovna Rada at 9 a.m." the notice said, "because survival of the Ukrainian language in Ukraine is at stake and we need to voice our opinions." The radio news the next morning over breakfast said that the planned protest was looking to be huge, but that in all directions around Kyiv police were stopping busses with protestors headed toward the city and turning them back. In two years of the Yanukovych administration, the tactic of limiting access to the capital had already become established as a hallmark method for limiting the voices of opposition. Another tactic, even more explicitly geographical, has been to limit access to protest sites. Before the Orange Revolution, much of Independence Square in the center of Kyiv had been redesigned with the addition of fountains, benches, greenery, and minor monuments arranged in a way that inhibited large gatherings, and then after the ascension of Yanukovych to power, other more novel ways were found to control gatherings and protests on the more open rest of the square. In Ukraine, as perhaps in other countries, too, he who controls the main public spaces can control what the news reports from those spaces and can therefore shape public opinion either for against any person or issue.

This protest was scheduled for the public space in front of Verkhovna Rada rather than for Independence Square about a kilometer away. I had been to many protests there before. This time, there was a surprise. I came with a friend and we arrived just after 9 a.m., and saw that the president had ratcheted up his strategy of controlling public space for protest to a new level. Overnight thousands and thousands of supporters of the Party

15   https://www.youtube.com/watch?v=ETU8Hdwh7Nc

of Regions had been bussed into Kyiv and brought by rail from Regionnaire strongholds and implanted from about 7 a.m. as a thick and densely populated human cordon between arriving protesters and the building in which the vote would be held. They waved blue-and-yellow Ukrainian flags and the blue-and-white flags of their party, and they looked like a loving crowd to the TV cameras. "Yanukovych, Our President" was a common placard sign and the slogan that was written on the backs of the blue raincoats that had been passed out on this day with a threat of rain. What is more, these particular citizens of Ukraine were contained within an iron fence of a type that is commonly used in riot and other security situations. The police (*militsia*) stood in a line within the fence with them to create still another barrier against arriving protesters, leading to a microgeography in which protestors had no recourse but to remain on the far side of a barrier while the police, an Iron Curtain, and a line of young Regionnaires who looked for all the world like thugs stood just behind the police and protected (or imprisoned, as some observers said) the mass of transportees inside. There was Ukrainian music broadcast over Regionnaire loudspeakers for the TV microphones to pick up, and speaker after speaker, speaking in Russian, who professed love for Ukraine but hatred for the Orange Revolution. Some pro-Ukrainian protestors shouted taunts across the cordon, and there were equally vile taunts that came back. At its basest, the dialogue was something like this: "Go back to Russia you communist bastards" from the Ukrainian side, and "Go back to Germany, you fuckin' Nazis" from inside the barrier. When the taunting seemed to escalate, still another layer of security was added between the two sides – a column of police in riot gear in close formation along the outside of the barrier to complement the layer of police inside the barrier.

I went inside; I always manage a way. I found a place along the fence where there was a narrow opening that was being guarded not by police, but by civilian supporters of the Party of Regions, and talked my way though. The "guard" who challenged me was no more than a tough-looking teenager in street-thug clothes. He had pimples. I intimidated him by aggressively reminding him that he was but a kid who was not bright enough to know who I was, and he simply stepped aside. Then until the rains came, I walked among the Regionnaires, looked, listened, and asked questions. They were paid to be there. Most people said that they were not paid when I asked and were suspicious of my question, asking if I was being paid by the opposition to ask it, but enough of them acknowledged that yes, they had been gathered for the event with the promise of money. The amounts that I heard were 135, 150 and 160 hryvnia for 9 hours of duty, about US$16 to US$20. Those who looked like students said that they cared not a bit about politics but needed the money. Old ladies and old soldiers denied being paid, and challenged me after hearing me speak Ukrainian or Ukrainian-accented Russian, and they wanted to have nothing to do with me except to heap abuse. And that some of them did. The oldsters are even more financially strapped than students, I think, and were paid, too, I am sure. I checked with a news crew and they seemed surprised that I even asked: "Of course, this is a paid audience. How can you not know that?" That was, of course, routinely the case in Soviet times, when the Communist Party was always able to guarantee a large and "happy" turnout whenever one was needed by inducements, threats, or both.

Some of the Regionnaires had traveled all night to be at their assigned places within the human shield, but others claimed to be Kyivans who had arrived spontaneously out of conviction for the cause of the Russian language. I caught one person in a lie about this, because it was clear that he knew nothing about the city. I can also conclude about this audience that they were totally disinterested in the speakers, paid no attention at all, and said to me again and again that it was just "blah-blah-blah" from the podium. There was little cheering, even when a speaker punctuated his speech with a loud "Hoorah!" into the microphone, and only some signs of audience participation with the music. Mostly, the crowd of Party of Regions supporters entertained itself with conversation. Like the audience at the Red Army birthday celebration described earlier, they had come in groups from given neighborhoods, cities, and local party committees, stood together in those groups, and chatted. Old people and heavy people sat on the supports of the riot fencing.

Meanwhile, the friend I came with did not have the luxury of being able to mix it up with Regionnaires as I did because she was a Ukrainian local. I could always rely on the American passport in my pocket to get me out of trouble, even though I have never needed it, and therefore could brave "foreign territory." I also have the advantage of being a senior citizen and, therefore, am harder to hit. My friend found her way to the far side of the Verkhovna Rada building where the main group of pro-Ukrainian language protesters had set up their activities in a park that is not normally used for such gatherings. There was little security there, and as many thousands if not more people than had been paid to shout for the Party of Regions. These protestors came freely and were much more animated. A number of mutual friends were there, including people we both knew from NaUKMA. Again, there was Ukrainian music, as well as readings of apt poetry, but in this venue the speeches were all in Ukrainian. The history of linguistic colonialism in Ukraine was mentioned prominently, as was this side's conviction that in the face of a history of Russian imperialism in Ukraine, the Russian language cannot be allowed to have equal status. A student from NaUKMA was wearing a T-shirt with a message in English on the back that was addressed to football fans from other countries who were arriving to see the 2012 European championship matches. She stood still for me as I photographed the text:

Dear guests of Ukraine!

We are united not only with our joy of football. Most Ukrainians want to see Ukraine in the commonwealth of European nations. We feel ourselves a part of Europe.

The Ukrainian Parliament intends to adopt a law that will exterminate the Ukrainian language at first, and then – Ukraine. Possibly this could happen during Euro-2012. We do not want to spoil your football holidays, but we love our country very much and cannot let out authorities destroy it. Therefore, we beg your pardon if protest actions and demonstrations somehow cause inconvenience for you and spoil your vacation.

We hope for your understanding.

Other speakers on the pro-Ukrainian side of the Verkhovna Rada building included representatives from the political party of Yulia Tymoshenko, the imprisoned political opponent of President Yanukovych who has caused such a global stir, and Vitaliy Volodymyrovych Klitschko in person, the reigning WBC Heavyweight Champion (boxing), holder of an honest PhD (in Physical Science and Sports) from the prestigious Kyiv National University of Taras Shevchenko, leader of the political party Udar and a possible opposition candidate for president. Interestingly, both Tymoshenko and Klitschko grew up speaking Russian and adopted Ukrainian as their main language when the country became Ukrainian. In another zone near Verkhovna Rada, another group of pro-Ukrainian language protestors had gathered, those affiliated with the right-wing Ukrainian political party Svoboda. This party is especially strong in the west of Ukraine. Their members often show little tolerance for Russians or other minorities, and one often finds lurking among them the same kind of mean-looking thugs that mark the Party of Regions.

Then came the rains. I requisitioned a supply of party-branded raincoats from the Regionnaires but have them still packaged in case I need to return them, and I watched as the Regionnaire crowds scattered. There were loudspeaker admonitions against leaving, but most of the "captives" within the official cordon took off just the same. I made a tough-looking police commander laugh when I asked whether the people were leaving because they had been paid for dry weather duty only. The Ukrainian side scattered, too, but not as quickly, and many stayed to continue their protest. Before long, it was announced that the parliamentarians had cast their votes and that the Regionnaire-sponsored measure had passed with 234 of 450 votes. Of the 234 yes votes, only 172 were cast by parliamentarians who were actually present in person; the other "yes" votes were cast by persons who were present on behalf of absentees. This is a common practice in the Verkhovna Rada but is against regulations. We also heard that there were more fistfights on the floor at the time of the voting, and that at least three members of parliament who were absent and were recorded as having voted "yes" have already protested that they had instructed that their votes should be "no."

I am not going to take you any further on the language issue, as I am writing these particular passages mostly on the day immediately after the event. News evolves, and I would be continually updating text. Readers who are interested know how to follow up on developments on their own. Instead, I want to return to the graduation ceremony for my students that also took place on this turbulent day, and to reflect on what I saw and heard there. Speakers did acknowledge that the day was a milestone (my term) in the history of the Ukrainian language, and then they challenged graduating students as the next generation of leaders in the country to build the Ukraine that they desired rather than accept the one that is orchestrated for them. There was sideways comment from the podium that graduates of NaUKMA are now in positions all over the world, contributing their energies and skills in new societies, and a reminder that they are needed for work in Ukraine as well. Some successful and wealthy NaUKMA graduates from previous years were introduced to give scholarships and research grants to top students and faculty, and to stand as models for building a good life in Ukraine and assisting the country.

These proceedings were all in Ukrainian, as Ukrainian is, along with English, NaUKMA's official language, but as students chatted informally afterwards among themselves and with proud family members, they did so in Ukrainian, Russian, or a mix of both. Because it is the national capital, Kyiv often becomes the scene of extremely heated passions between opponents who have gathered from various directions to shout about important issues, but its own population reflects all regions of Ukraine, as does the population of NaUKMA (at least somewhat), and local people use whichever language they want in unofficial communication. No one is on anyone's case about language except crazies from the extremes and, often quite visibly, aging Americans and Canadians of Ukrainian descent on visits to the homeland who were taught intolerance of Russian. Most Kyivans change and mix languages as they wish. Moreover, there is a manner of speaking called *surzhyk* that blends Ukrainian and Russian quite nicely on a day-to-day basis, with no punches being thrown and no one thinking twice about the other's preferred tongue.

A friend who visited me in Kyiv from St. Petersburg once introduced me to a lovely couple about my age, Vladyslava and Vladimir Dmytrenko. He had had a successful career as diplomat in various countries for the Soviet Union, and then until retirement was ambassador from independent Ukraine to a mix of African countries, some in turn and others simultaneously. The Dmytrenkos invited us to dinner in their beautiful apartment on a high floor in a tall building in Obolon, an up-and-coming prestige area north of the center of Kyiv, during which the subject of language in Ukraine came up. We were conversing in Russian, and I asked what my hosts thought would be the language of choice in Ukraine in the future. Vladimir had a ready answer and took me to the balcony to show me. Young people in Kyiv and other cities in Ukraine (and elsewhere in the planned housing estates of the former Soviet Union, I suppose) have an interesting way of flirting, passing "I love you" messages to one another, and wishing one another a happy birthday, etc., by writing graffiti on sidewalks and the rooftops of low kiosk buildings and garages in car parks, that can be read from the windows and balconies of apartments above. For example, when Uliana wakes up on her birthday, she can look out her window and see that her boyfriend or her circle of close friends had written birthday greetings on the sidewalk below. Residential areas such as Obolon have lots of such graffiti, and residential areas with lower incomes and less prestige might have even more. Vladimir explained this system of communication to me, and then asked me to pick out the various messages that could be read from his balcony on the 16th floor and tally them by language. I came up with six messages: three in Ukrainian, two in Russian, and one that could have been either. Ukrainian wins! According to this very intelligent diplomat's theory, this signals that the Ukrainian language will gain in the future, because these graffiti were insights to the language of free choice, of spontaneity, and of affairs of the heart for the next generation. I said something that it might mean instead that Ukrainian speakers are more apt to write graffiti, but he would not hear of that.

4.4   May 18, 2013

It might be too early to declare that this date is one for the history books of Ukraine, if only as a footnote, but it could well be that such will be the case. At least that is what I thought on that day. On this particular Saturday, two large rallies were held in Kyiv by opposing political factions in preparation for elections to be held in 2015 for president and other offices. It was also the Day of Europe celebration, so the three main opposition parties to President Yanukovych and his Party of Regions, the political parties named Batkivshchyna (Fatherland), Svoboda (Freedom), and the aforementioned Udar, selected this date to hold a mass rally to announce that they would unite to field just one candidate against Yanukovych to maximize their chance of defeating him. The three parties are normally rivals, but Yanukovych is so despised that they have endeavored to overlook their differences. The rally was scheduled to start in European Square, with marchers then proceeding up the slope to St. Sophia Square where a stage and speaker systems were set up for the signing of the agreement and the speeches. I was there for the entire event, from the time that protestors began to gather at European Square until the end of the programming in front of the St. Sophia historical site some four hours later, and stood in a pressing throng several feet from the podium to witness the three party principals affix their signatures to the agreement and shake hands. There was Arsenyi Yatsenyuk, the leader of Batkivshchyna, the party of the imprisoned Yulia Tymoshenko; Oleh Tyahnybok the charismatic head of Svoboda; and Vitalyi Klitschko, the iron-fisted champion of Udar. They waved to the crowd and smiled broadly, and they promised in their speeches to agree on one candidate for 2015, to make sure that "that criminal clan from Dontesk," as the Regionnaires are called by the opposition, is defeated. On the stage with them were almost all the opposition members of the Verkhovna Rada, those from their own parties, from other opposition parties, and some independents. There were chants of *"Yuli volyu!"* ("Freedom for Yulia!") and *"Bandu het!"* ("Out with the gang!"), patriotic Ukrainian songs, and flags of Ukraine, of each of the three parties, and those with a portrait of the braided-blonde Yulia Tymoshenko. The event was called *Vstavay, Ukraino!* (Rise Up, Ukraine!). Maybe the movement will lead to something (Figure 4.2).

   At the same time, the Regionnaires held their own rally in opposition to the opposition. They picked the same day and hours specifically to counter their three opponents, and they were joined by the Communist Party of Ukraine. Their faithful marched from where they had gathered near the Museum of the Great Patriotic War (Chapter 5) to European Square, which

Figure 4.2   Leaders of the three main opposition parties in Ukraine singing the national anthem after signing their historic accord. From left to right they are Oleh Tyahnybok, Svoboda Party; Arsenyi Yatsenyuk; Batkivshyna Party; and Vitalyi Klitschko, Udar. In between these men, we can see other dignitaries wearing T-shirts in support of freeing former Prime Minister Yulia Tymoshenko from prison.

had in turn been vacated by their marching nemeses. They called their event a "rally against fascism." Because their political base is the Russian-speaking east and south of Ukraine, the Party of Regions strategy is to demonize the opposition as dangerous Ukrainian nationalists, Nazi sympathizers, and bigots against all things Russian, including the very many Ukrainian citizens who speak primarily Russian. They are enabled in this strategy by the apparent affinity of right-wing Ukrainians, including quite prominently some tough-looking skinheads, for the Svoboda Party, and by Svoboda's own origins in 1991 as the "Social-National Party." Its logo at the time resembled a swastika. Svoboda denies that it is racist or Nazi, and Tyahnybok gives speeches that I think express love for Ukraine without being bigoted, but again and again I have seen and heard creepy people and disgusting words from those who attend Svoboda rallies. Maybe they are plants, maybe they are not, and maybe Svoboda itself is a plant in order to discredit the opposition. It seems that there are as many opinions on the subject as there are political commentators. All of this fits what we are discussing in this chapter: the convoluted, opaque, underhanded, and thuggish ways of politics in Ukraine, and what we call here "Soviet ways in post-Soviet days."

The two factions went at one another on May 18, not just with words from their respective podiums, but also with the fists of young toughs. The newspapers referred to them as "hired athletes" and "hired thugs." Exactly what transpired and who punched whom depends on who you ask, as the fights that broke out over the course of the day in various parts of central Kyiv are presented differently depending on the political leanings of the news source and the politics of people who claim to be eyewitnesses. The versions of police reports cannot be trusted either, as they are under the control of the Party of Regions. Thus, we note with some amusement that the official police estimates of the size of the crowds are 4,000 individuals at Rise Up, Ukraine! and, exactly ten times more, 40,000, at the rally of Regionnaires. This is the exact reverse of what the opposition has claimed: 40,000 at Rise Up, Ukraine! and 4,000 Regionnaires. I don't know the exact numbers myself, but can certainly vouch for the fact that there were tens of thousands at the opposition rally, and that I hardly noticed the presence of Party of Regions supporters among the postrally crowds in central Kyiv. As claims and counterclaims about numbers sort themselves out, it begins to look like roughly equal-sized rallies for both sides, perhaps about 20,000 to 30,000 participants each.

What was not equal, it seems, was the marchers' motivation. There is no reason to think that any of the people who turned out for the three opposition parties did so for any reason other than conviction. They came voluntarily and were not paid for their participation. The judgment about the Regionnaires rally, however, is quite the opposite, as a great many participants were paid, others were promised to be paid but were not, and a great many others were public sector employees who were told to turn up as part of their jobs. Circumstantial evidence for the different motivations for the two groups is that many supporters of the opposition could be seen hanging around and socializing in central Kyiv for hours after the programming had ended, while the Regionnaires crowd seems to have simply disappeared. Also, there are verifiable news reports that for a time quite a few of the Regionnaires' participants blocked a street in protest after the rally had ended because they had not been paid the 100 hryvnia (a little more than US$12) that they were promised. Also, it is known that many Rise Up, Ukraine! participants were prevented from going to Kyiv for the rally by police who diverted buses of protestors and boarded trains to tell people to get off. This tactic has been used by the Party of Regions before, citing issues of public safety in making Kyiv inaccessible, and it is believed to have kept many thousands of opposition protesters from reaching the city. There is often violence when this happens, vandalism to vehicles, and other forms of intimidation. A close friend from Mariupol, an industrial city on the Sea of Azov 16 hours away by train, was among many who were escorted from a train by police, only to see their seats to Kyiv taken by supporters of the Party of Regions.

Both rallies were covered by media and photographers, so there is plenty of reporting and many images of what transpired. There was an enormous police presence, including Berkut, a no-nonsense special unit of the *militsia* that is descended from the Soviet Union's special OMON forces, in full riot gear. I managed to photograph units as they marshaled early that morning in the belowground pedestrian crossings at Independence Square, as well as some of the fighting that took place hours later, but I have no shot as fortuitous as the one that was captured by a photographer for the news magazine *Ukrainskiy Tyzhden* (Ukrainian Week) of the "athlete" Vadym Titushko. He is captured in a fighter's stance seconds before he and about ten compatriots behind him attacked *Kommersant* news photographer Vlad Sodel and Channel 5 TV journalist Olha Snisartchuk and pummeled them bloody. The two had been photographing the gang in an attack on Svoboda party marchers. The photograph also shows a police officer standing calmly beside Titushko. It has become an icon of that day, documenting the entry of violent thugs into the political campaign and police inaction.

Thousands of photographs were taken that day and disseminated over the Internet. That is how Titushko was identified and how it was learned that he and his associates, as well as other violent gang members that could be identified that day, were working for the Party of Regions. Titushko and his gang came from a "sports club" named Budo in Bila Tserkva, a town outside Kyiv, and they were known "thugs for hire." Other monikers for such sports clubs are "security agencies" and "fight clubs" (Mykhelson and Velychko, 2013).[16] In addition to working for clients in politics, such "fists" also work for raiders who want to intimidate building occupants or business owners who will not make way, and for business interests seeking to move against competitors. At least one gang member has confirmed in an interview that he and others worked for the Party of Regions and that the orders came from the party's parliamentarians (*Ukrainian Week*, May 20-30, 2013). Svoboda is also known to employ "athletes." Their toughs made trouble

---

16   "Titushko" has since entered the colloquial Ukrainian vocabulary as a word meaning "thug for hire," as in "Many *titushkos* (or *titushky*) were bussed in to cause trouble."

on May 18 as well, and they sparred head to head with Regionnaire toughs. I have seen thugs from Svoboda engaged in violence at other events as well.

It is not a great leap to suggest that, as a whole, what transpired on May 18 was the start of what promises to be an extraordinarily hot election campaign, and that the fighting echoes what members of parliament do routinely in their own "fight club" (Chapter 3). Furthermore, there are political commentators who interpret the events of that day as evidence of a campaign by the Party of Regions to swing an election that they are likely to lose in their favor by unleashing banditry under the guise of a struggle against fascism. The *Kyiv Post* referred to the Regionnaires' strategy as "playing a dangerous antifascist card" (May 19, 2013), while *Ukrainian Week* captioned its close-up cover photo of Titushko and his gang with the words "The fascists of the future will be called anti-fascists" (Ukrainian edition, May 20-30, 2013; International edition, June 2013).

The reason that May 18, 2013, might be a date for tomorrow's history books is that it might be a turning point in Ukrainian history. If the united op- position succeeds in finding one candidate to win the election, the country could embark on a very different path from the one it is now following, specifically one with more democracy, more support for the Ukrainian language, and closer ties to Europe. There might even be a significant drop in corruption and a chance to enter the European Union. On the other hand, if Viktor Yanukovych succeeds in winning reelection in 2015, he and his party will be able to solidify their hold on the country and run it with an even tighter fist, like Vladimir Putin runs Russia. Ukraine would then be brought closer to Russia, perhaps even into the sort of post-Soviet union that Russia has been urging. The use of gangs in the campaign can either turn independent voters against the Party of Regions, or gain votes for the party by convincing voters that the opposition is a dangerous fascist alternative. The gangs could also intimidate voters to support the party in power. That would truly be "a Soviet way in post-Soviet days." Unfortunately, my soundings of Ukrainian citizens, as well as the results of public opinion polls, say that regardless of who wins in 2015, not much will change for the better, as all politicians in Ukraine are cut from the same cloth and care first and foremost about themselves.

4.5   Heorhiy Ruslanovych Gongadze

That the worst of the old Soviet Union is not necessarily fully in the past is seen in the tragic story of independent journalist Heorhiy Ruslanovych

Gongadze. His life was ended in the crudest of ways: they cut off his head. Despite the passage of more than a dozen years, exactly who *they* among Ukraine's not-so-democratic post-Soviets are and precisely why the crime was committed is still not known. However, there is evidence that points at very high levels and it would not be a surprise to many Ukrainians if it were eventually proven that the order to kill this crusading citizen came from the then-president of the country himself. That is where suspicions and mounting evidence lead. Here is the story in a nutshell: it is Ukraine at its messiest.

Gongadze was 31 when he died. He was cofounder of a website *Ukrayinska Pravda* (Ukrainian Truth) that disseminated news and opinions in opposition to the increasingly authoritarian administration of Leonid Kuchma, the second president of independent Ukraine. The website successfully sidestepped controls that the government was imposing on other media, and it was widely followed, especially because it exposed high-level corruption. Gongadze obviously got under someone's skin. Soon after publishing a series of open letters about the nation's lack of press freedoms and threats to himself and his family from the SBU, the Ukrainian secret police, he was kidnapped on September 16, 2000, and was never seen again alive. His decapitated body was found in a forest outside Kyiv some two months later. There is no sense in my going through all the details of what may or may not have happened in the case, as I have no information beyond what is available on the Internet to everyone. The important point, however, that underscores that Ukraine is excruciatingly far from heaven, is that the case did not stop with the arrest of four "pawns" from the intelligence surveillance unit of the Interior Ministry for the murder. Instead, suspicions via what has come to be known as the "Cassette Scandal" or "Kuchmagate" continue to point high: to President Kuchma himself, to his chief of staff at the time, Volodymyr Lytvyn, and to Kuchma's Minister of the Interior, that is, the boss of the pawns, Yuriy Kravchenko. Kravchenko was found dead on March 4, 2005, in his luxurious dacha in the Kyiv suburb of Koncha-Zaspa from two gunshot wounds that may or may not have been self-inflicted; while on March 24, 2011, Kuchma was officially and inexplicably charged with unspecified involvement in the murder, an act that some critics see as a public relations stunt by Ukraine's president, Viktor Yanukovych of the Party of Regions, to draw attention away from mess that is the rest of his country, or as crude retribution by Yanukovych for political disloyalty in the past on the part of the former president. Lytvyn, meanwhile, has ascended to be the speaker of the parliament.

The killing of Gongadze outraged the nation, which in turn helped to elect an opposition politician, Viktor Yushchenko, as Ukraine's third president.

His was the "Orange Revolution" campaign of the winter of 2004-2005, the time when Ukrainian voices were the loudest in recent history. He was the candidate whose face was famously disfigured by poison during the campaign. That is still another unsolved crime. There are those who suspect Yushchenko's political opponents at the time, including by name today's president Viktor Yanukovych, and/or machinations in Moscow, but there are also many who suspect that the poison, allegedly dioxin, was self-administered in order to gain voters' sympathies. A blood sample taken from Yushchenko in 2005 has mysteriously disappeared, and the former president has since declined requests for a fresh sample (traces of dioxin stay in the blood forever, apparently), saying that he wants to put an end to that chapter of his life. His health has since improved. Whatever is the truth, it is ugly. All of this is context for understanding the mess that takes place in Kyiv.

4.6   A Personal Warning?

It is hard to imagine that my work about Kyiv would attract the attention of security authorities in Ukraine, but it is indeed possible that it may have. That, too, would provide a context for understanding the situation in today's Kyiv. I think that I have a lot to say about what is going on in the city and about how good people suffer as a result, but there are no great exposés herein of official secrets or privileged details about corruption in high places or how oligarchs made their billions. Yet, it does seem that authorities might be interested in advance about what I might write, and that I have blipped onto their radar screens. If that is indeed the case, it would be because there are, in fact, huge secrets to protect in official Kyiv, and great fears that insiders' income streams from corruption could be compromised by the results of brave investigative reporting. Many other writers, and not just Gongadze, but also newspaper reporters and university-based scholars, among others, have been "visited" by inquisitive government officials, so why not me?

My suspicions began to crystallize just four days before a planned departure from Kyiv. Quite a few people knew that I was leaving because I had been making a round of good-byes and thank-you visits to key informants and academic specialists who had been advising me. This included various friends and contacts who are well-known "Kyiv activists" and regulars at various protests and public demonstrations. I had been to dozens of "actions" over the months, knew quite a few of their key people, and was quite well known by others in turn. Indeed, I had become accustomed to people introducing themselves to me at protests or at other venues such as academic roundtables on Kyiv topics, saying that they had heard that I was working on a book about the city and offering to share what information they knew. That is how some of the specific topics that I discuss here came to my attention. Mostly, the people who wanted to talk to me were fellow academics or activists affiliated with Kyiv-minded nongovernmental organizations (NGOs), or sometimes they were just ordinary citizens who thought that the demons who were undermining Kyiv needed wider exposure. But it was not until those last few days that I learned that, quite possibly, the police were also interested in me.

Four days before departure I received an email from a key informant/protestor-activist that I know especially well, telling me that someone named "Volodya" wanted to speak to me about my research and that I should call him. I did that immediately on instinct, trusting my friend and thinking that sometimes last-minute information can be the juiciest, and without asking any questions over the phone, agreed to meet the mysterious man the next day at a particular café. I had no idea what to expect. Volodya turned out to be a police official of middle rank who investigated official corruption. At least that is what he told me. He had heard from my friend "Oleg" that I was writing a book about demons in Kyiv, and he wanted to feed me a list of names of corrupt officials and to provide details about how money flows within a corrupt system. "I know where the money goes all the way to the top," he told me, and offered to lay it out. "Wow, what a large proposition just three days before I am scheduled to leave!" I thought to myself. Images of Gongadze flashed through my head, as did those of a hallowed martyr in Putin's repressive Russia, the much-beloved Anna (née Mazepa) Politkovskaya, an American-born Ukrainian woman who was a leading anti-corruption writer in Moscow until her gruesome assassination on October 7, 2006.

What would you do if you were in my position? I asked him why he was making me this offer and he said that he was frustrated that police work would not end the corruption, because the police force was itself corrupt, and that the problem needed to be made more public before there could be solutions. I asked why he was speaking to me specifically and not to someone else, and he said it that was because the topic is deadly dangerous both to him and to whichever writer reports on it, and I had more protection in being a foreigner than did local writers. That last point might be true, but my BS detector was already on full alert. What was his relationship to my trusted friend Oleg? Both Volodya and Oleg separately said the same:

they had met for the first time just two days earlier at a site where Oleg was making his own protests about goings-on in Kyiv, and Volodya started questioning him about the issues as an interested passerby. Oleg mentioned that I, an American, was writing a book that would include his own story, and Volodya asked to meet me.

So, here we are soon afterwards at a coffee shop in the center of Kyiv, and I have a proposal from a man who says that he is a police official who wants to give me confidential dirt about people high up. Again, what would you do? His topic is so enormous and I have only three days. I responded to him, suggesting that maybe he could find an investigative reporter who was a better fit for his information. I then quizzed him about police work, to focus the conversation more closely on topics that I am writing about and to assess his own statement that he really is a police officer. Asking for a badge or identification card would not have worked, because the conversation was, of course, on the QT, but I was able to establish that he knew police work well and that he knew personally what it was like to be on daily patrol in Kyiv. At my direction, he talked in detail about small-scale police corruption of the kind that I had seen many times, such as the shakedown of vendors and street musicians for cuts of their income, and about a particular crime – the beating by skinhead thugs of two dark-skinned foreign visitors – that had occurred about a month earlier not far from where we were. He spoke with authority and inside knowledge about these topics. Having passed my tests, he once more offered me the dirt. When I hesitated again, he asked me what was in my book if I was not interested in high-level corruption. In my reply, I focused on several of my central themes: today's pillaging of Kyiv by high-handed developers, environmental degradation, and the gaps in Kyiv society between the rich and the poor. He probed a bit, wished me well, and said, like other Ukrainian voices had said, that my book is much needed. As he doesn't know English, he wondered if it would be available in translation.

I will probably never know for sure what Volodya really wanted. Maybe, indeed, he was just a good citizen who was looking to expose corruption. Or, maybe as my instinct for self-preservation suggested, he was an agent of some sort who wanted to know in advance whether the book his bosses had heard about was going to cause any embarrassment for people who matter. It has not been too long since Ukraine had been a totalitarian police state with a prying security apparatus, so it would not be out of the question that there would be some official interest in what I was up to. Besides, it is said that the Yanukovych government was returning the country to Soviet-style policing and was proactively interfering with journalists' freedoms of investigation and expression, which also lends credibility to the Volodya-as-agent interpretation. To my mind, it is fifty-fifty as to who Volodya was and what he wanted. I did save his telephone number and took his email address, and I promised to contact him if I found a writer who was better prepared for the kind of information that he offered.

There is one more detail. Oleg did not describe me to Volodya. I checked with him about that afterwards. Yet, when I entered the coffee shop about 3 minutes after our scheduled appointment time, Volodya smiled knowingly as I entered the establishment and waved me to his table. Maybe my body language gave me away as the person he was waiting for, or maybe he knew in advance what I looked like. I know for a fact that many times in the last months I was being photographed at protests and public meetings. Sometimes the camera was almost literally in my face as the photographer snapped, and other times I could see a long lens pointed at me from some distance. Police? SBU? Maybe, maybe not. I take my own photos of participants at public events for reasons of my own, so why should not journalists and other writers, and members of the public who think that I am interesting looking or irresistibly handsome take snaps of me? But we know that in Ukraine police and SBU attend meetings wherever there are unhappy citizens, and that they are accustomed to making inventories of those present, so we know pretty much for sure that somewhere along the line I, a frequent attendee at protests, entered onto their radar screens and needed to be accounted for.

5 Historical Memory

5.1 Place-name Gymnastics

The Soviet Union was adept at branding, and it changed the names of places under its control at will, most famously replacing certain czarist-period names with new names that honored the Bolshevik Revolution (Wanner, 1998, pp. 172-199). For example, in 1924 Petrograd (formerly St. Petersburg and named at first after the name saint of Peter the Great and then after the Russian czar himself) became Leningrad after Vladimir Lenin, the revolution's main leader; in the same year Yekaterinburg, named after Catherine the Great, became Sverdlovsk to honor Bolshevik leader Yakov Sverdlov; and in 1925 Tsaritsyn, meaning "the czar's city," became Stalingrad, "the city of Stalin." In the industrial district of Donbas in eastern Ukraine, a growing city founded in 1869 that was named Yuzhovka (Yuzhivka in Ukrainian) after John Hughes, a Welsh entrepreneur who opened coal mines and built a steel plant in the region, was renamed Trotsk after Leon Trotsky for a few months in 1923, and was then quickly renamed Staline and then Stalino. All of these cities were renamed almost in a single stroke in 1991 after the fall of the Soviet Union: Stalino became Dontesk, Leningrad reverted to St. Petersburg, Sverdlovsk went back to Yekaterinburg, and Stalingrad became Volgograd. Furthermore, during the years of struggle for communist rule, young revolutionaries in their prime rebranded themselves personally: the man who was born Ioseb Besarionis dze Jughashvili became Joseph Vissarionovich Stalin, or simply Stalin (man of steel); while the man born Lev Davidovich Bronshtein in a small town near Kherson in the south of Ukraine eventually changed his name to Leon Trotsky. The new names, of course, are the names they took to their graves.

Instability of place-names has marked spaces *within* cities, too, with politically important changes being made at critical times to the toponymy of streets, urban districts, parks, squares, schools, factories, subway stations, and many other elements of the urban landscape. There are directories published for individual cities, including Kyiv, that help residents keep track of both newly approved names that they should learn and the banished names they should avoid, as well many traces in the cityscape itself of place-name transition. For instance, one often sees "ghost" lettering of a previous long street name if the new name is shorter, as well as instances where a new address marker with a new street

Figure 5.1   Sign with conflicting street names

name has been installed directly over the old address marker with larger dimensions. Furthermore, there are quite a few instances of "place-name wars" to be seen in which opponents of a given street name paste a printed sticker with a preferred name over the one they dislike, and then where opponents of the opponents either tear way the graffiti sticker, or slap one of their own atop it.

In Kyiv, the disputes tend to reflect different visions of the past and different roads to the future. Is the Soviet past to be honored with the street name January Uprising Street, or is the new name, Ivan Mazepa Street, a better choice? The latter honors a 17th- and early-18th-century Ukrainian Cossack leader who battled against the Russian Empire and was declared anathema by the Russian Orthodox Church. For some citizens, the one name is a painful memory, while for others the insult is in the other name (Figure 5.1). Table 5.1 gives examples of shifting names for some prominent streets, squares, and landmarks in Kyiv before and after independence. Additionally, I note from a guidebook published in Kyiv in the deep Soviet year 1965, that the main hotels in the center of the city also had very "Soviet" names: in addition to hotels named Ukrainia (Ukraine), Dnipro, Kyiv and Teatralna (Theater), there were hotels named Intourist, Moskva

(Moscow), Leningradskyi (Leningrad), Chervona Zirka (Red Star), and Persho-travenskyi (First of May).[17]

Table 5.1   Shifting Place-names in Kyiv before and after Independence

Prominent Streets

Name at End of Soviet Period	Name after Independence	Comments
Lenina	Bohdana Khmelnytskoho	From Lenin to Bohdan Khmelnytskyi
Kirova	Mykhaila Hrushevskoho	From Kirov to Hrushevskyi
Sichnevoho Povstannya	Ivana Mazepy	From January Uprising to Ivan Mazepa
Engelsa	Luteranska	From Engels to Lutheran
Zhdanova	Petra Sahaydachnoho	From Zhdanov to Petro Sahaydachnyi
Karla Marksa	Arkhytektora Horodestkoho	From Karl Marx to Architect Horodetsky

Landmarks

Name at End of Soviet Period	Name after Independence	Comments
Ploshcha Zhovtnevoi Revolutsiyi	Maidan Nezalezhnosti	From October Revolution Square to Independence Square
Chervona Ploshcha	Kontraktova Ploshcha	From Red Square to Contract Square
Park of the 22nd Congress of the Communist Party of the Soviet Union	Park Nyvky	
Headquarters Communist Party, Ukrainian SSR	Ministry of Foreign Affairs	Hammer and sickle symbol at cornice covered over with Ukrainian "trident" symbol.
Museum of Lenin	Ukrainian House	See Chapter 2

17   There are several excellent case studies about the political geography of monuments and place-names across Ukraine in the text edited by Lyudmyla Males, et al. (2010). The collection includes a study of World War II monuments by Andriy Portnov (2010); politically symbolic place-names in the city of L'viv by Viktoriya Sereda (2010); a study of state-sponsored historical memory in Donetsk by Oksana Mikheyeva (2010); and reflections about the renaming the city of Zhdanov-Mariupil by Yulia Soroka (2010). Also on this topic are the analyses of Kharkiv by Volodymyr Kravchenko (2009) and L'viv by Liliana Hentosh and Bohdan Tscherkes (2009) that are chapters in Czaplicka, Gelazis, and Ruble, eds., *Cities after the Fall of Communism* (2009).

Metro Stations

Name at End of Soviet Period	Name after Independence	Comments
Leninska	Teatralna	From Lenin (Street) to Theater (Street)
Chervona Ploshcha	Kontrakotva Ploshcha	From Red Square to Contract Square
Komsomolska	Chernihivska	From Komsomol to Chernihiv
Pionerska	Lisova	From Pioneer to Forest
Zavod Bilshovyk	Shulyavska	From Bolshevik Factory to Shulyavska

5.2   Remembering the Great Patriotic War

After the war, the Soviet Union spared little effort in memorializing the fight against the Nazis. There were monuments built in virtually every city and town, including on Soviet territory far beyond the zone of fighting. Some of the monuments were truly enormous and awe-inspiring, for example, those I have seen personally in Minsk, Kaliningrad, and St. Petersburg, and the memorial to the fallen at the Battle of Stalingrad that was erected at Mamayev Kurgan in what is today Volgograd (Adams, 2008). Twelve Soviet cities, including four in Ukraine – Kyiv, Odesa, Sevastopol, and Kerch – were designated "Hero Cities" for their valiant defense against the invaders. In addition, medals for heroism were pinned on the chests of soldiers, factory workers, and farm workers whose sacrifices made victory against the Nazis possible. All of these actions and more acknowledged the cause of the Great Patriotic War, as World War II is known in the former Soviet Union, and helped the Soviet cause afterwards by building a feeling of Soviet national solidarity vis-à-vis the enemies that had just been defeated and the new enemies of the Soviet state in the Cold War.

In Hero City Kyiv, we see a wide array of World War II memorialization. Among many examples, there is Kyiv's longest street (11.2 km) named Prospekt Peremohy (Victory Prospect), Victory Square at a key intersection along that street, and a high obelisk monument at that square that honors Kyiv's status as a Hero City; the beautiful and solemn Park Slavy (Park of Glory) on a hill overlooking the Dnipro in Pechersk District where another soaring obelisk honors the Unknown Soldier; and statues around the city that honor such heroes as Soviet military commander Nikolai Vatutin, the young war hero Zoya Kosmodemyanska (1923-1944), and the brave Kyiv footballers who played the legendary "Death Match" against the German squad Flakelf. There are also place-names such as Heroiv Dnipra (Heroes of the Dnipro), memorial tanks on pedestals, and countless memorial plaques affixed to older buildings all over the city. A map that I have that was published in 1982 lists a total of 79 monuments, memorial plaques, and museums in Kyiv that memorialized the Great Patriotic War. Even if not all of them still stand, it is not possible to spend time in Kyiv and not be reminded often about what transpired in 1941-1945.

Without question, the most dramatic reminder in Kyiv of 1941-1945 is the Great Patriotic War History Museum and the enormous steel-sheathed statue of a heroic female figure that rises above it (Portnov, 2010). It is called Batkivshchyna Maty in Ukrainian and Rodina Mat in Russian. While it may well be that Kyiv's greatest wonders of the built environment are the glorious golden domes of ancient churches and monasteries, it is also true that this particular museum and its statue, whose name means "Mother of the Fatherland," are extraordinary wonders, too (Figure 5.2). The museum and its grounds are awe-inspiring examples of the best socialist realist art and design, and the statue itself, well, what is there to say except to let one's jaw drop. Set dramatically on a high hill on parkland overlooking the Dnipro River and covered in high-quality stainless steel, the Mother of the Fatherland soars to the heavens, and whether lit by daylight sun or at night by flood lamps, it positively glistens. She stands erect in a heroic pose, with a sword held upright in her right hand and a shield emblazoned with the hammer and sickle emblem of the Soviet Union in the left, and looks protectively at the river and the endless flat lands of Ukraine beyond. In size, it ranks among the highest statues in the world. She is 62 meters tall and stands atop a 40-meter, three-story pedestal-museum, making this monument the 15th-tallest statue in the world, the third highest in Europe (after the crazy Peter the Great monument by Zurab Tsereteli in Moscow and the aforementioned World War II monument in Volgograd), and the 4th-tallest nonreligious statue in the world (after the two Russian monuments mentioned above and a statue of two former emperors of China that stand in Henan Province). The statue would have been a bit taller, but the tip of the sword was diplomatically lopped off at the time of construction so that it would not rise above the highest cross atop a church dome at Pecherska Lavra on the same bluff just upriver.

The main approach to the museum and grounds is from the direction of Pecherska Lavra. One walks past displays of tanks, planes, cannons, and other weaponry, to an enormous concrete chalice in which the "flame of glory" burns each year on Victory Day (May 9), and then with accompani-

Figure 5.2   Kyiv's iconic "Mother of the Fatherland" World War II memorial as seen from across the Dnipro River

ment by echoes of heroic martial music, through a solemn, cavelike stone chamber with oversized reliefs of determined soldiers and Soviet citizens in action against the Nazis. As is the tradition, the bronze automatic rifle of one soldier has been rubbed so often by visitors that its barrel glistens. When you emerge from this "underground" passage there are more oversized heroes in action poses, but now they are bathed by sunlight, and above them the awesome steel sight of Batkivshchyna Maty, much higher and brighter than anyone could be prepared for. As we come closer on this particular holiday, we see huge posters with images of still-living heroes of that war, elderly men and women with chests full of medals, and biographical sketches that tell of exploits as sharpshooters or grenade throwers, or workers in munitions or uniform-sewing factories, or in other critical industries. The posters are adorned with enormous bouquets of flowers and great ribbons, attesting to the reverence that citizens today have for those who had fought for the cause.

The museum itself occupies three stories and is made of chamber after chamber of exhibits about the war: the Nazi front across the Soviet Union, the rings of defense around Kyiv, the occupation of the city by Nazi troops and the resistance by Kyiv's civilians, the heroic recapture of the city, the death camps of the Holocaust, Soviet prisoners of war, and other topics. There are displays of crashed planes and shot-up jeeps, enormous maps of battles and landscape reliefs, dioramas, and tens of thousands of artifacts, photographs, propaganda posters, and cards with printed explanations. At the top level we enter a high, sunlit cone atop which stands the Mother of the Fatherland. All around us on the walls are the names of Heroes of the Soviet Union and Socialist Labor – thousands of them. As is the case with each of the other chambers in the museum, this one is watched over by an elderly woman museum attendant. These attendants usually sit passively on chairs in the corner of the room, but here where the chamber is circular, this attendant has no corner and becomes part of the display. This particular babushka amply occupies a sturdy wooden chair along a curve of the room and faces a simple wooden table atop which is just one thing: a solitary red rotary telephone.

One quiet day inside the museum, I listened in as a professional guide gave a personal tour to a young girl, aged about 10. The girl was accompanied by her father, but he hardly spoke. It was just the voice of the twentysomething male guide that the father had engaged for the tour and the occasional comment or short question from the girl – a private history lesson on dad's day to be with his daughter. In the last chamber of the museum before the top-floor chamber with the retro hotline, the 17th, a large and very sad room adorned with thousands upon thousands of genuine photographic portraits of soldiers and civilians who had perished in the war affixed along walls on either side of a seemingly endlessly long empty dining table lined with empty dishes and cups in place-setting formation, I heard the guide sum it up: "All of these people died for us. They died so that we could live today in peace, be with our families, and have the nice life that we have." Little "Lena" scanned the room and showed with her eyes and a nod that she understood; my own eyes were transfixed on these three people who were indeed the beneficiaries of great sacrifices and welled up.

When the museum opened in 1981, the top-most name in the top chamber was that of Leonid Brezhnev, Mr. Chestful-of-Medals himself, a top Soviet official from 1964-1982. However, his name was removed after Ukrainian independence as one of several post-Soviet changes. In addition, there is now a blue-and-yellow Ukrainian flag behind the statue of the soldier who stands in the lobby and looks over the broken remains of a Nazi eagle-and-swastika statue; there are printed explanations about the exhibits in Ukrainian rather than Russian; and new displays about Ukrainian nationalists and their own war against the Nazis. But all in all, this is still a Soviet show that is much respected and admired for technical competence, overall impact, and unforgettable lessons about the worst of all wars. I am glad that they built this museum and gave Kyiv the image of Batkivshchyna Maty as an icon. The alternative, discussed seriously in the big-thinking 1950s, would have erected twin statues of Vladimir Lenin and Joseph Stalin on the same hill, both some 200 meters high – more than three times the height of Batkivshchyna Maty and by far the highest statue in the world. It would have been quite a job in 1991 to dismantle them.

5.3   Babyn Yar

The other "most important" World War II memorial in Kyiv is that at Babyn Yar, a ravine in Kyiv where the Nazis carried out a series of massacres of Jews and others during their occupation of the city. The place is also known as Babi Yar, from the Russian, and in both languages means "old woman's ravine." This is where 33,771 Jews, representing most of Kyiv's Jewish population, were marched to be shot and buried in mass graves on September 29-30, 1941. It was the first mass crime of the Holocaust and its largest single mass killing. The Chief Rabbi of Tel Aviv, Rabbi Yisrael Meir Lau, who was one of several prominent speakers at the site in 2006 on the 65th anniversary of the executions, suggested that history may have been different had the world paid greater attention at the time:

> Maybe I am not a historian, but maybe, say, this Babi Yar was also a test for Hitler. If on September 29 and September 30, 1941, Babi Yar may happen and the world did not react seriously, dramatically, abnormally, maybe this was a good test for him. So a few weeks later in January 1942, near Berlin in Wannsee, a convention can be held with a decision, a final solution to the Jewish problem. We are a problem, of course. Maybe if the very action had been a serious one, a dramatic one, in September 1941 here in Ukraine, the Wannsee Conference would have come to a different end, maybe.[18]

In addition to the well-documented case of the 33,771 murdered Jews, Babyn Yar was also the place of death for an additional 100,000 to 150,000 victims of the Nazi killing machine: more Jews, plus Ukrainians, most especially

18   https://www.youtube.com/watch?v=d8topGeyXaE

621 members of the Organization of Ukrainian Nationalists (OUN), Russians, communists, a large fraction of Kyiv's Roma population, and civilian hostages. The bodies of patients who had been gassed at the Ivan Pavlov Psychiatric Hospital in Kyiv were dumped into the ravines, too. A detailed count of the number of victims is no longer possible because before they retreated from Kyiv, the Nazis ordered chained prisoners to dig up the corpses at Babyn Yar and burn them, and then to scatter the ashes and other remains over the farmlands of Kyiv oblast. Among the Ukrainians, the most prominent victims were poet and activist Olena Ivanivna Teliha (1906-1942) and her husband, the bandura player Mykhaiko Pavlovych Teliha (1898-1942). Before she was killed, Teliha wrote her last words on a wall in her prison cell: "Here was interred and from here goes to her death Olena Teliha."

The main memorial at Babyn Yar was designed by M. Lysenko and other sculptors, and was erected in 1976 in an area between the killing-ground ravine and the concentration camp in Syrets where many of the Jews and other victims were held before their deaths. It takes the form of intertwined and anguished human figures reaching skyward and stands on a high pedestal with a stairway for walking up to the base, as many people do with offerings of flowers. There are side-by-side plaques in Russian, Ukrainian, and Hebrew that read that at this place more than 100,000 citizens of Kyiv were shot at the hands of German-Fascist invaders in 1941-1943. No mention is made of ethnicity or the Holocaust, and there are no additional explanations. Once when I wanted to photograph the monument and got tired of waiting for some teenagers who had climbed amid the human figures to drink beer and do some kissing to finish and climb off, I asked them if they knew where they were. They seemed like nice kids from the neighborhood, and they responded to me with politeness. No, they did not know what the "statue" was, they said, and they looked embarrassed when I gave them a brief synopsis. The monument is not a great piece of art and it does a poor job of education, but at least it is there. In 1961, fully 20 years after the first killings at Babyn Yar, the Russian-Soviet poet Yevgeny Yevtushenko (b. 1932) began his now-famous poem, "Babi Yar" with these shocking words:

No monument stands over Babi Yar.
A steep cliff only, like the rudest headstone. (1998)

It has been a sore point among many Jews (and others) that the monument does not single out Jews as special victims of Nazi murders, and that it treats the 100,000-plus victims only as one. It has further rankled Jews and others that the monument does not stand at the ravine where the killings actually took place (Burakovskyi, 2011). That ravine is on the far side of a busy road that cuts through the park that contains Babyn Yar and is deep in a forest. Therefore, in 1991, as soon as Ukrainian independence made it possible, a second monument was unveiled at Babyn Yar, this one closer to the killing ground and in the shape of a Jewish menorah. Then, in 2001 another monument was constructed, this one close to the subway station that serves the park, in honor of the many children who perished at the site. Still later, in 2007, a simple wooden cross dedicated to Olena Teliha and other Ukrainian nationalist victims was erected on the Babyn Yar grounds as well. Yevtushenko's admonition was heeded, but now it seems that there are competing monuments and still no public education about what happened. The richly illustrated Ukrainian-language booklet by L. Ye. Drob'yazko, *Babyn Yar: Shcho? De? Koly?* (Babyn Yar: What? Where? When?) is a welcome step forward (Drob'yazko, 2009). There are frequent calls to build an information center and museum on the grounds and, as of 2010, a fund-raising effort to support construction of still another Babyn Yar memorial. There is a design competition under way at this writing, and at least one proposal for what might be called the ultimate Babyn Yar memorial, a deep pit lined with the concrete shapes of piles of human corpses. In a case of grossly irresponsible reporting, the UK newspaper *The Guardian* reported incorrectly on September 24, 2009, that Kyiv authorities were planning to build a hotel for Euro 2012 football tourists on the site of the 33,771 Jewish deaths. That is how that article phrased it (Beaumont, 2009), inflaming emotions and hurting the reputation of Kyiv and Ukraine.

While Kyiv waits for its monument to the Holocaust, a superb Holocaust Museum has opened in the large industrial city of Dnipropetrovsk located south east of Kyiv. The museum is within a building called Menorah, the world's largest Jewish community center. Opened officially on October 21, 2012, the structure is a sprawling 22-story complex of 50,000 square meters (538,000 square feet) that, thanks to many substantial private donations, most especially from billionaire Jewish community leaders Hennadiy Boholiubov and Igor Kolomoisky, vanguards the revival of the Jewish community in Ukraine. In addition to the museum, the complex includes a four-star hotel with 80 rooms, shops that sell Jewish religious goods, a concert hall, meeting and business facilities, and space for various Jewish organizations. The city's main synagogue, the historic Golden Rose that dates to the 19th century when the city was named Yekaterinoslav, is incorporated into the architecture of the complex. The building is called Menorah because with seven individual towers, the structure resembles the traditional Jewish candlestick. The museum is as expert in its displays and annotation as any educational museum anywhere, and it presents not only the Holocaust and crimes against Jews at Babyn Yar and in Dnipropetrovsk, but also lessons about the Jewish faith, Jewish customs, and Jewish history, and about the revival of Jewish life in Ukraine. Interestingly, even though Dnipropetrovsk is a largely Russian-speaking city, the language used in the museum to explain its displays is Ukrainian; there is no Russian, no English, no Hebrew – just Ukrainian. As the Holocaust Museum expands, it will include sections dedicated to other holocausts, including the Holodomor, the tragic subject to which we now turn.

5.4   The Holodomor Museum

While the Soviets were keenly aware of the advantages for nation-building of pointing to the crimes of the Nazis, they were expert at hiding their own atrocities and omissions, and they punished those who brought them to light. With the exception of occasional hints of truth or half-candid admissions, the Soviet Union was a world of official secrets and lies for 70 years. When the state began its final disintegration in the late 1980s, all sorts of previously forbidden topics entered the public discourse and the Soviet version of history began to be rewritten. Since then, previously closed archives have opened, new documents have been unearthed, and countless numbers of eyewitnesses have stepped forward to tell what they saw and, in some cases, what evils they did. Some of the most horrific stories are about the Soviet Gulag and many millions of innocents who were sent there to die, and about the names and locations of concentration camps in the north of Russia and Russian Siberia whose existence was previously only whispered. Other Soviet crimes took place in its war against religion and included the savage demolition of ancient churches, looting or destruction of priceless church art, and the killing of priests and other martyrs of the faith.

In Ukraine, the worst of all Soviet crimes, however, was the Holodomor. This is the famine that took place in 1932-1933 on the richest Ukrainian farmlands during the time when farmers were forced into collectives and all grain and other foods were confiscated by government officials. It was a man-made disaster that took several million lives, not just in Ukraine but also across the border in Russian territory. The most often cited estimates of the death toll in Ukraine range from about 2 million to 5 million, with a demographic loss (i.e., an additional deficit of births) of about 6 million more. Among the informed interpretations for why this happened is an attempt by Stalin to break the spirit of Ukrainian nationalists and counter any threats that might be brought as a result to the territorial integrity of the Soviet Union, as well as the creation of an opening for the settlement of Russians into depopulated Ukrainian lands. Despite millions of deaths and countless emaciated corpses of innocent men, women, and children on the streets of even the largest cities such as Kyiv and Kharkiv, the tragedy was treated as a secret. Even the most prestigious media outlets in the West, e.g., the reporting from the scene by Pulitzer Prize–winning journalist Walter Duranty for the *New York Times*, propagated Soviet lies and denied that a famine existed, much less reported the truth that the hunger was orchestrated deliberately by the top leadership of the Soviet Union (Conquest, 2001). Even decades later, the history of the famine was hushed up while the Soviets still ruled.

Now the climate has changed. The single-most important, most elaborate, and most expensive monument in Kyiv to the crimes of the Soviet Union in Ukraine is the Holodomor Monument (Figure 5.3). Inaugurated on November 22, 2008, by President Viktor Yushchenko, this striking memorial is located on a prominent bluff-top site overlooking the Dnipro River about midway between the Park of Glory obelisk that honors fallen Soviet soldiers of World War II and the domes of Pecherska Lavra. The stainless steel of Batkivshchyna Maty rises just beyond, making the Holodomor Monument a new centerpiece for the iconic landscape of Kyiv that one sees from the Left Bank. Its design is not at all subtle and perhaps a bit over the top, in my opinion reflecting a deep-seated need to tell all about this most gruesome tragic period. The main part of the structure is shaped like a white memorial candle capped with a golden flame. There are grieving angels at the gates and bronze cranes taking flight from behind iron bars. The pavement suggests a plowed field. Everywhere, there are millstones, and in front is an enormously sad statue of a young girl with braids, emaciated with hunger, and holding five scrawny stalks of wheat. Her oversized eyes are those of an adult who has witnessed more than enough of the world's evil.

One enters the monument by descending along the walkway and going through two sets of doors into a large circular room where the light is faint. Candles flicker in the center of the room. We are invited to light a candle of our own. Looping black-and-white documentary footage is projected onto the walls and is accompanied by commentary alternating between Ukrainian and English. The names of countless towns and villages in Ukraine that were decimated by the hunger appear in font size that accords with the death tolls, and around the perimeter there are memorial books by Ukrainian oblast in which are given the names of victims arranged by where

Figure 5.3   The candle-shaped Holodomor Monument and Museum and a statue of a hungry girl

they had lived. Visitors were diligently poring over the books. I observed that some of the older visitors appeared to be survivors; they searched the lists for the familiar names of neighbors and family members and to seek out other memories. Lingering in this somber, darkened space seems natural, and when we finally do emerge into the daylight, it is through a door opposite the way in and (on some days) into blinding sunlight. A view of the Dnipro and the exceedingly fertile flat lands of Ukraine stretch before us, and a large bell overhead is ready to ring in a new beginning.

5.5   The Legacy of Chornobyl

The Chornobyl Nuclear Power Plant (*Chernobyl* is from the Russian) is not far from Kyiv and never far away in the memories of Kyivans who are old enough to have lived through the scary and confusing times that followed the disastrous accident of April 26, 1986. One cannot write about Kyiv and not say at least a little about this event and its impact on the city. It is also important to mention that what happened at this site in the small town of Pripyat 93 kilometers (58 miles) north of Ukraine's capital should be considered one last Soviet crime before the Soviet system fell apart altogether. It is a crime because the power plant was badly designed from the get-go and had engineering flaws that should have been avoided; because the evacuation of nearby residents and warnings to the public at large after the accident were insufficient and dishonest; and because so much damage has been done to human life and health and to the environment of a wide swath not just in northern Ukraine and neighboring Belarus, but across large parts of Europe as well. Now, more than 25 years later, a wide area around the power plant with a radius of about 31 kilometers (19 miles) is still a dead zone where habitation is excluded. What happened at the power plant is a crime also because when Soviet authorities realized the extent of the disaster, they first warned their own insiders to evacuate their families, and then a next circle of well-connected Communist Party *nomenklatura* before finally telling the public in Kyiv and other areas that they were in danger.

I will not retell the story of what happened at Chornobyl because it is a widely studied topic about which there are many sources. Regarding Kyiv, however, it is worth mentioning that the city is forever linked around the world with the tragic word "Chornobyl" or, alternatively, "Chernobyl" from the Russian, and that this fact cannot possibly be helpful to the city's reputation or prospects for progress. Being in the shadow of the first great nuclear power plant disaster in the world is almost certainly a handicap for Kyiv, at least somewhat, as Fukushima is hurting Tokyo now. It would be an interesting project to examine this question further. The book by Iurii Shcherbak (1989), an acclaimed Ukrainian writer, physician, and environmental activist, includes vivid descriptions of what it was like in Kyiv in the days after the disaster:

> [T]he patriarchal, ancient city with its gold-topped cathedrals, preserving the memory of the ages, in about two weeks had changed unrecognizably, becoming closely united with the image of a new, atomic age ... The words "dosimeter check," "radiation," "decontamination," and all those "millirems," "bers," "rads," and so on firmly entered the vocabulary of the people of Kiev, and the appearance of a man in a special suit, with a gas mask on his face and a Geiger counter in his hands flashed everywhere, became usual, just like the jams of cars at the exits from Kiev: at all the control points there were dosimeter checks for cars. (p. 91)

> [Kiev] was a city of excited crowds around railway and airline ticket windows. There were days when even people who had tickets could not get through into the railway station. You had to get the police's assistance. The trains left with eight to ten people in four-seat compartments; speculators were charging up to a hundred rubles for a fifteen-ruble ticket to Moscow. (p. 92)

Second, Kyiv did pay dearly as a result of the accident with lives lost and damage to health, although that too is hard to quantify. Eventually, some 600,000 "liquidators" had been put to work to contain the damage at the power plant and undertake clean-up operations afterwards. They came from all over the Soviet Union, but Kyiv was a first and frequent source of labor for these dangerous tasks. Everyone in Kyiv who is old enough to have been there is close to someone who had been volunteered for Chornobyl duty, and who had either died an early death or suffers from resultant ailments. Another likely impact, although it too invites research investigation, is that the Chornobyl tragedy sped up emigration from Kyiv. The timing of the accident was when Jews were beginning to leave the Soviet Union for Israel, the United States, and other new homes. Kyiv was one of those cities from which such emigration was heavy because of its large Jewish population base; it would not be surprising if research documented that Jewish choices to leave were stepped up in the wake of the accident. Finally, it seems worth mentioning that there is a small economy of "adventure tourism" that has developed from Kyiv to the Chornobyl Exclusion Zone. It is mostly Western and Japanese tourists who make the bus trek which centers on a visit to the abandoned town of Pripyat and a chance to photograph empty homes, schools, and playgrounds, and a lot of weeds. Many tourists, regardless of where they are from, as well as many locals, purchase "Hard Rock Chernobyl" T-shirts from vendors of tourist memorabilia in Kyiv and other cities.

There are various monuments in Kyiv to Chernobyl victims, to firefighters who were at the front lines in Chornobyl, and to other heroes. The main memorial is a museum, the Ukrainian National Chornobyl Museum, located in an old firehouse in the Podil district of the city. It was opened on April 25, 1992, not quite a full year after Ukraine became independent, and it continues to be operated by the government of the country as a place where Kyivans and tourists alike can learn about the disaster. Funds from the government of Japan helped to open the museum and professionalize the exhibits. Groups of Ukrainian school children escorted by their teachers are a common sight. They ascend the stairs to the second floor exhibit rooms beneath road signs with the names of condemned settlements in the contaminated "zone of alienation," and see various photographs and scale models of the plant at various stages of the disaster, an impressive topographic model of the area centered on the power plant, and thousands of photographs of liquidators and, in another room, their children. There are also spooky-looking figures in radiation suits and gas masks suspended from the ceiling and standing amid exhibits, considerable Orthodox religious iconography, and a centerpiece exhibit of a small wooden boat like a canoe that is suspended by chains from the ceiling and is filled with worn children's plush toy animals. Beneath the boat is a glass surface that represents the water within which we see religious icons and beautifully embossed books of Holy Scripture. For me, a Philadelphian, it was especially interesting to see reproductions of two successive front pages of my hometown newspaper on exhibit. On April 28, 1986, two days after the explosion at the plant, the *Philadelphia Inquirer's* headline blared: "Soviet Reactor Burning out of Control, CIA Says. Roof Is Blown Out. High Death Toll Feared." In the next day's headline, we see the beginnings of Soviet disinformation: "Soviets Report Nuclear Accident. Tass Says Some 'Suffered Injury.'"

5.6   Rebuilding Religion

The Soviets destroyed churches but since 1991 post-Soviets have been reconstructing them, be they (i.e., both the churches and the post-Soviets) in Ukraine, Russia, Georgia, Latvia, Moldova, or any other of the former republics of the USSR. In Kyiv, the main example of a rebuilt church is the beautiful golden-domed St. Michael's Church on the bluff in what was once the oldest part of the walled city (Chapter 6), while in Moscow there is the famous example of the Church of Christ the Savior. There is also considerable construction of new churches where there had not been churches before, particularly in larger cities, as in Kyiv and other urban centers entire new sections of urban terrain were developed during the Soviet period without provision for places of worship. Church-building is stimulated as well by a proliferation of different faiths and different splinter groups in post-Soviet society, including the religions brought to Ukraine and other newly independent countries by missionaries from abroad, and by the competition between various indigenous and newly imported religious groups for the attentions of post-Soviet citizens. In Kyiv, as in Kharkiv, L'viv, Donetsk, and other Ukrainian cities, as well as in Russia and other countries, one sees a landscape of new church buildings and of construction sites for churches underway. People are now free to worship and many do so with great enthusiasm. In stark contrast to the anti-religion ideology of the Communist Party, many leading politicians of today, including President Yanukovych of Ukraine and President Vladimir Putin of Russia, as well as candidates aspiring to public office, wear religion on their sleeves in order to impress voters and project the desired public image.

A generation ago, there were no churches in Kyiv's suburban ring. The Soviets had done their best to eradicate religion in their territories, and they certainly made no allowances for the construction of places for religious worship in the sprawling *mikroraion*[19] neighborhoods that they developed around the edges of Kyiv and other cities. In fact, from 1929 through the 1930s, Stalin carried out a war against religion and blasted into oblivion scores of churches in Kyiv, if not more than a hundred (Hewryk, 1982). At least 69 churches were demolished in 1934-1937 alone (Bilokin, n.d.). Among the many losses was the original St. Michael's of the Golden Domes Church and Monastery which was looted and then dynamited in mid-1934. The few religious structures that were allowed to stand were converted to new, often expressly counterreligious uses. For example, the famous Brodsky Synagogue, the city's largest place of Jewish worship, was confiscated in 1926 and was made, first, into a meeting place for crafts workers and then into a puppet theater, while the Orthodox St. Sophia Cathedral and the Monastery of the Caves were spared demolition at the intercession of historians and other scholars, and were redefined as museums of architecture and history.

19   A *mikroraion* (or microdistrict) is a type of residential complex that was a key component of residential area construction in the USSR and some post-Soviet states.

However, since the end of the Soviet period, there has been a massive rebuilding of much of what was lost, including quite prominently the main parts of St. Michael's, and reconsecration of sacred sites that had been made into secular places. This, of course, is in the older parts of the city that predated Soviet rule. The urban core also has a number of new churches where none had stood before. But in Soviet-built "suburbia," where there had not been churches except perhaps village churches that predated *mikroraion* construction, churches are being constructed for the first time. Like shopping malls, commercial billboards, and automobile salons, they are coming to be elements of the new vernacular of the residential ring. There are Orthodox Churches of the Ukrainian Patriarchate based in Kyiv, Orthodox churches that answer to the Moscow Patriarchate, and so-called Autocephalous Ukrainian Orthodox churches, as well as Greek Catholic (Uniate) churches, Roman Catholic churches, and many demolitions of Protestant and evangelical churches, including at least one of the Mormon faith. There are probably other new places of worship as well. The geography of what has been rebuilt after Stalinist destructions, what has been built anew and where, as well as what is planned for the future, is uncharted territory for research that, in itself, could be material for an entire book.

Some of the new churches are quite spectacular and reflect both the importance of religion for the congregations that built them and the prosperity of a rising middle class. Good examples of beautiful new churches include two Orthodox churches along the Dnipro in the increasingly upscale Obolon neighborhood (the Church of the Intercession of the Mother of God near the end of Obolon Bay and the Church of the Birth of Christ on Natalka Bay near the mouth of Obolon Bay) and another, the Cathedral of the Holy Trinity, in Troyeshchyna, a bedroom community on the Left Bank across the Moskovskyi (Moscow) Bridge from Obolon (Figure 5.4). Likewise, Ukrainian Catholics have built the beautiful Church of St. Vasyl near the center of Kyiv off Lvivska Ploshcha (L'viv Square) that is, perhaps happily, greatly overcrowded every Sunday, and they have recently finished construction of their main cathedral for Ukraine, the Patriarchal Cathedral of the Resurrection of Christ, near the Dnipro on the Left Bank, close to Livoberezhna Metro Station. That soaring construction has especially symbolic geography. The center of the Ukrainian Catholic Church has traditionally been in western Ukraine, and the leadership of the faith has been headquartered either in L'viv or in Rome. The Cathedral of the Resurrection, however, reflects a decision to move the center of the church to Ukraine's capital, a city where the faithful in the Ukrainian Catholic Church had never comprised more than a small minority. What is more, the cathedral is set strategically

Figure 5.4   Cathedral of the Holy Trinity, a new church in Troyeshchyna

on the opposite bank of the river, i.e., symbolically in the east of Ukraine where the church envisions a greater national presence for itself. This was a decision that the hierarchy of the Orthodox Church opposed, particularly the Moscow-based Orthodox Church, on the grounds that Catholics were making incursions onto their turf.

Even more than the big churches, there is construction across the residential terrain of Kyiv of smaller churches for local, neighborhood needs. A typical pattern is to see a green wooden fence that defines the construction site, while within it is a partially finished church and an assortment of construction materials that await the next step in the building process. Construction often takes years, as funds are gathered slowly and the labor is often provided by church members themselves. Father Nicoli, an Orthodox priest (Kyiv Patriarchate) whom I know quite well because of his charity work, has walked me through the process for the church that he is building in a very poor community at the western margins of Kyiv. He looks high and low for donations of building materials from other construction sites in Kyiv, and then relies on donated labor from parishioners, plus his own very capable hands, to make incremental progress. Such construction sites often have a temporary chapel, usually wooden, outside the boundary of the green fence where services are held during the construction period, as well as signs on the fence that explain the construction project and show architectural renderings of what is to come.

The new churches in "suburbia" seem to be built on what had previously been public space. They often occupy public squares or parks, the green spaces between busier roads and the first line of apartment blocks set back from those roads, and the edges of new commercial developments. While there might be some protests from neighbors who oppose a loss of greenery in their surroundings or the inconvenience of construction activity, I am told that people generally welcome the presence of churches nearby because the grounds around them tend to be much cleaner and better maintained than neglected surroundings. Religion sociologist Anastasia Ryabchuk[20] has told me that her research shows that clean church grounds are havens for mothers with young children, and that some churches are providing neighborhood-level social services such as preschool and children's activities that had previously been the territory of the state.

I was fortunate enough to come into possession of two very detailed recent maps that show in great detail the pinpoint locations of all buildings in Kyiv that are, in one way or another, related to religion, as well as all such construction that is underway, all announced plans for construction in the future, and all religious buildings that have been lost over history for which reconstruction plans do not yet exist. The maps are at scales 1:10,000 with insets at 1:5,000 and are amazing for their thousands of details and complex cartography. The symbols on the maps come in all sorts of sizes, shapes and colors, and they are embellished with various numbers, asterisks, quotation marks, pound keys, and other "fontabilia" that add still more information. An enormous amount of work has gone into the making of this seemingly exhaustive inventory of religious real estate in Kyiv, but it also takes an enormous amount of work to make head or tails of it. The legends are incomplete and confusing, terminology is not defined, and there is no date on the maps nor information about the origin of the data. The identities of the cartographers are also not disclosed. The maps were simply given to me by someone who knew I would be interested. I assume that they originated with the Kyiv Department of City Planning and Architecture and that they are no more than two or three years old as

---

20   National University of Kyiv Mohyla Academy.

determined by details of content.[21] I spot-checked the maps with the field and consider them accurate.

Despite the deficiencies of the legends and the enormous numbers of symbols piled atop symbols, I managed some counts of overall patterns. While I may have missed something here or there, it seems accurate enough to report that Kyiv now has 360 religious structures, including churches and other places of worship, seminaries or monasteries, religious schools, church administration buildings, and other categories of architecture for religion. Of that number, 150 belong to the Ukrainian Orthodox Church, Moscow Patriarchate; 52 to the Ukrainian Orthodox Church, Kyiv Patriarchate; 10 to the Autocephalous Ukrainian Orthodox Church; 11 to the Roman Catholic Church; and 8 to the Ukrainian Greek Catholic Church. The fact that the Russia-based churches outnumber all other combined is because this confession has been especially energetic in signing up new members. It is rumored that the Russian government subsidizes Russian Orthodox expansion in Ukraine as a way to maintain influence in the country and keep Ukraine at least partly colonial. In addition to the churches already enumerated, there are also 100 loosely defined "Protestant" churches, church schools, and other structures, including Mormon and evangelical facilities; 8 Jewish religious structures (3 of which are synagogues), and 5 that are associated with the Muslim faith. The balance (16) is other (e.g., Buddhist, neopagan Ukrainian, etc.). In many of the 360 cases, there are multiple buildings per "religious complex" such as a church, a bell tower, and a chapel as part of one location for religion. In addition to the 360 existing religious complexes, there are 32 proposed structures, an additional 6 that seem to have suspended in the course of construction, and at least 129 churches and other religious buildings that were destroyed in the past and have not been reconstructed. Finally, in addition to the total of 360, I counted 30 cemeteries that are affiliated with various religious confessions, and 23 more sites where religion-based cemeteries had been located in the past. I am not sure what all these numbers say as a whole except to conclude the following: (1) there is, indeed, a lot of new religion in Kyiv; (2) religion is coming to be, once again as it was in precommunist times, a major landowner and land developer; and (3) once again religion is playing a part in the long-standing political and cultural divide between Ukraine and Russia.

---

21 My benefactor for these maps is not affiliated with the Kyiv Department of City Planning and Architecture.

6   The Center of Kyiv

6.1   A Taste of History

Kyiv has two hearts, maybe three. The undisputed historical center of the city is the site of the old walled city of Prince Volodymyr the Great (r. 980-1015), and the site of the enlarged walled city that was put together during the long reign (1019-1054) of his son Yaroslav the Wise. This zone was the capital of ancient Rus and stood high on promontories above the Dnipro River. The main hill is today called Volodymyr's Hill (Volodymyrska Hora) and the main thoroughfare is Volodymyr's Street. There are some remains of an old gate to Yaroslav's city called Zoloti Vorota (Golden Gate) enclosed within a museum-like structure, but the main treasure from early history is the St. Sophia Cathedral complex, a UNESCO world heritage site with origins that go as far back as the first half of the 11th century. There are many newer additions to St. Sophia as well, and also centuries-old reconstructions and expansions of earlier construction, so not nearly all of this complex is the product of the princely period. It is, however, one of the two main historic sites in Kyiv and is intimately identified with the glory of Rus and historic Christianity, and with the city's early reputation as a "New Jerusalem." The other most important historic site is the Monastery of the Caves Complex (Pecherska Lavra), also a UNESCO world heritage site. It is on slopes that rise from the river south of the first center and dates to 1051. It is the centerpiece of Kyiv's so-called third heart, the Klov Hill (Klovska Hora) and the Pechersk district. That area grew up around the nearby monastery, and then in the 19th century became known for a large fortification and munitions manufactory for the Imperial Russian army.

The second heart of Kyiv is Podil (Russian: Podol), a district of trade and commerce at the elevation of the river. It was a port and the distribution point for food that was brought into the city, and it came to be known in later centuries for its various trade fairs and for the sale of grain and grain futures, horses, and other livestock. Podil was connected to the "Upper City" by a path along a winding ravine that is the origin of today's Andrew's Descent (Andriyivskyi Uzviz), a popular and funky street of artists, tourists, and souvenir vendors. This district was also replete with religious sites and church domes, and it figures equally with the other two centers of Kyiv into the "domes" part of this book's *City of Domes and Demons* title. What is now the National University of Kyiv Mohyla Academy was founded in Podil in 1632. In the 19th century, Podil also became one of the centers of Jewish life in Kyiv and one of the city's main industrial districts.

The main street of Kyiv became Khreshchatyk. Before about the middle of the 19th century, it was little more than undeveloped stream bed in a ravine between the southern slope of the old urban core and the slope of Klov Hill, but it then developed quickly in the latter part of the century into the same sort of elegant avenue that was found in other prosperous European cities. The fuel for this was wealth from industrialization, and especially the sugar boom of the late 19th century. Along a course of about 1.2 kilometers (0.75 miles), there were exclusive shops, theaters, and top-scale apartment buildings, as well as banks and trading companies, the stock exchange, the main post office, and fine hotels such as the famous Hotel Yevropeyskyi (European Hotel; Hotel Yevrope-yskaya in Russian) from 1857. The Duma (City Hall) was also on Khreshchatyk, in a decorative neoclassical structure erected over 1874-1879. Its high spire was topped with a statue of the archangel Michael, Kyiv's patron saint, while for a total of not quite four years in the square in front stood a memorial statue of Russian Foreign Minister Pyotr Arkadyevich Stolypin (1862-1911), who had been assassinated in the city's beautiful new opera house. In 1910-1912, the tallest building in Ukraine, and indeed in the entire Russian Empire, was built on Khreshchatyk, the 11-story Dom Ginsburga (Ginsburg House or the Ginsburg Building), named after its owner and developer, businessman Lev Borisovich Ginsburg. Kyivans also called it *neboskreb Ginsburga* (the Ginsburg Skyscraper). It was a mix of shops, offices, and apartments, while on two of its levels was the private residence of the wealthy Ginsburg and his family.

Other prominent Kyivans built their mansions in Lypki, a leafy district on the slope toward Pechersk. The area is still an architectural marvel of beautiful homes with ornate embellishments. It was an area of privilege as well during the Soviet years and is still high in prestige. Among the most spectacular man-sions that still stand are "Chocolate House" (because of its color), which was once the home of timber baron Semen Mogilevtsev; the caryatid-rich "House with the Caryatids" at 3 Orlyka Street that was built in 1911 for the engineer and prominent Kyiv political figure Vsevolod Demchenko; the Versailles-like 4 Lipska Street, the home of sugar magnate Markus Zaks; and the "House of the Weeping Widow" at 23 Luteranska Street that was built in 1907 for Sergey Archavsky, a prominent merchant. The building is called such because of its decorative face of a beautiful woman who appears to cry when it rains.[22]

The main government district of independent Ukraine is located in this zone. It is centered on a the president's office building on Bankova (Bank)

---

22   Outstanding, beautifully illustrated books about the grandeur of Kyiv's architecture from the end of the 19th century and start of the 20th century are Byelomeysyatsev et al. (2012) and Skibitska (2011). Both are in Ukrainian.

Street, and on the neoclassical Verkhovna Rada building, erected as the city's main library in 1910-1911 and now the place where *nardeps* habitually punch one another (Chapter 3). Nearby are the beautiful baroque National Bank of Ukraine (1902-1905), the Stalinist Council of Ministers Building, and the Supreme Court of Ukraine in a beautiful old mansion at 8 Orlyka Street that was raided from the forlorn Museum of the History of the City of Kyiv (Chapter 2). The same district was a center of government for Soviet Ukraine as well, and also of the short-lived (1917-1921) and officially bilingual (Ukrainian and Yiddish) Ukrainian National Republic of which the eminent historian Mykhailo Hrushevskyi (1866-1934) was the first president. Before then, the area housed czarist government officials. An extant landmark from that time is Mariyinsky Palace, designed in 1744 by the eminent architect Bartolomeo Rastelli for Russian Empress Elizaveta Petrovna. It is now a ceremonial residence of the president of Ukraine. Nearby is President Yanukovych's notorious helipad (Chapter 3).

The old walled city was destroyed by Mongol invaders in 1240, ending the glory of Rus. The site was then marginal for some centuries in comparison to urban development in the city's two other hearts until it too was converted during the industrial and sugar age into an impressive ensemble of commercial and residential architecture, grand public buildings and monuments, and superb cultural and scientific institutions. Examples of landmarks that still stand from the period include the former Prague Hotel and the former Leipzig Restaurant at 36 and 39 Volodymirska Street, respectively, the Moorish Dim Aktoriv (Actors' House) that was constructed at the turn of the 20th century as a *kenesa* (house of prayer) for Kyiv's Karaim community,[23] and the iconic monument to Ukrainian Cossack leader Bohdan Khmelnytskyi that was dedicated in 1888. There was also urban grandeur outside the perimeter of Yaroslav's former walls, particularly to the west, where the czarist-era St. Vladimir's University stood and where the university maintained a large and beautiful botanical garden. That university was the precursor for the large and prestigious Taras Shevchenko National University that has its main campus at the site. A landmark statue of the famous Ukrainian poet stands in a square across the street.

Of all the rich industrialists in Kyiv at the turn of the 20th century, the most prominent was the city's widely acknowledged "Sugar King" Lazar Brodsky (1848-1904). His 20 refineries produced a quarter of all the sugar consumed in the Russian Empire. The son of Israel Brodsky, one of the early pioneers of sugar

23   Karaim are Turkic adherents of Karaite Judaism, a branch of Judaism that does not recognize the Talmud.

in Ukraine, he greatly expanded his father's business, opened other enterprises such as flour milling, and became Kyiv's largest employer as well as its most generous philanthropist. Much of his charity was targeted at the considerable needs of the city's Jewish population and included funds for construction of the spectacular Moorish-style Choral Synagogue (now commonly called the Brodsky Synagogue), expansion and modernization of the Jewish Hospital that his father had built, and a trade school for Jewish boys. There were also substantial contributions for the needs of the city as a whole: a tuberculosis sanatorium, the Kyiv Red Cross, a literacy society, and the founding of the Kyiv Polytechnic Institute, among other projects. He was also engaged in city sanitation works, the public transit system, and Kyiv's gasworks, and he was an official of the city's stock exchange. Many of his factory employees lived in company housing, where Brodsky provided much better accommodations than they would have had otherwise. He also looked after their health. Money that he left after his death established Bessarabskyi Rynok (Bessarabian Market),[24] the lavishly ornate covered food market at the opposite end of Khreshchatyk from where the Hotel Yevropeyskyi once stood. The market building is still both an architectural landmark and a popular place to buy fresh food (Tret'yakov, 2013). One of Brodsky's provisions at the time was that a portion of the profits from the marketplace would be donated for charity.

A second individual to single out is Vladislav Desideriy Horodetsky (Gorodetsky in Russian), arguably the greatest and certainly the best known of Kyiv's many outstanding architects of the time. He has been referred to as Kyiv's Gaudi. He was born in rural Ukraine in 1863 to a family of Polish landowners, was educated in St. Petersburg, and died in Tehran, Iran, in 1930, where he had designed the main passenger rail station. For 30 years he lived in Kyiv, and he left behind a memorable legacy: the already-mentioned Karaite Kenesa; the soaring twin-spired, Gothic St. Nicholas Roman Catholic cathedral that served Kyiv's Polish population; and the classical National Art Museum of Ukraine, with its high porch of Doric columns and huge concrete lions at the main entrance, among other buildings. His most famous structure, though, was his own residence in Lypki, the Horodetsky House or, more commonly, the House with Chimeras at 10 Bankova Street. Built in 1901-1903, it is perched atop a steep slope that rises from the Khreshchatyk ravine along an architecturally magnificent street of turn-of-the-20th-century apartment buildings that now bears his name, and it is without question Kyiv's most amazing, jaw-dropping building. Horodetsky was an avid big-game hunter

---

24   Bessarabia is an historical term for the region that is now more or less Ukraine's neighboring country, Moldova. Farmers from the region brought products to Kyiv to sell.

and author of a richly illustrated book named *In the Jungles of Africa*, and this structure, like the lions in front of the art museum, reflects his interest: an entire zoo of real and fanciful animals envelopes the outside as sculptural ornaments. We see huge serpents and crocodiles, as well as rhinoceroses, lizards, eagles, lions, frogs, and, at the very top, fantastic fishes with young girl riders. Horodetsky's friend, the Italian sculptor Elio Salya, executed the stunning décor, while Horodetsky himself took charge of the difficult challenge of positioning the building on a precipice. The structure now shares a plaza on Bankova Street with the main administration building of the president of Ukraine, and its main use is for official ceremonies.

World War II took an enormously heavy toll on Kyiv, most especially on the center of the city. The Nazi invasion of Soviet territory began on June 22, 1941, and advanced along a front 2,900 kilometers (1,800 miles) long. They reached the vicinity of Kyiv by mid-July, but they came across brave resistance from Red Army troops and private citizens alike. Three rings of defenses around the city slowed the German penetration, and it was not until September 19 of that year, after seven weeks of enormously costly battle, that the invaders managed to occupy the city. For the Soviets, the losses in defending Kyiv numbered in the hundreds of thousands in terms of lives lost and prisoners taken to German camps, while for Germany the victory was somewhat hollow because of their own considerable losses and the delay, which negatively affected the full assault on Moscow and deeper penetration into the Soviet Union. The extended defense of Kyiv proved to be helpful to the Soviet cause in that it provided time for the Soviets to remove critical industrial production for the war effort from the city and other parts of Ukraine that would otherwise have fallen to the Germans, and then to supply the needs of the Red Army from new factories opened to the east in the Urals Mountains and beyond. One of the key factories that was removed from Kyiv was Arsenal, the munitions works in Pechersk, which was then quickly brought into production in the Russian city of Perm in the Urals.

The center of Kyiv was all but totally destroyed. As the Red Army retreated from the city, it booby-trapped the buildings along Khreshchatyk, the main street, where they correctly anticipated that the Germans would take up residence and set up administration, and then on September 24 detonated their bombs from a distance, inflicting heavy casualties on the Germans and on their own civilians, as well as on the architectural fabric of the city.[25] The

25   Not all the explosions were detonated remotely; some were probably set off by agents of the NKVD, the Soviet secret police, which had remained in the city to subvert the German effort (Snyder, 2010, p. 201).

Germans were incensed at this ploy and responded by calling for the city's remaining Jews to present themselves and then murdered them at Babyn Yar (Chapter 5). There were an estimated 200,000 other civilian casualties in Kyiv at the hands of the Nazis, many of them caused by a deliberate policy of starvation that was imposed at Hitler's personal direction (Berkhoff, 2004, pp. 164-186), as well as deportations of some 100,000 Kyiv citizens to Germany as slave labor. All told, the demographic losses to soldiers and civilians were devastating, but finally, on November 6, 1943, nearly 26 months after the occupation began, Kyiv was liberated. As the Germans retreated, they destroyed much of what was still standing in Kyiv and set the ruins ablaze.

Rebuilding started immediately after liberation, even as fighting raged west of the city. There was a rush to restart industries that produced food and those that could contribute directly to the remaining war effort by manufacturing armaments and repairing tanks (Boychenko et al., 1968, pp. 426-427). The other priority was rebuilding Khreshchatyk. This task had enormous symbolic value and was a boost for morale. The job of clearing debris befell the surviving citizens of the city as a cooperative civic duty, while architects and professional planners began to sketch what might be next. There were cash prizes for the best designs, so quite a few hopefuls did their best to draw as grandiose an avenue as their imaginations could conjure. A wonderful, richly illustrated book by Yerofalov-Pylypchak about Soviet architecture in Kyiv has page after page of these illustrations (2010, pp. 285-335). The proposals showed a broad avenue with straight rows of trees, grand plazas with great monuments and fanciful fountains, and enormous buildings, some soaring and others blocky, but all richly over-the-top with combinations of columns, domes, arches, spires, statuary, or Soviet stars. There were also parade grounds and formal gardens, as well as relics of history and cities of the future. At least one drawing even offered long escalators from the high ground where Khreshchatyk meets river-bluff parkland at European Square to the level of the river far below. For those who toiled with picks and shovels while the thinkers drew, there was a popular song written in 1943 by Pavlo Tychyna soon after Kyiv was liberated. My own translation of the refrain is this:

> Beloved sister, dearest brother,
> Let's work together on Khreshchatyk.
> You start at that end; I'll start at this end.

What resulted was an eclectic mix of fanciful architecture and the harsh architecture of Soviet authority. The architects who won prizes for the best proposals for Khreshchatyk were not those whose work advanced into the next level of competition. Instead, three new proposals emerged from the inner track, those by architects Volodymyr Zabolotnyi, Oleksander Vlasov, and Oleksiy Tatsiya. In turn, these also fell by the wayside. Zabolotnyi's work was rejected because it was seen in Moscow as too reminiscent of Ukrainian baroque and not quite Soviet enough; Vlasov's concepts were apparently liked too much in Moscow and in 1949 he was "promoted" to work in that city instead of Kyiv; and Tatsiya fell by the wayside apparently because a fourth architect, the very talented Anatoly Volodymyrovych Dobrovolskyi (1910-1988), was appointed as director of architecture for Kyiv in 1950 and took over the main elements of the Khreshchatyk project himself. Somewhere along the line, the body of Nikifor Nikitovich Sholudenko (1919-1943), a Hero of the Soviet Union and the first Red Army soldier to set foot in Kyiv when it was liberated from the invaders, had to be removed from its resting place beside Khreshchatyk. He had been buried in the city center just after the battle for liberation, but now Kyiv's first subway line, long delayed by prewar bickering, was finally being excavated and he was in its path.

Dobrovolskyi (whose family name means "man of good will") is credited with initiating the main features of Khreshchatyk today. This includes the central square that is today Maidan Nezalezhnosti or Independence Square (it was then named Kalinin Square), the Khreshchatyk Metro Station nearby, and the huge hotel building that rises from a higher elevation to the south of the square and looms over the entire scene as if it were lord and master. That structure occupies the site of the former Ginsburg House. Its design was supposed to echo the Seven Sisters, a group of seven skyscrapers in Moscow designed in the Stalinist style, but it was never finished and lacks the wedding cake features and spires. The hotel was called Hotel Moskva (Moscow) at the time, but with independence in 1991 it was renamed Hotel Ukraina (Ukraine). Other postwar landmarks in the Khreshchatyk ensemble include the central post office for the city which is simultaneously neoclassical, Stalinist, and multicolumned, as well as blocky and oversized; the modernist, clock tower–capped Trade Unions House across the square from the post office; "Ukrainian House" (present name), constructed in 1982 as the Lenin Museum on the spot where a long time ago the European Hotel had stood; TsUM, the huge Central Department Store of Kyiv that was grafted in 1958-1960 onto what was left of a smaller retail store from before the war; the huge Stalinist city hall building erected in 1952-1957 at 36 Khreshchatyk; and various large apartment blocks for those who were elites among Soviet equals.

6.2   Ghosts

My own time in Kyiv has not been long but the transitions that I have witnessed with individual buildings and along specific streets are palpable and much larger that I had imagined they could be. There is no loss when decay is removed to make room for fresh growth, but I was dismayed to learn from many examples that neglecting old buildings and allowing them to deteriorate are part of the developers' strategy to gain access to land. I was disheartened to see architectural treasures from the past being replaced with soulless construction. I also observed that the center of Kyiv was being gentrified: taken from ordinary citizens and long-time residents to make room for expansion of a commercial center or for upscale and expensive residences for a privileged market. My street-by-street inventory of the territory on which the walled city had stood counted about 30 substantial buildings that were empty. Most are exposed to the elements and are rotting. Some of them might be affected by disputed ownership, but for most of these ghosts, as I call them, it is known that decay is a deliberate strategy by their owners. The goal is to assemble surrounding property into bigger development sites, and perhaps to make sure that buildings become decayed enough to frustrate arguments by historic preservation-minded opponents of demolition. If developers need to move fast with a building, there is always the tool of fire. I have no rock-solid proof that a blaze at any specific building was ignited by developer-induced arson, but can say with confidence that Kyiv has had multiple fires of suspicious origin and that neighbors simply *know* what happened: they blame the redevelopment-for-profit industry.

I was struggling to fall asleep one night (June 10-11, 2011) in an uncomfortable sixth-floor apartment that I had just rented for a short while in the old city. The bedroom faced Mykhaylivskyi Provulok (Michael's Lane), where just about midnight I heard glass breaking and people shouting. My first thought was that a bunch of rowdy drunks were passing, but instantly I recognized the smell of smoke. I opened the balcony door and saw that a building very near, 4 Vulytsya Alla Tarasovoi (Alla Tarasova Street),[26] was ablaze and that flames were leaping from top (sixth) floor windows and through the roof. It was so close and right at eye level! I quickly dressed, grabbed my camera, and came outside just as firefighters began arriving, and was able to watch from directly below as they ascended their ladders

---

26   The street is named after Alla Konstantinova Tarasova (1898-1973), a celebrated Kyiv-born theatrical and movie actress.

and began dousing the flames with water. I stood at command central snapping photos every which way until embers began showering us. That is when I moved to the other side of the barrier that fire department officials had set up and joined the crowd of onlookers. Before long, the fire was brought under control, the excitement died, and my neighbors and I returned to our respective quarters. I was impressed with Kyiv's firefighters and will always remember that night as an example of bravery, professionalism, and a job done right.

There are other reasons to remember 4 Alla Tarasova, too. It dated from the turn of the 20th century, and it had been a beautiful old stone-front apartment building, replete with ornate balconies, a graceful pattern of pilasters, and a high acroterion with window openings that stood proudly front and center at the roof. The structure had been certified historic for both its architectural merit and because notable people had lived and worked there when the building was still young. But in the last year, it was emptied of tenants by a new owner and now stood as a ghost building, awaiting whatever was next. The last tenants, who had apparently departed less than a month before the fire, had left a sheet-sized banner on their private balcony. It was in Ukrainian and read in bold blue letters *"Kyiany Peredusim!"* ("Kyivans First!" or "Kyivans above All!"), the name of an NGO dedicated to preservation of the distinctive historic character of the city.[27]

After the fire, neighbors told me that *bomzhi* had recently begun staying in the building as squatters. That is a word related to "bums" that Ukrainians apply to homeless people, particularly those who are alcoholics. I did not see these people, but the next morning as I listened in on conversations outside the charred ruins of 4 Alla Tarasova Street, some neighbors were blaming *bomzhi* for the blaze, saying that the cause was probably a cooking fire gone out of control or the result of drunkenness and carelessness. Others, however, were quick to point out the value to potential developers of having the site cleared, and they chimed in with assertions that the real estate industry often used *bomzhi* to get the development process moving. The truth of that type of statement I can't prove, but add that I had heard this same claim before from preservation-minded critics of Kyiv's new development. What I do know for sure, however, is that the side of Alla Tarasova Street where the fire had been was uninhabited all along the block before the blaze and had looked from the get-go as a redevelopment site in waiting. By stark contrast, only a few meters away directly across the street

---

27   By coincidence, I had visited the building on the day of the fire, June 10, and took what are probably the last preblaze photographs.

from Number 4 looms a side flank of the gleaming glass-faced Hyatt Hotel, "St. Hyatt" as we called it below, one of the buildings that stands out most as a symbol of Kyiv in transition. Apparently, hotel guests had an even better view of the blaze than I had had from just around the corner.

There are many other "ghostly" buildings in the center of Kyiv. In summer 2011, I counted 37 such "curiously empty" historic structures in the small section of the center of the city that I had marked out for myself as the historic "Upper City." That inventory had included 4 Alla Tarasova Street. The map that I put together showed a scatter of such structures throughout the district, but also the identifiable clusters, suggesting that builders were putting together larger tracts for construction. A *Kyiv Post* article that was coincidentally called "Ghost Town" presented similar observations (Stack, 2010; Shevchenko, 2012). It featured a collage of photographs of sad-looking, decrepit old buildings arranged across a map of Kyiv's center, and text about some of the most prominent examples. The lead example, well known to just about every Kyivan, is the soaring red-brick Gothic residence at 1 Yaroslaviv Val, an ancient street along which a wall of Prince Yaroslav's city extended (Figure 6.1). The structure dates to the sugary end of the 19th century, and for a time it was the residence of a wealthy landowner, M. Pidhorskyi. It is now privately owned again, although the specific identity of the owner seems to be a guarded secret, and except for security guards and some film people during its occasional use as a backdrop for filming, has been vacant since about the turn of the millennium. A distinctive architectural feature is the main door, above which two crumbling and evil-looking winged demons of stone seem to support three stories of turret. Just above these demons begins a network of horizontal metal screens to catch debris as it falls from above. As reported in the newspaper article, the owner, whoever he is, has an asking price of US$10 million for the structure, which realtors say is way out of line because any buyer would still need to add millions more to renovate the structure. From the historic Golden Gate nearby, an ancient remnant of the walled city, one can see that at least one happy young tree has taken root on the sunny side of the roof.

The story seems to be similar for other ghosts. Somehow the structures were acquired by new owners with hidden identities, often investment companies with mysterious initials or other combinations of capital letters as names, when the getting was good during the disorganized time that accompanied the collapse of the Soviet system. Some of the properties were then passed on to other mysterious owners (examples of names: "D.I.B." and "LLC House") who have done nothing with them but sit and wait. In the meantime, builders have preferred to work on vacant land, including

Figure 6.1   1 Yaroslaviv Val

parks and playgrounds and other public spaces that can be gotten under the table, where they hastily construct large buildings much more cheaply than the cost of restoration of old properties. The *Kyiv Post* article had phrased it nicely: "Developers prefer cheap and ugly greenfield construction to expensive and laborious historical renovation." Another option for developers is to build on vacant land or on sites in the center that are easy to clear, a process that an activist from the organization Save Old Kyiv, Inna Sovsun, described as "new pinpoint construction." The result of that approach is a landscape of incompatible buildings and destruction of historical ambience.

A major weakness is the lack of financial incentives in the tax structure for property owners to undertake historic renovation. At present, there is simply no reward for an owner or developer from the government for undertaking the difficult and costly job of maintaining the historic landscape in Kyiv. Moreover, the tax structure does not penalize an owner for doing nothing for years with her or his property, because taxes are unrealistically low. Under the new and inexperienced land tax system in Kyiv, the amount of tax that one pays is tied to the size of the property and not its value. That means that taxes on a wooden or aluminum shed in the middle of nowhere and a treasured architectural gem from history in the prized center of the city are the same low amount as long as the plot size is the same. In this way, an owner of a building such as the ghost at 1 Yaroslaviv Val can afford to wait forever to find his US$10 million buyer, or to have his building deteriorate to the point where it can be torn down despite the tears of historical preservationists. In fact, one of the laws of real estate physics in this regard is that the longer an old structure stands empty in wait of a buyer-renovator, the greater the chance will be that it will eventually be declared a hazard that needs to be taken down.

6.3   Maidan: Independence Square

The symbolic center of Kyiv is Maidan Nezalezhnosti (Independence Square) or simply "Maidan" (Figure 6.2). It grew out of the square that was in front of the pre–World War II City Hall and is actually a rectangle about the length of two football fields. It is aligned perpendicularly to the wide, 1.2-kilometer-long main street of the city, Khreshchatyk, which cuts through it and divides the "square" into more or less equal sized parts that are closer to being squares. According to Kyivan terminology based on the "flow" of Khreshchatyk from its "source" near the river at European Square, the two parts of Maidan are the "left side" (south) and "right side" (north). Prior to 1991, the space was called Kalinin Square and then Ploshcha Zhovtenvoyi Revolutsiyi (Square of the October Revolution). Its centerpiece was a large granite monument to Vladimir Lenin (Chapter 4). This is where the Independence Monument now stands. Both the square and the wide street that bisects it are emblematic of Kyiv today. They have their charms and can be great fun at times, to be sure, but both also reflect much of

Figure 6.2 Independence Square. Khreshchatyk crosses the scene and divides the square into two halves. The lower portion of the Independence Monument is on the right.

what is wrong. Put simply, reconstruction after World War II created an ill-conceived architectural ensemble that has never been undone and that seems to be getting worse as "improvements" are added. Moreover, Maidan seems to be a lot less "public" than it used to be, with increasing restrictions as to access and what can take place.

Maidan is a hodgepodge with all sorts of individually placed and uncoordinated architectural knickknacks (Jilge, 2010). It is bisected by Khreshchatyk, Kyiv's principal avenue for parades, protests, and pickups, and which is part of the Maidan ensemble. Except on Sundays and holidays, when the street is closed to vehicular traffic, pedestrians need to cross from one side of the square to the other via an underground concourse of shops, restaurants, kiosks, venders, and beggars. The subway entrance is there, too, the turnstiles for Maidan Nezalezhnosti Station. The Hotel Ukraina rises high from a slope beyond the southern end of Maidan's left half where the Ginsburg House had stood. At its feet is the main section of Globus, an enclosed multilevel shopping mall behind a high glass façade that forms the southern wall of the southern "half-square." It was erected in 2001. An earlier plan for the site called for a national museum and a pantheon of great figures in Ukraine's history to look out over Independence Square, but that did not work out and we have a shopping mall instead. In the evening hours when the lights of the mall can be seen through the glass from the outside, instead of seeing likenesses of Shevchenko, Hrushevskyi, Khmelnytskyi, and Prince Volodymyr the Great, we read names such as Swatch, Swarovski, and "Solo Pizza and Sushi." There are two large billboards atop Globus, one on either side as if to provide geometric balance to the spire of the Independence Monument that stands in front. The billboards are tacky, like those along a highway, and have advertised, among other products, Coca-Cola, a vodka bar located in the shopping center, and the bearded Kirill – patriarch of the Moscow-based Russian Orthodox Church. Another large billboard, this one a digital video monitor, faces the square from the side, across Instytutska Street, where it blocks the view of the stately former Institute of Noblewomen building that shares Hotel Ukraina's hill. This billboard, too, promotes commercial products and, sometimes, the Russian Orthodox faith to people on Independence Square.

The centerpiece of the left side is the Independence Monument, also dated 2001 like the shopping center. It stands approximately where granite Lenin once weighed heavily on the heart of Kyiv and is a fine monument to a country's independence. Indeed, it must be because other countries, most notably Mexico and Turkmenistan, have used essentially the same architectural format to celebrate a breaking away from colonialism. There is a columned base around which are marble steps, and from there rises a tall marble column that supports some sort of heroic figure. In Mexico City's case the column-rider is *El Ángel* (the Angel of Independence), whereas in Kyiv the top has a she – a bronze figure of a striking, emphatically Ukrainian woman that is 12 meters (39 feet) tall. She represents Berehynia, a folkloric female spirit associated with the protection of home or homeland (Rubchak, 2001; Kis, 2005), and holds aloft a branch from a *kalyna* bush (guelder rose), a plant that has long been associated in song and storytelling with the promise of Ukraine's emergence from a history of sorrows. From base to *kalyna* branch, the structure is 50 meters (164 feet) high. It took about ten years to decide on the design, which in the end was approved very quickly to avoid the embarrassment of not having a monument in place by the tenth anniversary of Ukraine's independence. The panel that made the choice almost certainly consulted photos of the monument in Mexico City. The construction was a crash project, too, completed just three days before the August 24, 2001, ten-year celebration. There are fountains nearby with water that runs sometimes, and three other monuments: one to the legendary founders of Kyivan Rus, the brothers Kyi, Shchek, and Khoriv, and their sister, Lybid; another to national folkloric hero Cossack Mamay (also written Kozak Mamay), a popular personification of the Ukrainian nation; and the third, a new one, an oversized bronze Valentine's Day heart. Visitors pose for photos in front of all three, or in front of a fountain when the water has been turned on.

As we move under Khreshchatyk to emerge on the other side to see the right-side "half-square," we see that it is just as much a hodgepodge – also the product of confusion, incompetence, and crass capitalism. As opposed to the glass façade of Globus, we now have glass domes that provide natural light for a long-axis extension of the shopping mall, also built in 2001, that runs underground. One of the domes is much larger than the others like that in many Orthodox churches, and illuminates a pizza-sushi-and-McDonald's food court. The construction of the underground shopping center unearthed the ruins of the so-called "Ladski Vorota," the southern gate to the old capital of Kyivan Rus. The relics could have been preserved and made into an historic landmark, but were in the way of mall building and by all accounts were hastily destroyed (Kovalynsky, 2004, pp. 325-345). Preservationists were outraged. Perhaps as consolation or from a feeling of guilt, a new city gate was erected as decoration on the square atop the mall. However, it resembles nothing in particular, goes from no place in particular to no other place, and just sits there as yet another people-blocking piece of architectural furniture, its base two steps higher than the level of the plaza. The prewar city hall building that once stood just at this part of the square had a statue of the archangel Michael atop its spire. That monument had been lost some time ago, but a new Michael was crafted and was placed atop the fake gate to nowhere. Nowadays, the structure is popular with skateboarders who like to sail through the gate and land with a thud on the pavement two steps down. There are graffiti there, too.

There are also fountains and green plants on right-side Maidan, as well as many benches bolted to the ground. All this furniture provides comfort or enjoyment for visitors; it also impedes mass gatherings, as there is no room. The "wall" at the northern end of this northern half-square is a cluster of five fairly similar Stalinist buildings with capitalist neon advertisements at their peaks: three ads are for land development or construction companies and two are for brands of beer. The signs are lit at night and are becoming new icons of the city, something akin to the neon signs and big billboards of New York's Times Square, but only a tiny fraction as grand. Before these buildings were built, one could see the bell tower of historic St. Sophia at the top of the slope to the north, but nowadays one has to climb the southern slope in order to see this landmark from the center. One of the five buildings is the Kozatsky Hotel, still a very Soviet-looking inn, while the neighboring building has a McDonald's restaurant at plaza level and offices of export-bride and escort agencies above. Until recently, Ukrainiskyi Khlib (Ukrainian Bread), was next door. It sold delicious bread and other bakery treats, and its layout was reminiscent of Soviet-era retailing. Now the premises house a sushi restaurant.

As opposed to what is *in* the square or behind it, the *flanks* of Maidan Nezalezhnosti seem more appropriate. On the left side, there is the afore-mentioned former Institute of Noblewomen, a former private school and now a theater, while across the square is the renowned Ukrainian National Academy of Music, also known as the Kyiv Conservatory, an imposing Ionic-columned educational institution and concert hall that is known around the music world. I was lucky enough to be a neighbor and often listened in on students' opera voices or the sounds of violin or other instruments as they wafted on warm days through open windows. Across Khreshchatyk, there are government buildings, most dramatically the monumental central post office of Kyiv and its two stories of Grecian columns (Corinthian in this instance), as well as Trade Union House, a landmark building strongly connected with Kyiv's history as a city of workers. Unfortunately, the post office suffered a notorious collapse of a large section of the colonnade on August 2, 1989, killing 11 people.[28]

We now turn to Independence Square as public space and note that this is, indeed, the symbolic center of Kyiv: it is where Kyivans often go on a holiday to stroll, see, and be seen; where Ukrainians have gathered in number for pro-tests since the time when the Soviet Union began to unravel; where there are staged concerts and other public events on holidays and many Sundays; and where tourists, Ukrainians in their capital city and foreigners alike, almost always visit when seeing Kyiv. There are clusters of souvenir and ice cream vendors at specific edges of the square, as well as an interesting row about 30 meters long along the length of the post office building of vendors, mostly elderly people, who sell symbols of Ukrainian nationhood (flags, lapel pins, postage stamps, etc.), nationalistic literature, or CDs of traditional Ukrainian songs and songs of Ukrainian guerilla fighters against Soviet rule. Some of these sellers have displayed anti-Semitic literature. In addition, there are also "characters" on the square such as those who proselytize publicly about political or social issues, or in favor of a particular religion, and those who

---

28   The debris weighed more than 700 tons and was testimony that the center of Kyiv was badly rebuilt after the war. Older Kyivans are especially aware of this and often walk on sidewalks closer to the street than to buildings alongside in order to avoid possible falls of brick or plaster.

make a living off tourists by posing with them for pictures in costume or picking their pockets or bags. The square is also "infested" with two dozen or more costumed characters dressed as bears, zebras, tigers, chipmunks, and other animals, Sponge Bob, Homer Simpson, Shrek, a stereotype Native American in feather headdress, etc., who mercilessly trouble passersby to have photos taken with them. These are mostly students doing part-time work for tips, but they work for a boss who keeps a close eye on them from a central perch and keeps them busy (see Chapter 8). There are also young people with doves who accost people to have their pictures taken.

The most critical aspect of Maidan Nezalezhnosti as public space is its role as a venue for public protest. This would seem to be a normal role in a country that has gone from authoritarian control of public expression to independence from foreign rule and the adoption of democratic institutions, and was indeed an emerging activity on the Square of the October Revolution even before the Soviet Union had fully crashed. However, the abilities of Ukrainians to gather freely in anger about the government have been recently diminished and the square now rarely functions in this capacity. Critical in this change were the large-scale protests took place in 2000-2001 against Ukraine's then newly elected second president, Leonid Kuchma, the so-called "Ukraine without Kuchma" movement by the grassroots. Issues included corruption in government, Kuchma's authoritarianism, and allegations in the "Cassette Scandal" that the president had a hand in the murder of journalist Heorhiy Gongadze (Chapter 4). The protests were eventually put down via mass arrests, which was followed by closure of the square for construction of the shopping areas. The square was off-limits for more than a year, which may have helped to disassociate it from the public mind as a place for gatherings. When it was finally opened in 2002, it was with the clutter of fountains and planters and benches and other architectural elements that made it impractical for large demonstrations. I heard many times that such was the deliberate design, especially for the right side of the square, where the "Ukraine without Kuchma" demonstrations had been centered.

The left side of the plaza, the area around the Independence Monument, retained a larger open space and has since been used successfully for various public protests, as well as for events that it was especially designed for such as holiday celebrations and officially sanctioned concerts. The Orange Revolution[29] took place there, as did large celebrations on December 26, 2004, the

---

29   The Orange Revolution refers to the December 2004 and early January 2005 encampment by citizens from all over Ukraine to protest a rigged runoff vote for president on November 24, 2004, that had given Viktor Yanukovych a short-lived victory over Viktor Yushchenko.

day when the Supreme Court voided a crooked election that had seemed to put Viktor Yanukovych in power as president, and then celebrations again when a second election gave Viktor Yushchenko ("the Orange Revolution candidate") a decisive and clearly honest win. The public had much freer access to the square during the Yushchenko years (2005-2010) and used it for protests, spontaneous gatherings, and making soapbox speeches on political and religious topics, and fun. But from later on in 2010, after Yanukovych came to power in the next election, the square has become markedly less "public" except under controlled conditions. That micromanaged concert of February 23, 2011, attended by Party of Regions conscripts and audience members who were paid is an example of the Yanukovych administration's controlling approach to the square (Chapter 4). When the government did permit protest (for example, the one in Fall 2010 by small business owners and vendors who were angry about new taxes and bureaucratic regulations), it came to regret what followed, because the numbers of protestors and anger grew as the days passed, and thousands of people were shouting about revolution and a downfall for the Yanukovych government. In the end, the onset of bad weather in December, the need for the protestors to return to earning a living, and some promises from the government that looked good at the time caused the gatherings to disband. Authorities made a big deal of the fact that some pavement tiles in the square had been damaged by tent stakes (many of the protestors had camped for day and night on end), and they arrested some of the leaders for wanton destruction of government property. Then, supposedly for repairs, a key part of the square was fenced off for months afterwards, and that was that.

I witnessed all this personally. I attended the business owners' protests and protest events (concerts, etc.) almost every day for the two months or so that the movement was active, and I spent many hours listening to speeches and talking with people in the crowd. They came from all parts of Ukraine, but with a distance decay effect reflecting the time and cost of travel, and represented regions that had voted blue (Party of Regions) as well as orange. Often there were reports that many more people would have been on the square except that police were pulling over buses with protesters heading to Kyiv and turning them back. The students who had been the energy of the Orange Revolution never truly joined these older, blue-collar demonstrators, who were said to be interested primarily in their own personal pocketbook issues, so the movement did not grow much beyond its original core. Besides, many Ukrainians, the students included, were still dispirited by the failures of the Yushchenko administration. As the holiday season approached at the end of 2010, the tired protestors broke up and the city put up a huge

Christmas tree and a silly commercial "holiday village" where they had stood. A news article in the magazine *Tyzhden* (The Week) was headlined "A Christmas Tree as a Tool of the Regime" (Mykhelson, 2010). My own notes about these developments include this:

> Exactly at the base of the Independence Monument is an inflatable baseball batting tee where three-year olds can hit a balloon ball with an inflatable bat against an inflatable wall. Atop this attraction is an inflatable baseball player holding a bat. The person who runs this particular concession (there are 20 or so of the same vein around the square) yells "Yes!" in English when a kid actually makes contact with the ball with his inflatable bat.

Protest at Independence Square has not been possible since, other than some small exceptions that slipped through the cracks. Requests for permits are routinely denied, and rallies that do take place are steered elsewhere: the park near the Kyiv National University of Taras Shevchenko where the statue of Taras Shevchenko stands, and the plaza in front of St. Michael's Church atop the hill in the historic center, among other places. Planned events and impeding architecture continue as be used as barriers to protest. Whenever there is an upcoming concert, for example, the square is closed off in advance as materials are brought early in for erecting the stage and other backdrop, and then it takes days later for them to be removed. By that time, it is almost time to prepare for the next event. In summer 2011, much of the left side of the square was closed for weeks on end because on weekends a television program of pop music and dance for young teenagers was being staged. Thousands of tweens and teens took part every weekend, singing and dancing along with their favorite pop stars, and thinking perhaps that the government that sponsored all the fun was cool. Once while I was standing and watching the kids in repeated rehearsal, an oldster about my age struck up a conversation that began with his rhetorical question: "Do you remember when we were forced to do this on Saturdays for the Communist Party?"

6.4   Khreshchatyk: Main Street Kyiv

Khreshchatyk is not quite 1.2 kilometers (0.75 miles) long, but it is Kyiv's best-known street by far and the city's nearest equivalent to what Americans call "Main Street." It runs from European Square close to the bluffs that overlook the Dnipro River westward to the Bessarabian Market, the colorful farmers' market structure that was mentioned previously. As such, the street runs – or "has run" to be more precise – from Lenin to Lenin to Lenin. First, European Square is where the aforementioned 1982 Lenin Museum (subsequently turned into Ukrainian House) is located. Second, Khreshchatyk then passed the granite Lenin in what is today Independence Square. Finally, the third Lenin is one who still stands – the statue that was described at the start of Chapter 4. This Lenin faces the Bessarabian Market and is on Khreshchatyk at the T-intersection with Taras Shevchenko Boulevard. Along its "Leniniferous" course, Khreshchatyk bisects Independence Square, as we have just seen, and passes the offices of Unian (a news agency), various hotels, banks, restaurants, cafés, and mobile telephone stores, as well as the central post office, Kyiv's City Hall, and the formerly Soviet TsUM Department Store at the T-intersection with Bohdan Khmelnytskyi Street. The street itself is quite wide, measuring about 27 meters (88.6 feet) across, and is often clogged with cars despite having eight lanes of traffic (four in each direction). The sidewalks on either side are wide, too. They have many small kiosks and benches for sitting, and except for the wee hours are always alive with strolling pedestrians. Cars clog the sidewalks, too.

Despite the bustle, Khreshchatyk is often a pleasant street and very pretty when lit up for holidays. It is extra nice when chestnut trees are in bloom. There are many enjoyable diversions: street musicians and religious speakers, break dancers and fire breathers, commercial promotions of various kinds, and good ice cream. There are also many free concerts that attract tens of thousands. The stage is usually on Independence Square, but sometimes it is erected in front of City Hall or in the middle of the street on days when traffic is prohibited. The concerts are paid for by the government of Kyiv and/or the national government, as well as via commercial sponsorship, and they always feature plugs for politicians and for whatever commercial product is being promoted. Often at the end of a concert there is a fireworks show. A lot of beer is consumed on the street, but crowds are well-behaved and there is typically little trouble. Police are present in case they are needed, but they usually maintain a low profile.

There is also much amiss on Khreshchatyk that, like aspects of Independence Square, presents Kyiv in a bad light. It is normal for a "Main Street" to have all sorts of people and activities, and to range across various shades of what is proper or appropriate. Khreshchatyk has these characteristics and then some, particularly in the direction of what is improper or not befitting of a great city, and it can be thought of as blend of all of the following: (1) a low-class boardwalk strip at an ocean resort; (2) a cruising strip for prostitutes and prostitute-seekers; (3) a home for the homeless and for people suffering from alcoholism, pathological loneliness, and mental illnesses; and (4) a place of opportunity for pickpockets, bag-snatchers, and perhaps even hat-snatchers. There are also plenty of petty vendors, "starving" street musicians, little old lady flower sellers and cigarette sellers, people with bathroom scales where you can weigh yourself for a tip, and professional beggars. Many Kyivans stay away. The street is used disproportionately by visitors to the city who throng the sidewalks to observe the zoo and who sometimes fall victim of the street's professional scammers and thieves.

It is ironic that a street that was occupied by the Germans in World War II after enormous loss of defenders' lives, was blown up by the retreating Soviets in order to kill Germans, and was then recaptured at enormous cost by heroes of the Red Army and rebuilt after the war with intentions of meeting the highest principles of Stalinist urban design, is – in independent Ukraine – a veritable mess. I am not referring to the many unfortunate citizens on the street who are somehow afflicted or truly impoverished, or who are unfairly marginalized in other ways: their plight is not usually their fault and they might have no other place to go. As a class, though, they do show an unfortunate side of Kyiv. What I refer to instead are the exploiters of people for whom Khreshchatyk is home turf and to entrepreneurs whose entrepreneurship brings down the cultural level of Kyiv's main street. The examples are many: there are human sandwich boards who stroll the streets promoting wives for export and curvaceous escorts for hire; rigged arcade games that tempt passersby with apparently easily winnable prizes; fake Russian Orthodox priests who collect donations for nonexistent churches; and professional beggars who are almost certainly not poor or who present themselves as someone they are not. A severely bent over old lady with trembling hands that can barely hold a McDonald's cup for donations is, in fact, much younger than she seems and could be a man; while some of the seemingly impoverished Roma (Gypsy) beggars can sometimes be seen behind buildings making calls on cell phones, or without the bulge of pregnancy that was there before and will be there again tomorrow. One Roma family exploits a wheelchair-bound child who seems to also have a serious cognitive deficiency by leaving her along the sidewalk or at the bottom of steps to a pedestrian underpass with cup in hand, day in and day out and into the evening.

There are also many sex tourists. They stroll alone or in twos or small groups, and accost young women who catch their eye, sometimes ignoring or dismissing solicitations from professional sex workers and focusing instead on young women who, to my eye, are out shopping or simply passing by. Some women like the attention and even decide to go on dates or do business, but many others hate the come-ons. More than one pretty young Kyivan has told me that she avoids going to Khreshchatyk because of the nonstop unwanted attention from foreign men, some of whom are excessively persistent. One said that she is sometimes followed into a store where she wants to shop, and is then hit on by men who pretend that they need help with their own shopping. Foreign men come to Ukraine for a short time with the aim of having a lot of sex, and they cast their nets widely. Some seem to go especially for teenagers. We return to these aspects of Kyiv's seamy side in Chapter 10.

6.5 TsUM in Transition

Rinat Akhmetov has bought TsUM (Tsentralnyi Universalnyi Magazin), the Central Universal Department Store, the one and only "main" department store in the center of Kyiv. It is located at a prominent street corner along Khreshchatyk, and it is going to be remade into a modern and upscale shopping mall (Faryna, 2012a). So read the announcements in the media at the start of 2012. A sell-off of the inventory followed and quick shoppers picked up bargains. Then the store closed for three years of redevelopment that is said to cost US$100 million (Interfax-Ukraine 2012b). Exactly what the new shopping center will look like is all part of the great unknown in Kyiv, as is the case with so much else that deals with real estate and the transfer of resources. This is, therefore, a good example to include in this sequence of chapters about Kyiv's emerging new landscapes, and to continue telling the story of transitions that, from the standpoint of the city's ordinary citizens, simply happen. Kyiv changes before our eyes, but very little of what goes on is ever discussed publicly beforehand or vetted: in most cases, the people are simply informed about a project once it is so far along that it is a fait accompli. Sometimes the outcome is positive, as has been the case of some new shopping centers that the public patronizes with enthusiasm, but in other instances the city loses. After it opens, we will see what the new TsUM brings to Kyiv.

The fact that it is Rinat Akhmetov (born in 1966 in Donetsk; his name is also written as Renat Akhmetov) who is behind the transition is significant, as he is arguably more powerful than either the whirlybird president of Ukraine or the Supreme Court – probably the most powerful person in the country and certainly the richest. *Forbes* has ranked him as 39th on the list of richest billionaires in the world in both 2011 and 2012, with an estimated fortune of

US$16 billion in both years, while *Korrespondent* has him as Ukraine's richest individual with a fortune in 2011 of US$25.6 billion. The money comes from metal and mining interests in eastern Ukraine, power generation, telecommunications, media, real estate, banking, among other endeavors, as well as ownership of Donetsk Shakhtar, the greatly popular and highly successful football club that plays in his birth city. He is the money behind President Yanukovych, who would probably cease to be an entity in politics without his support, the principle benefactor of the Party of Regions, a member of the Verkhovna Rada (parliament) representing the Party of Regions, and in some ways the heart of the economy of Donetsk and its industrial hinterland, Donbas. There have been reports in various media that he is a "scandalous oligarch" with links to organized crime, but Akhmetov has been able to win libel judgments against their authors and extract apologies, so we will travel no further down this road. In fact, it will help to round out this brief biography to add that Akhmetov is a major donor to charitable causes in Ukraine, enough so as to make him quite probably the country's number one philanthropist.

For Akhmetov, TsUM is just one of many investments and a smaller project than many others, but for Kyiv his acquisition of the landmark store is a big deal, because what he does with it will have a great impact on the city center. From the time it was constructed in the late 1930s as *the* fancy and comparatively well-stocked Soviet department store in Kyiv's downtown, the building has been a mainstay of downtown retailing. It occupies a strategic central site, the busy T junction where Khreshchatyk meets an end of Bohdan Khmelnytskyi Street, and has been an anchor of business for both busy streets. For a time, TsUM was a typical "Soviet" store where all goods were kept behind counters and could be examined only when it came to be your turn with the sales clerk. Then, the goods you wanted had to be paid for in advance at a cashier booth at the head of another line before returning to the clerk with a stamped receipt. Eventually procedures were liberalized and the layout of the retailing floors became more consumer friendly, as TsUM was privatized and modernized after independence, but it still cannot escape that feel that it is "yesterday's store" from a time and place where "yesterday" was harsh. Perhaps it is the building itself, a stern Stalinist-constructivist edifice designed by the dean of Stalinist architecture himself, Alexey Shchusev (1873-1949), a man who helped give Moscow its "communist look." Perhaps that explains why the structure seems to fit so poorly with today's consumers no matter how much the sales staff of today smiles and offers good service. Shopping has migrated to the malls, including to one that runs for quite some distance underneath Khreshchatyk starting near TsUM, and Akhmetov has seen an opportunity to profit from an update.

Although we cannot as yet know the specific details as to what the update will bring, we can be more or less sure that TsUM-2 (or whatever it comes to be called) will be quite impressive and comfortable, and it will give the center of Kyiv a facelift. As I write this, the entire interior of the structure has been gutted and the roof is gone, and only the exterior walls are standing. A construction crane hovers overhead and there is machinery everywhere. Whatever criticisms there are to be made about Akhmetov, they have nothing to do with urban architecture and design, where his tastes seem refined. The spectacular stadium that he built for his Donetsk footballers is a case in point (Suma, 2010). For the remaking of TsUM, Akhmetov has engaged the London-based design firm Benoy, which is widely known for premium commercial projects in cities all around the world. High expectations for TsUM-2 are also conveyed by similar projects in other cities where landmark Soviet-era department stores that have been converted into attractive, high-end commercial centers can serve as models or standards, e.g., both TsUM and GUM in Moscow and the historic TsUM at Theater Square in St. Petersburg.

The sneak previews that Akhmetov's development company, ESTA Holdings, has been releasing in measured public relations doses also promise a fine structure. For example, we are told that the façade of the present building will be retained for reasons of historic preservation, and we are shown in architectural renderings that the building behind it, as well as below and above, will be spectacular. There is to be a two-level car park beneath street level, a bright and sleek interior with a huge open atrium and blue sky that is seen through a glass roof, and a public space at the top where Kyivans can hang out and enjoy a panorama of the center of the city. The stores themselves are apparently not going to be the kind that can appeal only to the richest shoppers, as popular brands such as H&M, Banana Republic, Uniqlo, and Victoria's Secret have been mentioned as representative of what is to come (Faryna, 2012b). According to Andrei Sverchevsky, the manager assigned to the project by ESTA Holdings, and as reported by the *Kyiv Post*, the remade shopping center will target a broad public: "We want to reach the widest audience possible. Kyiv has about three million residents and we want that almost all of them become our customers. We want all of them to feel comfortable in TsUM regardless how much money they have in their pockets" (Faryna, 2012b).

TsUM-2 follows in the steps of changes in retailing structure that are already well underway in downtown Kyiv in which mass market stores from the West have been replacing commerce from the Soviet economy. Khreshchatyk already has a United Colors of Benetton, a Zara, a Marks & Spencer, and a Gap, among other imported brands. So in that sense, the remaking of the old department store is nothing revolutionary – only more of the same, but in a shell that promises to be extra nice. It is also a large-scale project, so it is much more of the same rather than just a little, and it does sit at the key, standard-setting intersection of retailing in the downtown where it will have considerable spillover impact.

Interviews with older Kyivans reveal a sense of loss about an institution that has passed and a store that had served them well. They also reveal a realistic understanding that the styles and goods of the new retailing will not be for them. Downtown Kyiv is becoming youth-oriented, everyone agrees, even as demographic trends point to fewer youth in the future and continued emigration, and an ever more aging society. Moreover, the workers who had served with distinction in TsUM for many years and are now unemployed know that there will be no new jobs for them in the new stores, as it is primarily sharp-looking young people who are hired as clerks into the new economy. Also missing from the new Kyiv as represented by TsUM will be locally made, Ukrainian products. To its credit, TsUM was known for its support of Soviet and Ukrainian manufacturing in the clothing and household goods that it sold, but that will almost certainly change when the new array of retailers takes over.

6.6   SS. Sophia, Michael, and Hyatt

The hilltop in central Kyiv where the walled cities of Prince Volodymyr the Great and his son Yaroslav the Wise once stood is a palimpsest of the city's history, from structures that still remain from the princely era, to those from the czarist period, followed by Soviet-era construction, and then new construction since the critical date of 1991. We can ascend the hill from various directions: from the south via a short walk from Maidan Nezalezhnosti, imagining an historic gate that once stood along the way to give us entry; from the west past an attractive square that has built around the remains of the last remaining gate to Yaroslav's City, Zoloti Vorota (the Golden Gate); up the steep and winding Andriyivskyi Uzviz (St. Andrew's Slope) from Podil and past St. Andrew's Church; or by the easy way from Podil, a fun ride on the Kyiv Funicular, a cable car transport that was built against a riverfront bluff at the start of the 20th century to connect the lower and upper cities. However we get there, we come upon a large open space that is the heart of the old city. To the one side is Sofiiska Ploshcha (Sophia Square), an open plaza at the gate to the St. Sophia Cathedral complex (Figure 6.3), while off to the other side, closer to where the funicular brings

Figure 6.3   The bell tower of St. Sophia Cathedral

you up the bluff, is Mykhailivska Ploshcha (Michael's Square), an open plaza in front of the gate to the St. Michael's Church complex. The two are connected by a short stretch of wide Volodymyrska Street and some green spaces at its sides. St. Sophia dates back to the earliest period of Kyiv history and is a UNESCO world heritage site, while St. Michael's is a new church built in 1999 on the site of historic Monastery of St. Michael of the Golden Domes that had been dynamited in Stalin's notorious war against religion. These spaces are often the site of public gatherings, protests, concerts, and other events, as well as destinations for camera-toting tourists and the various kinds of local entrepreneurs who look to make a living from them.[30]

In coming to this space, we have the opportunity to reflect back on the history of Kyiv and also to ponder what seems to be its future. There are domes from the past and domes that have been built in the lifetimes of our children, as well as other landmarks from across history. The very center of the space, for instance, is occupied by the aforementioned equestrian statue of Hetman Bohdan Khmelnytskyi, the mid-17th-century leader of the Ukrainian Cossacks in their fight against rule by the Polish nobility. In 1654, he was

30   There are both honest and dishonest entrepreneurs. I pass through these squares regularly and because I look or walk foreign, have been offered the service of tourist guides, interpreters, personal drivers, and sex workers. Twice, I was targeted by "dropped-wallet" scammers, about whom I had been warned in advance and for whom I was well prepared.

signatory to the Treaty of Pereyaslav, a military alliance between Ukraine and Russia in that struggle that Russia has forever since interpreted as a permanent union of Russians and Ukrainians into one people. The statue is an icon of Kyiv – one of the most famous monuments in a city replete with monuments. Its designer was Mikhail Osipovich Mikeshin (1835-1896), a Russian artist who was responsible for many outdoor statues in the major cities of the Russian Empire. Khmelnytskyi strikes the heroic pose of a determined military leader, and he faces northeast toward enemy Poland. The original plan was for a much more elaborate and more expensive monument, but Kyiv citizens failed to raise enough funds. We can be thankful for that, I think, because Mikeshin had hoped to cast a design that would have celebrated the demons of ethnic and religious hatreds of the times. In the model that he put forward that Kyivans rejected, Khmelnytskyi's horse would have been trampling a Jesuit priest, a Polish landowner, and a Jew. The czarist regime approved the toned-down Khmelnytskyi and took him in as a hero because of Pereyaslav. He then survived Soviet rule because he had brought Ukraine to Russia. Ukrainians like him because he fought the Poles, and in their estimation, did not mean to bind the nation to Russia for so long (Sysyn, 1988, 2003; Stampfer, 2003; and Vernadsky, 1941).

The building I call "St. Hyatt" was opened across the street from the Hetman in 2007. The term is a little poke at the Hyatt Hotel, a fine global chain that erected its Kyiv structure in this historic district almost precisely halfway between SS. Sophia and Michael. Like the two churches, it is a large and dominant building; hence, the beatification. Across the way, still another international hotel, the Intercontinental, was unveiled in 2008, completing the boxing of the open space between two churches and two expensive hotels. The Intercontinental has a façade that fits the late-19th- and early-20th-century architecture of Upper City Kyiv, so it has not gotten the same criticism from preservation-minded Kyivans as the Hyatt, which is showy, postmodern, and covered with a skin of mirrored glass. "Too flashy," some critics have said. On the other hand, the façade literally reflects the bell tower of St. Sophia and the horse-riding Bohdan Khmelnytskyi, which in a way doubles the amount of history that we see.

6.7   Remaking Andrew's Descent

Andriyivskyi Uzviz (Andrew's Descent or Andrew's Slope) is one of Kyiv's most famous and most historic streets, and for many Kyivans and visitors alike, a favorite place. It takes its name from the beautiful baroque St.

Andrew's Church at the summit, which in turn had been given its name because the apostle Andrew is said to have stopped in his travels at the site, erected a cross, and foretold the founding of Kyiv. It was once named Borychevskyi Uzviz, and is referred to by this name in the 12th-century chronicle *Tale of Bygone Years*. The street winds downhill from the church, possibly following the meandering channel of a diverted stream, but also possibly through a man-made ravine between two hills that were once one, and ends in historic Podil below. As such, "Uzviz" (The Descent), as the street is known for short, connects the bluff-top site of the old "upper city," where the walled capital of Rus once shone, with another face of Kyiv's history below, the trade-minded "lower city" neighborhood of Podil beside the river. Uzviz is nearly a kilometer long, is paved with coarse cobblestones, and has an average grade of about 15 to 20 percent. Until recently, the surface of the street and the walkways on either side were in notoriously poor condition, but a major reconstruction project that was undertaken before the expected flood of football fans/tourists in the summer of 2012 has made the surface smoother and safer (Figure 6.4). There is also considerable redevelopment of buildings and vacant sites. The upgrading is sorely needed because there

Figure 6.4   Andrew's Descent during reconstruction (Courtesy of Vladyslava Osmak)

have been untended infrastructure deficiencies and substandard building conditions for far too long. This assessment has included even the landmark church at the summit, which has been in danger of collapse because of erosion of its hill. It was recently the beneficiary of an extremely costly shoring-up project.

The origins of Uzviz date to the time before the Mongols destroyed Rus (1240), but the street's reputation and treasures of architectural heritage (other than the 18th-century church) are from the 19th- and early-20th-century boom. Quite a few luminaries lived and worked on the street in that period, particularly writers, artists, and educators, such that the street is sometimes referred to as Kyiv's Arbat after the contemporaneous kilometer-long street of literati in Moscow, or as Kyiv's Montmartre, the storied artists' and writers' district in Paris. Without question, the most famous resident on Uzviz was the Kyiv-born Russian writer Mikhail Bulgakov (1891-1940), whose residence was at Number 13, a building that is now a museum to his memory, but there were also the noted composer and musical director Alexander Koshetz (1875-1944),[31] the Ukrainian writer Hryhir Tiutiunyk (1931-1980), and many others. A tidy little museum near the foot of the street in Podil, the Museum of One Street, displays memorabilia from local history and tells the story of the street's people and buildings. Another noteworthy landmark is Number 34, the former mansion of Andriy Petrovych Slynko (1839-1919), owner of a popular clothing store on Khreshchatyk and one of Kyiv's richest businessmen. It is still a substantial building, although it has long since been stripped of much of its splendor both inside and out, and it no longer has the two huge, highly ornate cupolas that stood atop the five-story structure. Halfway up the hill at Number 15 is the street's most-recognizable landmark after St. Andrew's Church, the soaring-spired, gothic "Castle of Richard the Lionhearted." Actually a private home and never a real castle, it was built in 1902-1904, several centuries after the life of the English king. The nickname is often attributed to the Kyiv-born writer Viktor Platonovych Nekrasov (1911-1987), although it is known that the term was in use well before his 1967 essay "House of Turbines." Some sightseers with poor knowledge of history and architectural style take the building's name literally. The real story is that this massive structure was the private home of builder-developer Dmytriy Orlov (killed in 1911 in a train robbery in Siberia) and his family. Its many apartments were also a bit of a who's who among Kyiv literati. The structure has been empty and fenced off since

31   Oleksandr Koshyts. The different spelling of his name in the text is an Anglicized variant that he used after emigrating to Canada.

the mid-1980s, as long-held plans to convert it into a hotel have not been successful. In fact, one of Kyiv's legends is that "the castle" has bad karma, and that it is safer to stay away.[32]

Most visitors to Andriyivskyi Uzviz focus on souvenir shopping, clothes-line art sales, and art galleries, and the street's selection of restaurants and cafés. There are all sorts of treasures for sale: beautiful shirts with distinctive Ukrainian embroidery; a world of interesting crafts, paintings, and lithographs; old maps and books about Kyiv; and memorabilia from the Soviet Union such as old political banners, flags, and medals, and busts of Vladimir Lenin. There are also Soviet-era porcelain figurines; *matrioshka* (nesting) dolls; and beautiful nickel-alloy holders for glasses of tea served on Soviet trains. In addition to *matrioshka*s of President Yanukovych, Russia's President Putin, and President Barack Obama, one can buy nesting dolls of Michael Jackson, Harry Potter, and Elvis Presley, players on professional baseball, football, basketball, and ice hockey teams from the United States, as well as *matrioshkas* of players on American college football teams (such those in my beloved Big Ten Conference). Many of the souvenir items are made in China and pass through Russia before coming to Ukraine. In addition to being a place to shop, Uzviz is also a place to engage in people watching and to shoot photographs. There are street musicians and other interesting characters, and backdrops of well-worn historic architecture and high hills. Also, one can risk broken stairways and climb to hilltops on either side of the street for great views.

Many of those who love the street fear that an onslaught of gentrification-displacement, mass-market commercialization, and loss of unique character is in process. Local historians and preservationists, as well as many vendors, small business owners, and "starving artists," all complain that the restoration and redevelopment work that has been taking place on Andriyivskyi Uzviz is destroying its historic ambience and displacing small business in favor of big business and global chains, and that products from China displace authentic local crafts. There is ample precedent for such a course in formerly funky streets and urban districts around the world, and a great many business interests in Kyiv and elsewhere who see commercial possibilities in this setting. Community activist and historian Vladyslava Osmak spoke with great passion at a recent conference in Kyiv and showed dozens of photographs of the unwanted changes that are

---

32   The story of buildings and personalities on Andriyivskyi Uzviz is told nicely in the richly illustrated book by Shlonskyi and Braslavets (2008).

underway.[33] It is just a small story when a popular art gallery is displaced and a chain pizza establishment opens in its place, she said, but when these kinds of changes happen again and again on a short street with not many addresses, it will not be long before a distinctive urban space becomes pretty much like any other place for the mass market and special ambience is lost forever. Indeed, only three galleries remain open on Uzviz and the population of artists who live and work there is much reduced. According to a short article that Osmak wrote for a Russian-language design magazine, the street's reputation as an artists' district continues largely because of "inertia" – Kyivans are simply accustomed to thinking of the street in art gallery terms and pages of tourists' guidebooks about the street are simply out-of-date (Osmak, 2011). The rumored construction of a sizable hotel on Uzviz is sure to hasten the transition, as would a planned multistory office and business center near the base of the street.

Enter Rinat Akhmetov once again. He is the oligarch-businessman who is redeveloping the Soviet-era department store on Khreshchatyk. During the time that the street was blocked off for reconstruction, three old buildings near the bottom of the hill were unexpectedly demolished: 10A and 10B of Andriyivskyi Uzviz and 9/11 on the intersecting Frolivska Street. There was apparently no advance notice to neighbors, historians, and others, as well as no transparency about approval for demolition from Kyiv city government. It simply happened, and happened quickly. By the time protestors turned up, it was too late. The buildings were admittedly in lousy condition and were empty, but almost overnight they were gone and there was a large vacant lot in their place. One of them was a famous old clothing factory called Unist. The site is now surrounded by a high wooden fence and is guarded around the clock. Ironically, where the fence faces Andriyivskyi Uzviz, it is decorated with historic photographic images of the street.

The demolition was apparently carried out on contract from ESTA Holding, part of SCM Finance that is owned by Akhmetov. It was authorized not by city government but by an arm of national government, the Inspection of State Architectural and Construction Supervision, despite the fact that it contravened Kyiv City State Administration Decree No. 979 from May 16, 2002, which prohibits arbitrary demolition on this particular street (Maksymenko and Melnychenko, 2012). There is also a requirement that no one can undertake construction work on the street without prior approval from the Department for the Protection of Historical and Cultural Sites; that

---

33   Heinrich Böll Stiftung, Kyiv. "Strategies for Urban Development in Kyiv" conference, National Academy of Sciences, Kyiv, November 10, 2011. I also spoke at this conference.

approval is absent as well. Nevertheless, ESTA Holding announced plans to erect the office and business center mentioned above, a very modern seven-story structure to be called Andriyivskyi Plaza, and it circulated an architectural rendering of the project. Protests ensued. There was anger about the demolition, about the lack of transparency and lawful process, and about the idea of a steel and glass "monster" in a setting of old brick and new cobblestone. Akhmetov is said to have been moved by the hostile reaction to his project, and he is now reported to have asked for proposals from the grassroots for arts and cultural uses. He has indicated that he is willing to rework the layout of his building and to set aside even a majority of floor space for such purposes. It may not have been part of the original business plan for the site, but Akhmetov understands that his professional reputation is worth money, too, and he seems to be willing to take a bit of a beating on this project in order to win popular support. At least that is what his representatives have explained to the community activists that I am in touch with. Time will tell what actually happens.[34]

6.8   Podil at a Crossroads

We have mentioned Podil before, as it is a very historic district at river level below the walled city that once stood on bluffs high above, and as the district at the foot of Andrew's Descent. The neighborhood was once the city's main center for commerce and trade and was especially famous for its trade fairs and the Contract House, where businessmen signed agreements. Also, Podil was one of the main centers of Jewish population, particularly in an overcrowded tenement area to the north that was called Ploskaya Sloboda. The neighborhood still has a great many old churches and monasteries, such as the Frolivskyi and Pokrovskyi Convents, as well as other religious and historical landmarks, including a prominent synagogue. A landmark event was an enormous fire that swept through the neighborhood in 1811. The National University of Kyiv Mohyla Academy, which was mentioned prominently at the start of this book, is in the very center of Podil.

Podil is at a crossroads between whether it will remain a mixed, historic old city neighborhood, or will be converted, as many developers would propose, into a zone of upscale residential towers, office buildings, shopping centers, and international hotels (Figure 6.5). All of this is abuilding

---

34   A helpful chronicle of redevelopment and citizen action on Andriyivskyi Uzviz is presented in Tyshchenko (2012a).

already, with many more such projects slated for construction soon, so the neighborhood is poised between a future of thorough gentrification and the possibility that life and business opportunities for ordinary Kyivans can still be maintained. Also at stake at the crossroads is Podil as a neighborhood with an active student presence, artists and their studios and galleries, theaters, and many grassroots civic organizations, cultural institutions, bookshops and publishing houses, and charming cafés. As is the tragedy of many funky urban neighborhoods around the world, Podil's charms attract developers who profit from being next to the charms, but who then with time inadvertently or irresponsibly choke them and cause displacement. Podil is at a crossroads geographically, too, located at a choke point of automobile and bus traffic between the center of Kyiv above and the highly populated residential neighborhoods of the city to the north and to northeast across the river. Those to the north especially include some newly prestigious precincts, so Podil is seen by developers as a place that can serve the new rich at a location between where they live and where they work and play. This, too, adds to the development pressure on the neighborhood. Many residents of Podil, Kyiv history buffs, and much of the NaUKMA university community, among others, oppose many of the

Figure 6.5   **Podil at a crossroads, literally. This is a traffic tie-up approaching Post Office Square. There is construction underway in parkland on the bluffs on the left, the large new Fairmont Hotel at right-center, and some of industrial Podil in the background.**

changes underway, so the neighborhood is an active battleground between developers and preservationists, and in this regard is also "at a crossroads."

Podil is big enough to have districts and subdistricts of its own, so a full tour of what is taking place can be long and exhausting. Several highlights, however, capture the essence of the transitions and their credentials as "monsters." We begin at a place called Poshtova Ploshcha (Post Office Square). This is one of two main squares in the neighborhood, and it is the name of an eponymous Metro station that serves the square and its surroundings. It is an intersection for vehicular traffic as well, as the square is just where major roads that run along the right bank of the river connect with another main road up the bluffs to "city level" above, so the traffic is always heavy and sometimes hardly moves. Therefore, it is here where battles have raged between architectural proposals that would make more room for cars, enable faster through traffic, and provide more parking on the one hand, and opposing viewpoints that say, in essence, that Kyiv should be planning instead for a future with alternatives to automobiles. The pro-automobile lobby has the apparent upper hand, as the entire area around Post Office Square is torn up for construction of an elevated "flyover" stretch of road and a tunnel that are supposed to move traffic faster. We see from the square itself that Kyiv has been separated from the river that gave it birth by multiple lanes of automobile traffic and the billboards that speak to the inhabitants of automobiles, and that access to the river from the Metro station and elsewhere in the neighborhood is cut off except for a lone pedestrian bridge and a lone underpass some blocks away. The new elevated roadway will block views of the river as well as complicate access for pedestrians.

The square itself has two structures of note: a reconstruction of a small historic church that is remembered for a funeral ceremony that was held there in 1861 for Taras Shevchenko, and, when there was no interference from construction activity, an especially large and busy McDonald's restaurant. Across the way is an old sugar mill that was owned by the rich industrialist Lazar Brodsky (1848-1904), but it can hardly be seen because it is covered from just above street level to near the roof line several stories above with a banner that advertises a brand of coffee. Next to that is a new international hotel, the Fairmont Grand Hotel; it opened just in time to house Euro 2012 visitors. The hotel might indeed be five-star, but it loses many points among Kyivans because it was built at an intersection that was already one of Kyiv's most traffic-jammed, and it has virtually no parking or automobile/taxi access except for what was carved from sidewalks along its two street frontages. Consequently, pedestrians at a busy intersection and the vehicles that serve hotel guests vie for one space. Also noteworthy is the Kyiv River Port Terminal across the way, a landmark building from 1953-1961 that was once a busy station for passenger transport up and down the Dnipro and that is now eyed with envy by developers who want to make it into a shopping mall, or still another hotel, or a complex for nightlife. There are also proposals to knock it down altogether. At a roundtable discussion one evening in the Building of Architects, I witnessed a presentation by an architect to build a multilevel parking structure in the square to support a shopping center, to which a young critic in the audience replied that architects responsible for that drawing should have their hands cut off.

Moving in another direction from Poshtova Ploshcha and in the direction of the bluffs, we see still another upscale hotel, several multistory new bank and office buildings, and much new construction underway. Trees have been cut on the slopes, tracts of land are blocked off for private use with Kyiv's iconic green wooden fencing, there are construction cranes in place, and great piles of building materials. "New Kyiv" is moving up the slopes that historic Kyiv knew not to develop for environmental reasons. Some of the active construction is for offices, but higher up, almost halfway to St. Andrew's Church, they are building very large houses – "houses for oligarchs" is how a Kyivan described the scene. It is especially this construction that has imperiled the stability of the church building above, as well as the slopes in general, and that is responsible for new problems of drainage, flooding, and mud accumulation. The construction overwhelms water and sewerage infrastructure as well, and it causes a ripple effect of damage and inconvenience for some distance. I walk among the building sites and try to converse with builders and security guards. "What building is this that is being built?" and "Who are the owners?" are questions that I ask. "I don't know" is the answer that comes back almost always, except when the answer is "None of your business" or "Go away, old man."

As we depart Poshtova Ploshcha for the other main square in Podil, Kontraktova Ploshcha (Contract Square; also the site of an eponymous Metro stop), we pass other aspects of the neighborhood in transition. We walk along a busy commercial street named after Petro Konashevych-Sahaidachnyi (1570-1622), a celebrated hetman of the Ukrainian Cossacks whose equestrian monument stands where the street ends nearly one kilometer ahead, and observe encroachment into Podil of Kyiv's seamy side. While the street has many very fine businesses as well, including at least one restaurant that plays on Podil's Jewish history, there is now also a prominent strip club and banners across the street that advertise sex and escort businesses, and a restaurant that advertises that its "veal is always tender" by showing on its quite graphic street banner the backs of a bevy of topless women. Also, there are various newly opened Ukrainian, Russian, and Western chain restaurants along the street that have set up sidewalk seating that takes space from pedestrians and sidewalk car parking. When we arrive at the Sahaidachnyi statue at the end of the street, we see that several streets come together to make a wide paved area that has been made into a sizable mid-street parking lot. Cars are everywhere, and behind them are treasured historical and architectural landmarks of Podil between which developers are squeezing new buildings.

There are development conflicts aplenty in the heart of this neighborhood, not the least of which stem from proposals for still more shopping centers, multilevel office buildings, and parking structures, and still more threats to the area's historical character (Shlipchenko, 2011; Kravets and Sovsun, 2011). Some developers would encroach on the popular square where so many locals and university students come to sit, drink beer, and listen to performances of street music in the shadows of a beloved tall statue of Hryhorii Savych Skovoroda (1722-1794), a graduate of the Kyiv Mohyla Academy and famous Ukrainian poet, philosopher, and composer. A plaque affixed to a stone nearby identifies this square as the place where in 2004 NaUKMA students began the protest movement that became the Orange Revolution. The Blue Line of the Metro runs directly belowground, making the land vibrate just a bit when a train passes, so it is hard to imagine how there can be construction of anything sizable, much less an underground parking structure as at least one architectural rendering has proposed. Were there the funds to do so, NaUKMA itself would become a developer in Podil because the campus desperately needs new office and classroom buildings, laboratories, dormitories, and other facilities. Some of the new construction or renovation of old buildings in Podil looks quite nice, as the neighborhood had deteriorated quite significantly and many areas had looked shabby, but other construction seems to fit poorly and clashes with historic texture.

The current flashpoint, since May 26, 2012, is a building that borders the square that is called Hostynyi Dvir (roughly, The Welcome Courtyard) that I will discuss in detail in Chapter 11 as a key example of civic protest and grassroots activism against unwanted commercial development. Walk in any distance from this central point, and there will be new tall buildings piercing the neighborhood's low skyline, construction cranes standing ready for more erection, and many tracts of land that have been walled off by the green wooden fences that signal redevelopment to come. There are also many dilapidated historical buildings, mostly old residences, "ghosts" in the terminology we have used, that sit empty and exposed to the elements. Some have "For Sale" signs. When the time comes, these buildings will be torn down because they will be too far gone for renewal, and developers will put up something new. The closer we come to the river, the more we see that the land is prized, and the more we see evidence of redevelopment.

In the river just off Podil is a large peninsula that is called an island, Rybalskyi Ostriv (Fisherman's Island). It was shaped in part by the course of a right-bank tributary of the Dnipro called the Pochayna that no longer exists, and gets its name from a fishing village that was nearby in the 18th and 19th centuries. However, Kyiv mostly knows the district for its heavy industry, particularly the enormous Leninska Kuzhnya (Lenin Forge) shipyard that was once a mainstay, and for its port facilities. The area is still gritty-industrial, but its large size, central location, and potential riverside amenities have attracted the attention of developers who have proposed an enormous scheme that would not only transform Rybalskyi Ostriv, but also be a centerpiece for urban change in all directions. Called the "Kyiv-Siti" (Kyiv-City) project, the plan calls for more than 2 million square meters of office space, plenty of parking spaces, a mix of hotels, exhibition spaces, entertainment complexes, and other land uses that would be a new center for Kyiv, perhaps like La Défense is for Paris and Canary Wharf is for London. The architectural drawings show no less than 14 skyscrapers, all gleaming and postmodern, and nothing that looks like Kyiv at all.[35] Indeed, what I am reminded of most is the new district in the big city to the north of Ukraine called New Moscow. So far, "Kyiv-City" is just an idea seeking investors, but it does have considerable support, including apparently that of the country's president, so it might indeed be able to take shape. If it is built, the geography of the city would be significantly altered, because the project would be a centerpiece between the center of Kyiv to the south and emerging prestige neighborhoods along the river to the north (e.g., Obolon), and would have enormous spillover effects on already-gentrifying Podil, creating an extended zone of prestige and new development along the right bank of the Dnipro River.

35 Images of the project can be viewed via the SkyscraperCity online community at: http://www.skyscrapercity.com/showthread.php?t=283956.

7 A Geography of Privilege and Pretension

7.1 A Diamond Monster

The word *monster* is used in both Ukrainian and Russian to refer to intrusive new buildings that are built without neighborhood welcome. They rise up from the earth and devour the city, something like the monster Godzilla emerging from Tokyo Bay to wreak havoc on Japan's capital. In Kyiv, the most aggressive monsters tend to be high-rises for rich people. They wreck history, historic cityscapes, and the natural environment, and impose themselves on existing infrastructure such as transportation or parking spaces, where they wreak havoc as well (Figure 7.1). They are built without reference to any overall city plan, in part because Kyiv does a very poor job of planning where to build, as well as without attention to zoning, in part because Kyiv zones so poorly. They simply appear wherever a developer has

Figure 7.1   A glass-skinned "monster" rising from within historic buildings in the center of Kyiv. The building to the right is the city's famed Opera. Note also the traffic and the vehicles parked on sidewalks.

acquired access to a wanted site. Often, the construction is on public land: a park or playground, for instance, and proceeds simply because someone in the developer's pocket has issued papers, however dubious, that authorize construction. Thus, monsters and raiders are intimately intertwined. It's all very murky and secretive – a function of collapsed centralized decision-making and document issuance in the Soviet state followed by too long a period of free-for-all chaos in advance of any new order (Cybriwsky, 2012a).

A building called Diamond Hill is a case in point (Figure 7.2). It is a residential tower of 20 stories and 83 meters height that was developed by K.A.N. Development Ltd. on a prime site either on or immediately adjacent to parkland in the Pechersk District near Kyiv's center, and stands high on the same bluff as Pecherska Lavra and other prominent monuments. In our telephoto composition from across the Dnipro, Diamond Hill appears to loom over bathers at one of the city's popular beaches. The site had been parkland, but the builder had somehow managed to gain access nonetheless. There is a stone marker next to the building that reads in Ukrainian: "The Church of St. Michael stood here. It was built in 1690-1693 through the munificence of Ivan Mazepa, an especially renowned hetman of Ukraine. It was destroyed in the 1930s by the communist regime." When completed, which is to be soon, Diamond Hill will have 131 residential units, 299 parking spaces, and amenities such as a fitness center, and – oh, so conveniently – an unspoiled park next door. The asking prices for apartments start in the neighborhood of US$2 million but a high view of the Lavra complex is reported to cost US$9 million, while high river views are supposedly even more expensive.

Like the whirlybird pad in the park nearby, Diamond Hill enjoys front-and-center position in the iconic cityscape of Kyiv. Its residents will have unparalleled views of the city, the nation's main government buildings, the river, the city's main monuments, unspoiled parts of the park, and the far bank. It is called Diamond Hill most probably because the project is on a hill and developers want to emphasize its luster. They have advertised it in English as a "premium class residential complex in one of the most picturesque places in the City of Kiev." However, according to my notes, some bloggers were not impressed: "Shit, how grotesque," wrote one in response to a photo of the building as seen from across the river, while another commented that he wants to spit every time he sees the structure.

The shape of the building is symbolic: in addition to being big and looming, the structure has been capped with a dome of its own – not a golden, onion-type dome like atop a Kyiv church, but one with a glass roof, like above an atrium. Such domes are quite common nowadays atop new, prestige

Figure 7.2   Diamond Hill rising from parkland atop the bluffs of right-bank Kyiv

buildings for the postsocialist nouveaux riches across urban Ukraine, as well as in Moscow, etc., and they are sometimes called "oligarch domes." The one atop Diamond Hill actually looks very much like the dome that crowns Ukraine's Verkhovna Rada building just down the street. It is easy to imagine that architects wanted to make this particular association, and that it will actually be members of the Verkhovna Rada who will purchase many of the expensive units in the building and park their cars in its garage. I see symbolism, as well, in a photo shoot at the top of Diamond Hill during its construction that I bumped into while browsing the Internet about the project. While you and I cannot go on this site because it is private property and an active construction zone, at least one photographer and his nude model were somehow allowed to the top to take photos with Kyiv as backdrop. The symbolism is this: a porno-shoot is linked to a porno-building, and the porno-building, future home of oligarch *nardeps*, lacks respect for Kyiv. At least the model took the precaution of wearing a hardhat on the premises.

Diamond Hill is conveniently close to a Metro station (Arsenalna), but that detail seems to have escaped the advertising copy, perhaps because *nardeps* do not ride the subway. Also missing from the advertising copy is the project's correct street address. Instead of 11-A Vulytsya Ivana Mazepy (Ivan Mazepa Street), named after the late-17th- and early-18th-century Ukrainian hetman, or Cossack leader, who very prominently championed the Ukrainian national cause against the Russian Empire, K.A.N. Development's literature about Diamond Hill uses the old Soviet-era name for the street: 11-A Vulytsya Sichnevoho Povstannya (January Uprising Street), named after a workers' rebellion in the Russian Empire in 1905 that was a step toward the 1917 Russian Revolution. The company's unilateral rejection of the street's legal, postindependence name associates it with local anti-Ukrainian graffiti writers and sticker-hangers who continually deface the words "Ivan Mazepa Street" on street signs with the Russian-language version of "January Uprising Street."[36] It is also in step with the company's own spelling of Kyiv in advertising copy in the Russian way as "Kiev." Thus, in addition to being an architectural encroachment on historical landscape, Diamond Hill is a battleground in a "culture war" between Russian and Ukrainian identities. Many Ukrainian citizens notice such details, and they take them not just as slights, but also as part and parcel of calculated Russian campaigns to undermine Ukrainian distinctiveness.

7.2   Face Control in Arena City[37]

Arena City is a well-known commercial development that opened in the center of Kyiv in 2005. It was developed by billionaire-oligarch Viktor Pinchuk on an entire historic city block that was once an integral part of Jewish Kyiv, and sets a new tone for the center of the city. From the outside, the architecture looks historic, like Kyiv at the turn of the 20th century, but the complex is essentially new from the ground up. Additionally, it is not at all democratic like the people's neighborhood that preceded it. The term "Face Control" reflects the new era. At Arena City, if we don't like how you look, you don't get in and we don't have to tell you why. Welcome to the new, pretentious, and exclusive gated city that Kyiv is becoming.

Sholom Aleichem once lived on the Arena City block. The space was called Bessarabsky Kvartal at the time; the last of it was pulled down in 2001 to make room for Pinchuk's new Kyiv. The destruction of the historic house caused outrage in Jewish communities around the world. But have no fear: Arena City offers the Sholom Aleichem Museum in the precise spot where the genius behind Tevye the Milkman did his writing. There are treasures from the author's own life and other memories of Jewish Kyiv before the emigration,

36   Recall the discussion about this street name at the start of Chapter 5 and Figure 5.1.

37   An earlier version of this section has been published in Ukrainian in the periodical *Politychna Krytyka* (Political Criticism; Cybriwsky, 2012b).

but the museum space is smaller than once promised. That's because there is a strip club beyond an adjoining wall that needed more room.

Solid Gold is one of three so-called gentlemen's clubs in Arena City. The others are Zolotoy Nosorog (in Russian; the words mean Golden Rhinoceros) and the Arena Stars Cabaret. There is no reason for us to go to any of them because there is nothing to be seen that has not already been seen, but we note them nonetheless because they set the tone for Arena City. They are impossible to miss with their huge neon signs and suggestive advertising, and they take up much of the commercial space that comprises the complex. They run all night and attract big-spending businessmen from Kyiv and other cities, and big-spending foreign sex tourists. The beautiful women who come and go have long legs, the shortest of skirts, and the slimmest and highest stiletto heels. They need to know their way around the complex, because its walkways are carelessly interspersed with the worst of hazards for heels – steel grates that ventilate the parking garage below.

The nightclubs of Arena City are also about sex. The tourist books all say that, and so do websites that advise sex-minded tourists to Kyiv. The largest club has the big "Face Control" warning posted on its door. It is probably sufficient to have a fat wallet to be allowed in regardless of what face or fashion one presents. It seems well known that foreigners almost always get in, presumably because they can spend more money than most locals and perhaps because they can be taken for a ride more easily as well. However, at another club in the complex, whose name I won't mention because I am not advertising it, the selection of who may enter is said to be extra strict. According to an online review:

> Don't even think of trying to get in here if you are not dressed to the nines, nay, the tens. Face Control is notoriously strict at [name of establishment], one of Kyiv's top-end new clubs. Glamour and opulence are very much the order of the day. That and a dash of decadence.

This particular place is so exclusive that you need to know in advance where to find it: the unmarked entry is through a boutique.

You need a fat wallet for Mandarin Plaza, too. That is one of the two shopping centers in Arena City. Chinese is not widely spoken there. Nor are there mandarin oranges in the mall. It is *Mandarin* Plaza because it invites the new class of aristocrats with its high prices and put-on airs of exclusivity. In the old Chinese Empire, the nine classes of Mandarins were distinguished by buttons worn on their caps. Now, "New Russian" mandarins are known by their fashion: Gucci, Louis Vuitton, Armani... all the usual pricy brands that serve to separate the conspicuous consumers of the new social order from the faceless masses.

Mandarin Plaza has six levels of stores wound tightly around a central atrium. It is eerily quiet in the middle of a normal day. As I stand near an escalator and survey the scene, I see eight security guards from just the one vantage point, plus an array of CCTV cameras. There are almost no customers. Incredibly, the security guards outnumber shoppers. I know from return visits that this is normal. Except for the belowground supermarket, which is busier, a quick tour of the 50 or 60 stores in the complex counts a total of three people who are inside shopping. Sales personnel are ready to serve in every store, but they are visibly bored. They watch as you pass because for them that is an event. Some are reading. Others are thumbing their mobile phones. One is asleep in her chair behind the counter. The security guards are bored, too. They pace. They stare at you. They also thumb their mobile phones. "What happened?" I ask one of them in mock seriousness. "Where are the people and why is there so much security? Did something happen?" "What do you want, old man?" is the reply. "We are protecting the stores." "From me?" I ask.

The other shopping mall is even sparser. Not only are the customers gone, but so are many of the stores. On three floors of retailing I counted 14 stores in business and 11 shops empty. There is an almost comical Potemkin Village aspect to the scene in that sometimes goods from one store are displayed in the windows of a neighboring empty store to make the mall look more filled. A magazine kiosk is apparently out of business, as there is no sales clerk and the magazines on display are all outdated. Ubiquitous security prevents theft. I take some photographs of architectural details by the elevator. A guard arrives to tell me that photography is not allowed. I ask how he knew that I was shooting photos. He replied that I was being watched on camera and that he was instructed by earphone to speak to me. We had a little laugh at the irony, as I mentioned that now he too is being watched to make sure that he carries out instructions. Earlier I had taken the elevator to an upper floor above the shopping levels. I was met by a security guard as the elevator doors opened. "There is nothing here," he said before I could step out. "Were you standing here waiting for me?" I asked. "Yes, we watched you as you entered the building," he replied.

Maybe Arena City jumps at night. I don't, so I don't really know, but that is what I am told. In the day it is dead. It is also filthy. Trash does not get picked up, and grime accumulates atop of grime. There are unsecured dark corners with empty beer and vodka bottles, hundreds of cigarette butts, and the odor of urine. A railing outside the ground floor entry to a "sky bar" in one of the high turrets of the complex is wrapped in aluminum foil, apparently as a parsimonious way to add luster to rapidly tarnishing architecture. The "Sky Bar" welcomed me, but there were three sets of security personnel along the way to check my face: one at the street level entry; another in the next room where the elevators are located, and the third on the seventh floor, where there is the sky. They let me take photos of Kyiv and the inside arena of Arena City from the windows, and they offered me 30 percent off the price of my drink. I was the only customer but it was a Saturday afternoon.

In summer there are occasional concerts from a temporary stage in the central courtyard. They can be enjoyed by people with comfortable seating in the bars and cafés that surround the interior arena, but not by others because, incredibly, for summer 2012 they have erected a circular wall of cheap plywood (painted black) within the arena to separate those who pay for expensive seats and drinks near the stage on the inside from the public on the outside. An arena within an arena! Concentric circles of security and belonging! Boy George played recently on the inner-circle stage. I had not heard his name in a long time and thought that maybe he was dead. That, I am told, is the ultimate humiliation for a fading celebrity – to have people think that he had died. Somehow it seems fitting that Boy Georges perform behind cheap plywood walls (painted black) in an arena within an arena for "New Russian" mandarins and their stiletto-heeled dates.

Pinchuk has a foundation and an art center. He runs them with his wife, Elena, the daughter of Ukraine's (creepy) former president, Leonid Kuchma. The Pinchuk Art Centre is wonderful. Its exhibits showcase some of the most commercially successful artists in the world and they are free. The place is a maze of rooms and surprises behind closed doors, and the guards allow visitors to enjoy the art. It is a must-see for visitors to Kyiv. But it is in Arena City and has sex spots and sex tourists as neighbors, dark corridors with urine and drunks, and a shopping area where bored security guards and bored store clerks try to not look too bored because they too are on camera. But it does make sense to have such a fine place in such a poor complex. The oligarch-benefactor grants us encounters with a world of creativity beyond our reach to remind us that he sits at the top as the ultimate arbiter of high taste and sophistication, and that we are his subjects. Moreover, we should not criticize him, because he has a foundation that supports fine causes, and because his generosity grants us good art to enjoy for free.

Despite the high art and the gesture to Sholom Aleichem, Arena City does not serve Kyiv. It stole from Kyiv when it was constructed and serves primarily today's self-absorbed post-Soviet aristocracy, tourists from abroad looking for sex, and young women who like that kind of environment.

As such, the complex is a metaphor for what is wrong in Kyiv today, in Ukraine more widely, and perhaps in other parts of the former Soviet Union where impoverishment, emigration, and declining populations are norms. The complex milks consumers for money, and then when there is no more money to be made, the riches are taken elsewhere and the remains are left for whomever. Just six years after a grand opening, there are "for rent" and "for sale" signs all over Arena City, drunks pissing in dark corners, huge advertisements for commercial products that cover the faux-historic façade, and posted offers to cover still more of the exterior with still more billboards.

7.3   Men in Black

Once, a long time ago, Kyiv was a walled city with gates that could be closed to keep out invading forces; now, the city is gated once again, but internally, and this time the gates are to keep the majority of Kyivans themselves from privileged spaces within Kyiv. Gated communities, shopping facilities, nightclubs, and other gated parts of the urban experience are nothing unique to Kyiv in this day and age. As in other cities around the world, those who have fear those who have not, and they use some of their wealth to create separation. Even if there is no fear, there is some sort of perverse psychological need for separation. In this section, we will present a short ethnography of *okhorontsi* (security guards), which as far as I know is a previously unexplored topic. Because of how they are told to dress, we will call this category of security guards "Men in Black." They contrast with other *okhorontsi* such as the "men in camouflage cargo pants" who work among a wider public in large covered markets or at nonelite construction sites.

A sociologist friend in Kyiv once piqued my interest in this subject with astute responses to my comments about the overabundance of security guards that we saw one day when visiting the shopping zones of the Arena City complex. There were so many of them, I said, all in serious black business suits and plain white shirts,[38] all apparently healthy and strong, all connected by earphone to some command center somewhere, and all looking as bored as can be in a shopping center with no crooks to catch, no homeless people or rowdy teens to chase out, and very few clients. Not one ever had a smile. "It's part of the décor to make the mall look exclusive," explained Lyudmyla Males (Kyiv National University of Taras Shevchenko).

---

38   In summer there is a reprieve and the suit jacket comes off.

"They are props like the furnishings and the smartly chosen names for the business establishments – necessary ingredients for a mall that wants to be upscale." She described the *okhorontsi* as symbols of masculinity where women shop. "It's a man's world, this mall, despite the many women's stores," she said, "and these men are here to remind the shoppers of that." And so it is that in gated residential communities, shopping malls, and elsewhere throughout Kyiv, we see poorly paid but healthy and strong men dressed in black business suits employed as props for the rich. We also see many beautiful young women in a variety of supporting roles to add cachet and present a desired image for the place of business.

I could put together quite an interesting tour. We leave Arena City and cross the street to the Lenin statue where the two guards in camouflage watch closely as I reach into my backpack, and then relax when they see a camera and not a can of spray paint. I make a mental note that on this hot July day the guards are wearing camouflage suits that were designed for some snowy battleground in the Arctic, and walk on. At the end of the block is the Premier Palace Hotel. It is one of the city's costliest and most elegant hotels, with expensive restaurants and clubs, a rich-looking clientele, and a lot of beautiful young women in spike heels. Its guards are Men in Black. I am dressed nicely and have the body language of a foreigner, so no one pays me any special mind. The street outside is marked as parking for VIPs. It struck me that this is a public street, but that you have to be VIP to park there, so I asked a guard how he knows who is a VIP and who is not. He was baffled by the question and said that only VIPs park here, and that they are clients of the exclusive casino on the second floor.

Across the street is an exclusive women's fashion boutique. The shop itself is in the interior of the block and is reached through a gated walkway. A guard's booth with one-way glass is at the gate. I walk in and a Man in Black steps out and asks me what I want. "To go to the store," I reply. "It's a women's shop," he says. "I know women," I reply and walk on. Seconds later, the door opens just as I arrive and another Man in Black welcomes me in. He happens to be a black Man in Black, from Africa. I ask him how he knew to open the door at that exact moment, as it is solid with no window, and he just smiled. I noted the earpiece that he was wearing, and I reflected how in my earlier experience in writing a book about a nightclub district in Tokyo I interacted often with imposing black Men in Black from Nigeria who were security guards and touts in pretentious "international" Japanese dance clubs. I browsed around the store for a while, moving from salon to salon accompanied in each room by a different beautiful woman wearing an earpiece, and then thanked the last woman who then escorted be back to the black Man in Black. As he opened the door I spoke to him in English, "I bet that if you and I sat down somewhere else on your day off, you could tell me some awesome stories about this place." His smile changed to that of a fellow human being, rather than the paste-on of an employee, but he said nothing and I never pressed the point. He had a job and I am sure that he wanted to keep it.

A couple of blocks away is a new glass-skinned office tower that is built into the core of a once-prestigious turn-of-the-20th-century residential block (recall Figure 7.1). It is a beautiful old building with enormous windows for the high-ceilinged apartments and lots of ornamental masonry on the street-front façades, and in excellent restored condition because of renovations that had been made by the developer. The structure is across the street from the Kyiv Opera, also an opulent historic structure. The glass-skinned tower looks odd as it rises from the old building, but some people like it, I am sure, as a blend of old and new, and without the new, the old probably would have been left in poor condition.[39] Regardless of the architecture, I was attracted by the sign at a main door: "Leonardo Retail Entrance." The Man in Black at the door gave me the once over and let me pass. Inside I saw a very elite-looking travel agency with beautiful female attendants at beautifully designed work stations, and next door was an Aston Martin dealership with more beautiful women at their desks awaiting clients. I must have looked better today than before, because on another day when I tried to enter the Leonardo Retail Entrance, a Man in Black turned me back. "There is no retail center," he told me, as he motioned to the door.

Some blocks away, where we have visited SS. Sophia, Michael, and Hyatt, is another opulent residential building. It faces St. Sophia Square, has several designer stores at street level, very expensive apartments on the floors above, and still more expensive penthouse apartments on the new floors that have been added atop the original roof. Behind the building is a private park and playground for the residents of this exclusive building on land that had been taken from the St. Sophia Cathedral complex by moving back the wall that surrounds it. UNESCO was quite disturbed by this construction and threatened to remove St. Sophia from the list of world heritage sites as a consequence. There are Men in Black at every store front, at the gate to the gated playground, at the gate to underground parking, and most

---

39 This particular historic building and quite a few others like it have additional stories that have been added to the top in a way that blends with the original design. Those new top floors are then typically heavily ornamented with cupolas, figurines, and other art work that also imitates historical architecture.

prominently at the entry to the very exclusive health club and sauna that is part of this complex. Outside are Men in Black drivers of luxury cars awaiting the rich-looking club members who are inside, engaged in midday workouts. There is probably a lot of business that goes on there, too, as quite a few rich businessmen come and go all day and all evening long. There are also quite a few very fit and very beautiful women, who also come and go all day and all evening long. This place is not far from where I lived, and I considered whether it was the gym that I wanted to join when in Kyiv, but the way the Men in Black at the door looked at me told me that I did not belong.

My particular street and some of those nearby have quite a few very exclusive shops, mostly selling designer clothing, jewelry, and accessories, such as enormously expensive handbags and shoes. One shop that I referred to in Chapter 1 sells diamonds, but in the past it was some sort of Communist Party office. There is still a Soviet hammer and sickle emblem carved from stone in the pediment above the door. Huge windows display the wares. There are glass doors, too, that allow passersby to peer inside. Such architecture qualifies these stores as "transparent temples of design," a very descriptive term that I learned in Tokyo with reference to the characteristic architectural form of exclusive designer goods stores along exclusive shopping streets. Regardless of whether we are in Kyiv, Tokyo, or elsewhere, such stores typically have few customers at any one time, and at most times are empty except for the waiting staff. When a client does show up, the employees snap to attention to offer the best of service. The typical pattern is to have two fashionably dressed young females as the sales personnel. One sits at a desk or counter and the other stands or walks among the displays. The other staff member is a tall young Man in Black, the security guard and door-opener. His station is near the door, and he is always watching. The females watch, too, because there is little else to do. Interaction between them is minimal, as that would look unprofessional from the outside, and there are certainly no games being played or text messages being sent by staff on their mobile phones during the interminably slow waits between customers, as that too would be on public display in these transparent temples. Even though the store consists of one room, the Man in Black at the door wears a listening device and a microphone. I don't wear the fashions that are promoted by these stores and might appear to be too old to be a shopper, so not once in thousands of pass-byes did I get a friendly nod, much less what would seem like an invitation to shop. Men in Black never smile.

An ultimate example is a restaurant on the block where I lived, an Italian place named not Leonardo but Bellini. A Kyivan friend described it to me as the city's most popular hangout for "New Russian" rich folks, for oligarchs and those who want to be oligarchs, for rich insiders in the Ukrainian government, for the Ukrainian Mafia, and for the very beautiful women in whose company many of these men normally travel. There is outdoor seating during the warm months, so during the period that I lived on this block I was able to observe the goings-on quite regularly despite a hedge of greenery between the tables and the sidewalk. The place is, of course, a world encased by Men in Black. Outside their sphere of control is the rest of the city, including a small public square across the street where there often are hopeless drunks and boisterous teenagers, and a sidewalk scene that includes Roma flower sellers and beggars, and "women of the night" who work the block. But inside the cordon one can see men at business leaning across the table one toward the other to talk deals, and many very fashionably dressed women. On Fridays the place is packed and, it seems, outside is every Lamborghini, Bentley, Rolls-Royce, and Aston Martin in the country. Indeed, Bellini's décor is at one level the red-and-white awnings of an Italian restaurant, but an another level it is super-expensive cars parked directly out front, very beautiful and beautifully dressed women at the tables along the sidewalk and beside the windows, important-looking men doing important business inside, all enabled by gatekeeper Men in Black.

There is no need to continue the tour with more examples, as each stop would offer no more than a new twist on the wider point: in Kyiv (and elsewhere in our unequal world), we have two planes of existence in the urban landscape, the exclusive world and everyone else. They exist side by side but do not interact. We can look, but not too hard or for too long, while the privileged insiders never, ever see us. For them, the looking is done by Men in Black. They are experts at Face Control, and it is their job to distinguish between VIPs and hoi polloi, and to get it right. If they are uncertain about someone, then they offer the noncommittal "Is there something that I can help you with?" The person who passes the judgment of the gatekeepers is assured that he or she is on the plus side of society's divide, and as a result the place of business, whether it is an office, a bank, a transparent temple of design, or a place like Bellini, looks to be tonier.

7.4   The Strange New Neighborhood of Vozdvyzhenka

Vozdvyzhenka is a newly built neighborhood of approximately a hundred buildings along four somewhat ancient streets in a deep ravine that separates the main hill on which the old walled city of Kyiv stood from Castle Hill, another historic promontory (Shlipchenko, 2009, pp. 36-39). The total area is 42 acres (17 hectares). Three of the street names betray their roles in history: as we pointed out above, a street named Honchari (Potters) runs along an old stream course and was once the domain of potters and other artisans; Kozhumyaki (Tanners) Street, a bigger street in the area, was the street of leather workers and tanneries; while Dehtryanka Street, from a word for makers of pitch or wood tar, is a short street in a back corner of the district. The fourth street is named Vozdvyzhenka Street, the same name as a famous street in the Arbat neighborhood of Moscow, but named specifically after an Orthodox church at the end of the ravine, Khtrestovdvyzhenska (The Church of the Presentation of the Cross). Most of the structures that stood in this district at the end of the Soviet period were from about the turn of the 20th century, but there were also older, more historic buildings. The area as a whole was run down and lacked basic amenities and infrastructure. Consequently, there were many vacancies as one by one, residents left for new housing that was being built on the Left Bank, but there were also residents and businesses that remained. For a time, the area was where Kyivans went to purchase birds, dogs, cats, and other pets, as well as live chickens (Bakanov, 2011).

Like Arena City above, Vozdvyzhenka is annoyingly pretentious and, like Arena City, it is designed supposedly for elites with sophisticated tastes. However, this neighborhood is also an affront to the true historical land- scapes of Kyiv and is silly-looking (Figure 7.3). In fact, Vozdvyzhenka is sillier and would be laughable were it not for the fact that its construction displaced people and businesses that were vulnerable, paved over considerable history, and spoiled a significant piece of ground in the historic center of Kyiv. The development is also said to have cheated buyers of their money. Moreover, it seems to be of little use to anyone, even the rich-people market that it is targeted for. We saw that various parts of Arena City were eerily empty, even in the middle of a business day; Vozdvyzhenka is the same. Whenever we visit, there are very few people or cars to be seen. Despite having some hundred new or redeveloped buildings, most of them multi-unit structures three to five or six stories high, so the potential population is high, there are very few residents and very few workers or clients in the neighborhood's various office buildings and other businesses. In fact, it seems that most of those people that we do see in Vozdvyzhenka are *okhorontsi* – the Men in Black who guard the few places that are inhabited and men in camouflage who sit watch over construction sites. We also see construction workers. Incredibly, building activity continues despite the evident lack of demand, filling in gaps amid empty structures with more buildings and pushing at the foot of hills at the district's edges with still more dubious construction.

Figure 7.3   A view of Vozdvyzhenka from above

In the 1980s, while the Soviet Union was still extant, plans were cooked up to upgrade the district and to make it into an arts-and-crafts zone where tourists could visit the workshops and studios of woodcarvers, potters, metal workers, jewelry makers, painters, sculptors, and other artisans, and where these various crafts workers would also maintain residences. The idea was that this would be "Old Kyiv" as the city was in the 11th century, i.e., a theme park of history. Oleksiy Radynski (2010) cleverly referred to this plan as a Kyiv version of Disneyland-type fantasy zones and as the city's first postmodern urban project. By 1993, now in Ukrainian times, the City Council of Kyiv officially endorsed an amended vision that reduced the mix of arts and crafts in favor of an exhibit hall for archeological treasures, a center for "international communication," and, quite interestingly, a casino. In Radynski's words, this was "Kyivan Las Vegas." However, by the end of 2002 the plans had morphed once more, and the office of architecture and planning in Kyiv put forth an alternative idea – this for a "European Square" (or "Square of Europe" more precisely) featuring hotels and exhibit halls, cafés, restaurants, movie theaters, and various shops. According to the concept that was publicized at the time, this was to be a place where one could "enjoy a Czech beer, watch a Spanish film, and become familiar with the paintings of the Dutch masters" (translated from Radynski, 2010,

p. 92). There would also be community facilities such as a school, nursery school, and a medical clinic. The plan also proposed a funicular to connect the district with L'vivska Ploshcha (L'viv Square) above, and identified an "Austrian-Slovakian firm" to take charge of construction. That did not work out either, because for reasons that are unknown (*"po neponyatnym prichinam"*), the City Council transferred the land to a private firm called Kievgorstroy-1 (Russian-language abbreviated version for "Kyiv City Builders") that constructed what we describe below.

Kievgorstroy-1 built the Vozdvyzhenka that we see today. It is mostly new construction that is done in styles and at a size-scale of individual buildings to suggest historical urban landscape. There is also redevelopment of old structures, but there are fewer of these than buildings of new construction, and there is no true restoration. According to the main website that promotes the area and markets its real estate, there are three main elements: elite apartments; elite single homes; and commercial and office buildings. At the head of that website is the information that Vozdvyzhenka is a "fashionable real estate district" (Ukrainian: *rayon feshenebelnoyi nerukhomosti*). In order to give the construction an "elite" look, the district is replete with turrets and domes and spires and castlelike crenellations, as well as mansards atop of which are lots and lots of chimneys, almost all with multiple vents for multiple heating units and indoor fireplaces. Windows are big and ceilings are high. The architectural style is supposed to be Europe at end of the 19th century – maybe pan-European, because we see a mix of elements: baroque, modern, gothic, as well as more than a little French romanticism. Something smacks of Holland, too. Here and there we come across classical columns. All of this is brightly painted: we see blues, yellows, greens, avocados, ripe bananas, unripe bananas, hues of orange, beige, brown and others, all different one building from the next, and often with multiple colors per building. The paint is still fresh and the look is one that we might find in a collection of neatly arranged dollhouses, or in a gingerbread Victorian neighborhood. The streets suggest old cobblestone but are smoother, and the sidewalks are paved with yellow bricks. Many buildings have driveways and underground parking, a landscape plus perhaps, but not historic.

There is an unavoidable urge to compare what we see to other landscapes that might be similar. The "painted ladies" of San Francisco come to mind, but the scale and architecture are entirely different. We are also reminded of a Disneyland-type theme park as suggested by the first plan, but instead of a "Frontierland," "Tomorrowland," or "Main Street, U.S.A." we are in a constructed fantasyland that might be called "Europeland." In a real theme park, however, we would never be as alone as we are when we walk in Vozdvyzhenka. Another parallel is with Dubai where an expansive new housing development has been put up by hopeful investors on an archipelago of artificial islands that are collectively shaped like a palm tree. The similarity is that the Dubai project is also fresh and new, and is also more or less empty – a financial disappointment. Another thought, for which I am indebted to my friend, Kyiv expert Vladyslava Osmak, is that the scene resembles a movie set in waiting – it is new, clean, hastily put together, evenly aged, of similar materials – and empty of actors. If we return to any of the hilltops above Vozdvyzhenka and look down, we can't help but think about some sort of children's toy town. It could again be colorful dollhouses arranged in a row, or a model city made of plastic and held together with glue, or it could perhaps be a model railroad town except for the absence of tracks or trains. Then we snap out of these fantasies and remind ourselves that this is real and this is Kyiv.

We do not know the details about Kievgorstroy-1, how much they invested in the rebuilding of Vozdvyzhenka, where the money came from, or how much they made or lost. Kyiv is always a black hole for this kind of information. We also do not know exactly how many of the developer's properties have been purchased, how many are still for sale to first-time buyers, how many purchased properties have been resold or are now for sale again, how many tenants there are in multi-unit buildings versus vacancies, how many subleases there are in effect, and so on. We can only go on what we see and what others have seen and reported. Yes, there have been buyers, and yes people do live in Vozdvyzhenka and yes, there are businesses in operation, too, such as a bank that keeps normal banking hours and has customers coming in and out like a normal bank. But on the whole, as we have said, the neighborhood is eerily quiet and empty, especially when considered in the context of the center of a busy city. Most of where we look, we see For Sale and For Rent signs, windows without blinds or curtains, and lights that are never turned on. To anyone's eyes, much more of the development is devoid of human activity than any percentage that is inhabited. We wonder why this is and why they keep building. It cannot be to provide still more cute-looking urban background for wedding photos and model shoots, two popular uses of the neighborhood so far.

A sharp eye can tell that many buildings in Vozdvyzhenka are cheaply made. There are buildings with thick outer walls and heavy foundations to be sure, but others show signs of foundations cracking, cracks along outer walls, crumbling plaster, and prematurely peeling paint. Builders' economies can be spotted widely, even when look ing at the quality of the construction materials as they stand piled at new building sites, and are reported to exist even more glaringly inside where again, walls are cracking, there are wet spots in ceilings, and carpentry does not quite come together. For some buildings, the problem might be that greed has added additional floors to the tops of buildings without shoring up foundations to account for the extra weight and the trauma of construction. Investors who feel that they have been cheated by shoddy construction maintain a website where they trade horror stories and discuss tactics about fighting back.

Vozdvyzhenka is a quintessential capitalist-speculative town. It is built to entice buyers so that it maximizes profits for builders. The familiar formula for this is to cut back on development costs without making it appear that you have done so, charge high prices, and convince buyers to pay those high prices by telling them that they are getting value for money. By studying the content of advertising for Vozdvyzhenka, reading managed "news" pieces about the neighborhood, following blogs by people who have invested in the area, and walking the streets and striking up conversations, a fairly accurate picture of how the process works emerges. It is a process in step with what has been observed in other speculative land development ventures in place as far flung as Dubai, the overly hyped real estate market of Shanghai, and the promotion of gentrification in uncertain neighborhoods in the United States, among other places. The key ingredients of the strategies that developers use in these kinds of ventures are listed in the table below, with details about how I have seen them expressed in Vozdvyzhenka on the right. What we see is developer sleight of hand, promises that are plumper than reality, and unhappy consumers. Many of those who bought into the community find that their units are barely habitable and are engaged in legal action against builders or contractors. There are also quite a number of units that are on the market as resale, because first buyers have decided to get out.

Table 7.1   Selling Vozdvyzhenka

General Sales Strategy	Vozdvyzhenka Example
Select a name for the project that will assist with marketing.	"Vozdvyzhenka" rings of history and will associate the buyer with the glory of early Kyiv.
Tout whatever is positive about the site, be that topography, location, or history, focusing on what buyers might like to hear.	We are told celebrated writer Mikhail Afanasevich Bulgakov was born at 10 Vozdvyzhenka Street and was christened in the church after which the neighborhood was named.
From the start, present the project as elite and not for everyone.	Vozdvyzhenka was branded as a "fashionable real estate district" from the beginning.

General Sales Strategy	Vozdvyzhenka Example
Build the project with symbols of wealth, status, and enduring quality, even if they are cheaply made.	Vozdvyzhenka is replete with turrets, domes, spires, and castlelike crenellations, among other architectural embellishments.
Import symbols of wealth and status as props to use while working to attract buyers.	I saw a beautiful white Bentley parked in a prominent spot for all to see when prospective buyers were being shown around.
Focus costs and energies on the exterior, not on the interior.	Bright paint, clever color schemes, exaggerated façades, and brass address number plates add luster to what might be drab, unfinished, and badly arranged inside.
Tell prospective buyers that they will be joining other elites as buyers, and will have them as neighbors. Drop names, but say that you cannot confirm details because the principals insist on privacy.	In Vozdvyzhenka there were "unconfirmed reports" that early buyers included President Yanukovych, singer Oleh Skrypka, football coach Oleh Protasov, poet Yuriy Ribchinskyi, and relatives of the Surkis brothers, two famous Ukrainian businessmen and football executives.
Explain the emptiness of your development by telling buyers that they are among the early comers, getting in on the ground floor.	This is standard procedure if a buyer asks why no other buyers are in sight.
Save on development costs by cutting corners where unsuspecting buyers might assume that construction is up to normal standards.	Here, we refer to the complaints about Vozdvyzhenka that buyers have posted online: peeling paint, collapsed ceilings, wet basements, water seepage through walls, leaking roofs, faulty plumbing, faulty wiring, etc.
Hide from complaints, stay away from reporters, shift blame, promise that you are working on the problem, etc.	This, too, is standard procedure. For Vozdvyzhenka, such practices are confirmed by unhappy buyers as cited above.

7.5   Koncha Zaspa: Gated Hideaway

Our tour of the privileged side of Kyiv inevitably takes us to Koncha Zaspa, without question the city's most exclusive residential enclave for the ultra-elite. The neighborhood is in a heavily wooded area on the Right Bank of the Dnipro River at the southern margin of Kyiv and covers the former settlements of Chapayivka, Kozyn, and Plyuty. It is named for its two largest lakes, Koncha and Zaspa. The area started to become privileged place from early in the Soviet period with the construction of sanatoria for the communist *nomenklatura* of Ukraine, most notably the facilities named Koncha Zaspa, Zhovten, and Prolisok. From 1961, the popular Kyiv Dynamo Football Club has had its training facilities in this district, and in 1974, the "Base Koncha Zaspa," a state-of-the-art training and health center for Olympics athletes was opened in the neighborhood. It now serves the Olympic athletes of Ukraine. Another distinction is that Koncha Zaspa has the first golf course that was opened in Ukraine, the Golden Gate Golf Club that opened in 2000. In addition to the links, its facilities include a condominium hotel, a health club, a swimming pool, a river beach, tennis courts, villas, and an outdoor theater. The neighborhood has been referred to as Kyiv's answer to Rublevka (also Rublyovka), the super-rich district on the west side of Moscow whose very name means "money." Rublevka is said to be the Beverly Hills of the elite "New Russians," and its homes are called *kotezhi* (cottages) instead of the more direct "mansions."

The excellent Stolychne Shose (Capital City Highway) connects Koncha Zaspa with the main part of Kyiv. This is the road that was famously kept completely clear of snow during Kyiv's record snowfall in late March 2013, while elsewhere in the city, including on bridges spanning the Dnipro, traffic was paralyzed and cars and buses were abandoned by stranded drivers. We are free to drive on Stolyche Shose and visit Koncha Zaspa, but there are private security guards everywhere, as well as police patrols, security cameras, barbed wire, razor wire, and big dogs. Guards stir to attention when a car approaches and stare closely at this vehicle that they do not recognize. They might not know about the curiosity of social geographers, but they do fear journalists. An exposé about wealth in Koncha Zaspa in the media could cost a security guard his job. None of this invites us to pull over for a closer look. It is not exactly a gated community, as there is no gate, but almost every one of the houses is behind high walls and has a gate of its own, and security is ubiquitous. We see mostly the tops of houses and trees. Where the rich have built their mansions, the trees are in straight lines like sentinels along the high walls. Poplars are popular because they stand at attention. The roof lines reveal multiple chimneys per building, assuring us that everyone inside is staying warm, as well as that they love turrets and towers. We also see fake baroque and Italian Renaissance sculpture and other décor, including here and there a Greek or Roman god. Some buildings have classical columns and porticos, as if they were temples or museums.

The Google Earth view from above confirms all this and is fun (Figure 7.4). We see that a third or more of the houses have outdoor swimming pools and suspect that others have indoor pools. There are tennis courts as well, in some cases two adjacent courts on a single property, and private docks for pleasure craft. The network of waterways is convoluted to give water frontage to more properties, and there are canals behind lines of houses and between parallel streets, like in Miami Beach, to give homeowners a sliver of waterfront and a pier of their own. There are circular driveways at front doors with landscaped fountains or statues in the center, and driveways that lead to enormous garages. There are Newport or Versailles-like formal gardens and expanses of grassy lawn. Some places have sandy beaches, although such terrain along the Dnipro and its various indentations is supposed to be public. The occasional mansion could have been designed by an architect from Mars: their appearance is futuristic and very glassy, with bizarre shapes and footprint. I wonder what the owners of the over-the-top neoclassical or Georgian mansions next door think when a neighbor puts up an original monstrosity as opposed to a pretentions copy? Do they talk and share gardening tools across the high wall? Are they members of the same political party?

Koncha Zaspa is the neighborhood where every past and present president of Ukraine lives (yes, president Yanukovych lives here, too, in addition to being Lord of Mezhihirya), as well as so many other of Ukraine's richest and most influential leaders. Among the other people we have met in this book, Koncha Zaspa includes controversial Minister of Education and Science Dmytro Tabachnyk, former Mayor of Kyiv Leonid Chernovetskiy (when he is not on the lam), and former Prime Minister Yulia Tymoshenko (when she is not in prison). Other residents are current Prime Minister Mykola Yanovych Azarov, Head of the Verkhovna Rada Volodymyr Mykolaiovych Lytvyn, Prosecutor General of Ukraine Viktor Pshonka, former Kyiv Mayor Oleksandr Oleksandrovych Omelchenko, former Head of the Verkhovna Rada Oleksandr Oleksandrovych Moroz, and another former Head of the

Figure 7.4   The mansions of Koncha Zaspa as seen via Google Earth

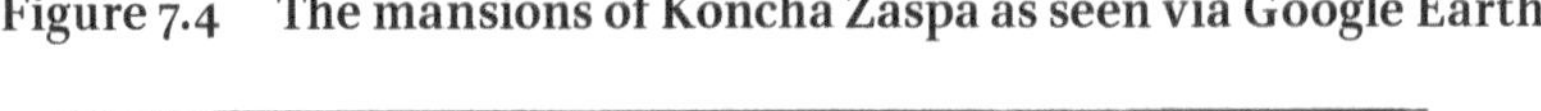

Verkhovna Rada, Oleksandr Mykolaiovych Tkachenko, among many other luminaries. All of them live in mansions that were built by the government of Ukraine and that the government maintains. The largest single one is apparently that of former President Kuchma; its grounds measure 1,226 square meters. There is also market housing for people who can afford the high end of Ukraine's real estate prices. An Internet search of what is available for sale shows nothing for less than US$750,000, with most properties in the range of US$1.5 million to US$6 million. As translated from the Russian, representative advertisements read as follows:[40]

Elite Single Home in Koncha Zaspa. House with expensive designer renovation in a cottage settlement. Contemporary style. Property size is 20 hundredths. Swimming pool. Prestigious cottage district with elite neighbors. Price: US$1,700,000.

VIP single home of a "deluxe" class in Koncha Zaspa. Tasteful designer renovation. The ground space of the single home measures 1,500 square meters on a designer-landscaped lot of 1.17 hectares. Swimming pool. Your own frontage on a private lake. A unique opportunity for connoisseurs of luxury. Price: Negotiable.

Unique house and residential property in Koncha Zaspa. Original architectural project and unique architectural solution – step out of your winter garden and into an interior covered courtyard with a waterfall, an alpine mountain, and a terrace! Price: US$6,500,000.

7.6   Bullies with Bentleys

The numbers of Bentley automobiles and other top-market automobile brands seem wildly disproportionate in Kyiv, given the relative poverty of the country, but such luxury vehicles are seen frequently in the center of the city and are key elements of Kyiv's landscapes of privilege. The Bentley dealership that I referred to in Chapter 1 has been open since 2005. My own short street near Maidan Nezalezhnosti regularly has as many as four Bentleys parked along the curb or on sidewalks, as well as a mix of Lamborghinis, Porsches, Land Rovers, Hummers, and other brands that are

40   http://dom-plus.com.ua/koncha-zaspa.html. Most advertisements for real estate for sale or rent in Kyiv are in Russian, especially for properties at the high end of the price range.

popular with the show-off nouveaux riches. The next street over has more such cars, including a sporty blue Bentley with a Ukrainian number plate that reads "Russia #1" in a kind of code. An even bigger concentration of such cars is just blocks away where Ukraine's top politicians park their cars: near the president's office building, beside the oversized, Stalinist Cabinet of Ministers building, and near the Verkhovna Rada. There is not enough room for them all, so sidewalks are taken from pedestrians for these cars, as are lanes of street traffic by double-parking. They have even cut mature trees so that drivers would have room to leave their cars. This is typical for Kyiv, where the rich and powerful consume space as they want regardless of the needs of others.

There are many stories to tell about rich people and their cars, and many examples of disdain on the part of the rich and well-connected for the rest of society and for the law, as expressed via automobiles. It is routine to see expensive cars with vanity license plate numbers (lots of 7s, low numbers, all the same digit, digits in numerical sequence, etc.) not just parked on sidewalks, but also actually driving on sidewalks in order to bypass street congestion, driving the wrong way in one-way traffic lanes for the same reason, not stopping at traffic signals, speeding crazily, and moving counter to directions given by traffic-control police officers. If they are stopped by police, drivers flash identification or bark something at the unfortunate soul who stopped them, and then drive off. Andriy Yushchenko, the teenage son of former President Viktor Yushchenko, was especially notorious. Unless he was in Dubai or Monte Carlo, or in some other foreign spot where he was known to entertain his girlfriends with lavish spending, his cars were seen daily speeding back and forth with impunity through the center of Kyiv, or parked directly in front of expensive restaurants and clubs. The succession of brands that he was reported to be driving included a Mercedes jeep, a Mercedes CLS 500, and then an expensive BMW M5. An article about him in *Ukrayinska Pravda* (July 7, 2005) was entitled "Andriy Yushchenko – The Son of God?" (Amchuk, 2005).

Kyivans seem to have a sixth sense about rich people's cars, always being on the lookout in case it is necessary to jump aside and make way (Figure 7.5). Sometimes, though, little people resist. Once I saw an SUV that was parked to block pedestrians outside a church that was pasted with preglued and preprinted stickers that read "I park like an idiot." In another insistence (this example is from Moscow where there are similar "class wars"), I saw a news photograph of a politically charged automobile accident: someone with an old rusty Lada, "yesterday's" Russian car, had driven broadside into an illegally parked Hummer, seemingly just for spite. The Lada was

Figure 7.5   This photograph was taken at an anti-corruption in government rally by the Communist Party of Ukraine in the center of Kyiv. The protester's sign reads "Caution! Oligarch at the Wheel." As is characteristic of Ukraine's communists, the language is Russian.

totaled, the brutish Hummer was barely bruised, but David had struck against Goliath.

I witnessed a similar "crash" on Khreshchatyk. It happened near the end of 2010 during the peak of a protest on Independence Square by owners of small businesses. The crowd had grown so large that there was no longer room on the square and protesters began spilling onto the street. Among the last cars to pass before the street was closed were two that may or may not have been involved in a minor fender-bender. As the protesters closed in on the traffic lanes and the remaining cars on the road became trapped, one driver, a man in his 50s in blue-collar garb, got out of his rusty yellow Lada, and started to yell at the driver of the shiny black Range Rover (license AA 8555X; a good number but not the best) beside him that she had struck his car. His car had dents indeed, lots of them, but the Range Rover had not a scratch. The very fashionably dressed driver of the Range Rover, much younger than the owner of the Lada, got out and insisted that there had been no contact between their cars. The crowd of onlookers grew as the two of them argued about dents and whether or not there had been an accident. Many onlookers were laughing. It may be that the man was trying to scam a wealthy person, or it may be that the woman was lying about a small accident that she had caused in the confusion; only the two of them know the full truth. The incident ended in an interesting way: the Range

Rover lady got on her cell phone while still on the street beside her adversary, talked briefly to the person on the other end, and then offered him the phone. He immediately declined to talk, hurried into his car, and hastily drove off as the crowd parted. I was lucky enough to have photographed it all from up close.

Another accident on Khreshchatyk was not so slight. It occurred on the evening of November 10, 2011, did truly involve a Bentley (Bentley Continental, license plate AA7777 IA, a top-prestige number), and resulted in injuries and a lot of expensive damage. I was on the scene just after the crash, well before emergency aid arrived, and recognized the Bentley as one that I knew from before on my street (I kept a log of such things). There are confusing and contradictory reports in the media about the details, probably at least in part to protect whomever was in the Bentley, but the following seems to be true. The Bentley was headed south on Khreshchatyk at high speed when a short distance away, at a busy street corner, the police officer who was directing traffic signaled Khreshchatyk cars to stop and the other cars to go. The Bentley, however, was being driven by a bully who did not stop and a nine-car crash ensued.[41] According to one witness, the Bentley had sped along Khreshchatyk as if it were a bullet in flight.

As a result of the impact, the Bentley was demolished, as was a top-of-the-line Mercedes SL500 head-on, and there were air bags opened in all directions. Some of the other six or seven cars in the accident were also badly damaged. The traffic policeman was struck as well, although it is not clear just by which car, but thankfully he survived. His worst injury was a broken leg. What else is known for sure is that the AA7777 IA car was registered to Vasyl Heorhiyovych Dzharty, a prominent former *narodnyi deputat* from Crimea and member of the Party of Regions. However, he had died from cancer not quite two months earlier. The Bentley's driver that evening seems to have been the family's chauffeur, Volodymyr Moskalyuk, who was hospitalized after the crash, and his backseat passenger was likely Dzharty's younger daughter, 23-year-old Olya. A young woman who looks very much like her was photographed on the scene by amateur photographers and phone-video cameras, and the "evidence" was been posted on the Internet. (She is not in my own shots.) However, Olya Dzharty has denied being in the car, and the injured Moskalyuk has refused to comment. Witnesses on the scene described a speeding Bentley that ignored a clear traffic signal from the traffic policeman, adding that the woman passenger was in a hurry and asked her driver to press on. How anyone not in the Bentley

41   Some reports say that the total number of cars in the crash was eight.

could know anything about that last detail is beyond me, but that was the buzz on the street and a characterization of what happened that entered the blogosphere.

The number of car accidents on the roads in Ukraine is staggering, as is the attendant death toll. There are bad road conditions and poor lighting, drivers who simply do not know how to drive safely, considerable drunk driving, and among the rich and powerful with expensive cars, a culture that there are no consequences for breaking traffic rules and killing people. To wit, a current member of the Verkhovna Rada, Vladislav Luk'yanov of the Party of Regions, has boasted openly on his Facebook site that he was able to drive the 441 kilometer (274 miles) distance from Kyiv to Odesa in only 2 hours and 40 minutes, a speed that he described as 241-250 km/hr (150-155 mph). The legal speed limit along the way is no higher than 110 km/hr (68 mph). A photograph shows him behind the wheel of his Audi A8 and a digital speedometer reading of 241 km/hr. When a reporter from *Korrespondent* pressed him on the issue, Luk'yanov expressed that he had been doing a public service to see how fast it was possible to travel between those two cities in order to set a new standard for driving in Ukraine. He further explained that he was not worried about a traffic accident because, frankly, car crashes happen at all speeds. He then backed off his preposterous boast and admitted that he had maintained the top speed only for short stretches of the journey as an experiment. The article that the reporter wrote was headlined "Regionnaire about High Speed: 'We Were Trying to See How Fast It Was Possible to Travel'" (Korrespondent, 2012). It gets worse: several days after that interview, Luk'yanov conducted a demonstration of his speeding abilities for news reporters and cameras, perhaps as compensation for having been forced to back off the preposterous boast of 2 hours and 40 minutes between Kyiv and Odesa. This time he drove a BMW sports car and conducted his demonstration on the highway between Kyiv and Boryspil Airport, where the speed limit is 130 km/hr (81 mph). As the cameras that were positioned along the way and in the car itself documented, Luk'yanov was able to reach 275 km/hr (171 mph) as he weaved through traffic and forced drivers ahead of him to clear out of the way (Ukrayinska Pravda, 2012).

Not all such bullies always get away with it. One who did not was Nikolay Pavlovich Lisin, another of Ukraine's high- and fast-living lawmakers, member of parliament, and member of the Party of Regions. Lisin was born in 1964 in Kriviy Rih. His was not a Bentley nor an Audi A8 but a beautiful black Lamborghini Gallardo (somehow I feel compelled to interject that the model name "Gallardo" is a breed of fighting bull) that was valued at about US$350,000. I used to see his car on Horodetskoho Street, usually on Friday afternoons when there were gatherings of elite Regionnaires at a particular restaurant. In the afternoon of April 17, 2011, he was charging homeward on Academician Zabolotnoho Street in the southern outskirts of right-bank Kyiv at a clip of some 200 km/hr (124 mph) when he apparently lost control of his vehicle, struck the cement curb, crashed through two lampposts, and came to eternal rest against the tall standard of a gasoline station's price board. He was reported afterwards to have been sober with respect to alcohol. However, like his Regionnaire buddy Luk'yanov, he may have been somewhat delusional about being indestructible because he had great wealth and power. When news about this one-car accident was broadcast, many citizens sniggered about him receiving his just deserts for being a have-all, take-all rich politician of the type that I call here a "Bully with a Bentley," and the Ukrainian blogosphere was alive with "dead Lisin" jokes and unkind commentary.[42]

42   Compare the episodes related here as "Bullies with Bentleys" with the chapter "Car Wars" in Stephen Graham, *Cities under Siege: The New Military Urbanism* (London: Verso, 2010).

8 Landscapes of Struggle

8.1 The Killing of Oksana Makar

Oksana Makar lived a difficult life and, at age 18, died a horrible death.[43] How she lived and how she died give insight to aspects of life among the poor in Ukraine, and perhaps also to special privileges enjoyed by the nonpoor. Put simply, this child of Ukrainian poverty and the social miseries that often accompany poverty had some questionable associations in her life, and in the end she was gang-raped by three young men and was then set afire and left to die. She survived for three weeks afterwards, but barely so, and then on March 29, 2012, succumbed to her horrible injuries. The next day she was buried in a wedding dress according to local tradition. The specific detail that these events took place not in Kyiv but about 480 kilometers (298 miles) away in the southern Ukrainian city of Mykolaiv is not very important for us; Oksana's story is a tragedy for all Ukraine, reflects the country as a whole, and may be a wake-up call in many respects about how to make the country better. I choose to tell this story also because it is very recent, and because Ukraine is talking about it, perhaps anxious to understand and learn.

Where to begin about Makar? Mykolaiv is a tough industrial city of about 500,000 known for shipbuilding and other heavy industry. It has not done well since the demise of the Soviet military machine that kept its factories busy and has offered its young citizens few prospects for a good life. Many of the most ambitious young people have left, either to go to Kyiv or other large Ukrainian cities, or just as often to seek work abroad. Others have fallen into poverty and some of the social problems such as alcohol and drug abuse that are often associated with economic hardship. The city's population has been declining in step with economic problems and outmigration. Oksana Makar was born into such a setting in 1993, two years after Ukraine's independence. She spent a lot of her childhood in an orphanage because her father was imprisoned for trafficking in narcotics and her mother for robbery. She completed only six years of schooling because she often ran away from the orphanage and was therefore not particularly employable as she approached adulthood. She had brushes with the law, including at

43   There are many Internet sources about this case, including Rudenko (2012) and Tomlinson et al. (2012).

least one arrest for prostitution. She probably ran with a tough crowd who were also from the underside of society in a poor city.

On the night of March 8-9, 2012, Oksana Makar was at a Mykolaiv pub called Rybka (a *rybka* is a small fish) where she met at least two of her attackers. She may have known one of the men before, although this has not been confirmed one way or another. Eventually, there were three men with her and she was in the apartment of one of them where she was severely beaten and then gang-raped. Her attackers apparently attempted to strangle her and then took her in an unconscious state to a construction site where they tried to hide what they had done by burning her. She was discovered by a passerby in the morning and taken to a hospital. There were burns on 55 percent of her body and her lungs were damaged from smoke inhalation. She was then transferred to a burn center in a hospital in Donetsk, where a she was operated on by a Swiss surgeon and had her right arm and both feet amputated to stop the spread of gangrene. It is worth pointing out that the cost of Makar's medical attention was paid for by Party of Regions billionaire oligarch Rinat Akhmetov, a man mentioned in a different light in Chapter 6. Makar's mother, Tatiana Surovitskaya, was with her during the hospitalization and at one point asked her daughter to describe her ordeal on video, which is now readily available online. The film runs for 1 minute and 19 seconds, and in it Makar tries to speak but either lacks the strength or decides not to continue after a few initial remarks. When asked what punishment should be meted out to her attackers, she said that they should have their balls ripped out and fed to dogs, and that she hoped that her attackers would be raped in prison (Antonova, 2012). Her mother has been criticized for making the video and posting it, as her daughter was in obvious pain and plainly was in no mood to speak. It is because Makar was filmed without her full and unequivocal agreement that I am not providing a link to the video.

Unfortunately, the attack on Makar was not an exception. It may have been more violent than most, but the instance of rape is high in Ukraine and violators often escape justice (Parfan, 2012). The country is still not far from the Dark Ages when it comes to protecting women from assault, both physical and verbal, and female victims are often treated as if it was their fault that they were unduly ogled, groped, or even raped. There is a culture among too wide a spectrum of Ukrainian society that believes that women are for sex, and that men who take sex are simply doing what is natural for men to do. It is that culture in which Makar's attackers were almost certainly brought up, and when they got good and drunk in the company of a woman they had chatted up in a bar, they did what they did. All three men were arrested soon after the incident. Two of them were released very quickly on bail, sparking rumors and news reports that they were politically connected. That turned out to be not true. Mykola Riabchuk, a journalist, author, and leading Ukrainian intellectual, has kept a personal log of violent crimes committed by Ukrainian VIPs and, especially, their offspring, and has written that although the rumors about the supposed high political status of Makar's assailants proved to be unfounded, "[Ukrainian] people have become so accustomed to daily lawlessness and the rampant impunity of the strong and wealthy that they tend, naturally, to overreact" (Riabchuk, 2012, p. 1).

On November 27, 2012, all three assailants were convicted of rape and murder and were sentenced one by one by the Mykolaiv court to terms of 14 years, 15 years, and life in prison. What we know for sure is that Makar lived a hard life and that she did not deserve to die.

8.2 Faces of Poverty

We know as well that Oksana Makar and her gritty hometown of Mykolaiv are all too representative of Ukraine today. A country with outstanding agricultural and industrial resources is much too poor, and far too many suffer. There is a grossly unequal distribution of wealth (although one that is far from the world's worst), and glaring reminders of Ukraine's poverty are seen daily not only in worn industrial cities or remote villages, but also in the very center of Kyiv. Amid the Bentleys that bully the city, and just outside the perimeters of privilege protected by gates and guards in black, as well as outside the gates of gold-gilt churches, are many of the city's poor. We see them one by one with paper cups begging for coins, poring methodically through trash cans for recyclables and food, asleep on benches in public squares, along sidewalks and in pedestrian undergrounds, or simply sitting alone with worn shopping bags overfilled with whatever possessions they have.[44] Nationally, the percentage of people living in poverty has been measured as high as 35 percent, the highest rate in Europe except for the 35.8 percent living below the poverty line in Armenia.[45] Of 157 countries

44 For an excellent study of begging in St. Petersburg, see Scattone (2010). The book in which this essay appears (Gdaniec, ed., 2010) contains several chapters that present research from Moscow and/or St. Petersburg that parallel my own observations about Kyiv.

45 Rankings and data vary somewhat according to source. Here, I am citing Index Mundi, a source that uses data from the *CIA World Factbook*: http://www.indexmundi.com/g/r.aspx? c=up&v=69.

that are ranked by Index Mundi, Ukraine is 56th in terms of percentage of population living below the poverty line, squeezed between Guyana (55th) and Paraguay (57th). Life expectancy at birth is 68.74, the second-lowest in Europe after Russia (66.4). The country ranks 152nd on this indicator out of 220 nations ranked by Index Mundi, just below Bangladesh, Moldova, Kyrgyzstan, North Korea, and Turkmenistan, in descending order, and marginally better than Mongolia and Belize, 153rd and 154th, respectively.[46] Furthermore, Ukraine has high rates of alcoholism, drug addiction, HIV-AIDS, and other afflictions, again among the worst in Europe and on a par with many developing countries. In addition, there are tens of thousands of "social orphans" in Ukraine, abandoned by their parents because they were born ill or deformed, or because the parents were impoverished, addicted to drugs or alcohol, or imprisoned. The country's orphanages are notoriously overcrowded and are often poor and depressing. Many children escape, preferring life on the streets where, all too often, they turn to drugs, alcoholism, crime, and prostitution. As we said at the start, Ukraine's citizens with options, such as my students who have graduated, prefer to move abroad, leaving behind a population that is disproportionately poor and poorly equipped for the future.

When I told Olena Zhelesko, the colorful street poet-protestor introduced in Chapter 1, that I was working on a book about the city, she advised me to go early on any morning to the Vokzal, Kyiv's central passenger rail station, to view the rhythms of activity and talk with people. I told her that I had been doing that already, because I knew from my travels that such a setting was geographical nexus between the countryside of a struggling nation and the possible promise of a better life in the nation's capital. Whether we are in Jakarta, Phnom Penh, or Vientiane in Southeast Asia, or Buenos Aires or Lima in South America, all capital cities in which I have observed the arrival of rural migrants up close, or in Kyiv, the rhythms at key passenger rail stations, inter-urban bus depots, and bridge crossings connecting countryside and city are all more or less the same: hopeful migrants from those provinces where there is no work arrive in the city risking what little they have in quest of a job, some seasonal work, or the chance to sell at a fair markup to a city market whatever it is that they brought with them from home. They are often greeted by someone with a need for their labor, as well as by an array of aggressive agents, touts, and operators who pull them this way and that with promises about income, an inexpensive place to live, and other opportunities. Often the migrants and sometimes those who await

---

46   Index Mundi, http://www.indexmundi.com/g/r.aspx?c=up&v=30. Russia ranks 166th.

them are keen for conversation, and almost always the conversations add up to the sounds of a nation's struggles.

Kyiv's *vokzal* is located in the center of the city in Solom'yanskiy Raion (ward) near Vokzalna Station of the Red Line of Kyiv's subway system. Its 16 rail tracks follow the valley of the small river Lybid, now invisible in the city except for underground pipes that channel its waters. The station is formally named Kyiv-Pasazhyr'skyi (Kyiv Passenger Station), which is what it says on tickets, but everyone calls it simply Vokzal, an abbreviated and fused word that means railroad building. It reads "VOKZAL" in bold Ukrainian and/or Russian letters affixed high atop the main building above the entrance (the word is written the same in both languages). The main building is imposing enough, although it is not one of the greatest and most beautiful in Europe, and was built in the late 1920s and early 1930s in a style that is said to be Ukrainian baroque mixed with constructivism. Vokzal is actually a sprawling complex that includes a second big entrance on the opposite of the main station building, the so-called Southern Station, as well as the Vokzalna Metro Station, and the various tunnels, underground passageways, and above-track skywalks that bind it all together. In front of the main building is a large public square that is called Vokzalna Ploshcha (Vokzalna Square) where licensed taxis, pirate taxis, minibuses, and larger buses await passengers, and where new arrivals in Kyiv begin their search for where to go and what to do. Adjacent to the square is a crowded McDonald's restaurant, reported to be the third-busiest in the world, with 2 million orders sold in 2010, and an unrelated outlet of the Ukrainian fast-food chain McFoxy that makes its living by catching spillover from neighboring golden arches. A March 11, 2011, article in the *Kyiv Post* pictured the two together in a feature article about brand piracy under the headline "Faking It with Impunity Is Way of Doing Business" (Panova, 2011).

Olena Zhelesko urged me to mix and mingle in this landscape, and I did. Vokzal hums all day and all night, as there are commuter trains that pass through, Kyiv-area intra-urban lines, and longer routes that reach distant cities in Ukraine and cities outside the country such as Minsk, Moscow, St. Petersburg, and Berlin. The hours near dawn, however, seem busiest and most interesting, as it is then when trains from the corners of Ukraine tend to arrive. Passengers of all ranks spill out, including business travelers, students on the move between home and campus, and Ukrainians coming to town for reasons such as business visits to government offices, specialized shopping, medical treatment, transfer to the international airport, and planned protest rallies. There are also migrants from rural areas who come to the capital to search for work, if not to start a new life.

Such migrants also arrive by bus, which is cheaper, and are often dropped at Vokzal, which also acts a terminal for bus routes. It is they who linger near Vokzal Square to find what is next. Especially in summer, they have that weathered look of people who have worked in the fields or outdoors in construction. They look strong (Figure 8.1). There are also Kyivans who make a living off the arriving passengers: bus and taxi drivers, food and drink vendors, apartment and rooming house agents, labor recruiters, and others. There are also bag thieves and pickpockets. And, finally, there are the destitute: those who ran out of money and hope, and are begging for fare to get back home; those who arrived without money and are begging for a handout to get them through the next day; those who have been robbed or cheated in Kyiv and have nowhere to turn; and those who simply pretend to be in any or all of these unfortunate circumstances.

People who are struggling seem to be everywhere in Kyiv. They are camped on benches in public squares and along main streets, work as petty vendors in pedestrian underpasses and on their stairways, and live in back lots, in derelict houses, and other hidden spaces. Away from the center, there are even more poor people, although densities might be lower. There are districts with low rents and poor-quality housing, inexpensive apartments

Figure 8.1   Laborers gathered around a recruiter for day work outside Kyiv's central rail station

that get overcrowded, and a maze of exurban villages and other settlements where almost no one seems to have any money. There are people who live in the city's parks along the river, even year-round in this four-season climate, and in the forests at the urban edge. Some are homeless loners, but quite a few others, such as ethnic Roma, have established camps along dirt trails in the forests outside the city and live in communities of a hundred or more. Many of the most desperate people suffer from alcoholism, mental illness, or physical ailments such as lost limbs. Some are panhandlers and beg for a living while others sift through trash bins or roam the streets in search of bottles and cans. On several occasions on Maidan Nezalezhnosti I was moved to see bottle collectors working furiously in competition with one another to put as much as they could into their various bags after a crowded concert or some other event had broken up and the people begin to disperse. There are also those who sing or play musical instruments for tips at Metro stations, along sidewalks, and in pedestrian underpasses, as well those who hand out advertising leaflets to passing crowds about sales at nearby stores, tasty fare at nearby restaurants, information about car insurance or driving lessons, and advertisements for everything from the services offered by Internet or mobile phone providers to discounts on new windows for drafty apartments. Some workers become human signboards and wander amid the crowds along sidewalks and near Metro stations as mobile advertisements for pawn shops, international marriage agencies, nearby stores that have sales going on and nearby restaurants with empty tables, schools of English language, and other businesses. Once I thanked an older woman in English who was wearing a front-and-back signboard for an English school and who handed me a leaflet for classes, but she had no idea what I said. Another memory is of a very old woman, at least in her mid-80s and small and frail-looking as can be, pacing outside a Metro station in a residential district as a signboard advertising an automobile driving school. There are a hundred or more such occupations; no one enters them by plan or choice – it is always a matter of poverty and necessity.

My notes have many entries along these lines. For example, there is Volodya, a second person with this name in this book, whom I met on a Khreshchatyk walkway where he worked by weighing people on a bathroom scale for tips. He had called out to me with a question about where I was from after seeing me pass by again and again over a period of weeks and said that he had noticed that I was both a regular in the area and, by looks, a foreigner. He spoke in Ukrainian and was very polite. A conversation ensued, the first of many that we had over a period of months. Volodya 2 was just 18. He had recently "been graduated" from living in an orphanage in the Volyn region of Ukraine, and having nowhere to go, came to the capital to start a life. He was slight and did not look the type for construction work or other labor, and he may also have had some deficiencies upstairs. Nevertheless, he was nice, friendly, and open, and he seemed honest. I took a liking to him. He had bought the bathroom scale at a flea market and had entered the "weighing occupation" in order to support himself. He kept regular hours at a spot that he had selected for himself near an older woman who sold cigarettes, who was also pleasant and poor, and simply waited for customers to step on the scale. He quoted no prices, as he worked for tips, and was sometimes cheated by kids in his age group who did not pay and who made fun of him. Every day at 7:00 p.m. on the dot, he packed up his business and headed to a side street where he caught a *marshrutka* that took him to near the rooming house beyond Kyiv's limits where he stayed. By 11:00 a.m. the next morning, he had commuted back to work. After I bought him a nice digital scale, he said that his business picked up.

Another example concerns the various furry animals, Bart Simpsons, and Sponge Bobs that I mentioned earlier in this book. They work Maidan Nezalezhnosti and Khreshchatyk for tips from tourists with whom they pose for photographs. They are much too aggressive and are annoying because they pester passersby and sometimes don't easily take no for answer. However, another perspective is that these creatures are hard at work at low-paying jobs that they themselves despise. Quite a few of the dozen or so who work the central square at a time are only teenagers, aged perhaps 16 or so. As "Tiger" and other animals told me when on break with their tops off, it is unbearably hot in the synthetic fabric costumes that they are made to wear, especially so during the heat wave of summer 2012, but their breaks are short and few, and they are carefully measured. A boss watches continually from a central vantage place and complains if they are not aggressive enough in chasing after possible tippers. At the end of the day, each gives him the money he or she has collected and is then paid a cut that is supposed to be proportionate with how hard the boss thinks they worked. They then file off to a nearby apartment where they change to their own clothes and leave the costumes behind. Earning 100 hryvnia (about US$12.50) is a good day, but on many days the pay is half that amount. "Why do you put up with such work?" I ask. "Have you got a better job for me?" is the reply. When I complain on the street about being pestered yet again by some furry creature who proposes to pose with me for a photo I do not need, the response is sometimes a plea: " I don't want to do this either. Don't you know how hard it is to earn some money?"

Next is "Svetlana," an 84-year-old taxi driver, the first female cabbie that I encountered in Kyiv. I entered her taxi for the first time for a ride from Pecherska Lavra to my home in the center in a sudden rainstorm after the first two cabs I tried wanted exorbitant sums for the short distance. However, when I asked at the window of a hulky, ancient white Volga with a cracked windshield, Svetlana said that the fare was a very reasonable 40 hryvnia (US$5), so I hopped in. The cab was not only ancient, but the driver looked old, too, and her dashboard was a world of icons and holy cards that also suggested the past much more than the present. She told me that she had been working as a cabbie for 40 years and that when she started, she was Kyiv's first female taxi driver ever. She was not welcomed into the profession and is still not particularly welcome among male drivers, if only because of her pricing. It was a much easier job than the farm work she had done as a young woman, she explained, and was now her means of supplementing an inadequate pension. I watched nervously as she drove very slowly, shifted gears very slowly, and made choices about turns and lane changes very slowly, so I asked how old she was. When she said 84, she added that she could not afford to stop working because of the rising cost of living. Her personal needs were not great, she said, except to top off a pension, so her prices were what prices should be rather than extortive. I rode with her several times since, always slowly and always knowing in advance where she might be parked, and then one day she was gone. It has been more than a year since I have seen Svetlana, so I assume that she is no longer driving and may not even be with us. She had told me that she expected to drive until the end.

There are many other elderly people who could or should be enjoying a restful retirement except for economic circumstances that force them back to work. A disproportionate number are women who have outlived their husbands and are impoverished in widowhood. For everyone, pension payments are small and do not keep pace with rising prices. Some old folks have been abandoned by children who are themselves poor or have moved abroad, while others work because their children or grandchildren have needs. In a culture where hard work is the norm, at least among those with rural roots as opposed to those from urban proletarian occupations, we see older women as petty vendors of everything from cigarettes by the smoke to lottery tickets to small bouquets of wildflowers to cups of fresh raspberries or other seasonal fruit. Sometimes in the morning, we encounter sellers struggling with bulky bags of wares as they board crowded trolley buses or subway cars during the morning rush. Often, no one seems to see them and no one offers to help, even to the slightest of old ladies with the biggest bags, or to the most overweight babushka who can barely lift herself onto the bus, much less her goods. I break rules of social-scientific participant-observation and intervene when I can. Older women also comprise much of the workforce as eyes in the corners of rooms in museums, the eyes on escalators in the Metro system, and as the city's army of gardeners, leafrakers, street sweepers, and custodians of public toilets. They work silently with dignity and with little interaction with the public, and are often regarded as if they were invisible.

One particular incident was especially eye-opening. I was about to move from one apartment to another in Kyiv and decided to give away various household goods and refrigerator contents that I did not want to lug. I put them into a beat-up wheeled suitcase that I no longer wanted either, and then pulled it behind me into the courtyard of a nearby abandoned building where I knew that homeless people were living as squatters. It was well after dark when I arrived because my packing had taken a long time, but I knew the layout of the place from an earlier photo excursion and managed to penetrate quite deeply into the complex with little light. The sound of the rolling suitcase got residents' attention and I was greeted by an older woman who was the first to emerge from the ruin. She gave me the once-over, welcomed me, and began to offer a place to live. I should have known better. When I explained my intentions, she was shocked, and then asked me a question that shocked me in return: "You know that we are bums, don't you?" She had most likely detected from my speech that I was a foreigner, and wanted to make sure that I knew where I was. She used the word *bomzhi*, which does indeed translate as "bums." That is what society thinks of her and her neighbors, and it was simply not conceivable to her that someone from the outside, whether foreigner or fellow citizen, would be giving them things. "Yes, I know that that is what they call you," I said, "but these are things that I no longer need and I thought that you might have a use for them. There are some perishable food items," I added, "but they are fresh from the refrigerator and still cold. If you eat them soon, it will be alright." I am too embarrassed to elaborate on the great thanks and prayers to God that gushed forth. I came back a little later with a second load, and this time there was a handful of well-wishers and thankful "bums" to greet me.

There are few "soup kitchens" and residential shelters to help such people in Kyiv or in other Ukrainian cities (although there might be marginally more in the west of the country than in other regions), so "*bomzhi*," as they are called almost universally in the country,[47] are more or less on their own.

---

47   For example, see the article about street children in the Ukrainian city of Makeiivka (Russian Makeevka, as in the article's title) by Naterer and Gordina (2011); and the 2007 article about homeless construction workers by Anastasiya Ryabchuk.

When the notorious Leonid Chernovetskiy (Chapter 3) was mayor (2006-2012), he initiated some programs to help the homeless as part of his populist platform, but that was early in his term of office and the programs withered away before long. Where there is help, it is often the work of churches or other religious organizations such as the Embassy of the Blessed Kingdom of God for All Nations mega-church of which Chernovetskiy was a prominent member and some, but not nearly all, Catholic or Orthodox parishes.

In my own experience, I was privileged to visit an exceptional help center called Logos on several occasions and to get to know some of its key people. It is located in a forested area just outside the western municipal limits of Kyiv and is a "Christian center of spiritual renewal" that has transformed an old school building into a haven for neighbors in need. It operates a soup kitchen that feeds 45 to 50 poor people each day and a free medical clinic, and provides a very comfortable and nicely equipped shelter for people in need of a place to stay. Its facilities also are used for religious retreats. Father Nicoli Ilnytskyi, the young Ukrainian Orthodox priest who had dedicated himself to this project, has plans for additional programming and the expansion of its facilities, and is building a church nearby as well. Funds and materials are from donations, with a good fraction of the help coming from evangelical Christian churches in the United States. There are few such places in Ukraine, Father Nicoli explained, but the needs are enormous. I can testify that Logos's "clients" are in disbelief, at least initially, that there is help for them without a catch. That is, you do not have to pray to eat, nor pay. Logos is in a "forgotten" part of the metropolitan area where poor people live as if in exile from the city. Housing conditions are poor, as are community services, and many neighbors reside, quite literally, as campers in the forests with no running water or other urban services.[48]

These kinds of experiences took place again and again. Wherever there was someone who was in need and who had caught my eye for whatever reason, when I offered help over and above a few coins or low denomination bills tossed into a cup, the response was disbelief that someone was being nice. Indeed, I found that some people mistrusted me for trying to be helpful and assumed that I must have ulterior motives or a scam up my sleeve. My foreignness is what sometimes got them to believe: that is, no one from their world would pay them any mind and only an outsider could be so kind. For example, there was a man about my age (60s) who was wandering in the underground corridors of Khreshchatyk Metro Station. He was carrying seven sizable plastic shopping bags filled with belongings in his hands and

48   The website of Logos is http://www.logos-kiev.org/.

a bulging old backpack on his back. His jeans were torn, his shirt was dirty, and he looked very tired. I watched from a distance as he walked back and forth, put his bags down, read some ads on posters in detail, picked his bags up again, and wandered in circles a little more. "You look like you might be lost," I said. "Can I help you?" "I am not lost" was the blunt reply. "Well maybe there is something else that you need? Are you alright?" "I am fine. I do not need anything." I looked at him for a moment, and then said bluntly: "Maybe you need some money?" "Money? For free? Of course. Who would say no?" I handed him 200 hryvnia that I had prepared for the moment (only about US$25, but to him a substantial sum) and walked away to a barely audible "Thank you." I then watched him from a distance from behind a post as he examined the two 100 hryvnia notes again and again. He finally folded them into an envelope and put them deeply into a pocket. I knew that he was aware of me, and I turned my back. Within a moment he was there beside me: "You are Polish, right? You are not one of us. You sound like you are Polish." A conversation ensued, but I kept it short, as I did not want to make him explain his poverty. He was from the south of Ukraine and had studied in Moscow where he became an engineer. He worked on "Soviet rockets and stuff," he said, and had lived all over the Soviet Union, especially in remote launch and research sites, but now there was a new world. What was past no longer matters, he continued, and no one cares who he is or what he had done. "What do you do now? I asked. "I am in transition," he said. "It is a time of transition." I took the next subway train as it came by, and he presumably has gone to wherever the transition is taking him.[49]

I have many photographs of people who struggle: not this gentleman with his bags, but ice-breaking babushkas, street-side beggars, dispensers of toilet paper, sellers of flowers, and weighers of passersby, among others, but they are all sad photographs and are mostly not for show. The looks on some faces remind me of the faces in Ilia Repin's *Barge Haulers on the Volga*, a famous painting from 1870-1873 showing "Volga Boatmen" pulling a ship up Russia's great river. Printing a photograph of an old woman or someone else who is struggling through life might be another form of exploitation, although the situation is so common in Kyiv that not showing it would constitute an omission. Likewise, I also have photos of charlatan beggars, but it is not my function to expose them. I wish that I had a photograph of Svetlana at the wheel of her cab, if only for myself, but I never got up the nerve to ask if she minded, so there are no pictures of her. That was a mistake. However,

---

49   For a wider study of social costs of postsocialist transition in Ukraine and Russia, see Round and Williams (2010).

there is Misha, a middle-aged man I met one day during one of my long walks through Kyiv. He did not mind posing and gave permission when I explained that I was a book author-professor. I had met him at the edge of the Svyatoshyn neighborhood, a residential area in the western part of the Right Bank, where he was at work in the fairly sizable yard of an older single home cutting branches off trees that had been felled. The property was fenced in but the house looked like no one had lived there for a long time. I took an initial photo from a distance and then when he looked my way, I approached him and we talked from opposite sides of the fence.

No, it was not his house, Misha explained with a laugh; he was just a handyman who had been picked for this job from among other hopefuls that morning at Vokzal. He has worked at hundreds of odd jobs all over Ukraine and in Russia, and has just arrived in Kyiv once again from his home village in Poltava oblast, where he also works on the family farm. There was less to do there at this time and always a need for money, so he was on one of his many ventures into the capital to earn some cash. This task will take another two days, he said, and because the weather is good, he might decide to simply sleep on the grounds where he was working. He does not know the area nor who owns the land he was on, but was driven to the site by the labor recruiter who recognized him from an earlier gig. He had been handed a small chain saw and other equipment, and his job was to cut limbs and branches into smaller pieces, and to stack them. We surmised together from the setting that it was all coming down to continue the expansion of urbanization in the district, and that he was doing clean up after the tree-cutters had taken down some monsters before other machines would come in to remove stumps. I did not ask how much he would be paid, but he said that it was good work and that he was pleased with it. Other

Figure 8.2   **Misha the handyman**

work is downright dangerous, he said. Removing branches from a downed tree is far better that cleaning up chemicals on the sly as some jobs offer, or work at some construction or demolition sites. I mentioned that I had once seen a construction site where the workers came out at the end of the day covered head to toe in some sort of dust, and that they looked to be only teenagers. *"Take buvaye"* ("Such things happen"), he said with a nod. Before I left, I took some photos of Misha in the setting in which he worked and decided to use one of them here to finish this section with something more upbeat (Figure 8.2).

8.3   Petty Traders

There is hard work and little pay as well in petty trade, another occupation in which we see Kyivans of all ages struggling to make a living. There are vendors at pretty much every venue where the public gathers or passes: the central train station, Metro stations, bus and *marshrutka* (minibus) stops, pedestrian crossings and underpasses, busy sidewalks, the fronts of

Figure 8.3   One of the countless petty vendors in Kyiv, a great many of whom are elderly women

shopping centers, supermarkets, and other stores, as well as at the gates of churches, in popular squares, parks, and beaches, and at events such as concerts, fireworks displays, political rallies, and sports competitions. What is sold is just about everything a person could have a use for that can be carried or consumed. You won't normally buy a double-door refrigerator or a sofa bed from a petty vendor at street side, but there are cigarettes by the pack and the single smoke, as well as fresh vegetables and eggs, prepared foods, chocolate bars, drinks, lottery tickets, flowers, minutes and cases for your mobile phone, batteries, newspapers, shoes, socks, sunglasses, sunblocks, shampoos, shopping bags, scouring pads, scissors, stockings, and bras, among countless other items (Figure 8.3).

There is an important distinction between those petty traders who work for themselves and those who have bosses who assign them to spots for which they had previously or concurrently arranged with authorities. The former are always in danger of being shaken down or chased by police, and are sometimes victims of such actions several times in a day from different locations, while the latter work for a pittance for a business owner who keeps a sizable chunk of the proceeds and also pays off police who decide which businesses go and which stay. At the end of the day, employee-vendors need to square proceeds with inventory and are personally responsible for any shortfalls. Quite a few business owners operate multiple kiosks such as for drinks, ice cream, or newspapers and magazines in various parts of the city that are duly licensed and pay taxes, and they pay their employees an hourly wage. Small motorized "barista" vans that brew espressos and other kinds of coffee are increasingly common in off-street locations. As they expand their businesses to new locations, kiosk operators often put pressure on competitors who lack official protection, and have them chased away. Kiosks, in turn, can be the scourge of store and shopping mall operators who oppose the competition out front and employ their political pull to free up the sidewalks from so-called MAFs (*mali arkhytekturni formy* [small architectural forms], as they are officially classified). From time to time, one sees or reads about anti-vendor and anti-MAF campaigns in Kyiv to rationalize business and provide more space on sidewalks for pedestrians and cars (Krasnohorodsky, 2012). Thus, there is a game of musical chairs of sorts in Kyiv in which bigger businesses with better connections exert pressure on smaller businesses in contested territories, and where the ultimate losers are the smallest and pettiest of self-employed entrepreneurs who have no one to turn to and lack the proceeds with which to buy administrative support. They are chased around Kyiv and stay in poverty. As in other cities around the world, especially in developing countries, many of the vendors are young people who are striving to *build* lives, but in Kyiv and other cities in Ukraine the ranks of street vendors also include countless elderly people who are struggling to *continue* lives.

My notes contain countless references to vendors. One day I stepped out from Zoloti Vorota Metro Station and saw a middle-aged woman selling nice quality plush animals. There was a frog that I liked as a gift for someone I would see soon, so I negotiated a price and said that I would return in a few minutes because I was plumb out of cash and needed to go to a bank machine. She told me to hurry because she expected the police to chase her away at any minute, and told me where to look for her if she were gone. Sure enough, ten minutes later, she was no longer there but was down the block and around the corner looking for me to come back. It is a daily, day-long routine for her, she said, and she did not think that it was right to pay the police for a place to stand. Another example concerns street musicians. Some seem to have a given hour or two that is theirs day after day at a given spot, after which they move on to another place. Their "permits" seem to work this way. Others apparently are almost literally forced to share the take. I remember listening to two students of violin performing at a Metro station entrance and then seeing the two police officers on patrol look hungrily into the violin case with coins and small bills. The two of them stayed put a few feet to the side of the musicians to watch as donations accumulated. I left before the "take" was executed because I sensed that I had become an object of interest, too, but when I saw the same musicians the next day and made a respectable donation, I asked them about the day before. "Yes, of course, what do you think? Everyone wants theirs," was their answer to my question about whether the police had taken a share of their proceeds. The amount that police expect to be paid varies with how lucrative a business seems to be, and there are many cases where the police are corrupt *za kopiyky* (for small change) only. I have also heard that at least in some precincts, members of the rank-and-file police are given quotas with respect to how much money to bring in from such shakedowns, and that the money works its way up a chain of power. The police, in turn, might solve disputes between competing traders or musicians and assign one to a better spot and another to a place further away, depending on the price they get for their services.

Among the new "small businesses" that have appeared this year (2013) along Khreshchatyk and other busy parts of the city is a game to challenge your strength: pay 20 hryvnia (about US$2.50) to play and you can win ten times that amount – simply hang for two minutes from a horizontal bar above your head without letting your feet touch the ground. It sounds easy for those in shape, but no one ever wins; very few make it to the 60-second mark. The best that I have seen was someone who came within six seconds of being a winner. The bar is simply rigged: it is not fixed but turns to work hard against you, and makes something that looks easy at first to be nigh impossible. Every day there are several of these games in operation along the 1-kilometer length of Khreshchatyk, and every day their operators find young male after young male who tries the challenge and fails. Perhaps some of the takers are naïve "country bumpkins" who have recently arrived in the capital. Business picks up with nightfall and increased alcohol consumption; the concessionaire makes good money to be sure.

I tell this story because I have seen how the police want their cut of this action, too. One sunny Saturday afternoon I see that there are two horizontal bar devices and their unhappy operators "imprisoned" behind a traffic control barricade off Khreshchatyk alongside the post office building. At first, three police officers are standing guard and then there are five. I decide to play dumb. I walk up, shoot a photograph, and turn to the policeman who looks to be in charge (conversation in Ukrainian):

Me:	What's going on here? Why are these men being held? I see these gymnastics devices all over Kyiv.
Police:	We are waiting for them to produce permits for their games.
Me:	You need a permit?
Police:	Of course. What business is it of yours?
Me:	I am not from here. I see these games everywhere. I am simply interested in your system. I am surprised that you need a permit. If I wanted to make a living on Khresh-chatyk, would I need to get a permit?
Police:	You know the answer full well. Why are you asking?
Me:	Why are you smiling?
Police:	Because I know that you know the answer full well.
Me:	How does one get a permit?
Police:	It's on the Internet. Go to the site of the City of Kyiv.
Me:	It must be a serious thing, this permit. There are five police officers here guarding these two men and their two devices. That's a lot!
Police:	(Just laughter)
Me:	Once when I was in Cambodia I saw something that looked like this. Only it was not about a permit. It was about paying bribes to the police. I am glad that it is different here.

Police:	(Now laughing loudly) Yes, this is not Cambodia. But I think that you know where you are.
Me:	I am just a foreigner, so I did not know about the permit system.
Police:	Yes, we have a permit system.

I then questioned him a bit more about "permits" for vendors, street musicians, and others. Another of the police officers had edged closer to listen in. As I spoke, I put the word for permit (*pozvolenya*) into finger quotes. He tried to get away by pretending that his phone had rung, but he knew to be polite to me. At one point, he even laughed at himself, after making the absurd comment that the reason for the protective barrier was to provide safety from any automobiles that might drive past. We both knew that we were standing well back from the street, against a building and behind a portico, and that on that day Khreshchatyk was a pedestrian zone that was closed to motor vehicles. I needed to be polite to him, too, as I was vulnerable at that particular time in not having my passport on me, so I thanked him for his time and disappeared into the crowd. But I kept watching. Someone came to one of the "imprisoned" game operators and handed him something. That person then signaled the police officer I had spoken to and the two of them stepped outside the perimeter for about 30 seconds, during which time he handed something to the police officer. It must have been the "permit," because the barricade was moved aside, the five police offers left, and the two released prisoners reclaimed their devices and returned to Khreshchatyk. I would not tell you this story if I did not know that it was an everyday occurrence.

In the same vein, I remember seeing a lineup of 10 to 15 elderly men and women vendors who would come regularly to sell clothing and various household items along a busy one-way subway pedestrian concourse that I used regularly when commuting to work in the mornings. They stood several feet apart on the same side of the walkway, and whenever one of them at the end saw police approaching, everyone would pack up instantly on signal and the entire group would disappear into the crowds. Their wares included women's clothing items such as sweaters or blouses on hangers, stockings and bras, and doodads for hair, as well as small mirrors, kitchen tools, and various toiletries. Every time I walked past as part of the commuting throng, I wonder who would buy a bra at such a time and place, and I never actually saw such a sale occur. I also wondered who among the morning commuters would step out of the moving tide to pick up a hand mirror or a vegetable grater on the way to work. Yet, the sellers returned day after day. On the days when I did not see them, I assumed that they had already been chased, and on the days when they were there, I always noticed how observant they were to the ends of the concourse, looking for approaching police. Eventually, I accepted that the items they sell are normal for areas where commuters pass, both in underground walkways and outside under the open sky, including men's and women's undergarments. Not everyone can afford to shop at Victoria's Secret, I began to understand.

I have special respect for those who make a living on the subway itself. There is a dour army of sad-looking sales agents that moves from car to car at station stops in order to renew pitches for the products that are offered for sale. Others who work the subway cars break into song or play a musical instrument for tips. The products that are sold range from batteries to maps of Kyiv, magnifying glasses, plastic passport covers, driving test manuals, folding fans for the sweaty, as well as various toys and other gadgets. One man bounced a plastic ball as he walked through the subway car, showing how it lit up in many colors with each impact. When another vendor demonstrated a toy helicopter that lifted on spring power from his hand into the air, I imagined that he was President Yanukovych heading for his beloved helipad. There was, in fact, a physical resemblance, and I wanted to comment to the stranger next to me but held back. My respect for the subway vendors is because they work so hard, moving all day long from car to car and then speaking up without embarrassment from amid the standing passengers as soon as the doors close to begin the ride to the next station. In a matter of seconds, they recount the advantages of the product that they are selling, note the amazingly low price, and ask who would like to buy. They speak in Russian or Ukrainian (no apparent pattern) and try hard to make a sale or two in the short time between stops. They never look prosperous or upbeat, are typically middle-aged or older, and make me think that they must be desperate for any honest work to take jobs such as this. Usually no one buys, but when one person does, then others often follow.

One subway seller made a lasting impression. I refer to my notes from November 9, 2010. He was young, about 20-22, was not dour like the others, and began his sales pitch just as the train cars doors closed for the start of the ride. He was selling a simple peeling device for potatoes, carrots, etc., and was carrying a supply of vegetables in a large plastic bag that he had at his side. As he spoke, he pulled out a carrot and began to peel it, showing how well the device works. I thought that it was funny to see a carrot being peeled on the subway and had to hold back laughter. A woman to his back was laughing, too. But elsewhere, people were minding their own business, not really looking at him, noses buried in their books or mobile phone screens, or looking dead ahead. Then in a flash he pulled out a cabbage and showed how well the device could make slaw. Carrot and cabbage parts flew into his bag. The price is only 20 hryvnia (about US$2.50), he said, and the device cannot be had in a store – not one this good. "Who wants one?" he asked? Soon we will be at the next station. To my surprise and to my admiration, in the next few seconds he sold five units to five different people. That's 100 hryvnia (US$12.50) in 3 minutes or less. The car slows to a stop, the door opens, and he switches to the next car. I was impressed. Surely, so many people could not be in need of a slaw maker; I assumed that buyers were rewarding him for his energy and efforts.

Being exploited is the norm for petty vendors. Comparatively few are in business for themselves, as Volodya the bathroom scale master apparently is, and most, including the popular carrot guy, actually work for a boss. In a society rife with corruption, it is hard to be your own business, because if you actually start making money, the crooks will muscle in. So, like the rabbits and tigers who struggle to get a fair cut of the take at the end of the day from their handler, there are poor people everywhere who report to a boss who takes the lion's share of proceeds. He, in turn, supplements the incomes of police officers on the beat from money that he does not pay his sellers, and some of that is passed upwards. Some bosses are big enough to live off the labors of not just a dozen teenagers in furry suits, but maybe dozens or hundreds of struggling underlings. The old lady who sells cigarettes by the pack or by the individual smoke from off an inverted cardboard box does not work for herself, but is one of many other such people who sit all day at some assigned crossroads of pedestrian traffic on behalf of some king of cigarettes who pays off authorities to monopolize that business. She needs to account for every cigarette with either money or unsold inventory. Once at about 11:00 p.m., I felt sorry for a stooped old woman selling flowers on the street, so I bought her entire inventory so that she at last could go home. What she did instead, I observed, was to go to a parked van not far away to take an even larger load of flowers from the flower boss, and then return right back to where she had been. Ice cream vendors also work for bosses (and are required to weigh ice cream as it is put into a cone), as do vendors of minutes for your mobile telephone, vendors of *kvas* (a popular nonalcoholic beverage made of fermented rye), and vendors of many other products. They are part of a chain that is "owned" by someone else. We conclude that once the nation worked for a screwed-up state; now many of its neediest citizens work for *biznesmeny* (businessmen) who screw them. The businessmen, in turn, are screwed by the foot soldiers of the state, the lowest police officers, whose job it is to collect the petty cash that accumulates and moves up and up the hierarchy.

8.4   The People's Markets

Kyiv has had public markets since well before Soviet times, and then since the fall of the Soviet Union and the rise of hard times for so many citizens, has seen the development of new markets where poor people work as vendors and other poor people shop for bargains. This pattern, too, is reminiscent of the Third World, and reflects a society with widening gaps between rich and poor and increasing spatial segregation. I call them people's markets because for so many citizens in Kyiv, literally tens of thousands of them, they are a source of livelihood, and for many tens of thousands more are a source of necessities at lower prices. The words "informal markets" also apply, although not necessarily to all examples of such markets because some of them are officially sanctioned and are, therefore, not quite informal. Those markets are more accurately simply "public markets." In Ukrainian, the word for market is *rynok* and the plural is *rynky*, and the words *stykhiynyi rynok* are the closest translation for informal market. Many of the sanctioned markets are in dedicated structures with roofs and can, therefore, be called covered markets, *krytii rynky* in Ukrainian.

There are various categories of people's markets, including: (1) those that are located in covered market structures that were erected in Soviet times or even earlier; (2) informal spillover markets from those "official" public markets; (3) periodic farmers' markets; (4) large, bazaarlike markets in residential zones and near Metro stations that have come under the private ownership of a landlord to whom vendors pay rent; (5) so-called *sekond-hend* (secondhand) markets that specialize in used clothing; (6) periodic flea markets; and (7) specialized markets such as the large market that sells both new and used books near the Petrivka Metro Station, and a pet market in the Kurenivka neighborhood that is named Ptychka after the sales of birds there. There is some overlap between these categories as well as differences within them, so this list of 1 to 7 is simply a rough guide.

As with the case of individual vendors, these markets are also vulnerable to displacement by redevelopment or other forces, and also face the additional costs of corruption and bribery from officials who insist on a piece of the proceeds, even if those proceeds are very small. In Kyiv, as I have seen as well in the Third World, people's markets have a precarious existence. This applies to informal flea markets where poor Kyivans gather to sell some of their possessions in order to raise money, as well as to markets that are large, popular, well-established, and well-known. They can all be made to close when someone else wants the land, or when other retailers, for example, those who pay rent to a shopping mall, use their influence to get rid of competition. Informal markets where the sellers refuse to leave have had a way of catching fire in Kyiv, much like in the case the flaming ghosts of Chapter 6, or have been shut by force by armed police.

As an example of how unstable it can be in Kyiv for business people at the bottom of the economic hierarchy, the popular Lukianivsky Market located in central Kyiv not far from heart of the city recently fell victim to raiders who simply took the place for themselves during an ownership dispute. Specifically, the market was reported to have been "seized" on May 20, 2012, by some 300 "unknown young people" who simply told the vendors to leave and then turned off the market's utilities. Police are said to have looked the other way, and officials in City Hall were unresponsive except for words that sounded empty. A spokesman for stall operators explained it this way: "Raiders from Kvitkova Haliavyna Ltd. aren't letting us work calmly – they're threatening us by saying 'get out of here, take your stuff away, we want to come and change the management.' They don't tell us what they want to do, they just want to seize it [the market]" (Interfax-Ukraine, 2012a). The land will almost certainly be put to other uses soon, perhaps even for construction of a "monster," and the people who worked there are simply out of luck.

Some of Kyiv's public markers were established decades ago in order to sell food products, and continued through Soviet times to supplement what was sold at government stores with products from private plots on collective farms and dacha allotments. With time, such markets expanded to include various black market and imported goods such as clothing and household items in addition to meat, fish, produce, bread, and dairy products. Some of the markets were in specially built structures for such trade and actually have a fairly long history, while others have a more spontaneous look to them, like a bazaar with narrow lanes and cubby holes for business. Perhaps the best known of Kyiv's markets is the picturesque Bessarbskyi Market, popularly called "Bessarabka," at the end of Khreshchatyk across the street from "Bessarabian Lenin." It predates the Soviet period and was constructed in 1910-1912 as a market for food that was brought in from the Russian czarist region of Bessarabia in the south of Ukraine. It still has a bit of an ethnic and regional flavor, as well as architectural charm from a century ago, and is a popular photo stop for tourists to the city. It is not an obvious "landscape of struggle," although it may well be that many tenant-vendors do not make a strong living from their work, as rents are high and the potential numbers of shoppers has declined with changeover of the surrounding area from residential to commercial land uses.

Another landmark is the Zhytnyi Rynok (Rye Market) at the edge of Podil. Its origins are linked to a local historic church and monastery and go back several centuries, but the market now has a retro-Soviet look, as since 1980 it has been housed in a covered structure adorned on the outside with enormous socialist realist representations of historic scenes, landscapes, and famous faces from around Ukraine and the former USSR. The interior has orderly rows of vendor tables arranged by product type where shoppers can easily compare one seller's cuts of meat or tomatoes to those offered by another, and an upper mezzanine level that specializes in the sale of clothing. Outside this market, the look is more chaotic, as still more sellers of food items, household goods, and other products have crowded as close as they can to the building, and compete with one another and against the sellers inside for customers. Here we do get images of struggle, as in the case of old women who sit apparently all day long offering no more for sale than a meager inventory of potatoes, radishes, or raspberries, etc. Sometimes they plead with passersby to make a purchase.

On Saturdays there are many more of these sellers, and they expand the marketplace to the walkways and grassy area between opposing lanes of traffic along the wide street Nizhnyi Val. This is an example of a "periodic market" in Kyiv, of which there are many. Such markets are open only on particular days of the week or month such as on Saturdays, on "third Saturdays," or on every other Tuesday, along a designated street in a residential area or near a Metro stop. Neighbors know to schedule their purchasing accordingly. Such markets tend to specialize in fresh food, although other foods are sold as well, as are items of clothing and household goods. Many vendors follow a circuit of periodic markets, and sell their meat, eggs, honey, or inventory of socks or sunglasses at many locations over the course of a month. The vendors police themselves, if only informally, with respect to which vendor occupies which spot in the market and clean-up of the area at the end of the working day. "Tips" for local police are often managed centrally, that is, via a representative of the sellers as a group. Quite a few of these periodic markets have been at the same site on a regular basis for decades and seem stable. However, urban change and redevelopment have done away with others, or at least shifted them to new locations, and the possibility of market closure is always present. There is increasing upmarket redevelopment along Nizhnyi Val near Zhytnyi Rynok, and it would not be a surprise to see a reconfiguration of the outdoor market in the future if not outright closure. Such was the fate of a similar market called Sinnyi Rynok (Wheat Market) close to L'vivska Ploshcha (L'viv Square) near Kyiv's center. In addition to sellers of vegetables, bread, meat, and shoes, among other "basic" items, there was also a flea market with a reputation for unusual objects and a cast of Bohemian vendors, but the entire place was closed in 2004 and later demolished to make room for a new-style commercial center (Belorusets, 2010).

The situation is more precarious for other categories of markets. For instance, since the Soviet period, there has been an explosion of bazaars that specialize in sales of used clothing and other secondhand goods. They are popular with bargain hunters who look for just the right item, even a famous brand, at deeply discounted prices. Some of the goods originate as items that had been worn locally, but most of the inventory comes from abroad, and much of that had been donated by foreign charities with an interest in helping the poor. Foreign aid shipments, in turn, have a way of being hijacked by shady entrepreneurs who sell what they have taken instead of distributing it free, with the result that in cities and towns all over Ukraine (and in other poorer parts of Europe and other continents, too) there are booming "secondhand" markets where people know to go for used clothing in good condition and foreign cachet. In Kyiv, the biggest such markets have been at Shulyavska and Lisova (Figure 8.4). Both are names of Metro stations, with Shulyvaska being on the Right Bank near the huge Bilshovyk (Russian: Bolshevik) industrial complex that was once a key

Figure 8.4   **A view of a table at the secondhand market at Shulyavska before the market was burned down**

producer of machinery and armaments for the Soviet military, and Lisova on the Left Bank in a district where the expansive apartment complexes of the 1970s and 1980s end and the forests (*lisy*, hence "Lisova") outside Kyiv begin. There are also many secondhand sellers at Troyeshchyna Market, Kyiv's largest public market, also on the Left Bank. It has a reputation much wider than just secondhand goods, and during its peak in the late 1990s and at the turn of the millennium, had as many as 5,000 stalls and employed as many as 20,000 Kyivans (Riaboshapka, 1998, p. 4; and Ruble, 2003, p. 145).

All of these places and other secondhand outlets in the city have been periodically raided by authorities, with goods being confiscated by police. If the goods are ever seen again, it is at another market where the inventory is resold after it had been purchased from corrupt officials. The large secondhand section of the Shulyavska Market burned down at least five times from the start of 2006 through April 2007 (Boksha et al., 2010, p. 80), and then again on March 20, 2012, with the causes never resolved. However, workers at the market are convinced that the fires were started deliberately to drive them out of business and free up the land. The market was closed altogether by police on March 16, 2012 (Tuchynska, 2012a). Hundreds of workers were displaced as a result, many of them immigrants from West Africa and other foreign regions. When questioned, Kyiv's municipal officials cited structural problems with the highway bridge above which the Shulyavska Market had developed as a reason for closing the market. They are almost certainly accurate in their assessment of a bridge that, even to my untrained eye, looks to be in need of repair, but there are infrastructure hazards galore in Kyiv and elsewhere in the country and there seems to be no explanation as to why this particular deficiency caught engineers' attention.

Many reasons are given for officialdom's constant war with the secondhand markets in general. "Official" reasons have included that the markets lacked required permits, that used clothing is said to be unsanitary, that a bad image of Ukraine is presented when citizens wear cast-offs from other countries, and that the goods being sold had found their way to the market through less than honorable means. On the other hand, vendors at these markets, for whom livelihoods are at stake, as well as purchasers, for whom the markets provide much reduced prices, have protested, saying that the true reasons for anti-secondhand campaigns are (1) to support the formal retailing sector and Ukraine's lobby of struggling clothing manufacturers; (2) that someone else wants the land; and (3) that police and other officials are not satisfied with their cuts of market income. It is also said that at least some secondhand markets (and other categories of markets, too) are controlled by mobster owners, allegedly foreigners from the Caucusus, Russia, or Israel, who operate independently and pay for the privilege in taxes or bribes. Indeed, vendors speak poorly of their landlords, saying that they are extortive, but then fear being evicted should the landlord be able to identify the source of criticism.

Racism is also a factor in the precarious existence of some markets. At the Troyeshchyna Market, for example, where there have been a reported 500 workers from Afghanistan, "several hundred from Pakistan," more than 120 from Bangladesh, and "many from China and other countries," police have routinely conducted roundups of vendors and hauled them away in buses to detention centers even though many of them were Ukrainian citizens or applicants for citizenship. While in lockup, they filled out endless forms and faced other harassment until they paid the required bribes. In a series of such raids in 2010, it was reported that a bribe of 50 hryvnia (about US$6) would move a detainee ahead of others in the processing queue, while double that amount would buy one's release. Some vendors have been arrested multiple times, only to be released each time by a judge who understood that the arrest was nothing more than a shakedown attempt by police. At first, a police official explained to news reporters that such actions were necessary because "amid entrepreneurs who work legally, illegal immigrants often hide," but then when no illegal immigrants were found in the operation, he modified his explanation: "Even if they are citizens of Ukraine, what positive contribution are they making to this country? None. They ... sell goods of bad quality" (Tuchynska, 2010).

I saw similar disdain for non-European ethnics at the Shulyavska Market before it closed. As mentioned previously, a sizable fraction of the approximately 350 vendors there are of African origin, especially from Nigeria (Figure 8.5).[50] Some of them had come to Ukraine to be students, or to Ukraine via Russia as students, and were now university graduates without jobs other than at the market. A number of Africans dealt in secondhand goods, but most stall operators sold new clothing, especially shoes, jackets, and hip-hop fashion. One day, I was interviewing "Michael," a Nigerian "boss" among the African vendors, who had just begun telling me some details about police racism and corruption when there was a commotion nearby in the aisles between stalls. "There, look," he said in English, "That is exactly what I am talking about! Bastards!" I saw that two uniformed police officers and a security guard for Shulyavska Market that I had made note of before were manhandling an African vendor, and taking him away as he protested. "What is going on?" I asked, "Why is he being arrested?" "Oh, it's

---

50   For an excellent paper about discrimination against African migrants in the post-Soviet world, see the case study of St. Petersburg by Svetlana Boltovskaya (2011).

not an arrest. He's done nothing. They are harassing him for money, and he refuses to pay." I had a camera with me and asked if I could shoot pictures. Michael encouraged me to do so if I dared, and as the gathering crowd of Africans saw me, they parted so that I could have a clearer shot. I had just started to do well when one of the policemen saw what I was doing and began shouting at me. He and his compatriots rushed to Michael's stall to confront me. "Give me the camera," one of them demanded (in Russian). I was about to make a case for why I would not give him the camera when the police were distracted by a new commotion, this one a ruse by African vendors, in the aisle outside. As they looked away from me, an African I did not know said in English "Quick, give me the camera." Instinctively, I tossed it to him across the stall, and then it was gone. When the police returned their attention to me seconds later, they demanded the camera again. Michael whispered to me in English that I never had a camera, and that is how I replied to the police, again and again, "What camera? There is no camera. I have no camera," I pleaded. Before long, as many as ten other police officers arrived and began a search of the market, not just Michael's stall amid the shoes and jeans that he was selling, but also neighboring stalls up and down the aisle and in next aisles. "If you give us the camera, we will simply delete the pictures. But if

Figure 8.5 African vendors and their merchandise in the under-highway section of Shulyavska Market

we find it on our own, we will either smash it or steal it," is how my main interrogator put it to me. I kept denying that I ever had a camera.

How did it end? Although they never asked for identification or even my name, I think that my being a white American scared the police off. After about a half-hour of questions and searching, they simply left. The African vendor who had been harassed for money was among those who remained after the commotion died down; he thanked me for intervening. Michael told me that I was now one of them, and that I was welcome at the market any time. As a "chief" among the vendors, he gave me his blessing to study the market and interview his compatriots. He told me not to worry about my camera and that I would get it back. Sure enough, about an hour after the police had dispersed, Michael and other African vendors encircled me and walked me back to the Shulyavska Metro Station, with Michael in telephone communication with someone who was walking ahead as lookout. When we reached the turnstile of the subway, one of my escorts reached into his bag and handed me the camera. Michael told me to come back, but not for at least a week to make sure that the incident was truly over. I looked at my photos on the subway ride home. Everything was just right with my camera. A couple shots of the police harassment turned to be quite good in quality, but I decided to not print them to avoid trouble for the vendors who are shown, including "Matthew," the individual who was the object of police attention at the start of the incident. Not long after all this the market was shut, so I lost the place as a venue for research. The feelings of friendship, however, remain.[51]

8.5   The Scourge of Prejudice

Racism is indeed a fact of life in Kyiv, as are other prejudices (Starr, 2010). Most Ukrainians are wonderful people and are warm to others, just like any other ethnic group or nationality, but among them there are those who are unacceptably ignorant and bigoted, and a few who would do violence to people of other races or religions, to sexual minorities, and to women. As we have seen with respect to workers of color in the markets of Troyeshchyna and Shulyavska, police can be part of the problem rather than a source of help

---

51   Ironically, it is because of a camera incident that I met Michael in the first place. I had wanted to find the boss of the market and did so by arriving one day and shooting photographs without permission. An African challenged me and said to follow him. He took me to Michael and reported with concern that I had been taking pictures of the market. When Michael asked me why, I reported that he was welcome to delete them and that I simply wanted to meet him because I want to learn about the market and its people. Obviously, the strategy worked.

or protection, perhaps routinely so. Furthermore, the legal system often fails to protect women from violence or to bring even rapists and killers to justice. Racism, sexism, classism, homophobia, and other prejudices (e.g., against ex-convicts) are found in probably every society, and Ukraine or Kyiv are not any worse than much of the rest of the world in this regard. Nevertheless, it is necessary for us to consider these problems in Kyiv in order to present a balanced view of society, as well as to acknowledge that for a great many residents of Ukraine (and for foreign visitors, too) there are both hazards in daily life and additional obstacles to long-term success in Ukraine that stem from prejudices. The long history of strained relations between Ukrainians and their Jewish neighbors (Brandon and Lower, eds., 2010; Meir, 2010; Reid, 2000, pp. 139-168) is another reason to underscore that prejudice has been a persistent scourge in Ukraine. However, I also point out that it has been only a little more than 20 years since Ukraine became an independent country, and that prior to then, Ukrainians themselves were targeted as victims of discrimination and ethnic violence on their own lands, not the least of which were the Holodomor and Russian and Polish campaigns against usage of the Ukrainian language (Reid, 2000, pp. 112-138; Subtelny, 1988; Yekelchyk, 2007). That is, the hatred has been directed against Ukrainians, too.

Soon after I came to Kyiv to start this book, I encountered a middle-aged man with dark skin sitting at the edge of Independence Square in a puddle of his own blood. His equally dark-skinned companion was pleading in English for help. It was about 10 a.m. and they were literally sitting in the same light that bathed the Independence Monument. They were visitors from Pakistan who had arrived earlier that day for an academic conference, and had just walked from their hotel nearby for a first look at the attractions of the city when they were jumped by some 8 to 10 young thugs and were beaten. There was no robbery, only a thorough beating and kicking, and some shouting at them that the victims did not understand. The victim who was not in a daze had been trying to get help for his bloodied friend for some minutes, he said, but people simply scattered as he called to them. That was my experience, too, even as I asked in Ukrainian for someone to call the police and an ambulance. Eventually, help did come, but for both ambulance and police car, the help was slow and the drivers made sure to park carefully in a good spot and turn off the headlights before approaching the victims. A first question from the police was whether the man who was bleeding had done something to provoke the attack.[52]

52   This is my own account of the incident as I witnessed it personally. Additional information was reported in Grushenko (2011).

Other incidents have been reported against people of African origin, Middle Easterners, and other foreigners, as well as against Jews and Jewish landmarks, as anti-Semitism in Ukraine, long a scourge, is reported to be on the rise (Brym, 1994; Mirsky, 1994; Rudling, 2006). Because of the history of anti-Semitism in the country (Bartov, 2007; Carynnyk, 2011; Gross, 2001; Himka, 2011; Potichnyj and Aster, eds., 1990; Redlich, 2002), watchful Jews worldwide are alarmed, and worry that Ukraine is once again becoming a dangerous place. For example, the newspaper *Jerusalem Post* has recently published an editorial entitled "Hatred in Ukraine" that posits that "little has changed" in the country over the decades with respect to anti-Semitism, and argues that hatred of Jews is once more "vulgar and in-your-face – as it was before the Soviets temporarily held the genie [of hatred] in the bottle" (Jerusalem Post, 2012).[53] With respect to Kyiv, the article focuses on the reported beating of Alexander (Aron) Goncharov, a 25-year-old yeshiva student who was apparently attacked by neo-Nazi thugs after he left the Brodsky Synagogue on the night of April 8, 2012. Likewise, the New York-based *Jewish Daily Forward* has also reported about anti-Semitism in Ukraine, although it appears open to the possibility that one or more of the most virulent recent attacks against Jews, including the alleged attack against Goncharov, may not actually have been motivated by religious or ethnic bigotry. Still, as one of that newspaper's Jewish informants, the principal of a Jewish school in Bila Tserkva, a medium-sized town about 80 kilometers (50 miles) south of Kyiv that has long and rich history of Jewish settlement, explained, "Anyone who says there is no anti-Semitism [in Ukraine] is living with their eyes closed."[54] Among other evidence, there is documented vandalism against Jewish cemeteries and synagogues, and common usage of the offensive word *zhyd* (Yid) when referring to Jews, especially in western Ukraine where relations between Ukrainians and Jews have historically been most strained.[55]

53   The charges of "hatred in Ukraine" might well be true, which is why I write about them here, but it is also true that the article could have been entitled "Hatred *of* Ukraine," because that is how it reads: Ukraine, Ukrainians, and especially western Ukrainians are all painted unfairly as murderous anti-Semites with a broad, black-smearing brush that oozes with undiscriminating hatred.

54   See Berger (2012). The article refers to the name of the town as Belaya Tserkov, the Russian name. Usage of outdated Russian spellings reflects the usage that Russian-speaking émigrés living in the United States are more familiar with, but is also said to reflect a certain antipathy to things Ukrainian.

55   This is not the place for a detailed account of anti-Semitism in Ukraine or of Ukrainian-Jewish relations. However, it might help to consider the succinct summary of Ukrainian-Jewish relations by Orest Subtelny in his widely praised *Ukraine: A History* (1988):

It may be that the recent rise of the political party Svoboda (Freedom) is also a manifestation of Ukraine's scourge of prejudice. Led by a charismatic and talented speaker, Oleh Tyahnybok, who insists that the movement is pro-Ukraine only and not racist or prejudiced against any group, the party, which has its origins in western Ukraine, has recently won its first seats in the Verkhovna Rada and, until recently, seems to be gaining in popularity as an opposition alternative to the Party of Regions. However, critics say that Svoboda is racist and anti-Semitic, and equate its brand of nationalism with fascism and collaboration by western Ukrainians with the Nazis in World War II. The Jewish media sources cited earlier are most emphatically alarmed about Svoboda's rise. The party was founded in 1991 as the "Social-National Party of Ukraine," and until 2003 used as a logo a swastika-like symbol that was explained as an interlocking of the capital letters I and N (without serifs) standing for the Idea of Nation. The symbol was commonly seen as being neo-Nazi and so the logo was officially dropped. In 2004, the name of the party was changed as well (formal name: All-Ukrainian Union "Svoboda") in a further attempt to separate itself, at least for public consumption, from the neo-Nazi and anti-Russian elements that it had come to be associated with. Time will tell exactly what Svoboda is, but for now I conclude that there is reason to be wary because creepy people with creepy placards and banners, including the spooky I/N symbol, do show up in numbers at Svoboda rallies and marches.

There is also the issue of homophobia. I am disappointed to report that a person needs to be either exceedingly brave or simply foolish to be openly gay or lesbian in Kyiv (and even more so elsewhere in Ukraine), as harassment is common and even routine, and unprovoked beatings of LGBT people[56] take place all too frequently (Matiukhina, 2012). A prominent LGBT activist in Kyiv told me that a first step when planning any event is about security to make sure that "right-wing thugs" (such as those associated with Svoboda) do not show up and start beating people. Usually, this involves

[T]he relationship between Ukrainian and Jews was not – nor could it hardly have been – a friendly one. For centuries, the two peoples found themselves in structurally antagonistic (yet mutually dependent) positions. To the Jew, a Ukrainian represented the backward, ignorant village; to a Ukrainian, a Jew epitomized the foreign, exploitative city that bought his produce cheaply and sold farm goods dearly. Ukrainian peasants feared Russian officials and hated Polish landlords; Jews, for want of other means for making a living, often acted as their representatives or middlemen. Culturally, the Jews and Ukrainians had little in common, and their religions only widened the gaps between them. (pp. 277-278)

Also see the article "Ukrainians and Jews and Ukrainians and Jews..." in Alexander Motyl's always interesting blog (2011b).

56 Lesbian, gay, bisexual, and transgender.

maintaining secrecy about the exact place and time of the event until soon before it takes place, and dissemination of information via targeted channels such as email lists and SMS messages. They might also maintain a lookout on the street to warn of the possible arrival of thugs. But thugs do arrive nevertheless and beat gays, typically with impunity.

The story of a Gay Pride parade that was planned for central Kyiv on May 20, 2012, is illustrative. Called KyivPride 2012, the "coming out" event was to be the first of its kind in Kyiv, and was purposefully planned for a date close to the start of the Euro 2012 football tournament when European eyes would be on the country. Organizers believed that it might be safer for participants to march while Europe was watching and also that Kyiv authorities would give them permission to march for the same reason. Permission they got, as homosexuality is legal in Ukraine (as of 1991) and discrimination against homosexuals is illegal, but the outcry against the event was instantaneous and scary. There were two prominent anti-gay protests in the city before the event, one on April 27 in front of the office building of the president of Ukraine and the other on May 10 at the large plaza in front of St. Michael's Church in the heart of historic Kyiv. As reported by the Religious Information Service of Ukraine, groups who called themselves the "Parents' Committee" and "Youth for Healthy Life" were in the forefront with placards reading "No to Sodomite Sin" and "Homosexuality = AIDS" (RISU, 2012). Political leaders and clergy also weighed in with opposition. The comments of Communist Party of Ukraine parliamentarian Yevhen Tsarkov are representative of commonly held attitudes: "Our society is traditional and just does not tolerate homosexuality. If some people are suffering from the mental illness of homosexuality, they should not display it in public and promote it to children" (Tuchynska, 2012b). After threats of violence against the marchers mounted on the Internet along with calls for "tough men" to break up the event, KyivPride 2012 was called off.[57] This was the advice that the police gave to the organizers of the event instead of a promise to beef up protection. But even still, there was violence against gays, as the "tough men" who showed up just in case found some march officials in conversation with members of the news media and attacked them even with cameras rolling. The beating and stomping of Sviatoslav Sheremet, head of the Gay Forum in Ukraine, by a gang of vicious toughs hiding behind masked faces and baseball caps is evident for all to see (Tuchynska, 2012b).[58] Then, about

57   The first ever Gay Pride parade in Kyiv was held a year later on May 25, 2013. Because of the threat of violence, it was a small event.

58   Sheremet was bloodied but was not seriously injured. No one was arrested for the attack.

a full month later on June 22, 2012, Taras Karasiichuk, the main organizer of KyivPride 2012, was attacked with no warning as he walked at night from the Metro station to his apartment by a masked man who asked if he was a "fag" (*pidor* in Russian) and then kicked him in the head and jaw before fleeing (Human Rights Watch 2012). Months later, during a Human Rights Day march in the center of Kyiv on December 8, 2012, gay marchers were attacked, beaten, and sprayed with tear gas by tough young men from the Svoboda political party, which boasted on its website two days later that "thanks to the five nationalists [who conducted the attack], the Sabbath of 50 perverts was broken up" (Tuchynska, 2012c; 2012d).

With this as backdrop, it should not be surprising to learn that social opportunities and nightlife for gays in Kyiv are quite different from those in many other European capitals. Whereas other cities have many LGBT institutions and an open LGBT nightlife, as well as residential neighborhoods that are identified as being heavily gay, Kyiv has very few places that are known openly as gay or lesbian spots and no areas in the city that gays can call their own or even regard as a safe zone. Rainbow flags are almost nonexistent, and there are almost no symbols on the doors of cafés, pubs, and other business establishments that signal a gay-friendly environment. Displays along these lines would invite vandalism to property and physical harm to proprietors and clients. The gay night spots that do exist operate more or less clandestinely, although there are three or four places that get mentioned fairly prominently as gay bars or clubs when doing an Internet search about gay Kyiv. Some places have a "LGBT night" on a given day of the week, while in other cases the venues where gays gather rotate from place to place so as to not offer a fixed target. LGBT people typically dress like everyone else in the city so as to keep a low profile, but when they do dress differently or know that they can be identified in some other way as a sexual minority, they are especially careful about their surroundings and keep an eye open for possible trouble.[59]

8.6   Roma

Kyiv has many thousands of Roma people in its population. How many thousands is anyone's guess, as I have heard wildly ranging estimates from about 5,000 to 15,000 to 40,000 and maybe even more. The wide range reflects the fact that little is known about this population in general and that reliable

---

59   For an engaging parallel discussion of lesbian spaces in St. Petersburg, see Sarajeva (2010).

statistics are lacking. In fact, even the numbers given here are uncertain, as I simply repeat them from a source that does not explain their origin and that may or may not be accurate (Chekmenov, 2011). In Kyiv, in Ukraine, in other European countries and elsewhere, Roma or Romani people as they are often called nowadays,[60] or Gypsies as they were commonly called in the past, are prominent minorities, more so than numbers alone would dictate, and are at or near the bottom economically in whichever country they live. In Ukrainian they are called *tsyhany*. They are targets for inordinate prejudice and discrimination, but are also seen, perhaps through lenses of prejudice, as people who willingly reject sincere offers of help and chances for full integration into society. Their history is long and complicated, has taken them in various migrations across a wide map, and has included attempted extermination in the Holocaust and forced expulsions from communities, cities, and even entire countries. This is not the place to repeat the story of the various people who are collectively known as Roma, and readers are steered instead to fine studies such as those by Fonseca (1995), Hancock (2002), and Liégeois (1983). It is appropriate, however, to say at least a little about Roma in Ukraine and their place in Kyiv.

Kyiv, like most other Ukrainian cities, has only a very small percentage of the population that is Roma (5,000 to 15,000 of 2.8 million is about 0.02 to 0.05 percent; 40,000 is about 1.4 percent). Even in Uzhorod, a Ukrainian city on the border with Slovakia and near the border with Hungary that is said to have a high concentration of Roma population, their percentage is only about 1.5 percent of the total. In Ukraine as a whole, the Roma population is 47,587 as counted in the census of 2001 (0.01 percent of the population), although estimates say that their actual numbers are closer to 400,000. Whatever their number, Roma are more visible than population totals because they stand out by how they dress and comport themselves, because they are often seen in groups rather than individually or simply in pairs, and because their habits and occupations often bring them to urban centers where visibility is maximized. Paradoxically, at the same time, many Roma live isolated from the rest of society, sometimes in remote camps in forests at the margins of cities. Most speak one or another of the dialects of Romani among themselves rather than Ukrainian or another national tongue, and may or may not know the national language. Many of their children do not attend school by choice of the parents or ethnic habit, which isolates the minority all the more even as it stands out for its differentness.

60   The two words are often used interchangeably as synonyms, although technically Roma are a subgroup of Romani. There is considerable variety within Roma and Romani populations.

In Kyiv, Roma are seen daily in the center of the city, especially along Khreshchatyk and some side streets, where they work as beggars and petty vendors. They tend to be the same people over and over again, and are part of a clan that is transported almost daily from an outlying camp to work all day and often deep into the night among the passersby in the city center. Roma are also said to engage in crimes such as theft and pickpocketing, but I have never seen this personally and have not seen data to support such a contention. In my experience, the worst is perhaps pretending to be more needy than is actually the case, as in the case of a "pregnant" beggar who is mysteriously not pregnant when seen later, and then suddenly pregnant again when kneeling on the sidewalks the next day and asking for handouts. Also, there are instances of child labor among Roma that could be classified as crimes, because Roma children are often seen begging or working long hours as vendors at very young ages. Other Roma are sometimes visible in the center of the city as musicians – sometimes as street musicians who work for tips and other times as hired acts in popular live music venues where customers pay an admission charge and for food and drinks. Thus, for many Roma the urban center is a resource for making a living. I can't know this for sure, but it is also said, and seems plausible, that the right to work in the center is something that was negotiated by one or more clan heads or Roma barons with city officials who receive payments in return. Other Roma groups are not part of the deal and do not work this turf. The barons make money off all the men, women, and children who work under them, and can become exceedingly wealthy. Apparently, some barons also operate narcotics businesses. Among the attractions of the city center for Roma, in addition to a higher density of passersby, is the presence of many foreigners. They are more inclined to give than the local population, if only because they are less aware of beggars' scams. It is not my role to undermine anyone's way of making a living, but honestly it seems that some of the most pathetic and most poor-looking Roma beggars are simply actors that Ukrainians are wise to and that foreign visitors feel sorry for.

Although there are Roma leaders who own businesses and live in luxury off the labor of their underlings, as well as professional thieves and beggars among Roma for whom honest labor is something foreign, there are also many Roma who work extremely hard at physical jobs and struggle to make a living in the face of a wider society that does not give them an honest chance. It is a complicated topic to discuss job discrimination against Roma, because one reason that not many hold steady jobs is because not many want such jobs, preferring to be independent without a boss and without scheduled hours for work. On the other hand, there is prejudice against

Roma as well and widespread assumptions that they are not willing to work, so the only alternatives are to work independently. In Kyiv as elsewhere in Europe, many Roma make a living as scrap collectors, particularly of metal (Figure 8.6). They haul it from where old buildings are being demolished, rusted factories, trash bins, and other sources, and sell it to recycling companies. I have seen numerous instances in which a strong Roma man is carrying a load of metal on his back or in a cart of some sort, and heads with his treasure into the forest. In some cases he is accompanied by a pregnant wife, so the image is one of a young couple working hard to make a living.

Roma camps sometimes have sizable piles of rusted and twisted metal that await truck transport for sale. Those same camps are also known to have terrible housing conditions that are sometimes nothing more than plywood or cardboard, or a rusted auto body, and essentially no running water and no sanitary facilities. They are squatters' camps on public land, and are often cleared by authorities against residents' protests on grounds of public health. There are also quite a few instances where Roma camps have been set on fire, presumably by racist neighbors who want the Roma to leave. In fact, there are reports that some such fires are started by the police on behalf of neighbors, or that police simply look on when a fire does take place and Roma scramble to retrieve possessions (TSN, 2012). Because of these and other experiences over a long history, Roma tend to be mistrustful

Figure 8.6   A Roma husband-and-wife team of metal scrap collectors at work

of people outside their communities and can seem insular. They are often portrayed in the media as impossible to assimilate into society (Basarab, 2010; Lazareva, 2010; Zavhorodnya, 2010), and as a subculture of scammers, liars, and thieves (Chekmenov, 2011). Perfect strangers sometimes shout unprovoked insults at them and yell that they should go away, so the Roma draw inward and tighten their defenses. The circle is vicious, to be sure. However, also to be sure, I know personally that Roma can be warm and welcoming once initial suspicions have passed, and are actually pleased that an outsider takes an interest. My own experiences with Roma, both in the city as along Khreshchatyk, and in and near the forests at Kyiv's margins have been normal and positive. Being introduced by someone the Roma trust was especially helpful.

9 "Suburbia"

9.1 The Residential Ring

I am not the first urbanist to write a book about a city and focus disproportionately on a small area in the historic center at the expense of a vast outer ring of urban development. The center always draws those who love cities, has more history, more variety, and more action per unit area, and disproportionately distinguishes the city from other cities. But the zones beyond the center are important, too, and we now turn to a profile of Kyiv's "residential ring" and its changes in post-Soviet time (Kravets and Sovsun, 2012; Skubytska, 2012; Tyshchenko, 2012b). I write "suburbia" in quotations because not all of the places that we will discuss here are actually beyond Kyiv's municipal limits. A great many of Kyiv's bedroom zones (*spalni raiony*) are well within the city.

We can think of Kyiv as essentially two residential zones: (1) a central core in which the majority of dwellings are older apartment structures such as those from the late 19th and early 20th centuries, but within which many new tall, modern residential structures are being built; and (2) an expansive outer zone of newer apartment buildings, most generally taller than the older ones in the core, that is the ring of "bedroom suburbs" around the city. Another fair generalization is to say that much of the development of the outer zone began after World War II as a response to the housing shortages that were caused by wartime damage in the city and postwar rural-to-urban migration. Construction was stepped up in the 1970s and 1980s in connection with the Soviet government's efforts to ease the housing crisis that was exacerbated with extra-rapid population growth and industrialization, and to improve the quality of urban housing. The majority of these buildings are in planned *mikroraion* developments that characterize Soviet city planning. These neighborhood units were all pretty much the same, not just across Kyiv but also within Soviet urban space more generally, as were the individual apartment structures and the individual apartments.

The most fundamental change in the housing landscape is the shift from state ownership of most housing to the private sector, and the concomitant emergence of a society that is increasingly one of home and apartment owners as opposed to tenants. Most Soviet-built apartment complexes still remain, but the vast majority of units is now in private hands, although they might be rented to tenants. Indeed, it became common for Kyivans to have acquired an apartment from the state when that was first being done at extremely favorable terms, but then to rent it and live elsewhere. Many landlords reside abroad. A great number of the older structures are in poor condition, particularly common areas such as mail rooms, elevators, and lower stairways in buildings, with many renters living in crowded, old-fashioned, and poorly equipped apartments (Ryabchuk, 2010). Some buildings are actually unsafe. There have been substantial renovations within many buildings by apartment owners who have transformed small, drab Soviet apartments into sprawling and luxurious spaces by purchasing neighboring units. In addition, there has been a boom of construction of new market-based housing since the Soviet period, most often in buildings that are taller than the Soviet six-story structures nearby, a little sleeker looking, and better equipped with respect to amenities, both common and those within individual apartments. Central air-conditioning, however, is a rarity in even top-end buildings, and their exteriors are marked with a patchwork of cooling units protruding from windows and through openings that have been cut through masonry. Many of the newer buildings fill vacant spaces between previous residential structures, while others are in new clusters of residential towers at the edges of existing urbanization. Although they might offer better housing than older structures, there are often complaints that the new structures have intruded without compensation or plan onto existing neighborhood facilities, and add unfairly to demands on everything from spaces for children in schools and playgrounds to flows of traffic and places to park, as well as infrastructure for water provision and sewerage. Such "socially irresponsible development," as it has been called, has also infringed on people's views from windows and balconies and access to direct sunlight without consultation or compensation.

It is mostly the newly built places that Kyivans are told to buy now and pay for later, and see advertised most often as hallmarks of a better life. Often the residential lifestyle that is packaged in the ads is represented as the "European Dream" or a "new standard in European living." Such terminology helps potential buyers to distance themselves in their self-conceptions from the poor housing standards of the wrong side of the Iron Curtain from which they hail. Everything "European" is good: European kitchen cabinets, European toilets and faucets, European hot water heaters, and the amazing furniture and goods that are sold in that amazing blue-and-yellow logo "European" (Swedish) store, IKEA. Although the example is not about housing, I was recently amused to see a small kiosk in a working-class housing district that offered "European fashions from Poland and Turkey," while the women's wear shop in the kiosk next door blared on its sign that it offered Ukrainian prices. In keeping with the observations above about advertising for new automobiles among pedestrians and bus passengers, there is also a push to advertise new housing specifically to commuters to and from work. I saw this in Japan, too, where commuters were fed a steady diet at train and subway stations for cars and better housing to be bought on credit. In Kyiv, as I have observed in Tokyo, once cold-looking pedestrian walkways in the underground system have been transformed into virtual walks through bright landscapes of new housing developments and park-like greenery, with exhortations for trudging commuters to contact the development companies or real estate agencies in charge. Another favorite example is the many *marshrutkas* that have been transformed into roving billboards on all sides for new lifestyles in new housing. A specific example is seen in Figure 9.1: An attractive and positively beaming family of four points happily at a rendition of a new high-rise housing complex beneath the printed exclamation *Rozpochny evropeyske zhyttya!* (Start Living like a European!).

In addition to planned clusters of apartment buildings, the residential ring around Kyiv also includes a second type of housing landscape, one of

Figure 9.1   A minibus (*marshrutka*) decorated with an advertisement for "Comfort Town," a new housing development in Kyiv's residential ring. The text reads "Start Living like a European!"

sizable clusters of small single homes (*osobnyaky*). Many of these areas are vestiges of old pre-urban villages on the outskirts of Kyiv that have since been swallowed up by municipal limits and have become incorporated within the city. They are not all the same, and within any one village area, houses differ one from the other in design, size, and aspect. In general, however, during Soviet times the houses were small, mostly single-story, and on generally equal-sized plots of ground that were big enough for some outbuildings, a small vegetable plot, some fruit trees, and room for a cow, pigs, goats, or some chickens, in addition to the main house. Individual allotments were fenced, with the front fence and gate along the narrow dirt road often being sturdier and somewhat decorative. Quite a few such villages were swallowed up by the expanding city and no longer exist except in the names of the housing massifs that replaced them. Some of these places were previously important as a source of fresh farm products for the urban market.

Another landscape of single homes in Kyiv is that of the dachas (small country homes). While these getaway places for city residents are usually located some distance from the urban area, such districts also exist within Kyiv's limits, even within sight of the main landmarks of the city center. Their land plots are generally smaller, typically 6/100 of a hectare (approximately 0.15 acres), and were arranged in many cases in straight lines along dirt roads that were laid out in a planned grid. With time, quite a few dachas have been transformed by owners into year-round housing, so dacha territories are to be counted now as part of wider residential landscape. The biggest such area is the Nyzhni Sovky dacha allotments in Left Bank Kyiv along the Dnipro just downstream from the center of the city. It contains several thousand individual houses, and has a geographical area that is larger than some of Kyiv's ten administrative districts (*raiony*). Also on the same side of the river but in the upstream part of the city is Rusnivski Sady. This zone also has more than 1,000 houses. The Berkovets dacha area in the far northwest is the largest dacha zone in Kyiv on the Right Bank. In all three of these cases, the dachas were once outside the city but then became part of Kyiv when city limits were redrawn.

Both the old villages and the zones of intra-urban dachas also have changed greatly since the Soviet period and are also part of a new, emerging postsocialist residential landscape. What stands out the most here is the replacement of small, simple homes with residential structures that are much larger. Often the construction follows original property lines, in which case the new building fills the yard except perhaps for space to park a car or cars, while in other instances the construction spans adjacent properties as in the case of apartment renovation after owners acquired the apartments of neighbors. What also stands out is the ostentatious nature of many of these new homes. These are McMansions Ukrainian-style, or perhaps Moscow-style, as such architecture is quite common among the nouveaux riches in the Russian capital, and are adorned with the same kinds of turrets and towers and castlelike crenellations that we saw in that "strange new neighborhood of Vozdvyzhenka." As opposed to more neighborly design of the houses and gardens that they replace, these new suburban single mansions hide behind high walls and solid gates, and are secured as well by CCTV cameras and signs that warn of large, angry dogs. One sign says "Angry Dog, Call in Advance," while another reads "My dog can get to the gate in 2 seconds. How fast can you run?" Clearly, there is no neighborliness here. All of the dacha areas within Kyiv are undergoing at least some transition to more showy housing, but the most dramatic changes of this type seem to be taking place in Nyzhni Sovky among properties nearest the river. The presence of a subway station nearby adds to the desirability of the real estate (Figure 9.2).

As apartments and single homes are remade by owners, a sizable business sector has emerged to provide materials and services. The strip shopping areas that stretch along thoroughfares in the residential ring have many

Figure 9.2   A large new private home close to Dnipro River beaches in an area that was reserved for modest dachas during Soviet times

"home center" stores that sell everything from lumber and roofing materials, to toilets, floor tiles, kitchen cabinets, lighting fixtures, paint, and tools. One chain in particular has stores that are positively huge. There is a variety of furniture stores, too. Also common are small enterprises that offer the services of handymen. Often, they are just one-man operations. Do you need new windows? A European-style kitchen or bath? Your rooms painted? A shipment of sand or cement? Topsoil? A ditch to be dug or a tree to be cut down? Old housing materials or construction waste to be hauled away? Such businesses commonly offer phone numbers on tear-away slips that flutter from the main message above. Some walls have literally hundreds of such advertisements, and reflect both the large scale of change in the surroundings and the large number of people who anxiously look for a niche in the new economy. Such ads also hang on tree trunks and light poles along roads where new construction of private homes is taking place, and within the landscape of high-rises. Companion ads are for loan agencies that offer short- and long-term credit. Some entrepreneurs paint their ads as stenciled graffiti onto sidewalks so that prospective clients can read them as they walk or see them from the windows of their upper-floor apartments. A corollary to the landscape of active home remodeling is one of trash from the past. In various spaces that fall outside of the geographical boundaries of social control and responsibility, one encounters the piles left behind by owners and contractors: old doors and windows, bags of broken tiles or masonry, old toilets, kitchen sinks, and cabinets – all blights on neighborhoods that say, ironically, that inside individual apartments or homes, there are lots of new fixtures.

9.2   Commerce, Cars, and Billboards

In addition to changing housing landscapes, there has also been a proliferation of private-sector commerce since the demise of the Soviet/socialist economy. A considerable number of stores of all sizes and descriptions have arisen along main streets and near Metro stations, including those in fancy enclosed shopping malls, along strip malls, and in hundreds upon hundreds of small scattered kiosks that bureaucrats call MAFs (*mali arkhytekturni formy* [small architectural forms]). There are huge supermarkets, furniture stores, and bright new emporia with electronics goods like wide-screen televisions or the newest models of personal computer, digital camera, or mobile telephone, as well as new and used car showrooms and inventory lots, and a range of businesses that service automobiles from garages for repairs, to automated car washes, dealers of new tires, and multipump gasoline-filling stations. There are multiplex movie theaters, and a mix of restaurants, cafés, and bars, large and small. Among all of these businesses, many are locally owned and unique, existing as just that one outlet, but increasingly the landscape is one of commercial chains, including those from abroad that are known globally.

Supporting all this is a landscape of commercial advertising. Not only are there often big and bold signs on the businesses themselves and golden arches that reach on poles to the sky, there are enormous billboards everywhere. They stand on poles along busy streets as far as the eye can see, stretch as banners across roads from one utility pole to another, are perched atop shops and other buildings, and surround Metro stations and highway cloverleaf interchanges. Other advertising hangs as banners on unfinished buildings that occasionally reach 15 or so stories in height. There are also bright neon signs along roads and atop the tallest buildings that are kept illuminated well into the night. In contrast to the past, when signage was sparse and focused almost exclusively on public service information or political messages from the Communist Party, the landscape now reads that we should buy, buy, and buy more. It is a text of consumer society rather than the values of socialism. Increasingly, that society lives on credit. "Buy now, pay later" is an exceedingly common kind of advertising, not just in the signage of the residential ring, but also in the center of the city, on posters in buses and subway cars, in print media ads, and in commercials on television. If you do this, you can have the beautiful new apartment that your family deserves, a world of stylish furniture, a nice automobile, a vacation trip to a Red Sea beach in Egypt, as well as surgery to correct that awful nose of yours. Thus, both the advertising landscape and the landscape of businesses along the streets and in shopping centers is also one of banks, more banks, loan agencies, and pawn shops.

Another striking change is the prevalence of the automobile and the enormous changes to landscape that automobiles have brought on. While private ownership of cars was already on the rise in the last decades of socialism, there has been a spectacular jump since, and cars have come to clog Kyiv (and other cities) both in the center and the outer rings. In Kyiv, the number of privately owned automobiles is reported to have increased from 200,000 in 1990 to some 700,000 in 2006, and is expected to grow to 827,000 by 2020. It is estimated that now (2012), there are 1 million cars in the city each day when one includes those that have arrived from elsewhere. There are chronic traffic jams, and because there far too few spaces to park, there are massive invasions by automobiles of sidewalks, crosswalks, and grassy areas. Residential complexes are ringed with cars parked outside the buildings where owners live, and are plagued at night by faulty alarm systems that keep going off. Most alarms sound alike and every sleepy owner seems to assume that it is someone else's and not his own car that has disturbed the neighborhood. Air quality has declined as well, and there is more urban sprawl. I once heard a Kyiv city officer explain that he and his colleagues in City Planning had recently been to Moscow to study how that city addresses the growing problem of traffic congestion and parking. He outlined a list of new roads, wider roads, new bridges, overpasses, underpasses, etc., that Kyiv would need as a fix. He did not seem to understand when someone from the audience pointed out that in the long run it makes more sense to plan for a city without cars than for planning for more cars, because that comment was probably too "green" for him.

As corollary to the growth in automobiles, there is heightened bifurcation of society into those with cars and those without. To my mind, among the most striking and most symbolic scenes in the residential ring are the contrasts between the many Kyivans who still trudge long distances from home to Metro station or bus stop, and who wait in long lines at bus stops for their particular *marshrutka* to pull up on the one hand, and the many others who zip by encased in fast-moving steel, glass, and plastic. Even more, there is a striking contrast in scale between the human forms that stand at curbside waiting for buses and the enormously high steel poles with huge and brightly lit billboards that rise above them that promise all the happiness in the world to those who buy a beefy Toyota Highlander SUV or a Czech-made Škoda Octavia A5, to cite two specific examples from different prices ranges. It seems that it is a business strategy of automobile dealers and manufacturers to promise car purchasers relief from the twinned hells of mass transit and the vast, impersonal character of the preautomobile apartment block residential landscape. Furthermore, as in other societies, having a classy car has emerged as a status symbol. In response to the advertising, many Kyivans go deep into hock to purchase an automobile, and often buy one whose cost is far disproportionate to their income level.

9.3   The Middle Class and the Malls

Just as it is common for writers about a city to focus disproportionately on the urban center at the expense of a much larger residential ring, it is common to focus on issues of rich versus poor when writing about urban society and to express solidarity with the poor, but to not write enough about the population in the middle. Ukraine is, indeed, developing a middle class, even as we correctly despair growing inequality and income gaps between the extremes. Kyiv is the one Ukrainian city where this development is most visible. Detailed social statistics are not possible yet in Ukraine, as most official data are still too "Soviet" and avoid the subject of class separation, but there are recent sociological studies that cast light on the middle class with attempts at definition, estimates of numbers, and comparisons with other countries. Depending on the source, estimates range wildly from about 5 percent to not quite 50 percent of the population, and show either little change over a recent ten-year period or steady growth in Ukraine's middle-class population. What is not at issue is that Kyiv is in the lead in Ukraine in terms of its middle-class population.

Not only does Kyiv have a middle class, but there is also what looks at least a little like a familiar middle-class suburbia in the residential ring. As is common of Europe, more people live in multi-unit structures than in single homes, but there are quite a few fine single dwellings that might be Ukraine's architectural variants on middle-class suburban housing in the West nonetheless, as well as many nice-looking apartment and condominium complexes in pleasant settings for middle-class family life. As we have seen, some of these homes are built out of older Soviet-era apartments or dacha allotments, but many other are brand new on newly urbanized ground or where redevelopment has taken place. Furthermore, as we have seen, everywhere there are advertisements that promote such a landscape: billboards along city streets and along interurban highways that show new apartment complexes or planned developments of single homes in green settings, advertising posters in buses and in subway cars, leaflets that are handed out on sidewalks or that are inserted into newspapers and magazines, and ads in print and television media. If you agree to go into long-term debt, you too can partake in the new society. What can be more emblematic of a campaign to promote the promise of a middle-class lifestyle than Figure 9.1, the earlier photograph of the bus that is itself an ad asking people to start "living like a European."

We look at Kyivans themselves and see among the population a comfortable prosperity. A great many people are attentive to fashion and are nicely dressed. We see them on the subways and buses with shopping bags from upscale stores, moving to the beats of music heard from expensive handheld players through expensive ear phones, thumbing late-model telephones, and sliding screen after screen on new iPads and other devices. Many have also been abroad, looking not toward a less expensive or less exotic vacation in Russia, but more to the capitals in the west and center of Europe and the beach resorts along the Mediterranean and Red Seas. Turkey, Israel, Egypt, Tunisia, and the Maldives are especially popular because of sun and uncomplicated entry. Furthermore, Ukrainians buy expensive concert tickets (Madonna recently played in Kyiv's big football stadium; I heard Joe Cocker), speak English and other foreign languages, and are fully in tune with the latest Hollywood blockbusters and gossip, popular foreign singers and novelists, the stars of European football, and a great many other aspects of global popular culture. While some super-rich Ukrainians think that they own it all, and far, far too many Ukrainians are mired in poverty and do not share in this world, there are many, especially in Kyiv, for whom global lifestyles and middle-class consumerism are the norm.

Perhaps no place displays the middle class as vividly as a shopping mall. At the extremes, there are markets for the poor and places that only the rich can afford to frequent, but in Ukraine as in other countries, there are also modern, enclosed malls for the middle class. Kyiv has several, plus some that are under construction and will open soon. These and other malls are found on both sides of the river, in residential areas, and in the center, and are typically quite popular. As happens as well in other countries where English is not the main language, the names of malls are often in English and are written only in Latin alphabet. The same applies for most of the stores, although there are also store names that are in French, Italian, and other languages. Clothing and accessories outlets predominate, but there are also other kinds of shops and food courts with worlds of cuisine. Most of the stores are Ukrainian- or Russian-owned chains, but there are also stores from Western Europe, the United States, and Japan. As in the United States and elsewhere, malls have two or three levels, large stores as anchors, and small kiosk-type establishments in atrium spaces that sell inexpensive jewelry, doo-dads for mobile telephones, and other items. The sales staff consists mostly of young people who hope to earn enough to be shoppers in stores nearby, while most of the shoppers are other young people and young families with children. With the exception of a custodial staff of older women who clean public restrooms and the like, there are very few or no oldsters employed at the mall, most certainly not as sales staff or at cash registers. Perhaps this adds to the image of mall "middle-classedness," since in a prosperous society both grandma and grandpa should be either shoppers or at home enjoying hobbies and rest. Shopping malls in the center of the city like Globus Mall at Independence Square and Metrograd in the underground near the feet of "Bessarabian Lenin" are dependent on shoppers from the subway system, while more distant malls are primarily automobile-oriented and have sprawling parking lots or multilevel garages.

At Lybidska Station on the Metro a new shopping mall that is now in advanced stages of construction promises to revive the economy of a tired industrial district. It is being called Ocean Plaza and will be themed by an aquarium as anchor.

Dream Town has everything. It is my favorite Kyiv mall because it is in many ways original despite the generic nature of malls in general, and is a great place for watching nice people having fun. The name of the center is hokey, but it conveys something positive about Kyiv nonetheless. The crowds are happy. We see friends and family members enjoying themselves while shopping or simply hanging around. I have taken non-Ukrainian guests to this mall just to show a different face of Kyiv: a city without the extremes of poverty and "New Russian" arrogance, and without rudeness, dour faces, graffiti, grime, and crumbling stone that is too common elsewhere. The place is, simply, normal.

The mall is in Obolon (Kravets and Sovsun, 2012), and was put together in stages over 2008-2011. It was superimposed on the median strip between opposing traffic lanes of Obolonskyi Prospekt, the central boulevard that Soviet planners had designed through the heart of this large zone of *mikroraion* districts, and stretches for about 540 meters (1,772 feet) from near the Obolon Metro station to near Minska Station. It is anchored at one end by a large supermarket and sporting goods store, and that the other end by, hooray, a sizable bookstore. In between are well over 200 other stores, kiosks, restaurants, cafés, and other businesses on three levels that make Dream Town a shoppers' or browsers' paradise. The third level is most fun, because in addition to restaurant choices that range from sushi to the cuisine of an American Western-style saloon, there is a world of recreation: a roller rink, an ice rink, bumper cars, a simulated space capsule ride, a bowling alley, kiddy rides, a games arcade, and (trust me, I am not making this up) a regulation-sized sheet for playing what is known as "that roaring game," curling. Nearby is a small zoo with live animals and next to that is a shooting range where enthusiasts can fire "real guns."

Also distinctive about Dream Town are its five "exotic zones." That is my term for the tacky but good clean fun theme park-like décor for the escalator and elevator areas. Each area has as a centerpiece a café that sports the zone's distinctive theme. Zone 1, near the "Oscar" multiplex movie theater, suggests Hollywood with its giant King Kong figure, a big fiberglass dinosaur, a flying Spiderman, a suspended Batman, and bevies of sizable Oscar statuettes and mock movie cameras. The next exotic zone is a jungle environment. There are "realistic-looking" plastic crocodiles, an enormous python wound around a tree limb, a waterfall, and plastic palm trees, plastic ferns, and plastic moss. Zone 3 is Asia or China: There is a pagoda, "Ming" vases, a large Chinese lantern suspended from the ceiling, and faux bamboo framing for the mall's elevators. The fourth zone is either ancient Greece or ancient Rome, or possibly both: There are Corinthian columns, charioteers, a fountain with a statue of Poseidon, and a world of Greek gods and Greek art. Zone 5 (as we move from south to north) is a parody of Paris with a mock Eiffel Tower, the stained glass of Notre-Dame Cathedral, Napoleon's crest, and gargoyles who watch us as we sit in a sidewalk café. It all echoes Las Vegas without the gambling. It is much more cheaply built, but is fun nonetheless. A generation ago, there were only government stores and portraits of V. I. Lenin to enjoy.

9.4   Four Photographs

In order to illustrate the changes in the residential ring, I selected four additional photographs for this section. Figure 9.3 looks west from the roof of a late-Soviet-period apartment building that is located at an edge of the

Figure 9.3   Troyeshchyna village and parking garages from the roof of a high building

sprawling high-rise residential complex on the Left Bank named Troyesh-chyna. The high-rises of the Right Bank are seen in the far background across the Dnipro (also visible, but faintly). The large middle ground is what is left of the green village of Troyeshchyna that predates the high-rise landscape. There are fields, small farm houses, smaller outbuildings, and tall trees, as well some larger structures that have intruded more recently amid them as comfortable homes in the "suburbs." The new houses that are clustered in the center of the photograph on the far side of the high wall are oversized "suburban" homes on undersized plots that had once been part of village Troyeshchyna. Some or all of them were probably erected by a developer on speculation, while others are homes that people put up for themselves on land they had bought from a speculator. The structures that are arranged in the horizontal pattern in the foreground are parking garages for private automobiles. They are rented spaces, but some could also be owned, and some could be used to store belongings other than an automobile. There are hundreds of spots in this garage complex. It provides secure, gated, and guarded parking for owners of cars who live in the high-rise buildings such as the one from which I took the photograph. While

Figure 9.4   Traffic circle and Metro terminus at Heroiv Dnipra, north of the city center

some people might use their automobile daily, garages such as these serve primarily the weekend driver. It could be a good 15-20 minute walk between home and garage, so parking complexes such as this one have little appeal for most daily automobile commuters.

Figure 9.4 was taken in a residential complex called Heroiv Dnipra (Heroes of the Dnipro) at the end of a subway line on the Right Bank. Most of what we see was built in the Soviet 1980s as new, improved housing for Kyiv's upwardly mobile citizens. The subway stop is beneath the circle and is designed as the hub of the neighborhood. Wide streets extend from the traffic circle around the Metro circle and lead to various planned *mikroraion* developments in all directions, each of which houses thousands of residents. Units within the buildings are now privately owned. Some of them are quite large and spectacular in design, although that cannot be seen from the outside, while elsewhere the apartments might be decrepit and old-fashioned, and common areas might be in poor repair. This photograph also shows the landscapes of commerce and automobiles. We see various small businesses both within and outside the central circle, cars parked

Figure 9.5   New residential high-rises, commercial strips, billboards, and harsh distances for pedestrians in the Osokorky neighborhood on the Left Bank

every which way, and billboards on sturdy standards. Small shops and kiosks crowd competitively along the walkways that connect the Metro circle with adjacent *mikroraions.*

Figure 9.5 looks across a slice of the Left Bank Osokorky district along a stretch of a wide highway (Brovarskyi Prospekt) between Osokorky and Pozniaky Metro Stations. This is a fairly new district with considerable ongoing construction. We see busy traffic on the road, tall new apartment and condominium buildings beyond, a series of new commercial structures (offices and shopping) at their feet, and a rising forest of billboards. The foreground, by contrast, is a world of pedestrians on long walks to the subway or bus stops, and some of the small, table-top businesses that serve them. The pedestrian who does not own an automobile is at a disadvantage, as the scale of the neighborhood and the distances involved are better suited for automobiles. Windy days, driving rains, the colds of winter, the summer heat and humidity all make this a miserable world for pedestrians. It seems ironic that such a difficult terrain was conceived by Soviet planners before people in any numbers owned automobiles; at least there was equality of suffering.

Figure 9.6   **Kyiv relaxing. The photo is of the walk along the beach in Obolon.**

Finally, Figure 9.6 shows the middle class at rest. The scene is from Obolon, the Right Bank residential area in Kyiv beside the Dnipro that was mentioned above. It is not far from the Dream Town shopping center. The area was developed in Soviet times as a *mikroraion* for the masses, but has since emerged as a distinctively middle-class area and, in parts, as one with a bit of cachet and wealth. Locational advantages are that the area is easily accessible to the center and that it borders the river. There are beaches and green spaces, cleaner air, and much more quiet that elsewhere in the city. The apartments nearby command higher prices, especially those with fine views. The photo shows Kyivans enjoying themselves along the pedestrian walk that parallels the river. There is a lower walk, too, that goes along the beaches and past places for volleyball, fishing, picnicking, and other activities, but this is the "high road" past restaurants and terrace cafés, where families stroll with their children, parents or grandparents wheel baby carriages, children ride bikes and scooters, people walk dogs, and vendors sell ice cream, soft drinks, beer, cotton candy, and rent bicycles. There are old men playing chess, lovers holding hands, joggers, and happy teens. The place is especially popular in the after-dinner hours during the long summer daylight of this somewhat northerly city, while on weekends young people play music, drink beer, and kiss long into the night. The scene is generally one of comfort and contentment, with people having a good time and where life is pretty much the way it is supposed to be.

10   Seamy Stories

10.1   "No More Heroines"

No More Heroines? (note the question mark) is the title of a very interesting book about changing conditions for women in post-Soviet Russia (Bridger, Kay, and Pinnick, 1996; also see Engel, 2004). Even though it is about Russia and not Ukraine and is now more than a decade old, it applies to a very large extent to the experience of women in Ukraine as well, and still speaks to us today. The book makes a pithy comparison between the heroic image of women in the Soviet period and the unfortunate images that have emerged since the Soviet Union ended. The discussion accords with my own observations and opens a topic here about sex and sexism in contemporary Ukraine, and in Kyiv specifically.

In the propaganda of Soviet times, women were portrayed as being strong, confident, central to the economy, and during the war against the Nazis, heroic defenders of the homeland. Whether she was Olympics gymnast Olga Korbut (actually an ethnic Belarusian) or a female cosmonaut such as Valentina Tereshova or Svetlana Savitskaya, to mention the three names that are listed as examples in *No More Heroines?*, the popular image was "overwhelmingly one of achievement ... In production, in sport or at home with the family, the Soviet woman ... was strong, progressive and capable of anything" (p. 1). We see this in Soviet propaganda posters, for example, in which she joyously called her community to join the collective farm; she was seen as a determined factory worker in a black landscape of belching smokestacks; or as in a 1931 poster by G. Shegal, she broke free of the drudgery of kitchen work and stepped into the bright light of modern Soviet urban life ("Down with kitchen slavery! Let there be new household life!"). In World War II, she sternly (and now famously via a popular poster) sushed her countrymen against gossiping (*Ne boltai!*), unwaveringly sent her only son to war with the charge to be a hero (*But heroem!*), and supported the troops by laboring in field and factory. A 1942 poster by Viktor Ivanov shows the Soviet woman driving a tractor and the inscription "A tractor in the field is worth a tank in battle." After the war, we see her calling fellow citizens to rebuild: "We defended Leningrad. Now let us rebuild it!"

Socialist realist painting presented similar images. One striking work by Yuri Pimenov (1903-1977) shows a woman skillfully driving her convertible automobile through the traffic of 1937 downtown Moscow, while another, from 1962 entitled *Wedding on Tomorrow Street (Svadba na zavtrashnei ul-*

itse), has her as a bride walking happily with her groom on a temporary path of planks past stacked sewer pipes in the muddy landscape of a high-rise residential district under construction. Also in Soviet times, women were awarded medals for their heroic contributions (e.g., "Heroine of the Soviet Union," "Heroine of Socialist Labor," and "Heroine Mother" among other titles). Furthermore, I remember a positive and strong image of women that was depicted on the postage stamps from the Soviet Union that I collected as a child. Even *Wedding on Tomorrow Street*, sewer pipes and all, was depicted on a postage stamp, albeit in 1973 and past my childhood.

Contrast these various images with what we see today. There is still hard work for women – way too much of it – but much of the respect that women once enjoyed for that work is now gone. Also gone are most heroines, at least from official recognition, as well as much of the enthusiasm that women had had for hard work. As described by Bridger, Kay, and Pinnick, Russia (or Ukraine) is now part of the world of Samsung, Philips, and McDonald's, and the images that we see most often of women today are those of models for commercial products. Their smiles are posed, and they are hired because of their looks. Furthermore, nowadays, it is "young prostitutes and strippers [as well as] middle-aged women forlornly offering items for sale on the street [and] angry pensioners with their pictures of Lenin ... [that] are flashed around the world to create a new visual lexicon of life for the women of Russia" (p. 2). Indeed, even though Soviet sources typically presented an overly idealistic perspective on women, and today's media sometimes seem to forget that there are still very many women of achievement, talent, and strength, there is more than just a little truth to these generalizations. As we saw in "landscapes of struggle," there are far too many women who have no alternatives other than the likes of selling flowers, radishes, and potatoes at the margins of the economy; and as we will see in this chapter, there are far too many of the younger women in Ukraine who are at the margins of society as sex workers at home or abroad, and as export wives for lonely men from far away. There are also the countless untold stories of women who find themselves "marginalized by suburbia" – that is, in bleak housing block developments that are more or less remote from the pluses of the city, and that lack cultural life and opportunities for themselves and activities for their children. The old Soviet Union was not truly open for women's advancement either, at least not in most occupations, but now in post-Soviet times, women's options are often much more constricted, there is less respect and support, and the social order resembles disorder and is screwy in new ways.

There is ample proof for all this, including scholarly studies and anecdotal evidence. Among the former is the book about women in contemporary

Ukraine edited by Marian Rubchak (2011) and the special issue of the Ukrainian-language sociological journal *Spilne* entitled *Hender i Pratsia* (Gender and Work; no. 6, 2013), while for the latter we can go to the very top in Ukraine and consider what the highest leadership in the country has to say about Ukrainian women. Putting aside his acerbic relationship with political rival Yulia Tymoshenko, whom he clearly despises, as that is a long, separate topic for another book or for a feature film about political intrigue, we look instead at President Yanukovych's love of travel. Since taking office, he has taken virtually every opportunity to visit as many countries as possible, and enjoys being a regular at international conferences where world leaders gather. There, he strives to stand as an equal with other presidents and prime ministers and to represent Ukraine in a positive manner. He often seeks the floor to try to attract foreign investment to Ukraine, as was the apparent objective of his ill-fated book *Opportunity Ukraine* (Chapter 4). Now, in the context of this particular chapter, consider Yanukovych's attempt to sell Ukraine to global business and political leaders who had gathered in late January at the 2011 World Economic Forum in ski-happy Davos-Klosters, Switzerland. He spoke at a luncheon that was organized by the Viktor Pinchuk Foundation (Pinchuk is an extremely wealthy Ukrainian businessman), and invited listeners to taste Ukraine's borsht, vodka, and *salo* (delicious raw fat), but also urged them to be sure to enjoy the unclothed beauty of Ukrainian women. The startling quotation is as follows:

> In order to get to know Ukraine, I want to say that you should see it with your own eyes, particularly when the chestnut trees begin to bloom in Kyiv. And, at that time when it starts to be warm in Ukraine's cities, Ukrainian women start to disrobe. You will see such beauty. It is quite wonderful.[61]

The outcry from women in Ukraine was instantaneous. Some argued that if this is how Ukraine's leadership views the nation's women, then imagine how backward the attitudes must be among the common folks. On the other hand, other outraged critics expressed an opposite view and expressed no surprise at the comments, pointing to what they say is Yanukovych's long record of both insensitivity and stupidity. Maria Popova, a member of FEMEN, referred to the president as "Sexist-in-Chief" in a newspaper editorial after this incident. Sociologist and gender scholar Tamara Martsenyuk was quoted in the media as saying that the president's comments

61 https://www.youtube.com/watch?v=zYxut3y5COE

were a tacit endorsement of sex tourism to Ukraine, while legal expert Maria Yasenkovska regretted that his words were yet another blow to the international image of Ukraine. That Ukraine's image has been spoiled in this regard is seen in a recent broadcast on Dutch television that showed images of scantily clad Ukrainian women and offered tongue-in-cheek advice that Dutch wives and girlfriends should not allow their football-fan men to travel to the country for the Euro 2012 football tournament because of the temptations that they would face. If they did go to Ukraine anyway, they could have brought home souvenir T-shirts that were available at many kiosks in the games cities: the text reads "Welcome to Ukraine" in bold letters (in English) and below are cartoon color images of some dozen or more topless young Ukrainian women. In addition to frontal views of bare breasts, there are braids, flowers, and ribbons in the hair, and Ukrainian embroidery for each of the portraits, as well as inviting smiles and typical Ukrainian names: this one is Olena, that one Oksana, and the one next to her with the wavy hair is Olya.

That Yanukovych considers the beautiful women of Ukraine to be a national resource to be tapped for some sort of gain was reflected in how the country was prepared under his watch for Euro 2012. As an example, we cite an article in the London tabloid newspaper *Daily Mail* to which I was alerted by an article in the *Kyiv Post*. Descriptively titled "Border Control Ukraine Style: Glamorous Airport Guards Who Look Like They've Just Walked off a Fashion Show Runway," the British article is built around a series of photographs of attractive, young women newly hired to be passport inspectors at Kyiv's Boryspil International Airport, and shows them getting advice from experts about hairstyling and how to wear make-up. They are all in uniform, but the photographs show a lot of leg and thigh as well. I do not fault the young women who are shown at all. They look to be of the age of recent college or university graduates and should probably be congratulated on new jobs and the start of a career. There is also nothing wrong with looking nice. The point is that an arm of the Ukrainian government, the State Border Guard, may have discriminated in hiring by favoring a certain look for its employees, and then had them take part in an imitation fashion photo shoot for a base tabloid in a country known for rowdy soccer fans and stag-party sex tourists to East European capitals.

We can also reintroduce Dmytro Tabachnyk, a prominent member of the Party of Regions and Ukraine's outspoken Minister of Science and Education under President Yanukovych. We met him in Chapter 1 as the target of a slap in the face with a bouquet of flowers by the angry young student Daria Stepanenko. He was once a member of the Verkhovna Rada but was forced to resign, apparently because he had padded his résumé by falsely claiming for himself the title of military colonel (Markulevich, 2010). On May 17, 2012, he voiced still more stupidity from the top about Ukrainian women today by opining that in the better graduate schools of the country there "are girls who have a less bright, less attractive, and less model-like appearance." There was no apparent reason for his making any comment at all about this topic, and of course no data to support his view. It was simply a comment that shows that sexism is alive and well at the top in Ukraine and that even the education minister needs an education.

Deranged images of modern Ukrainian women are found widely on the Internet and in other media, both domestic and foreign. If you type the word "Ukraine" into the Google search engine, the first result at the top is, as expected, the Wikipedia entry about the country. Entries immediately below that are legitimate, too: travel sites, reference sources, news information, the *CIA World Fact Book* site about Ukraine, etc. But just to the right of this list are advertisements that present the other picture of Ukraine: their headings are "Single Ukraine Ladies," "Budding Brides Ukraine," and the like. Turn to Ukraine in Wikitravel and to the side is an elongated ad featuring a leggy brunette, truly a beauty, announcing the availability of a "first class Russian dating service." Turn to the website of the *Kyiv Post*, a very fine newspaper that I read daily, and the front page is at times emblazoned with a photo of a beautiful blonde and, from the same dating service, the message "Find True Love with a Russian Woman." Click on "Ukraine" at that site for up-to-date news from the country and spread across the top will be four more hot photos and a chance to "chat" with Alexandra, Galina, and Anna in Odessa (sic) and Ekaterina in Nikolaev (sic). Then, type "Ukrainian girls" into the Google search engine instead of the one word "Ukraine" and the list of dating and marriage agencies offering Ukrainian women to foreigners is endless, running for page after page. If you dare, click on "Images" instead of "Web" and a page full of portraits turns up: all beauties with beautiful smiles, some in bikinis, some in traditional Ukrainian embroidery, and some in lingerie. None are actually "girls"– they are all young women, but somehow the Internet has made them into girls. One is an athlete in Ukraine's Olympics garb. Most of the photos are individual portraits, but some models pose in beautiful complementary pairs. Additionally, it does not take much skill on the Internet to find lots of other Ukrainian women who are completely undressed, or to see photographs or videos of them engaged in sex. I have heard that there are even porn actresses who are not Ukrainian who are presented to aficionados as Ukrainians because the "brand" is popular.

The image of Ukraine in global consciousness is at stake. Presentation of the country as a place that is worth attention mostly because of beautiful women, accessible sex, and transportable brides is so pervasive on the Internet (as read from the United States) that one could suspect the existence of some sort of ulterior agenda. When I traced the sources of some offending ads, I was repeatedly taken outside Ukraine to Russia, that is to "dot ru" Internet addresses. That might help to explain another characteristic of the advertising: frequent conflation of Ukraine and Russia. For example, ads might offer "Beautiful Russian ladies in Kyiv" or invite prospective tourists to study Russian in preparation. One Russia-based advertiser who seems to be especially prevalent, popping up with ads for sex services or "Russian" brides (even when I typed "Churches in Kyiv" into a search engine as an experiment), seems to have an especially nasty business reputation. A check showed the following grades: Trustworthiness – very poor; Vendor Reliability – very poor; Privacy – very poor; Child Safety – poor.

Even uglier is the trafficking of Ukrainian women to countries abroad for sex work. It is one thing for women to go far from home willingly to earn money as sex workers, as many Ukrainian women in fact do, but a cruel crime when unscrupulous entrepreneurs trick women into thinking they will be working at jobs such as child or elder care, housekeeping, or waitressing, but then hold them captive and force them into work as prostitutes. Yet, this happens to unspeakable numbers to women not just from Ukraine, but also from Russia, Poland, Moldova, and other countries who wind up as slave laborers throughout the Middle East, in Japan, Shanghai, Hong Kong and Guangzhou, Western Europe, and even in the United States. In Ukraine, 70 percent of the victims of trafficking are reported to have been enticed abroad by sham offers of work or study-abroad opportunities, and other misrepresentations (Denisova, 2001, p. 33). The problem of human trafficking from Ukraine is presented with especially chilling impact in a short book by UK journalist Dan Archer and Fulbright scholar from Ukraine Olha Trusova (2010) that I saw one day in April 2011 on poster display in Taras Shevchenko Park. Designed to be a public service project, the book is called *Na Mezhi* (On the Edge). It combines Ukrainian-language text with accompanying pages of comics illustrations to tell the tragic stories of seven victims of cross-border trafficking.

Such programming for the public is necessary to make sure that gullible young women are aware of the dangers that await them. For instance, on Khreshchatyk we can readily observe foreign men making advances to young women not just to ask about companionship for the evening, but also to broach the topic of traveling and working abroad. I know this from my students and other young women who told me about such exchanges, and who added that they are quite frequent. Again, Turkey and other Middle Eastern destinations (e.g., Dubai) seem to be most prevalent. Over a period of months, I tracked a middle-aged Turkish man who operates this way along Khreshchatyk and near university campuses nearby, but never challenged him directly. I know his business because I asked some girls (in this case, "girls" is the more appropriate word instead of "women") that he had approached about what he wanted. Likewise, I have observed local men (as opposed to foreigners) stopping attractive young women on the street with offers of sex work. Some are recruiting for strip clubs and local brothels, I know for sure, but there also openings for work abroad. Khreshchatyk is known as one of those places where wide-eyed young women from the countryside and small towns encounter the big city and its multitude of opportunities. There is a lot that is harmless and even good, of course, but there are demons, too – many of them.

10.2   Visitors from Abroad

The Internet takes us to places we wouldn't go otherwise and shows us what otherwise would not be seen. And so it is with a video clip that a friend alerted me to that shows sex tourists from Turkey on their way by bus from the airport to the center of Kyiv. Someone seated in what looks like about the middle of the bus shot the scene toward the front and recorded the sounds, almost certainly with a cell phone. We see purple seat covers and the backs of about a dozen black-haired male heads, and can hear the native Turkish escort-guide as he explains in Turkish how to pick up women for sex in Ukraine, what it costs, and what the risks are. There are subtitles in English. Who provided them is a mystery, just like we don't know who made the film. The clip is 7 minutes and 25 seconds long, starts abruptly in mid-lecture with warnings about ways that prostitutes can steal money from clients' wallets, and ends just as abruptly in mid-sentence about laws of supply and demand in the sex trade. I image that about 30 to 40 individuals are on this particular bus, probably first-timers for sex in Ukraine as evidenced by the text of the lecture. There might be other buses like this on this same day, maybe even from the same flight from Istanbul, plus buses of sex tourists from other countries: Egypt, Iran, and the Emirates in the Middle East among other places; from China and Korea in Asia; and from Germany, the UK, Italy, and other countries in the EU. Ukraine attracts them all. They come from the United States, too, and are quite visible on Khreshchatyk and other streets in the center of Kyiv because of their distinctive Americanisms, both visual and auditory, but they arrive perhaps not by the planeload or busload. No one knows how many sex tourists there are in Ukraine, much less how many come to Kyiv versus other cities (Odesa is also known for sex tourism), nor how many there are by nationality, but the numbers are doubtlessly in the hundreds of thousands annually, if not low millions. Yes, a fraction of the Ukrainian population eats because of prostitution: not just the direct providers of sex, but also hotel operators and employees, nightclub and bar employees, tour operators, taxi drivers, and drivers of buses with purple seat covers, among others.

I found the video clip to be disgusting and culturally fascinating. Men chuckle as they are told what to do and what not to do with respect to finding a partner for sex. Among the options that are mentioned are women who hang out in hotel lobbies, women who can be hired via escort magazines (hotel staff have copies for distribution), and the exceptionally beautiful women who work in top casino-nightclubs such as one on a Dnipro River boat that is mentioned by name. The guide could also have mentioned the give-away tourist maps in English that are found virtually everywhere in the city that might have a concentration of foreigners: the airport, all levels of hotels, certain types of bars, nightclubs and restaurants, many tourist attractions themselves, etc. In almost all cases, the maps of Kyiv's highlights are framed by advertisements, and the majority of those are about sex. It is as if there were no other reasons for a foreigner to visit Kyiv!

Another option for meeting women, presented as the third in the film, is simply this: asking for sex from the women one routinely encounters, but only on the second night, not the first. To wit:

> The third method, this is the most beautifull [sic] one, the most kind one. In a gentle manner, wherever you are, do not hesitate to get closer to the girls. This can be the sales woman, can be the waitress and the restaurant, McDonalds or friend chicken. Get close nicely, with language, and become friend. You go out on the first night. She never sleeps on the first night but she sleeps on the second ... This is proven by experience.

This method must be very popular, because one can see it in practice daily by Middle Eastern men on Khreshchatyk and in the cafés and restaurants in the city center (Figure 10.1). Much of the time they are rebuffed immediately, but often one sees that a longer conversation is taking place and sometimes even a joint departure. My female students and other young women I know

Figure 10.1   Foreign men "shopping" along Khreshchatyk at Independence Square

in Kyiv tell me that they are continually accosted by foreign men when they are in the city's center, most often and most obnoxiously by Turks and other apparent Middle Easterners. Some women have said that they no longer enjoy going to Khreshchatyk for this reason.

To my mind, the most interesting part of the clip is when the guide emphatically tells his charges to behave and to do nothing that would damage the reputation of the Turkish nation: "Listen to what I am telling you. We will act according to the Turkish Nation, Turkish Culture. We won't bring any bad words to our nationality." It seems that for this eager group of tourists, behaving as they would be expected to behave with respect to Turkish women in Turkey who work in McDonald's or some shop or other, is obviously not an option.

10.3   Sex Tourism

But it is not just Turks who come to Ukraine for sex; sex tourists come from other countries, too. There are plenty of Egyptians, Iranians, Arabs, and others from the Middle East; Europeans from, I suppose, just about anywhere in the EU (most especially perhaps from the UK) as well as from non-EU countries; and also Koreans, Japanese, and Chinese. There are also quite a few of my own fellow Americans. They are easy to identify because they tend to be much louder than others, even while sober. One countryman I saw on Khreshchatyk with a willing-looking young woman in a miniskirt had his American passport dangerously on display, poking out of the top of his back pocket, but I decided not to warn him about it. There are probably other ethnicities, too, maybe even sex-tripping Russians. Wherever they are from, the visitors are guided through Kyiv by sex tour organizers such as the speaker on the bus; by explicit details on the Internet about where to go, how to get there, and whom to contact for a personal escort from the airport; by taxi drivers, hotel concierges, and doormen; and by the advertisements for escort services, strip clubs, and other sex-oriented businesses that frame virtually every map of Kyiv that is available as a giveaway to foreign visitors. Even travelers who want nothing to do with commercial sex on their visits to Ukraine are confronted with this, as the free tourist maps look as if tourists came to Ukraine mainly to purchase sex: the actual maps are sometimes smaller in size than the total space given to circumferential advertising that is, disproportionately, advertising for escort agencies, strip clubs, and other sex businesses.

One American whom I confronted initially in Russian for approaching a girl on the street who was way too young tried to pretend that he was from the United Arab Emirates. He responded in English, and probably thought that his darker complexion as an Hispanic American would allow him to pass as a Middle Easterner, but his distinctively American accent gave him away. He was from California and was taken aback when I changed from my mock Russian-accented English to native US English and told him off. "What do you want from me?" he asked. "I am not bothering you. Live and let live is the American way." I replied that "propositioning minors is not the American way," and added that "we take no pride in Americans who travel halfway across the world just to get laid. There must be something wrong with you that you can't find sex in California." "I like Ukrainian girls," he said as he turned to walk away. I chose to drop it, knowing that harassing him further would not change anything and settled for simply knocking him off stride for a few minutes.

The Internet shows Kyiv to be presented quite prominently as a best-choice destination for stag party travelers, particularly from the United Kingdom, a country where boys'-night-out getaways are something of a tradition. It may be that Kyiv and other cities in Ukraine are especially popular for such travel not just because of comparative prices or whatever extra charms Ukrainian women might have, but also because Ukraine actually seems to welcome and encourage such excursions. This contrasts with other places in Eastern Europe that have had enough. For instance, Riga, the capital of Latvia, has grown especially impatient with stag-partiers from Western Europe, and its mayor, Nils Usakovs, has singled out British men for special scorn and a crackdown. In complaining about drunks from the UK who make a sport of urinating on Latvia's Freedom Monument and climbing it nude to pose for souvenir snapshots, Usakovs said this in an interview in 2009:

The only problem is that we have a large share of those British tourists.
If we also had other tourists, then British visitors who piss about all
the time would not be as noticeable. Let's not be politically correct.
Unfortunately this is their specialty" (Press Association, 2009).

In Kyiv, there are many agencies that offer to organize stag parties and to
provide services to meet revelers' needs for nonstop alcohol, nightclubs,
daytime fun (go-carting, paintball, Kalashnikovs), and sex with the most
beautiful Ukrainian women. At least one company offers limousine service
for party groups with stripper entertainment during the ride from the
airport, while others offer strippers during limousine or minibus tours of
the city as entertainment between scheduled stops. One boys'-night-out
entrepreneur, distinguished for the cheeky writing style of his promotion
materials, asks prospective revelers "Are you a Dynamo or a Chicken?" and
then describes Kyiv as follows:

> Situated in the north of Ukraine along the Dnieper River and home to
> 3 million fiercely independent brothers and sisters is the surprise stag
> packet of modern times, Kiev. Formerly the third biggest city in the
> old Soviet Union, this intoxicating landscape of frozen lakes and lush
> green parks packs the kind of sledgehammer punch you'd expect from
> a major producer of iron, steel and heavy artillery. Breathlessly beauti-
> ful in winter (when all thoughts of traditional British stag nakedness
> should be abandoned if you ever wish to see certain parts of your
> anatomy again), and passionately party-minded whatever the season,
> Kyiv Stag Weekends are more chic than bleak, providing the boys with
> a platform for devilment that we promise will not disappoint.
> From Shevchenko Park and St. Sophia's Cathedral to Khreschatyk
> Street and October Palace, this is a firecracker of a city, smouldering
> with incident and crackling with atmosphere; a place where astonish-
> ingly gorgeous women are the perfect-cheekboned norm. Set your
> collective chops to Drool Factor 12 before you arrive, gents, for stag
> weekends in this city promote heavenly aesthetics at every conceivable
> turn. Truly, God broke the mould when he assembled his Kiev cast list,
> and I for one would like to have the guidebook.[62]

---

62   I omit the citation on purpose as I have no respect for the source and do not wish to
advertise it.

10.4   Export Wives

A related topic concerns Ukraine as a source of brides for foreign men. Agencies that specialize in this are also all over the Internet, on tourists' map and brochures, and on signposts that hang outside their offices in central Kyiv, Odesa, and other dating centers. In the center of Kyiv, there are even women wearing front and back signboards advertising these services as they walk the main streets and across Independence Square. There is at least one book, this by an American, that is a guide for readers of English about how to find a Ukrainian or Russian bride. I saw it at a flea market in Kyiv and was so put off that I choose to not cite it as a bibliography item. The humor publication *The Onion* has published a country-by-country world atlas in which the entry for Ukraine is introduced by the headline "Bridebasket for the World." The accompanying photograph of a container ship being loaded with export brides is both funny and a reason to cry. One can also be angry. In the same vein, a radio station in New Zealand held a contest in which the prize was the trip for a male listener to travel to Ukraine and meet attractive prospective mates.

There are legitimate needs being met, of course, by bridal agencies that bring together people who need one another and come to be close, and a great many happy stories about Ukrainian women who have found happiness abroad with foreign men who care for them. One can only cheer when people find one another and embark on happy lives together, and applaud the professional matchmakers who knew how to make it happen. But the good stories are a minority, it seems, outnumbered by profound disappointment by men and women alike, financial loss to scamming agencies by both sides, and financial loss that is sometimes enormous by men to scheming women who are no more than gold diggers. Dating agencies that scam true-hearted clients are the worst kind of demons, as they prey on the loneliness of innocent people and set up the happiest of human hopes before the crash. There are also the tragic stories of women who go to live abroad with their new husbands only to find a life of loneliness or worse: miserable living conditions and a second life in poverty, physical or psychological abuse, previously undisclosed sexual aberrations – even death by murder. A celebrated case of the latter occurred in my own back yard in the United States, in the New Jersey suburbs of Philadelphia, when 60-year-old Lester Stuart Barney slashed the throat of his wife Alla, aged 26, a native of Mykolayiv, the same gritty city where the late Oksana Makar had lived, in front of their 4-year-old son. The bridal search agencies are unregulated, and it is truly consumer beware in this Wild West of sexual services and matchmaking. A recent ethnographic investigation of the bridal agency business in Ukraine by activist/cultural studies scholar Nadia Parfan linked the phenomenon to the feminization of poverty in the country and the globalization of the "Ukrainian brand" via new media consumption by patriarchal capitalism (Parfan, 2012).

The publicly seen interactions between foreign men and Ukrainian women who for them are prospects either for hot dates or as brides make for fascinating ethnography. As the center of Kyiv is a prime meeting place for such dates, I have had ample opportunity to observe and listen in, and would be happy to see some graduate student in social anthropology or sociology undertake such a study in detail. It is interesting, for example, to observe that women who are selling sexual services either look straight ahead when walking with their dates or are wholly attentive to conversations with them, but never appear to look around or to make eye contact with passersby, while on the other hand, women who appear to be on marriage agency dates do make wide eye contact as if looking for signs of approval or disapproval. Likewise, I observed that some women walk proudly with the flowers that they had been given by their dates, others act as if they wish the flowers weren't there or hide behind them, and others still firmly reject an offer of flowers. It would be interesting to sort which women behave one way or another about flowers under which conditions. "I hate flowers. Don't buy me any. I always hated flowers," I heard one young woman scold the date that she clearly did not want to be identified with or beholden to. On the other hand, I have also seen Ukrainian women who look to be exceedingly proud and happy as they walk with their foreign dates or sit with them in restaurants or cafés. At the airport, I have observed those who look to be truly sad as they say and kiss good-byes to dates who, for now at least, are returning home.

Coffee shop talk is also interesting. One place in particular that is directly across from a busy marriage agency seems to have many "first conversations." Often, there is a language gap, as one party or both speaks very poor English, their only common language, sometimes resulting in embarrassingly loud conversations in chop-sentences and hand signals that everyone in the place can see. More often than not, it seems, the Ukrainian woman client is disappointed from the get-go, while the man presses on with a sales pitch. "I came here to find a good wife," one American English-accented man said so loudly that everyone in the place was embarrassed for him and for his greatly embarrassed date. On another day I heard a fellow countryman drawl Texas-style to a young woman who was already bored and embarrassed and may not have understood his English anyway: "I thank

God every day when I say my prayers that I was born an American." The flowers that he had given her were on the floor beside her feet, perhaps as an expression of her opinion of him for the people at nearby tables.

10.5   River Vice

Until about mid-2010 when there was a government crackdown for reasons that I speculate about below, Kyiv's beautiful river, the Dnipro, was lined at certain banks with some 20 or 24 (sources are inconsistent) floating hotels, restaurants, nightclubs, and until they were banned in Ukraine in 2009, casinos (Figure 10.2). In Ukrainian, such boats are called *debarkadery* (singular *debarkadera*), "landing-stages." They were most heavily concentrated near the center of the city along the right bank of the river in Podil and beneath the city's beloved bluffs and golden-domed historical landmarks. They floated on the river but were not necessarily navigable. Almost all were permanently moored to the shore and were accessible by gangplank. Not all of these places were openly associated with the sex trade, and some were probably quite respectable, but others are remembered mostly as "floating brothels." This was especially the case for the notorious *River Palace*, a barely navigable vessel that was opened in 1995 as a combined hotel, restaurant, sports bar, casino, and nightclub. It was especially popular with foreign male visitors to Kyiv who regarded it as a paradise of especially beautiful and willing women, and referred to it as the "Love Boat." Travel websites wrote it up prominently with enticements such as this:

Figure 10.2   Former restaurant-nightclub boats docked in limbo along the Dnipro River

Do you like girls? Do you like a wide variety of girls? Do you want to make sure you go home with one of them at the end of the night no matter what you look like? If the answer is yes to all of these questions, then River Palace is for you! For many expats, River Palace is one of the biggest reasons of what keeps them in Kiev ... Not to say that non professional girls occasionally visit, it's just that your odds of running into them at River Palace are about the same as winning a lottery ... Even on slow nights your jaw will be dragging along the floor due to the sheer quantity of available babes. Prices have gotten relatively cheaper.[63]

Other famous craft had names like *Baccara*, *Faraon* (Pharaoh), *Perlina Dnipra* (Pearl of the Dnipro), and *Admiral*. I cannot vouch for or against any of them, except to say that websites describe hotels that seem quite normal and restaurants that seemed to be among the city's most popular. More than one specialized in sushi. The hotel on the *Perlina Dnipra* was reportedly a favorite of the popular Russian singer Alla Pugacheva, a very highly respected woman whose professional career is a half-century long.

"Love Boat" or not, all the ships fell equally on the wrong side of Kyiv authorities and the Ukrainian Ministry of Transportation, and were raided, closed, towed away, or left on their own starting July 8, 2010. The first to close was the *Murakami*, a floating sushi restaurant belonging to the prominent Kozyrna Karta (Trump Card) chain of restaurants and night-clubs. It was taken across the river and placed "under arrest" off Rybalskyi Ostriv (Fisherman's Island). *River Palace* was closed in dramatic fashion on July 29 by plain-clothes police who arrived that day at 7:45 a.m. There are wildly confusing accounts as to exactly what happened. The ten or so cooks, waitresses, and security guards who were on board at the time were reportedly forced on shore (no information about customers or any possible hotel guests), the chains that moored the vessel were cut, and the vessel itself was the disengaged from the shore in a way that damaged both the pier and the vessel itself. Then *River Palace* was taken away. The same news story said that there was not even opportunity for the owners to empty the contents of the boat's safe. Other sources say that in the night before the 7:45 a.m. confiscation, the vessel was full of foreign male customers and entrepreneurial local young women, and that many "men in black" had come aboard and took the women away in one bus after videotaping them, and the foreigners without passports on their person in another.

63   Again, I omit the citation on purpose.

Before long, all the boats were gone. What happened? We already know not to expect definitive answers in Kyiv because much is simply murky, and that with some topics it is better to not ask and even better to not know. There is something quite Mafia-like about the whole episode of boat-removal that keeps us at a distance, but that in itself teaches about Kyiv. A likely scenario of what took place is this: The 20 to 24 boats in the water, whether they were honorable businesses or not, had too much of a free ride on free space, and were making too much money to not share it. Not only were tax coffers not getting their dues, but there was also a shadowy economy of corruption that was not being paid. That economy had and continues to have the power to cite breakage of rules and use government resources to muscle in. If I knew who the players were, I'd likely be dead. Here is how it looks to me: we remove the boats from the shore because they were not supposed to be there and were not paying dues. Some of them are made to sink, others are left to rot, and others still make it to a safe mooring. Then, we selectively rebuild the boat economy in new places, but this time under our control. The *Baccara*, for instance, wound up across the river off Hidropark, a large public park with public beaches. Its mooring took river frontage from the park, including a bit of beach, with no known compensation to the public or justification. It is, however, a fine hotel where I enjoyed a month-long summer stay in a room with a private deck that faced the river while working on this and other parts of the book. There is a strip club onboard, but it was entirely possible to ignore it and to enjoy the riverine setting and a comfortable room instead.

10.6   The Voices of FEMEN

I have mentioned the women's protest organization FEMEN before and now turn to a closer consideration. The group is quite visible at protests in Kyiv and other cities in Ukraine, as well as increasingly abroad, and is controversial because its beautiful young activists call attention for their issues by baring their breasts in public. The approach is simple: the power structures that make decisions are comprised disproportionately of men; the media professions that can be used to publicize issues are also heavy with men; men like to look at breasts. Therefore, to get men in power to see your issues, let them see your breasts. Not everyone agrees with this strategy, of course, for many reasons, not the least of which are that the net result might be to call more attention to FEMEN as an organization than to their issues, and more attention to breasts than to the messages written on their placards or to what they voice with clever chants. Many people do not take the organization seriously and think of the group as whacko, meaningless, and tasteless. Others, however, see a brave and revolutionary strategy in which women's voices are empowered by the weapons of toplessness. It might be worthwhile to have a closer look.[64]

The organization was founded in 2008 by three young women from Khmelnytskyi, a small Ukrainian-speaking city of about 300,000 in western Ukraine: Anna Hutsol, Oksana Shachko, and Oleksandra (Sasha) Shevchenko. According to what they tell interviewers and what has become common lore, they "spent long evenings discussing philosophy, Marxism and the situation of women in post-Soviet society ... [and] decided that instead of getting married, they would bring about change" (Neufeld, 2012). They founded a group called New Ethics, moved to Kyiv, and began their protests. The first actions were in September 2008 and were against sex tourism (Table 10.1), with particular venom against the very rude and aggressive sex tourists from Turkey who made it impossible for "normal women" to walk along Khreschatyk without someone asking them for sex (Neufeld, 2012). For that protest at the Embassy of Turkey, the FEMEN leaders were dressed as street prostitutes and carried placards with the message "Ukraine Is Not a Bordello!" Later protests took on the business of export brides. They turned to toplessness as a calling card because bare breasts attracted journalists and an audience, and were tools for spreading their message. The group adopted a very clever logo. It focuses on two circles, one blue and one yellow, as in the Ukrainian national colors, that can be imagined either as breasts or as eyes. In the case of the latter, a vertical line between the circles represents the nose and the word FEMEN written across below is the mouth. I like that, because it suggests FEMEN as a "voice" in Ukraine.

The group claims some 300 members and says that 30 or so are active at protests. I normally see many fewer and often the same 5 or 6 individuals. Regardless of numbers, they have used a popular café in the center of Kyiv as a base, and routinely met there to plan future protests and to give media interviews. Until recently, a display case showed mementos from past FEMEN events and promoted sale of FEMEN souvenirs. There are now FEMEN offshoots in other countries, including reportedly in Poland, Italy, Brazil, and Israel, as well as a fake version of FEMEN that appeared in Moscow in April 2011. Oleksandra Shevchenko described it in the news-

---

64 I positioned my observations here at the end of a chapter about seamy topics because FEMEN protests against what is seamy in Ukraine, not because I think that the organization is seamy. I think no such thing.

paper *Ukrayinska Pravda* as an attempt by the Russian nationalist group United Russia to discredit activism by Ukrainians (Shevchenko, 2011). Now, in addition to protests against the sex industry in Ukraine, FEMEN has broadened its issues to include matters of democracy and social justice more generally. Also, the group has protested at foreign embassies in Ukraine about the treatment of women in those countries, and has traveled abroad to protest on behalf of women's issues or issues of democracy. I myself saw FEMEN protestors once at Maidan Nezalezhnosti where they bombarded a portrait of Belarus President Alexander Lukashenko with tomatoes fired via erotic slingshots in which their legs formed the V shape. According to the protestors, Lukashenko's sin was that he was a sexist pig with power.

Other memorable protests were in Italy against sexist Prime Minister Silvio Berlusconi; in Paris on behalf of freedoms for Muslim women and, separately, against Dominique Strauss-Kahn, the big-time banker who was accused of raping a hotel worker in New York City; in Kyiv when FEMEN activist Yulia Kovpachik grabbed the Henri Delaunay Cup that is awarded to the winning team in the European football championship and posed topless with it for photos with the words "FUCK EURO 2012" written on her body. Perhaps the most daring act was an attempt in the Moscow action by a topless Oksana Shachko to steal the voting box that contained the election ballot that had just been marked by Vladimir Putin, then a candidate for president of the Russian Federation. She was caught on the spot and arrested, spent several days in jail, and was then deported and reportedly banned from Russia for life. It was not the first time and will probably not be the last that a FEMEN activist is arrested for a protest, be that for public nudity or for the brazenness of a political act in countries where leaders have no sense of humor.

Because FEMEN has gained such a media following and notoriety, it has come to be the subject of serious discussion and debate among feminists, as well as insightful articles by sympathetic interviewers such as the one for the German publication *Der Spiegel* by Dialika Neufeld that was cited above. At issue is whether the tactics of FEMEN are effective and helpful for women's causes, or whether they do the exact opposite because much of the public focuses on breasts more than issues, and through FEMEN looks at women as beings with breasts rather than human beings with something important to say. Another dimension of debate concerns FEMEN's choice of issues, and whether they have done well to broaden both the geography of their attacks and their subjects of complaint. On the one hand, it might be smarter to attempt to "change the world" by adding new strategies to a more global women's movement, or smarter instead to focus on combating the very noisome sex industry in Kyiv that runs rampant within blocks of their café headquarters. Some of this debate was captured recently in the popular Ukrainian intellectual magazine *Krytyka* in which feminist scholars Maria Dmytrieva (2011), Maria Mayerchyk and Olha Plahotnik (2011), and Yulia Soroka (2011) were among those who weighed in with opinions, and in a more recent review article in English by Jessica Zychowicz (2011).

Table 10.1   Protest Activities by FEMEN, 2008-2012

Year and Month	Location (Kyiv unless specified otherwise)	Main Issues
2008: September	Embassy of Turkey	Sex tourists from Turkey
2008: October	Maidan Nezalezhnosti	Sex tourism; shut-off of hot water in Kyiv homes
2009: February	Maidan Nezalezhnosti	Sexual harassment in the workplace
"	Maidan Nezalezhnosti	Sex industry advertisements
2009: April	Maidan Nezalezhnosti	Sex tourism
2009: May	Maidan Nezalezhnosti	In favor of making the men's side of transactions with female prostitution also a criminal offense
2009: August	Khreshchatyk	Abuse of children in prostitution and pornography
2009: November	Maidan Nezalezhnosti	Against political exploitation of influenza threat
"	Khreshchatyk	Against stress; to promote a "cheerful" mood during influenza epidemic
2009: December	Intercontinental Hotel	Miss Ukraine Pageant
"	Mykhailivska Ploshcha	Euro 2012 ("Ukraine Is Not a Bordello!")
2010: February	Kyiv: A polling station	Lack of democracy in Ukraine
2010: March	Cabinet of Ministers	Lack of women in government positions
2010: May	Embassy of the Russian Federation	Against special privileges in Moscow for "blue-light" VIPs (breasts painted blue)
2010: June	Maidan Nezalezhnosti	Freedoms of assembly in Maidan Nezalezhnosti (protestors were dressed as police officers)
"	SBU Headquarters (Secret Service of Ukraine)	SBU harassment of FEMEN
"	Embassy of Saudi Arabia	Against the rules in Saudi Arabia that prevent women from operating motor vehicles

Year and Month	Location (Kyiv unless specified otherwise)	Main Issues
2010: July	Maidan Nezalezhnosti (at a fountain)	Against high prices for water and shut-off of water in Kyiv homes
2010: October	Ukraine government area	Against Russian President Putin's alleged personal relationship with young Russian gymnast Alina Kabayeva ("Ukraine is not Alina" and "We won't sleep with midgets")
2010: November	Ukraine House and at Lenin Statue on Khreshchatyk	At Iranian event; protest against the treatment of women in Iran
2011: January	Khreshchatyk	Arrest of FEMEN leader (free hugs; protest fully clothed)
"	Paris	Against Dominique Strauss-Kahn; outside his home
2011: February	Kyiv: A residential balcony	Against a new rule that during Euro 2012 Kyivans need to be properly dressed to go out on balconies
2011: March	Kyiv: A park popular for wedding photos	Against the "export brides" business
2011: April	Maidan Nezalezhnosti	On the occasion of an international conference on radiation hazards, a reminder that "Yanukovych is worse than radiation"
"	Ministry of Health	Women's health issues
2011: May	Maidan Nezalezhnosti	Against Belarus President Alexander Lukashenko
2011: June	Pechersk Court	Lutsenko trial
2011: July	Verkhovna Rada	Pension reform
"	Embassy of Georgia	In support of a photographer detained in Georgia
2011: August	Khreshchatyk	Tymoshenko trial
"	Maidan Nezalezhnosti	Celebration of Ukrainian independence
"	Cabinet of Ministers	In support of democracy
2011: September	Kyiv: Press conference by Paris Hilton	Against brothels
"	Olympic Hotel	Against the uptick in prostitution that is expected to come with Euro 2012
2011: October	TsUM department store	
"	Paris	Against Dominique Strauss-Kahn; outside his home

Year and Month	Location (Kyiv unless specified otherwise)	Main Issues
2011: November	Rome: In front of Vatican, St. Peter's Basilica	Roman Catholic policies against women
"	Rome	Against Italian Prime Minister Silvio Berlusconi
2011: December	Olympic Stadium	Against Euro 2012
"	Minsk	Against dishonest election in Belarus
2012: January	Residence of Ambassador from India	Against an alleged comment from India's consulate that Ukrainians go to the country to be sex workers
"	Davos, Switzerland	Globalization (economic summit is a "Gangster Party")
"	Sofia, Bulgaria	Human trafficking
2012: February	Moscow: Gazprom HQ	Russian gas pricing policies
2012: March	Moscow: At a polling station	Russia's dishonest election
"	Istanbul: In front of Hagia Sophia	Turkey's treatment of women
"	Paris: At Eiffel Tower	In support of Muslim women
"	President's office	In support of Oksana Makar
2012: April	Near Bell Tower, St. Sophia	Against proposed abortion ban in Ukraine
2012: May	Dnipropetrovsk	Euro 2012
"	Khreshchatyk	Euro 2012 ("Fuck Euro 2012")
2012: June	Warsaw	Euro 2012
"	Olympic Stadium	Belarus President Lukashenko's planned trip to Kyiv for Euro 2012 final match
2012: July	Kyiv: Boryspil Airport	Protest against the arrival in Ukraine of Russian Orthodox Church Patriarch Kirill

Source: Internet news items and personal encounters

11   The Defenders of Kyiv

11.1   Hero City

The title of this chapter and "Hero City" are terms that are not to be taken lightly, because in history the city has faced the worst of demons and many heroes have sacrificed their lives to defend it. The time of World War II is indelibly etched most strongly in the narrative of Kyiv, as the suffering at the hands of Nazi aggressors was unprecedented, and the defenders who fought against them in the "Great Patriotic War," as the struggle is known in the Soviet/post-Soviet sphere, are remembered forever with reverence and thanks (recall Figure 5.2). These heroes encircled the city with rings of defenses and held strong for seven weeks before the Nazis eventually took over Kyiv, were deliberately starved during German occupation, and then fought valiantly to retake the city on November 6, 1943. Hundreds of thousands of citizens gave their lives in the fight for just this one city, earning Kyiv the Soviet designation as "Hero City." There are great monuments in Kyiv to these heroes that are much beloved, most especially the Museum of the Great Patriotic War that is capped by the dramatic 62-meter-tall stainless steel statue of Batkivshchyna Maty (Mother of the Fatherland) (Chapter 5). Other memorials are Park Slavy (Park of Glory) with its obelisk honoring the heroes of the Second World War and eternal flame to the Unknown Soldier; another tall obelisk on Prospekt Peremohy (Victory Avenue) that honors Kyiv as a Hero City; and various Soviet tanks on pedestals throughout the city and statues of generals, soldiers, and sharpshooters. Still more remembrance is via street names (e.g., Prospekt Peremohy; Prospekt Heroiv Stalingrada [Heroes of Stalingrad Avenue] in Obolon), names of subway stations (e.g., Heoriv Dnipra [Heroes of the Dnipro]), and annual holidays, parades on Khreshchatyk, and staged events in Independence Square (e.g., November 6 is the day for honoring the 1943 liberation of Kyiv). We see aging heroes on the street sometimes, men and some women, proudly wearing their medals. Their honorable service may have been in the defense of Kyiv or it may have been elsewhere in the war; regardless, other citizens offer smiles and sometimes nod or a bow of appreciation.

With full respect to these heroes, living and dead, and also to those who defended Kyiv and other Ukrainian lands from the brutality of Stalin's assaults on religion, history, and Ukrainian nationhood, we can now speak about a need to defend the city once again with new heroes. This time the enemy comes from within, sings songs of money, and assaults Kyiv by raids against buildings, parks, squares, and courtyards in residential developments that it covets, as well as against hilltops, hill slopes, and riverfront property, and against individual businesses, institutions, communities of residents. Their weapons are corruption, intimidation, and connections to power, all of which individually or in combination have the ability to destroy. They are the demons in this book. Fortunately, the weapons for the defense of the city can also be powerful. They include courageous journalism and well-documented exposés, solid academic research, good friends in high places, and educational programming about the issues for the general public. There are also the tools of public protests, mass gatherings, and if need be, civil disobedience.[65] Once at a protest rally I encountered an older gentleman whose T-shirt caught my eye. He allowed me to photograph him. The message on the shirt was in Ukrainian and read: *Nasha zbroya intelekt*, roughly "Our best weapons are our brains."

11.2   The Grassroots

It is fair to say that most Kyivans do not think very much or often about the problems that are described in this book. They simply go on with their lives. Some of them are doubtlessly satisfied because for them life has been good. On the other hand, many others are simply too busy with the struggle of making a living to consider wider questions about the condition of their city or society, and to become involved. There is, however, an energized grassroots as well, and a fair representation of Kyivans who care deeply and make time to become activists. It is to them that we now turn.

We begin by positioning grassroots activism in Kyiv within a wider context. Most importantly, I do not mean to suggest that it is only now, 20-plus years after the fall of the communist state, that Kyivans (or other citizens of the post-Soviet world) are beginning to speak up about what is wrong around them. Not only were there the famous dissident leaders in Ukraine, Russia, and other republics who openly challenged the Soviet state beginning in the 1970s and earlier and whose actions contributed mightily to the landmark events of the late 1980s and early 1990s (e.g., Browne, ed., 1973; Chornovil, 1968; Kolasky, ed. and trans., 1974; Pavlychko, 1992; Kuzio and Wilson, 1994), there were also apparently some less visible and less commonly reported challenges in late Soviet times by groups of neighbors and

65   Natalia Moussienko, a friend and mentor in Kyiv, has recently published an excellent article in English about the demons and the defenders of Kyiv (2013). I recommend it as a complement to this book.

other ordinary citizens at city and district levels against unpopular urban planning decisions. Much less is known about this dimension of protest, although it did exist, if only in specific circumstances. For example, once at a recent presentation of a newly released book about Kyiv in the 1970s, I heard its author, Stanislav Tsalyk (2012), respond to a question about protest from the audience by referring to the anger that many Kyivans expressed about the demolition of more than 700 buildings, including those with historic value and those in which they lived, in preparation for Kyiv's role as one of the hosts of the 1980 Olympics (sometime referred to as the "Moscow Olympics"). I had not heard of this incident before, and Tsalyk acknowledged that the episode is fading into distant memory and needs to be investigated more closely.[66]

Second, I acknowledge once more that there have been true heroes who have given their lives *since* Soviet times for the cause of right, even if not about Kyiv land development specifically, and that monuments to them exist already. For example, in Chapter 4 we met the activist journalist Heorhiy Ruslanovych Gongadze who was killed near the end of summer 2000 almost certainly because of his reporting about corruption in Ukraine. He was the founder of the website *Ukrayinska Pravda* (Ukrainian Truth), which continues to report exposés about dishonest dealings in the country and which I have cited many times as a source in this book. Gongadze was awarded the posthumous title Hero of Ukraine by President Viktor Yushchenko in 2005, and in 2008 a monument to him and 11 other journalists who were killed since Ukraine's independence was unveiled in a Kyiv park (Table 11.1). Like Gongadze himself, almost all of these victims lost their lives during the corruption-rife administration of President Leonid Kuchma from 1994 to 2005. None of their killers has ever been brought to justice. There is also the matter of Viacheslav Chornovil (born 1937), a prominent Soviet-era dissident and advocate of Ukrainian independence who then became a member of the Verkhovna Rada from the People's Movement of Ukraine Party (often simply called Rukh [The Movement]) and was positioned to run for president against Kuchma until he was killed (along with his assistant Yevhen Pavlov) in a car crash in the outskirts of Kyiv on March 25, 1999. An investigation by the Ministry of Internal Affairs concluded that foul play was not involved in the accident, but many supporters disagree and continue to call for new investigations more than ten years later. Like Gongadze before him, Chornovil, too, received posthumous awards, including a fine monument in his honor in a prominent spot near the center of Kyiv in 2010.[67]

---

66 June 7, 2012, at the bookstore Ye.
67 There is also a prominent monument to Chornovil in L'viv.

As I edit this book, I learn that yet another journalist is in danger, this time because she had been asking too many questions for too long about a questionable development plan near Kotsiubynske at Kyiv's western outskirts. The tract is public land in the Bilychansky Forest, and measures some 4,000 hectares (nearly 10,000 acres). Developers want to cut the trees and build. In a corrupt system, access to the land and permits for construction can easily be had by someone with the right connections and enough pocket cash. In this case, STB Channel investigative journalist Iryna Fedoriv apparently got too close to uncovering details about the development. As reported by Oksana Faryna (2012c), the land has a potential value of US$2 billion, so for the developers a lot is at stake. "You are covering the wrong topic. Drop it," Fedoriv was told by an unknown voice on her cell phone. "I know you have a lot of influential friends and acquaintances but they won't always be with you and your family," the voice continued. "I hope that you will sleep well tonight." The journalist and her family have gone into hiding, while her supporters and activists for the preservation for the forest have turned to placard-waving protest at the office of President Yanukovych, asking that he chase the developers away by declaring the forest to be a national park. This is quintessential Kyiv: corruption and lawless development; gangsterism; unspecified and broad presidential powers to do both good and bad; citizens caught in the middle.

Table 11.1 **Journalists Killed in Ukraine, 1995-2010**

Date of Death	Name	Affiliation	Place of Death	Comments
April 1995	Volodymyr Ivanov	*Slava Sevestopola*	Sevastopol	
May 1996	Ihor Hrushetsky		Cherkasy	
March 13, 1997	Petro Shevchenko	*Kyivskiye Vedomosti*	Kyiv	Found hanged in an abandoned building after writing exposé articles about mayor of Luhansk and Ukrainian Security Services
Aug. 11, 1997	Borys Derevyanko	*Vechernaya Odessa*	Odesa	Shot twice and killed while on way to office
May 16, 1999	Ihor Bondar	AMT television station	Odesa	Shot with automatic weapon while driving in residential area
Sept. 16, 2000	Heorhiy Gongadze	*Ukrayinska Pravda*	Kyiv oblast	Kidnapped; found beheaded in forest; investigated corruption

Date of Death	Name	Affiliation	Place of Death	Comments
June 24, 2001	Oleh Breus	*XXI Vek*	Luhansk	Shot outside his home after threats were received by his weekly magazine
July 7, 2001	Ihor Oleksandrov	TV and radio station TOR	Slovyansk	Killed in his office by four men with baseball bats; he had been reporting about corruption and organized crime
Nov. 27, 2002	Mykhailo Kolomiets	Ukrainian News Agency	Belarus	Found hanging from a tree
Dec. 14, 2003	Volodymyr Karachevtsev	*Kuryer* newspaper	Melitopol	Found at his home hanging from the handle of his refrigerator
March 3, 2004	Yuriy Chechyk	Radio Yuta	Poltava	Killed in mysterious car crash
August 2010	Vasyl Klymentyev	*Novyi Stil*	Kharkiv	Is missing and is presumed dead; he had been investigating corruption

Source: Committee to Protect Journalists and http://en.wikipedia.org/wiki/Georgiy_Gongadze

Third, I emphasize that protest is now commonplace in Ukraine, not just in the capital but in other cities as well, and that reasons for citizens' anger include not just scandalous construction projects like those that threaten the forest outside Kotsiubinske, but also a great many other topics, both admirable and not. The Orange Revolution, for example, was focused on dishonest elections and the need for a fair vote for president. Other issues that have brought Ukrainians out in numbers include economic concerns such as onerous taxes and bureaucratic regulations on small, private enterprises (Figure 11.1); issues about pension payments for retired persons; political repressions including very centrally the mean-spirited imprisonment of Yulia Tymoshenko and other political opponents of the current presidential administration; declining freedoms of the press; political and business corruption, including the allegedly widespread corruption that has accompanied preparations for the Euro 2012 football tournament; support for the arts, museums, and cultural institutions that are underfunded or threatened with eviction; various issues of women's rights and freedoms such as protests in favor of abortion choice; and protests

against racism, homophobia, and sex tourism, among others. There have
also been protests from the other side such as marches against abortion,
against homosexuality, against immigration to Ukraine by people of color,
and against participation in Ukrainian football by players from Africa and
South America. There is anti-Russian bigotry, too, sadly under the banner
of Ukrainian patriotism.

A Kyiv-based NGO called Tsentr Doslidzennya Suspilstva (the Center for
Research about Society) monitors protest events in Ukraine. The group is
made up largely of faculty members and graduate students at the National
University of Kyiv Mohyla Academy. Their website (http://cedos.org.ua)
publishes quantitative summaries by category of protest as well as write-ups
about individual protest events and the issues at hand. With respect to
anti-development protests, specifically such as those that we have concentrated on in this book, a printed publication by this organization indicates
that there were at least 278 such events in Ukraine as a whole between
October 2009 and September 2010; 10.3 percent of the protests nationally,
with Kharkiv leading the list with 43.2 percent of all such protests (Tsentr
Doslidzennya Suspilstva, 2011, pp. 29-33; also Dutchak and Ishchenko, 2010,

Figure 11.1   Photo of angry citizens in demonstration. The sign reads, "If
you don't like Ukrainians, get out of Ukraine."

pp. 102-103). Some part of this high figure is attributed to a particularly virulent protest campaign against the construction of a particular highway through a city park (Verbov, 2010), and to the presence in the city of an especially active NGO concerned with human rights, the Kharkiv Human Rights Protection Group.[68] Kyiv was second in numbers of anti-development protests with 16.2 percent of the total, followed by L'viv with 9.4 percent and Odesa with 7.2 percent, adding up 76.0 percent of protests having taken place in just four cities.

Who are the protestors? To be sure, their numbers include regulars who come often to *aktsii* (actions, demonstrations) wherever they occur in the city, including "professional" community organizers and activist-volunteers affiliated with NGOs such as Save Old Kyiv (see below) that take lead roles in staging events and drumming up a turnout. I know quite a few such individuals personally, and have heard some of them speak at rallies several times. In addition to the colorful Olena Zhelesko with her entertaining, extemporaneous politically charged poetry (Chapter 1), I am sure that I can mention by name the examples of Inna Sovsun and Ihor Lutsenko, lead personages with the Save Old Kyiv organization who are often at the microphone at anti-development rallies and in the front line of protest marches; Oleksandr Bryhynets, a poet, writer, and member of the political party headed by Yulia Tymoshenko who heads the Kyiv City Council's committee on culture and tourism; and Maria Lebedeva, a journalist and committed activist, and organizer of some of the programming at protests. My friend Vladyslava Osmak is another ubiquitous presence; another Kyiv activist described her to me as "the conscience of Kyiv." There are also assortments of Kyiv historians and history buffs, experts from local universities, and a procession of speakers affiliated with vote-seeking political parties. When the protests are at specific sites that are being contested, there are local experts and neighborhood leaders who speak from the microphone and give interviews to journalists. At the "Theater at Teatralna" site (Chapter 2), for instance, one always sees Natalia Moussienko as a central figure, while at Andriyivskyi Uzviz (Andrew's Slope) and in the heart of Podil (Chapter 6), it is often Osmak who, among others, has the microphone. Journalists protest, too: for example, the Stop Censorship group has posted a handsome map of corruption in Kyiv on its blog at wordpress.com and has printed it in English on one side and Ukrainian on the other for free distribution.[69]

---

68   http://www.khpg.org/en/.
69   http://stopcensorship.wordpress.com/.

There are regulars as well among the placard-waving public who face the speakers (Figure 11.2). In contrast to some of the Party of Regions-managed rallies that were discussed earlier (Chapter 4), no one is paid to attend and no one takes attendance. These protestors come of their own volition out of conviction. I know many regulars personally and we have had good conversations. A close friend who is herself a regular at both the megaphone and as a rally participant insisted that as I write this section, I do not neglect to mention the demographic diversity that characterizes Kyiv's protestors. I would have done so anyway without the advice, because, indeed, one is struck by the range of people who turn up in support of the city. It is neither men nor women who run the rallies, but both genders who work together. Nor is it just the firebrand young who are seen front and center, but there are also many people of middle age and many oldsters as well. As a senior citizen, I did not feel at all out of place at any of Kyiv's rallies. There are also mothers and fathers with small children, and sometimes rally speakers with children in hand. Many gays and lesbians know to keep a low profile in Kyiv (Chapter 8), but one also sees many of the recognized leaders of the city's the LGBT community who are open about their sexuality as supporters at anti-development protests. Ukrainian is the main language at the microphone, but Russian is heard often and both languages are respected. I also recognize many of the same journalists who cover protest after protest, as well as members of the plainclothes security forces of both Kyiv and Ukraine who watch from the side. Their photographers document everything and everyone, and zoom in on individuals' faces. More than once I have zoomed my camera onto the lens of one tracking me and offered a wave of greetings to a never-smiling counterpart.

Figure 11.2   "This city is not for sale!" (right), "Keep your hands off of my city!" (center), and "Hostynyi Dvir – A Space for Culture" (right) (Right image courtesy of Vladyslava Osmak)

The main objective of anti-development protests is to gain a greater voice in decisions about changes in land use and other aspects of city planning. To this end, activists are learning how to organize and fight back, how to make use of courts, legal documents, and trusted connections in politics to press against unwanted development, as well as how to work with the media and with experts on architecture, history, and city planning. They gather signatures and email address at protests, and then spread the word electronically about new issues and upcoming events. Various NGOs, including Save Old Kyiv, Kyiany Peredusim! (Kyivans First!), the Visual Culture Research Center that was once affiliated with the National University of Kyiv Mohyla Academy, and the Heinrich Böll Foundation (see below), operate professional quality websites that are updated regularly and offer links that help readers understand the issues and know how to help.[70] Members of these NGOs and other grassroots organizations are learning to work together to support one another's specific goals, because, in the end, they all have the same goal: a voice in the city and the right to the city. For example, we increasingly see activists from feminists' groups, the LGBT community, arts advocates, and others at anti-development protests, and return support by urban activists for social and humanities causes. There are also advances in guerilla tactics: how to dismantle a security fence and knock it down, how to climb to the summit of a construction crane and post a sign, and how to occupy a site to prevent or delay illegal or unwanted construction. I have spoken personally with some of the "nighttime" operatives of the anti-development movement, and am impressed as well with their knowledge about how to fight at the margins of what is legal. They have learned by experience and from the study of people's movements around the globe.

The Heinrich Böll Foundation has been an especially helpful organization for promoting dialogue in Kyiv (and also across Ukraine, in Russia, and elsewhere). The organization was founded by the German writer Heinrich Böll, and is affiliated with the German Green political movement. It opened its office in Kyiv in 2008 from which it administers its programming across Ukraine. Activities include speakers and roundtable discussions, public meetings about planning issues, and publications that present viewpoints about social issues and city planning by multiple authors. The stated objectives are to support democracy and political education, the protection of human rights, the promotion of gender equality, and the protection of the environment. I have attended quite a few events that the organization

---

70   In the order of how they are listed in the text, see their websites: http://saveoldkyiv.org/, http://www.peredusim.kiev.ua/, http://vcrc.org.ua/, and http://www.ua.boell.org/web/40.html.

has sponsored, beginning with an impressive program in German and Ukrainian that was held over several days on a stage in the center of the street on Andrew's Descent where speakers, panelists, displays on poster boards, and passersby all exchanged opinions about how to renovate the street. The attendance was enormous because of heavy pedestrian traffic on this popular street, and I was impressed at how eagerly Ukrainians took to debate and the democratic process. Afterwards, I attended a dozen or more roundtable discussions and panelist presentations that were held most often in the Building of Architects or in the National Academy of Sciences. There, the programs centered on proposals for renewing places such as Kontraktova Ploshcha in Podil, Pochtova Ploshcha, or Evropeyska Ploshcha at the head of Khreshchatyk,[71] the Kyiv Plan for 2020, and other planning issues. Speakers included various experts, most often architects and students who presented architectural renderings of what might be, as well as an assortment of the Kyiv activists described above, and quite often, representatives of the Kyiv government and construction/development companies. I have also been on the program as a speaker.

These events were normally quite well attended and lasted into the evening longer than planned, and commentary from the audience was generally animated, plentiful, and rich with difference of opinion. Like with the protests, many of the same faces came again and again, including a number of the individuals who have been helping me most with this book. Perhaps because they had learned by experience that they would be subjected to criticisms and anger by urban experts and members of the public, representatives from government and the building industry who were on the program often did not turn up or would leave the proceedings with an excuse about schedule conflicts after making their own presentations. One of my favorite moments at one of these events was when a speaker from the Kyiv government about traffic problems said that he had just returned from a conference in Moscow where he had heard new ideas about building roads and bridges to ease congestion and was ready to apply what he had learned to needs in Kyiv. He spoke in Russian. Immediately after he finished, a young person from the audience, about half the speaker's age, commented in Ukrainian, making two brief points that delighted the room but sent the government representative packing: (1) "Since when has there been anything good for Kyiv coming from Moscow?" and (2) "Don't you know what has been learned around the world that the only way to beat traffic congestion is to provide alternatives to motor vehicles, and that planning for more motor vehicles only always makes matters worse?"

71   Contract Square, Post Office Square, and European Square.

11.3   Save Old Kyiv

Among the NGOs that have been most active in Kyiv's anti-development
protests is an organization called Zberezhy Staryi Kyiv (Save Old Kyiv).
The organization was established in September 2007 in response to a plan
by builders to construct a high-rise building at a place called Peyzazhna
Alleya (Landscape Lane), a protected green zone on a hill near the site of
Desiatynna Church (Chapter 3) and other historical sites, and from there
it branched into actions against illegal construction activity around the
city. Arguably, it has since become the best-known and widest-reaching of
several grassroots organizations in Kyiv that are concerned with local ecol-
ogy, historical preservation, and citizens' rights to urban space (Dutchak,
2009). I have seen Save Old Kyiv in action many times and know a number of
its principals, and acknowledge that what I learned from this organization
has influenced both the content and the tone of this book. The group's logo,
an image of a bulldozer with a red circle-slash atop it, summarizes quite
effectively what the group is about, as do some of the text banners that
often accompany the logo: "Save Old Kyiv: Join us in the streets and recoup
your city" and "Are you still destroying Kyiv? Then we are your opposition."

As spelled out in the group's website (http://saveoldkyiv.org/), Save Old
Kyiv is made up of ordinary people of various ages, of various professions,
and with diverse interests. What they have in common, the "Who are
we?" part of the website continues, is a sense of care about the city. The
organization is nonpartisan politically, receives no funding from political
parties, and as must be necessary to point out in a society where protestors are often paid for their time, its activists are not paid for their efforts.
Moreover, in a society where Mafia-like tactics in business and politics are
not unusual, the activities of Save Old Kyiv are not part of any blackmail
scam against builders to provide them with reprieves from bad publicity
or costly protests and delays. Citizens come out only because they support
the aims of the organization: to stop the ruination of the city's architectural
fabric, monuments, and scenic landscapes; to stop the raiding of museums,
galleries, theaters, publishing houses, children's centers, bookstores, and
other aspects of cultural life; and to stop assaults by developers against
urban greenery, public squares, children's playgrounds, and common spaces
adjacent to residential buildings. Again according to the website, what Save
Old Kyiv favors is renovation of old buildings whenever possible, allowing
new construction when it accords with regulations and approved plans, the
development of more parks and open spaces for the public, diversification of
land uses in residential zones to provide more employment and recreational

opportunities, regulating access by automobiles to the city center and keeping them off sidewalks, and making the city more friendly for bicyclists. These are mostly green goals and accord with sustainable city principles.

The Save Old Kyiv website is worth a close look not only because it defines the group and announces coming events, but also because it reflects in its professional quality the high level of sophistication that grassroots organizing has attained in Kyiv. We see that Save Old Kyiv builds coalitions with other organizations that have similar goals. For example, there are hot links to the websites of Zabudovi.NET (a loose translation is Intrusive Buildings: No!); Forum Spaseniya Kieva (Russian: Forum for the Saving of Kyiv), whose banner shows an iconic photograph of Kyiv's golden domes and the Dnipro River under the protection of a photoshopped image of the Archangel Michael; and Zelyonyi Front Kharkova (Russian: Green Front of Kharkiv). There are links as well to readings and discussion groups about community organization in general, the history of Kyiv, urban environmental topics, relevant law and bureaucracy requirements in Kyiv and Ukraine, and so forth. The website also publishes a "black list" (*chornyi spysok*) of companies and organizations that are accused of irresponsible development in Kyiv, as well as of specific individuals. The former list has more than 30 names, while the number of individuals on the black roll is about two dozen. Clicking on company logos or on the photos of black-listed people opens pages with additional information.

The centerpiece of the website is a log of "hot button issues" (*haryachi tochky*) in Kyiv. There are 40 or so at this writing, and for each we can click on separate pages that provide location maps, background information and explications of issues, photographs, contact information for local activists who are most engaged with that particular battle, information about the developers who are said to be at fault, and running updates about what is newest and upcoming events. The center of that centerpiece is an impressive map of Kyiv with color-coding to define historically and ecologically protected zones of Kyiv and color-coded "pins" that mark the location of the 40-plus hot button issues and categorize them as to just how "hot" they are. Table 11.2 provides a selection from those that concern Save Old Kyiv at present.

Table 11.2   Examples of Save Old Kyiv Hot Button Issues

Name	Address	Status	Comments
Billa supermarket	Trostyanetska 1-a	under construction	The site is in a residential zone on the Left Bank and was previously a park and playground

Name	Address	Status	Comments
European Plaza Kiev[a]	Khreshchatyk 5	planned	48-story, 160-meter-tall high-rise that will alter Khreshchatyk and mar iconic the view of Kyiv from the river
Diamond Hill	Mazepy 11[b]	under construction	Elite residential tower that takes from parkland and mars iconic view of Kyiv (Chapter 7)
Sofitel	Kruhlouniver-sytetska 9	under construction	Trees and children's playground removed for upscale hotel site
Fresco Sofia	Honchara 17-23	under construction	Elite residential building within St. Sophia historical zone; UNESCO is opposed
Zhovtneva likarnya	Shovkovychna 39/1-a	canceled	17-story, 100-meter-long building proposed on a slope beside a medical clinic
Sadyba Murashko	Mala Zhytomer-ska 12	planned	Threatened demolition of historic building; see "Oleksandr Glukhov's Apartment" below
Teatralna Metro Station	Bohdana Khmelnytskoho 7	completed	Museum of Kyiv history (see "Theater at Teatralna" in Chapter 2)
Peyzazhna Alleya		canceled	Defeat of proposal to build a high-rise in a green zone
L'vivska Ploshcha	L'vivska Ploshcha 8-b	under construction	Shopping center being built in place of square and fountain

a Russian-version spelling of Kyiv, as with advertisements for Diamond Hill (see Chapter 6).

b Developer uses the preindependence name for the street, January Uprising Street, instead of Vulytsya Mazepy. (Source: http://saveoldkyiv.org.)

The activities of Save Old Kyiv are the subject of a reflective article in the sociological journal *Spilne* by Oksana Dutchak and Volodymyr Ishchenko (2010). The conflict over the proposal to build a high-rise building at Peyzazhna Alleya gets particular review, because the conflict was extra intense and was a landmark case in propelling Save Old Kyiv to prominence. The conflict was also significant because it resulted in a victory for citizens. Instead of an intrusive monster, the site was cleaned up and artists put in street sculpture, artsy benches, and a creatively designed playground for children, converting a once-neglected space into a favorite spot for Kyivans and a new entry in tour books for visitors. The site became a rallying point for Kyivans who had had enough of the city's real estate development corruption, illegal construction projects, and raiders' incursions onto parkland and historical landscapes. The winter of 2007-2008 saw numerous protest activities at Landscape Lane and demolition by protestors of protective fences that builders had erected. This was followed almost immediately by the remaking of Peyzazhna Alleya by the grassroots into a new public space. The actions had an unmistakably anti-capitalist tone, with protestors flying a flag of Che Guevara and displaying a portrait of Karl Marx in a Zorro mask with the words *het' kapitalizm* (capitalism out) below. Thus, we see this protest as yet another example of conflict that can be framed in the context of Kyiv's transition from socialist city to one where the market economy, accompanied by boundless corruption, holds sway (Figure 11.3).

11.4   The Republic of Hostynyi Dvir

The most recent (2012-2013) hot spot for Save Old Kyiv and many other activists, including a fast-emerging new NGO called Pravo na Misto (The Right to the City), has been a place called Hostynyi Dvir (roughly, The Welcome Courtyard or The Hosting Place) (Figure 11.4). Since early in the 19th century the building has served as a commercial center where craftsmen and traders from other cities could come to Kyiv and have a place to set up workshops or studios and to sell their wares. The structure is located

Figure 11.3   A controversial new construction site. The Ukrainian Orthodox Church, Kyiv Patriarchate, is building the new office building that is shown on the billboard in an historic part of the city, on the site of old buildings that had been taken down. The Jesus Christ with thorns placard reads, "Dear Lord, help us to save Kyiv from illegal construction."

in the heart of Podil, where it is a prominent local landmark for locals and visitors alike. At issue is that a development company has recently received approval from Kyiv City Council to reconstruct the building into a modern office building and shopping center. From the standpoint of local residents and Kyiv anti-development activists, this plan came out of nowhere and did not include input from the public. According to critics, approval by Kyiv government means nothing because that decision was made without transparency and the public was not consulted. The protestors want the construction to stop, at least until a decision about Hostynyi Dvir becomes a democratic decision, and undertook a bold new tactic for Kyiv activists – round-the-clock occupation of the site and simultaneous remaking of Hostynyi Dvir into a public, community space. The situation is current and continues to evolve (Butkevych, 2012; Zawada, 2013), although as we will see below, the protestors have been evicted and the occupation is now by the builders.

The background is this. First, Hostynyi Dvir is indeed in the very center of historic Podil (Chapter 6). It is near the Kontraktova Ploshcha Metro Station that serves Podil, and is surrounded on all four sides of its rectangular footprint by other major landmarks. Its immediate neighbor to the north, in the direction of the subway station, is Kontrakova Square and its landmark statue of Hryhoryi Skovoroda. To the south is a companion square that is centered by another landmark statue, that of Hetman Petro Sahaidachnyi

Figure 11.4   Kyivans encircling Hostynyi Dvir in a symbolic action to defend the building from developers (Photo courtesy of Viktor Kruk)

in heroic pose on horseback. The two squares were once one until the 1808 construction of Hostynyi Dvir divided them into two. To the east, in the direction of the Dnipro River, is the campus of the National University of Kyiv Mohyla Academy, with the main administration buildings and the oldest buildings where the school was founded being directly across the street. A set of stone steps on the side of Hostynyi Dvir opposite the university has been a place for students to sit and read or to socialize between classes. Directly across the street to the west, where Hostynyi Dvir faces the base of Andrew's Descent and the lofty Upper City, is the historic 12th-century Church of Our Lady Pirogoshcha that the Soviets had destroyed in 1935 and the post-Soviets rebuilt in 1998. The Fountain of Samson is also just across the street in this direction. It was built originally in 1748-1749 under the direction of architect and NaUKMA graduate Ivan Hryhorovych-Barskyj (1713-1785), a leading proponent of the Ukrainian baroque style, as an element in Kyiv's water distribution system, and was then destroyed in 1934 or 1935 by the Soviets for spite. The present structure, which like the first features a statue of Samson and the Lion, was reconstructed in 1981.

The building itself covers what is essentially a full city block. It has a sizable rectangular open space, the *dvir* or courtyard, in the center. This is the space that the protestors occupied. The *dvir* is invisible from the streets, has open sky above, and can be entered via gates that open toward NaUKMA in one direction and the Church of Our Lady of Pirogoshcha in the other. The building itself was designed in 1808 by Italian-Swiss architect Luigi Ruska (1762-1822), and features a classical style with thick Doric columns and covered porticos on all four sides, along both the exterior and interior. The site is sloped down toward the river, so the building is perched at an elevation above the surroundings in that direction, and the aforementioned stone steps are required to enter. At its peak around the end of the 19th and start of the 20th centuries, there were about 50 shops and studios in the structure. Ruska had planned two stories for Hostynyi Dvir, but initially only one was built. The second story that we see now was added in 1980-1982, at the same time as the Fountain of Samson was rebuilt, as part of a wider fix-up of Kyiv on the occasion on the city's 1,500[th] anniversary. The history of the site, including details about architecture and the history of construction and reconstruction, the range of businesses and crafts that operated there, the tragedy of pogroms (e.g., in 1905) that were waged there against Jewish merchants, and the use of Hostynyi Dvir as backdrop for period movies, has been told engagingly and with illustrations in the periodical *Istorychna Pravda* (Historical Truth) by the respected Kyiv historian Mykhailol Kalnytskyi (2012).

Hostynyi Dvir is in much worn condition. Until recently, it housed a commercial bank, as well as the V. H. Zabolotnyi Government Library of Architecture and Construction, a popular cosmetics and beauty store, and one or two cafés. There were some other businesses and offices, too. The structure had been allowed to deteriorate, probably in preparation for redevelopment, and the courtyard was mostly closed to the public and was becoming a dumping place for trash and abandoned vehicles. The first official sign that change was coming was on August 15, 2011, when the Cabinet of Ministers of Ukraine, in decree No. 1380, unilaterally removed the structure from the list of historically registered landmarks. This was followed by a handover by the Kyiv government to a well-connected company with the ironic-seeming name Ukrrestavratsiya (Ukraine Restoration) of rights to remake the building into a modern office and shopping center. Adding to the irony is that "Ukraine Restoration" is 91 percent owned by a company registered in Cyprus, Afridreko Holdings, Ltd. The deal was announced on May 26, 2012, but the terms were not disclosed. Most business in the complex closed about August 15, 2011, but the bank and the library held on for some time afterwards until the winter of 2012-2013. The courtyard was trashed with broken furniture, display cases, advertising posters, and other equipment from departing tenants.

The protests began as soon as the announcement was made to remove the building's historical status. Not only were activists upset about the lack of democracy, they also feared the possible or likely loss of historical architecture in the center of Podil. If Hostynyi Dvir can be taken, what about all the other structures nearby that also make up the character of this historic neighborhood? Thus, on the same day that the unhappy May 26th announcement was made, someone broke the locks to the courtyard, and members of Save Old Kyiv and Right to the City, as well as other groups and individuals, came together in Hostynyi Dvir to say no. It was Kyiv Day that day, an official city holiday that is held annually near the end of May, and that is marked by concerts and fireworks at Maidan Nezalezhnosti. Here, the holiday became an "alternative" Kyiv Day gathering. There was music and speechifying, and much conversation, followed by a decision to stay put to protect the site. They began calling it the Hostynyi Dvir Republic, founded on May 26, 2012. A core group of activists took turns, several at a time, living and sleeping under the colonnade in the interior of Hostynyi Dvir, while during the day, they and others worked at cleaning up the mess. They collected funds contributed by supporters into a jar in the middle of the occupied site for the safe disposal of the debris, and began their own project of landscape architecture and planting in the open space. They also initiated conversion of some interior space, namely the former site of a popular café, into an art gallery. For a time, it housed a display of photographs from Save Old Kyiv activities and photographs from the history of Podil.

Supporters of the occupation brought in tools and other equipment to aid with the restoration. A portable toilet was brought in and a jar was placed outside to collect funds for its maintenance. Some basic rules and a list of daily chores that need to get done were posted on a wall under the colonnade. Other supporters brought food for the sleepers and workers. In order to build public support for the cause, there was a rich array of programming every day (more so during good weather months), to bring people in. Large signs at the one open gate, the one across from the Church of Our Lady Pirogoshcha, announced that the courtyard was open and that the public is welcome. Another sign listed a schedule of events. In addition to the burgeoning art gallery, there were speakers about Kyiv history and architecture, musicians, lessons in English, lessons in Ukrainian (mostly for Russian speakers), concerts, nighttime film screenings against a stretched-out white sheet, picnics, and games for children, among other events. Protestors used their contacts in the media to inform the public about the cause and build support, as in the nicely illustrated newspaper article about the many public programming events that had taken place recently in Hostynyi Dvir by Maria Lebedeva (2012). In December 2012, when it looked like developers were set to bring in heavy equipment and a contingent of police turned up, the protestors responded with a strong man in a high place: Vitalyi Klitschko, world heavyweight boxing champion, leader of the political party Udar and a parliamentarian in the Verkhovna Rada, turned up with television cameras in tow and diverted what was apparently going to be an assault by tear gas.

We do not know what the future holds for Hostynyi Dvir. The republic grew stronger every day, but it was known all along that it could be crushed at any time and that reconstruction would follow. In a way, it would not be such a huge change to have an office and retail center in the center of Podil, because that is what Hostynyi Dvir has been all along. It might also help to have the architecture library in a different location, because Hostynyi Dvir is prime real estate with very high pedestrian traffic outside, almost none of which ever sets foot in the library. The defenders of Kyiv who occupy the Republic of Hostynyi Dvir made it clear that they did not oppose an office and shopping center at the site, nor renewal of the worn-out facility. What they want is for the people to decide what the site should be as opposed to a closed-door decision without citizen participation, and assurances that the renewed structure will preserve the historic architecture. They also want respect for the library, citing the famous eviction of the Museum of the History of the City of Kyiv (Chapter 2) as an example of how cultural institutions get trampled in Kyiv's aggressive land development process. There is an additional fear among activists that the two-story exterior of Hostynyi Dvir might remain intact along with its columns, colonnades, and stairs, but that the open space in the center will become the basis for construction of a steel-and-glass skyscraper. Such a structure would surely mess up the heart of an historic district, even if its mirror effects magically multiply the numbers of historic buildings in Podil. Such tricks have been effected by developers elsewhere in Kyiv and beyond, but the determined occupiers of Hostynyi Dvir are wise to them.

We now know more. While protesters were asleep during the night of February 8-9, 2013, a fire broke out on the second floor. It consumed a good portion of the roof and a number of rooms. The activists called the fire department but the response was slow, suspiciously so they said, and the firefighters seemed to work slowly once they arrived. There are reports that they did not have all the usual equipment with them when they respond to a fire. The cause of the blaze has not been determined, and is said by activists to be extremely suspicious. The occupation, however, did not cease, and activists continued to live in the portico of the courtyard despite the cold, the wet, and the smell of a fire-damaged building. Then, just ten days later, a large force of strong young men dressed in black broke through the gates, roughed up the occupants, and turned them over to police for arrest. To put it plainly, the raiders had come and the protesters were gone. So were their belongings, the speaker system, film projector, the works in the art gallery, and tools. Everything was gone and nothing was returned. The gates were locked anew, and a cordon of police was put in place to prevent reoccupation. Soon, the iconic high green wooden fence that says "land use transition in progress" was erected around the site. Construction equipment and construction workers arrived and, at this writing, have been chipping away at the stucco inside and out to expose the original brick. A very high crane is within the enclosure and is poised for big work. The protestors did what they could, but the builders succeeded in getting a court injunction against them that prohibits protest activities in the area. So, the Republic of Hostynyi Dvir is now in exile. Protests and public programming continue elsewhere, but there are also guerrilla strikes in the night: graffiti on the green fence, graffiti in the neighborhood nearby, and graffiti on an immobilized old truck that was left mysteriously near one of the gates. On May 25, Ihor Lutsenko (Save Old Kyiv) and a companion climbed to the top of the tall crane with a protest sign and were then arrested as they came down. My friends say that the battle for Hostynyi Dvir is not over, but what I see is a lot of construction going on behind a protected barricade. The fight seems to depend on the courts now and friends in high places.

11.5   Oleksandr Glukhov's Apartment

Oleksandr Glukhov lives at 12-A Mala Zhytomerska Street, less than a hundred meters from the northern rim of Independence Square (Figure 11.5). That puts him squarely within the once-walled old city, in an historic district with potential historic ambiance. His building is one of those impressive sugar-era structures of Kyiv, a thick-walled, once-ornate five-story apartment building that was built in 1909. The structure was badly damaged in World War II but was handsomely refurbished afterwards, and then for nearly a half-century enjoyed a second life as a fine apartment address in a prized central location for lucky Soviet citizens. But now there are new owners of the land and 12-A Mala Zhytomerska is endangered, as its site has been targeted for redevelopment. If the new owners, a company called Pantheon Investments whose true principals are not easily identified, succeed in emptying the structure of residents, they will erect something new, probably in conjunction with the site of the building behind, which has been rotting in ruins since it was consumed a few years back in an unexplained fire, and the structure next door, 14-A Mala Zhytomerska, another ruin where only the façade remains standing. Put together, the three sites would make for an ideal location for a prominent bank or office tower, or for a new hotel. Indeed, it seems that Pantheon Investments has bought the land under not just 12-A and 12-B Mala Zhytomerska and 14-A, but also at 14-B (the building behind) and on Mykhaylivska Street that borders these properties. 14-A is noteworthy in history as the former residence and studio of Oleksandr Oleksandrovych Murashko (1875-1919), a distinguished Ukrainian painter at the turn of the 20th century. The development project could potentially be truly huge. But 12-A Mala Zhytomyrska is an historically certified structure, and tearing it down would be in violation of historical preservation law.

Glukhov is in his 50s and is a mathematics professor at one of Kyiv's well-known universities. He writes his name Glukhov instead of the Ukrainian Hlukhov or Hlukhiv, because his name was always spelled the Russian way when he was growing up. In addition to his technical subject, he knows the law and the rights of citizens under the law, and understands the value of a carefully chosen fight for principle. He and his wife Tatiana are the last two residents of 12-A Mala Zhytomerska Street. They have lived in

Figure 11.5   Oleksandr Glukhov in his cold apartment

their unit on the second floor since 1992, and have indisputable proof of ownership. They have been to court and have won in proceedings against Pantheon Investments, but still the "owners of the land" persist and want the Glukhovs out. The inhabitants of the seven other units in the building took buyouts and left, or simply succumbed to harassment, and their apartments have been sealed with iron bars and iron doors to keep out squatters, but Oleksandr and Tatiana Glukhov have resisted the pressures and stay put. They could be more comfortable elsewhere, but for them the struggle is not just about their rights to the apartment they own, but also to save a fine old building from destruction. Indeed, their quest is to save historic Kyiv. They avoid eviction by not leaving the apartment untended. In their fight, they have had to endure periodic shutoffs of water, light, and gas, and threats from armed security personnel. Recently, Pantheon Investments has begun stationing guards at the entrance to the building 24 hours a day, seven days a week, to keep watch on the Glukhovs' comings and goings, on their adult daughter who tends the place when both parents are out, and on visitors such as myself. It's a standoff situation.

I have used the Glukhovs' correct names and true address with permission. They have made their fight public and are quite well known in

"Save Old Kyiv" circles, so there is no violation of privacy involved. Indeed, they broadcast their struggle as widely as they can by periodically staging licensed protests with information signs in front of City Hall, and with a sheet-sized banner that hangs from the balcony of their apartment. In bold font it calls *Kyiany*! and then in smaller letters below reads *Ne damo zruynuvaty budynok pam'iatku arkhitektury*! *Vul. Mala Zhytomyrska 12-A* (Kyivans! Do not allow the destruction of this architectural treasure building! 12-A Mala Zhytomerska St.). Ironically, the balcony itself is crumbling and looks about to fall, while much of the ornate stone artwork that once graced the façade around the sign has already fallen or been lopped off. Just to the right of the sign, for instance, is a window-sized frieze of an eagle: its wings and feathers are intact, as are both claws, but the head is simply gone. At street level below the sign, two sheets of standard-sized A4 paper hang on the door to the building, just where the guards work. One is a photocopy of the 1982 designation of 12-A as an historical property, and the other a photocopy of the Ukrainian law that makes it illegal to destroy such structures. There had once been an official brass marker on the front of the building that had identified the building as historically certified, but that disappeared sometime in the mid-1990s (it was probably taken by "hooligans," according to Glukhov). Passersby see the big sign above the balcony and then often pause to read the two A4 notices. I was doing just that and taking photos when Glukhov came out of his apartment and introduced himself. He was in a hurry, so he invited me to accompany him to City Hall a few blocks away to join his protest and hear the details. I went, of course, and wound up passing out leaflets for him. That started a friendship and opened doors for me to understanding other sites in Kyiv where monsters invade.

11.6   The Ordeal of Oleksandr Hudyma

Let us meet still another Oleksandr, one of several in this book, a good citizen who led protests against illegal evictions of neighbors, the demolition of their perfectly good apartment buildings, and the construction on the site of luxury housing for the rich. All this took place on Lesya Ukrainka Boulevard near where another of our Oleksandrs, Oleksandr Borysovych, had railed against Bentleys and oversized condominiums for government officials. The present Olesksandr is Oleksander Hudyma, a pensioner in his 60s, a former elected member of the Verkhovna Rada, and a founder of an activist group in his neighborhood. He introduced himself to me on May

14, 2011, in front of the Verkhovna Rada at a very angry "Day of Anger" rally against parliamentary shenanigans and the Yanukovych government and invited me to witness the continuation of his trial five days later in Pechersk District Court. He had been charged with vandalism to the private property of the land developer at 9 Lesya Ukrainka Boulevard and with physical assault against the security guard on the site, and thought that both his cause and my book would benefit from my presence. It was an eye-opener!

On the day I attended, the witness against Hudyma was the arresting police offer. The judge began by asking him to recount what happened on the day in question. He replied that he did not remember because the events had taken place months before. She prodded him again and again, and he always replied the same. Then, in exasperation, she read aloud the report that he had signed that specified the accusations of vandalism to the fence surrounding the construction site and Hudyma's beating of the security guard. The report was long and she read rapidly, but still it took 10-12 minutes to get through it. I remember that the report was well-structured, and that it employed complex sentences and sophisticated vocabulary. I noted that because after I heard the "author" speak in microsentences and one-word utterances, I knew that he could not have written the report. The security guard who was allegedly assaulted was in the room and was about half Hudyma's age and weighed considerably more. The judge asked if the report that she read was accurate and the policeman replied that yes, it must be because he had signed it. She then asked him questions about details that she had just read:

Judge:	"Exactly where on the premises was the guard when the accused beat him?"
Witness:	"On the other side of the fence."
Judge:	"How did the accused get to the guard?"
Witness:	"He climbed the fence."
Judge:	"Did you climb the fence, too?"
Witness:	"No."
Judge:	"Did you see Mr. Hudyma beat 'Mr. Milov' with your own eyes?"
Witness:	"Yes. It says that in the report."
Judge:	"Then how did you see that Mr. Hudyma beat Mr. Milov if you did not climb the fence?"
Witness:	"I don't know."

After yet another scolding of the witness for having a faulty memory and providing inconsistent testimony, the judge exclaimed to the courtroom in general: "If such idiots represent our police, then God help Ukraine. Who hired this guy anyway?" The back and forth then continued:

Witness:	"I was wrong. He did not climb the fence. He tore it down. That's how I could see him beating Milov.
Judge:	"He tore the fence down?"
Witness:	"Yes."
Judge:	"Are you sure? With what? How did he tear the fence down?"
Witness:	"With his bare hands."
Judge:	"He tore the fence down with his bare hands? What was it made of?"
Witness:	"Iron."

There is audible laughter among Hudyma's supporters, more than before, and a look of panic on the part of the prosecuting attorney, a dashing young man who looks to be on the rise professionally in his crisp beige suit. For some time he had been nervously fingering his pen, his mobile phone in its case, and all the papers within reach on his table directly across from the defense. At a key point, he looked quizzically at the bench where representatives of the development company were also shrugging their shoulders. Meanwhile, the judge was red-faced with anger, perhaps because spectators were laughing, but certainly also because the witness was, indeed, an idiot. I couldn't see his face because he stood facing the judge with his back to the courtroom. When he looked over his shoulder to make eye contact with other police officers who had also been called to testify, the judge screamed at him to look straight ahead. At one point, Oleksandr Hudyma looked directly at me to make sure that I was taking it all in; he seemed pleased that I was. Nearly three months after that amazing day, the trial was still proceeding, moving at a glacial pace perhaps because Hudyma can't be convicted on the evidence, but also because he can't be allowed to win vis-à-vis the development company. I thought that the judge seemed like a reasonable person who would make a reasonable ruling, but perhaps she was caught in something outside the reach of her courtroom. But then, what do I know? I was a just one-day spectator. What I know for sure is that I don't want to be arrested in Ukraine. I imagined that charges were trumped up against Hudyma because he and his protestors were getting in the way of an expensive construction project, and that a less-than-bright police officer had signed his name to an arrest warrant that he had little or nothing to do with. Its true authors probably never imagined that their little pawn would be called to testify. Pity the police officer, too, an expendable entity in an aggressively capitalist Kyiv.[72]

11.7   The Last Farmstead in Pozniaky

Pozniaky was a farmers' and boyars' village south of Kyiv on the Left Bank at least as far back as 1571, its first known mention. As Kyiv grew near the end of the Soviet period, the rustic aspects all but disappeared, as did those of neighboring villages, and vast tracts of new high-rise residential towers were built on the land. Because the water table was high and conditions were often mucky, enormous quantities of sand were piped from the Dnipro to raise the elevation of the surroundings by several meters. For a time, nothing grew, not even the new buildings, and the Left Bank looked like a flat Sahara. But then in the late 1980s, tall buildings began to rise from the sand, becoming apartment homes for displaced farmers, as well as for suburbanizing Kyivans and urbanizing Ukrainians. The Left Bank in general became a zone of generic Soviet *mikroraions*, each with an allocation of just so many residential high-rises, so many floors per building, so many units per floor, and so many barely sufficient square meters per unit, all as if specified in a master manual. The Pivdennyi Mist (Southern Bridge) was constructed across the Dnipro in 1983-1990 and made these expanses much more accessible to Kyiv' core, and then in 1993 the area became even closer to the center when the Green Line of the subway was extended to Pozniaky and beyond. Pozniaky became one of the stops on the Metro, and the road from the bridge became a busy highway, so now in post-Soviet times some part of the area is taken up by shopping malls and other commerce, strips of automobile dealerships and fast-food restaurants, and growing forests of billboards that promote postsocialist consumption.

Amid this suburban scene is the last farmstead in Pozniaky (Figure 11.6). It is about 10 to 15 minutes' walk north west of the Pozniaky Metro Station near what was put through as Vulytsya Anny Akhmatovoi (Anna Akhmatova Street), named after the brilliant modernist Russian poet. The tract stands as a lone holdout from the past against a tide of suburban

---

72   For an account of the charges against Hudyma and other aspects of the proceedings in Ukrainian, see Gnap (2010). The dialogue presented here is my translation of what was said in Ukrainian at the trial as reconstructed from notes that I took while the speakers were speaking.

development. I have visited the site several times, always marveling at the contrast between this unusual small space (about the size of a football field) that the Yurchenko family still farms, and the vast scale of the tall buildings and thousands and thousands of citified new neighbors that surround it. It is the topography that is most striking, because the Yurchenko farmstead is, quite literally, in a hole. It sits five or so meters lower in elevation than the immediate surroundings because urban Pozniaky is built on thick layers of recently imported sand. When you approach the site from across the flat surroundings, the first thing you see is tree tops poking from below. The environment of the new neighborhood on sand is sterile, supporting little greenery except for some scrawny new trees and worthless patches of weeds, while the last farmstead in Pozniaky is on dark and mucky earth, and is thick with greenery and alive with wildflowers, roses, wildlife, and farm animals. There are birds and bees, as well as chickens, a dozen or more pigs, and several goats. In addition to the main residence, which is a typical old village farm house, there is another house as well and a mix of rustic outbuildings, including an outhouse, a greenhouse, a shelter for livestock, a workshop, and a sauna. Mothers from the city neighborhood bring their young children to the edge of the precipice to look down at the

Figure 11.6   The last farmstead in Pozniaky

wonders in the hole below, as do grandmothers and grandfathers with the grandchildren they look after. A flag of Ukraine rises on a mast from the roof of the Yurchenko house; like the tree tops, it just barely pokes above the base elevation of the surrounding neighborhood.

There are lessons to be seen everywhere. As we walk through urban Pozniaky to reach the Yurchenko property, we see that new owners of the now-privatized apartments in the area have been remodeling what the Soviets had built. Not only are there ads posted everywhere by contractors who want to furnish them with new windows or flooring, or with updates to kitchens and baths, there are also quite a few stores along the way that specialize in sales of materials for home improvement. But instead of getting a positive feeling from the upgrading, we note also that many of the weed-infested spaces between buildings are where thoughtless homeowners and their contractors have dumped old windows, toilets and other construction waste. The lesson is about an atomized society in the city, where people live in their own private spaces behind locked doors high up in tall buildings, and relate not at all to their surroundings. Even the Yurchenko property has been littered, as contractors have dumped waste onto the corners of their property from the edges of the urban precipice. As is normal for farmsteads, the Yurchenko property has a fence around it and a gate; what is unusual though is that the fence is not the plank fence that one sees in the countryside, but is one of old doors from the old homes of their former neighbors in Pozniaky village. In contrast to their citified neighbors, the Yurchenko household is tied to the land, as Ukrainians were throughout history, and remembers the past. Perhaps, too, the old doors are memories of neighbors who have departed.

One of my former colleagues at the National University of Kyiv Mohyla Academy, Oleksiy Radynski, has done some research on this particular place, and has reported that the Yurchenko family has experienced many pressures over the years to give up and get out. Builders would like to fill in their hole and put up new structures, but the Yurchenkos seem to be asking for a sum for their property that builders are not accustomed to paying. Their goal, according to Radynski, is not to stay put as farmers, but to get for their land the kind of compensation that accords with the levels of profits that the urban sector will realize once they are gone. That would mean that this Ukrainian family would exchange life on the land for a realistic nest egg to start life in the city. By contrast, too many other Ukrainians left the land poor and stayed poor after moving to the city. In the meantime, the Yurchenko farmstead has housed the homeless and other outcasts from the city in exchange for labor on the farm, and for a time until they were deported, sheltered some undocumented immigrants to Ukraine from Georgia (Radynski, 2010, pp. 86-87). The essential story of this property is one of holding on to one's right to the city in the face of powerful forces of urbanization and, simultaneously, demanding a fair share of the financial benefit that comes to those engaged in transformation of a socialist city to one based on a market economy.

12   Reflections

12.1   A Souvenir and a Song

We begin with an inexpensive but telling souvenir that I once brought home from Kyiv. It is a work of junk art which may be legally exported from Ukraine (as it says explicitly, tongue-in-cheek on the back), and is printed on a small block of "ecologically clean wood" (as it also says on the back). The front is an image of Ukrainian faces in shades of white and grey drawn against a gloomy black background. In the center is a familiar portrait of a young Taras Shevchenko, the beloved "bard of Ukraine," representing the heart and soul of the nation. There are also some church domes, such as those in the title of this book, and a small rendition of the heroic statue of Batkivshchyna Maty (Mother of the Fatherland), the enormous Soviet-built World War II monument. However, most of the images and all of the larger ones other than Shevchenko suggest the "demons" side of the book's title. There are big-breasted beauties sipping cocktails (one has vampire teeth); a creepy-looking gangster with a shaved head and a cigarette in his mouth; someone dancing with the face of death; and a mix of symbols of consumer society (the front of a BMW automobile and an advertisement for Coca-Cola reflected on the sunglasses of still another shady character). I could not resist buying this "art" because as soon as I saw it I envisioned this paragraph. Instead of calling on comrades to join the famers' collective or win the war effort, as the heroines of Soviet society had done so famously, the caption to this image says (in English): "Welcome to Ukraine: Not Smiling Country!"

Yet, a popular song that is heard often in the city, "Kyeve miy" ("My Kyiv"), carries a refrain with the rhetorical question: *Yak tebe ne lyubyty, Kyeve miy*? (How can one not love you, my dear Kyiv?).[73] The melody is catchy. The 11 notes for the 11 syllables of the refrain play on Independence Square in the center of the city as a clock tower chimes the hours. The song is also heard, with or without lyrics, over the speaker systems in subway concourses and platforms during the morning rush, and want to or not, it is easy to wind up carrying the tune around all day afterwards. I at least, if not others, sometimes smile with appreciation for the city when I hear it.

Indeed, Kyiv is easy to love, truly so. I say this because we have read about one thing after another in this book that is wrong in the city – inexcusably wrong – so a declaration of love and an explanation for why one loves the city

73   Music by I. Shamo and lyrics by D. Lutsenko.

is necessary. We focus on the problems because we care and because we want solutions. We love Kyiv for many reasons. The city reflects in its landscape more than a millennium of rich history and architectural landmarks even though that history was itself marked by enormous tragedy and the worst urban destruction, and is still beautiful despite imposition of Soviet sameness to its vast housing estates and, as we have seen, shameless disorderly urban development after independence. Despite appearing to be dour at first impression – something that is said to be an outcome of living within the rigors of Soviet society – the people of Kyiv are genuinely warm and friendly and the city is welcoming. Cultural opportunities are everywhere, and life in Kyiv can mean having to choose between too many concerts, too many theatrical or ballet performances, too many art gallery shows, and too many good speakers at university campuses and learned societies at once. Despite poor city planning, much of what is new in the city is good, too: improved housing choices for those who have found a foot in the economy; better shops and a full choice of goods; economic links and opportunities to the global world; good restaurants and a bustling nightlife; and new freedoms to travel and to pray. There is also increased use of the Ukrainian language in Kyiv and patriotism to Ukraine, both of which the Soviets had suppressed as they had suppressed travel and prayer. There are other pluses, too.

To my mind, the single most spectacular feature of Kyiv is the city center, where the mighty Dnipro River cuts through the middle of Kyiv and divides it between the historic Right Bank and the much more recently developed Left Bank. It is an enormous green zone with parks, forests, meadows, wetlands, and countless sandy beaches (Kyiv Urban Design Studio, 2006). Some of the beaches are big and public and others cozy and secluded. In a section of this vast zone that is called Hidropark, the area near the Metro stop has countless food, ice cream, and beer kiosks, restaurants and nightclubs, an amusements and rides section for children, and designated places for an enormous variety of sports: volleyball, tennis, ping pong, weightlifting, gymnastics, basketball, and others. All of this is left over from the Soviet Union. There is also bungee jumping, a zone on sandy dunes for dirt bikes, and jetboat rentals, among newer diversions. Other cities have great beachfronts or enormous parks, too, but no other city anywhere has such an enormous and diverse green center to which citizens converge from all directions during their free time. Indeed, in other cities people scatter in all directions when they have days off. But uniquely, in Kyiv, when the seasons allow, they come together in the city's heart (Figure 12.1). There, they enjoy themselves in each other's company. From here especially, one can sense great potential everywhere for Kyiv, if only the demons that now trouble the city could be brought under control.

Figure 12.1   Kyivans in the sun together

12.2   A Messy Period

We had come to Kyiv during what a friend has called (in English) a "messy period" in its history – that period of time between the end of one system of social order and replacement by a new order that works. I have used terms such as "difficult transition" and the "Wild West" in text to describe the situation, and highlighted it early in the book with discussion of a graffito on an escalator in Kyiv's subway system that proclaimed that "Ukraine Is Far from Heaven." It has been more than 20 years since Ukraine became unexpectedly independent and Kyiv became the national capital for the first time in a very long time; now it is clear that 20 years is not enough time to replace mess with success. Few countries in history have been fortunate enough to be born without trauma, and many have taken much longer than just one generation to forge the kinds of societal agreements that work for the country. Ukraine will be a mess for a while longer, and Kyiv will continue to be picked apart by the greedy and self-interested. Lamentably, recognition of Kyivans' rights *to* their city and the institution of effective protections for them by rule of law *within* their city are still some way down the road. Also sadly, much of the social security that socialism had provided such as steady work for all, decent shelter, and at least a modicum of social equality for all, if only at a lower level, has been eroded, and people live with increased uncertainty, unfairness, exploitation, corruption, and disorder. In this book, we have documented many of these ills and given examples.

Let us hope that when order does arrive, that it comes from within Ukraine and not, as has been the tragic history of the country, one that is imposed from outside. Having an assertive and acquisitive big neighbor next door has made it that much harder to build Ukraine into a truly independent country, and has retarded as well achievement of the national dream that perhaps at last, Ukraine could be both free of foreign rule and prosperous. It has also hurt that, in a lingering vestige of the old Cold War, the West covets Ukraine, too, and would like to drive an ever-wider wedge between the country and its long-term cousin, Russia. Unfortunately, the country's political leaders have not been talented enough to successfully play off one suitor against the other for the benefit of the nation as a whole. Instead, during the messy period, far too many politicians have concentrated on taking care of themselves and their cronies, have become fabulously wealthy, and in many cases have planted at least one foot (if not both) in a comfortable country abroad in preparation for the time when they will need to emigrate. It is often said in Ukraine that the robbers will eventually run from the law or a change in government, or when there is nothing more left in the country to steal, whichever comes first. Like the American robber barons of the latter part of the 19th century and their "cottages" in Newport, Rhode Island, there are super-rich Ukrainians (and Russians, of whom there are more in this category) who are now prominent new residents in the communities of super-rich expats from around the globe in places like Mediterranean Spain or France, the ski resorts of Switzerland, and prestige neighborhoods in London. I can imagine the opulence of these privileged spaces as being the transplanted wealth of Ukraine (and Russia), as it has also been the product of the oil wealth of the Arabian Peninsula and Nigeria, among other sources of global fortune. I also see these landscapes as the twinned obverse of the depressing "landscapes of struggle" that are now so extensive throughout Ukraine.

A main theme throughout this book has been the injustices that have been aggravated since the end of the Soviet period by rich *bizensmeny* (businessmen) making huge additional profits for themselves at public cost. Such practices are global, of course, and have gone on throughout history, and are not limited to today's societies in transition from socialism. They are also not limited to capitalism. They are, however, emblematic of our times. A short essay in the latest book by noted urban scholar David Harvey entitled "London 2011: Feral Capitalism Hits the Streets" makes this point:

> We live in a society where capitalism itself has become rampantly
> feral. Feral politicians cheat on their expenses; feral bankers plunder
> the public purse for all it's worth; CEOs, hedge fund operators, and
> private equity geniuses loot the world of wealth; telephone and credit
> card companies load mysterious charges on everyone's bills ... A politi-
> cal economy of mass dispossession, of predatory practices to the point
> of daylight robbery – particularly of the poor and the vulnerable, the
> unsophisticated and the legally unprotected – has become the order of
> the day. (Harvey, 2012, pp. 155-157)

Thus, much of what I have said about Kyiv is only one's city's twist on a story
that is familiar worldwide. There are demons who muscle for what they want
in all corners of the planet, and everywhere there are legions of ordinary
people who pay the price. From my earlier research, I could elaborate with
examples about how top-down redevelopment has taken Japaneseness out
of Tokyo, about how incursions by multinational business and development
companies from abroad have taken livelihoods from ordinary Khmer and
Cham citizens from along the riverfront and lakes of Phnom Penh, and about
the toll that developer-led gentrification has taken from community life
in neighborhoods in my home base of Philadelphia. My life has now taken
me to Kyiv where the pattern continues, but in a framework of transition
from Soviet socialism. Because that is a new type of transition that affects
a vast region with many cities, it is a story whose details are especially
worth presenting.

There was inequality within Soviet society, too, as Community Party leaders found ways to satisfy their own needs while the rest of the population
struggled with long lines and shortages of commodities. Now, however, in a
fairly short period, the inequalities have become truly obscene. A new class
of "millionaires against the people" has taken the country and its capital,
and lives as it wants at the cost of the masses. Ironically, this was the case
also in the Russian Empire near the turn of the 20th century, albeit under
different circumstances, when members of an idealistic intelligentsia began
talking about revolution against excessive czarist privilege and exploitation
of workers by capitalist industrialists. While it is only a minority of people in
Ukraine (and in Russia, too) who would seem to favor a return to communism
(and for some of those, the true motive is said to be to return to the special
privileges they had lost from when they were communist chiefs), the truth is
that communists now have a "we told you so" platform to run on in national
elections. It is campaign season for local political offices in Ukraine as I write
this, and the Communist Party of Ukraine is optimistic about making gains in

the Verkhovna Rada with election slogans about the unfairness of capitalism. The large red billboard that one sees now across the city that reads (in Russian, not Ukrainian) *Vlast millionam, a ne millioneram!* (Wealth for the millions, but not for the millionaires!) might resonate well with much of the public.

Kyiv, as we have seen, has been a particular object of theft. The transition from state ownership of land and buildings to an environment of private ownership has produced lopsided distributions of profit and other benefits in favor of those who are most aggressive at business, toughest, most powerfully connected, and most lacking in conscience. Many ordinary Kyivans who had happened to live on real estate that a "new oligarch" coveted found themselves to be poorly protected during this messy period and were rudely displaced. The same is true for many museums and other cultural institutions, and countless popular bookshops, cafés, restaurants, and other small businesses. There have been inadequate protections as well for city squares, parks, playgrounds, river frontage, and promontories with prized views, and for the preservation of historic buildings and landscapes. While there are many aspects of "New Kyiv" that are welcome and positive additions to the urban scene, there is so much else that is shamefully destructive of lives, livelihoods, and landscapes that it is not too much of an exaggeration to say that the ancient city of Kyiv is once again being pillaged.

I wish the following were not true but it is: there is a children's board game for "ages 10 and up" (as it says on the box) that is called "Kiev Capitalist." I have transliterated the title from the Russian language, the language of the game. Hence, "Kiev" and not "Kyiv." I saw it for sale in the children's section in a bookstore selling mostly Russian books, and almost bought it until my conscience caught up. It is a takeoff on the board game Monopoly. The object is to move through the tourist landmarks and historical sites of Kyiv, acquiring as many of them as possible before your opponent does, and to wind up with all the property and all the money. The box cover says something about learning about the city's past, but the title of the game and its definition of ultimate victory are taken from the culture of raiders and not from the culture of those who love cities. To my mind, this is another bit of proof that the capital city of Ukraine is nothing more than a commodity for the new, postsocialist class of oligarch-capitalists, and that in such a context it is perfectly fine for children to be taught such hooey. Yes, indeed, Ukraine is still far from heaven, and there are demons who would keep it that way. Reclaiming the city for the people will take many years, indeed. If I were in charge, I would draw a line around Castle Hill and in the sands of the banks of the Dnipro, and say that it is here that the defense of Kyiv should be concentrated and that from here, the rest of the city can be won.

12.3   A Book Review

It is not unusual for an author to close a book with a review of what has been said. I have done some of that already. But, if I may, since this has been a somewhat unusual book from the start, as well as one that has been quite personal, I close not with a review of my own words, but with a review of another book that, in a very different way, says much of what I have strived to convey. This is an ambitious new book that came out after I had already finished and edited advanced drafts of my manuscript, so this review is an afterthought. It is written just days after the book was presented publicly for the first time in the lecture hall of Ye, the Ukrainian-language bookstore near the Opera House in the heart of Kyiv. As I listened to the various speakers, these afterthoughts began to take shape.

The book is called *Kyiv Zhyvopysnyi/Kyiv Pictorial*. It is bilingual Ukrainian–English, like the title, and is a large-format, coffee-table book with 255 color reproductions of recently commissioned paintings and engravings of Kyiv scenes by selected artists from all over Ukraine. Almost all of the work was done in 2011. Some of the painters are established stars with global reputations, while many others are young talents whose work is seeing wide exposure for the first time. Some knew Kyiv extremely well, while others, perhaps a little like me, were drawn from elsewhere to a city that they did not know well to record their impressions. The official reason for the volume is to celebrate the 200th anniversary of the birth of the Ukrainian poet and artist Taras Shevchenko (1814-1861), so there are numerous quotations from the beloved bard throughout the book about Kyiv and its river. The goal is also to draw attention to the city's charms and beauty which are, unfortunately, being eroded. As expressed in the introduction, "just two years from [when the project started in 2010] the Capital looks different. It changed immensely and not always for the better" (Oslamovskyi, Lytvynenko, and Zayika, eds., 2013, p. 10; punctuation error corrected). At the book's public premier, one of the speakers opined that, these days, young people seem to always have their concentration on their mobile telephones and no longer see and appreciate the city around them or their fellow citizens. But art is a medium that they respond to, and artists have unusual power to sway the public's thinking.

There are a variety of subject themes in this collection, many of them more or less to be expected: the city's historic churches and golden-gilt domes; its parks, fountains, and places to sit; high points with panoramic views; and the hubbub of Khreshchatyk both during the day and after dark. There are also paintings of the river and its iconic bridges, popular beaches, the city in various seasons, famous monuments and other landmarks, and chestnut trees in colorful bloom. The paintings are, for the most part, excellent, and the book is, like Kyiv itself, a joy. I wanted to show the same in my book, too – that Kyiv is beautiful and easy to love. But, also, I wanted to show that Kyiv is worth saving from the demons of destructive urban change that are all too prevalent.

Kyiv Zhyvopysnyi/Kyiv Pictorial does this, too. I heard speakers at the book's opening lament that the city's cultural institutions are being undermined for profit elsewhere, and that there are significant losses of historic buildings and authentic historical urban texture, and of the city's outstanding and ample greenery. So, while the majority of the artwork in this handsome volume shows well-executed scenes that are "to be expected," there are a number of other artists' contributions that depict a new and unhappy side of Kyiv. There is a painting of the motorcade of President Yanukovych disrupting traffic at the congested "crossroads in Podil" – billboards and all; another painting that is matter-of-factly entitled "Everyday Life in the Capital" that shows two giant billboards on high poles being erected on a new residential district where pedestrians are dwarfed by the distances that they need to walk and the height of the advertising (see my Figure 9.5); and a painting of vernacular architecture in historic Podil that centers on a large vacant lot surrounded by the iconic green wooden fence that anticipates new construction. For most Kyivans, the expectation is of something incompatible with their needs – a "monster" of some sort or other. There are no artworks about sex tourism, official corruption, "Bullies with Bentleys," or many other problems, but there are paintings of a city full of cars, including an oil of the bell tower of St. Sophia that seems stranded in a sea of automobiles. It is called simply "Evening." Another painting by the same artist shows cars parked on a sidewalk. Likewise, there are no overt depictions of poverty or other human misery, but there is a painting of a very heavyset and angry-faced old woman sitting alone on a wooden crate on a sidewalk in freezing winter weather and selling sunflower seeds, another of a hungry cat rummaging in the night through a garbage bin, and a third of a stray dog lurking in the dark shadows of a gritty interior courtyard of an old housing complex.

There are not as many of these "alternative" views of Kyiv in the book as there are paintings of happy scenes, but there are enough of them to signify to lovers of the city that, in Kyiv, there are problems. The balance of representations in my book was the reverse. I have written on and on about things that are wrong, and spent only some pages here and there about Kyiv the good. But as I listened to the speakers at the book's public debut and began to pore simultaneously through the contents, I realized that despite the differences in media, my book and theirs shared the same message: we have a great city that is enormously undervalued, and that will be stripped of its value unless Kyivans intervene and others help.

Postscript

With the situation changing so rapidly in Ukraine as I write this from Kyiv in mid-March, 2014, the best option for current information is this epilogue. Instead of repeating what has been widely reported in the global media about the ouster of Viktor Yanukovych from the presidency, the brazen Russian aggression in Crimea and the march of Soviet-like propaganda that is being used to justify it, and the escalating tug of war over Ukraine between Russia and the West, I will focus on updates about the specific people and places in Kyiv that were most prominently mentioned in the previous twelve chapters. A format akin to bullet point will suffice.

The Euromaidan demonstrations continue on Maidan Nezalezhnosti (Independence Square) despite the victory over Yanukovych. The numbers of people, however, are smaller. Even during the worst of the storming of Maidan during February 18-20, 2014, during which more than 100 defenders were killed by government forces, Maidan held, albeit for a time in much reduced territory. The stage from which there had been so many speeches, songs, and prayers during the three months before the attacked never yielded, and was a scene of fervent ecumenical prayer as fires raged and snipers' bullets flew at any human targets within sights. Now that Ukraine's interim government is headed by pro-Maidan activists, the Berkut police units have been dissolved, and there are no hostile militias or hired *titushky* in sight, Maidan is being rebuilt once again, and again as a grassroots encampment. The goal now, after Yanukovych is gone, is good government. For many Maidan activists, that means a complete turnover of membership of the parliament (Verkhovna Rada), the various ministries of government, the courts and other justice institutions, and local and oblast offices across the land, including the office of the mayor of Kyiv. Moreover, quite a few of the buildings around and near Independence Square are occupied by protestors and self-defense units, including the large Hotel Dnipro, various government buildings, and many retail premises along Khreshchatyk and other streets. The Trade Unions House (Chapter 6) was all but totally destroyed in a fire during the height of the fighting, with many deaths. Its blackened ruins loom over Independence Square as reminder of what had taken place.

Even more than before (Chapter 6), the word "Maidan" has come to mean a gathering of the citizenry to effect change for the better, and the specific space that is Maidan Nezalezhnosti has come to be emblematic of such activity. Furthermore, because there were so many deaths in defense of

Maidan and the Ukrainian cause, Maidan Nezalezhnosti is now thought of as sacred space. It is still ripped up and charred from the conflict, but it is slated to be repaired, apparently at the donated cost of billionaire businessman and likely candidate for president Petro Poroshenko (Roshen chocolates). The base of Independence Monument is also charred and needs repair. I imagine that the design of the square will be changed, perhaps in a way to encourage public gatherings (as opposed to the planned design that had deliberately impeded large gatherings in the past), and to present a more dignified space for the center of Ukraine's capital. On a different note, however, on March 9, 2004 I heard Yuriy Lutsenko, a former Minister of the Interior, former prisoner under Yanukovych, and a central organizer of Euromaidan (for which he was beaten on January 11, 2014 by a gang of police and hospitalized), speak to a huge crowd on Independence Square and say that the new pavement needs to be of stones that fit neatly into the palm of a hand "in case we ever need to start throwing again." The crowd cheered. His serious point was that all future politicians will know why the stones are of a particular size, and will therefore behave themselves.

At present, Independence Square is a shrine to the fallen, Nebesna Sotnya, the "Hundred in Heaven" or "Heaven's Batallion." There are memorials everywhere, thousands and thousands of candles, religious icons, and enormous piles of flowers, as well as countless photographs of the dead. There are photos and flowers at the precise spots were bodies were found. Visitors stream through by the thousands, speaking silently to one another, taking photographs, and pausing again and again to pray. They see where government snipers had taken positions, where their heroes had fallen, and the great many bullet holes that scar the trunks of trees, signposts, and the sides of buildings. Nearby is an assortment of captured government water cannons, personnel trucks, and burned buses, as well as displays of weapons that had been used against the people such as percussion grenades. There are still enormous barricades that surround Maidan, and mountains of tires and other flammables that will be burned if the defense of Maidan once again calls for walls of fire. There are also countless high piles of bricks, stones, and Molotov cocktails for defenders to use. The most blood was shed on Instytutska Steet beside the square. As seen in new street signs, it has been renamed the Heroes of Nebesna Sotnya Street. Granite monuments are up too, less than two weeks from the time of the shootings. Symbolism matters greatly in times of conflict.

The previous acting mayor of Kyiv (technically Director of City Administration), Oleksandr Popov (Chapters 2 and 3), was suspended from office by Yanukovych on December 14, 2013 and then fired altogether on January 25,

2014, as a result of the wholesale beatings of peaceful Maidan demonstrators on November 30, 2013. At the time, the majority of demonstrators were college students. Popov's dismissal was not because he ordered the beatings of students, which he apparently did not, but because he responded to a reporter's question about who did by pointing the finger, apparently accurately, at Viktor Pshonka, the Prosecutor General of Ukraine and one of President Yanukovych's closest allies.

Elections for Mayor of Kyiv are scheduled for May 25, 2014. (So are national elections that will determine the next president of Ukraine and the membership of the Verkhovna Rada.) Two candidates have been announced so far, Lesya Orobets, a member of parliament from the Batkivshchyna (Fatherland) Party and prominent Euromaidan activist (who was not mentioned previously in the text), and Ihor Lutsenko, a prominent activist with Save Old Kyiv and other protest movements (Chapter 11), including Euromaidan. Kyiv will be in much better shape in the hands of either.

Ihor Lutsenko was one of the many Kyivans who was very helpful to me as I worked on this book. On the night of January 21, 2014, he escorted his friend Yuriy Verbytsky to a hospital for treatment of injuries that he received from an attack on Maidan by *titushky*. The both of them were then kidnapped from the hospital by unknown men dressed in black, and taken to a wooded area outside Kyiv where they were interrogated, beaten, tortured, and left to die. Verbytsky did not survive, but Lutsenko, who did not know that Verbytsky was nearby in the same forest, managed to crawl for help. He survived, but barely so. Yuriy Verbytsky's death adds the scandalous body count of those who had opposed the bad governments that Ukraine has suffered since independence. (There were, of course, even more deaths during Soviet times when opposition to the Communist Party was truly dangerous.)

A few days before my March, 2014 trip to Kyiv, I attended a public lecture given by Myroslava Gongadze, the widow of the murdered Ukrainian journalist Heorhiy Ruslanovych Gongadze (Chapter 4), in a packed hall at the Law School of New York University. I also had the privilege of speaking with her afterward in a room where refreshments were being served. She lives in the United States now, along with twin daughters, and speaks English well. Despite the large audience, you could have heard a pin drop as she spoke about her ordeal when her husband went missing, and her ordeal again in seeking justice after his body was found. The Yanukovych government had not yet fallen when she spoke, and her message was not just about the worst period in her life, but also about the rapidly escalating dangers to democracy and press freedoms that Ukrainians were facing. She spoke about Lutsenko and Verbytsky, and about other activists who were being beaten and kidnapped by an army of thugs in the pay of the government. Most especially, she spoke about the recent ordeal of Tetyana Chornovil, a journalist affiliated with *Ukrayinska Pravda* (Ukrainian Truth), the online newspaper that her husband had founded and paid for with his life.

Tetyana Chornovil (also written as Tetiana Chornovol) was almost another victim. She was the fearless investigative reporter who climbed the fence of Yanukovych's Mezhiyirya estate to photograph the riches on the other side (Chapter 3). She had also been investigating the construction of a new "Monaco-like" palace for Yanukovych on a promontory above the Black Sea in Crimea (referred to as "Mezhihirya 2"), and together with Ihor Lutsenko, who is also a journalist by profession, took photographs of the construction from above, below, and the sides. Then, on December 25, 2013, she was run off the road near a shopping center near her home, and was severely beaten by a gang of men in black and left for dead. She survived and became a *cause célèbre* on Maidan where photographs of her severely disfigured face after the beatings helped to swell the crowds to new levels. Incredibly, the official investigation into the case offered a conclusion that she was the victim of nothing more than a road rage incident. After Mezhihirya was vacated by Yanukovych, photos of Tatyana Chornovil were found on the premises, along with a detailed description of her automobile and information about her personal schedule and frequent whereabouts. I saw these with my own eyes.

Yanukovych's Mezhihirya estate proved to be much more luxurious and over-the-top lavish than people had imagined. The grounds were opened to the public after its "lord" had fled (Chapter 3), and Ukrainians have come ever since in great numbers for a personal look. On some days there are traffic jams. Not only is there outrage about how much the estate must have cost the public, but considerable laughter at its bad taste. A fake pirate ship on an artificial pond is a favorite target. The premises also sport a golf course, an equestrian club, yacht club, swimming pool, and tennis courts. The private zoo that had previously been a rumor is there also. In one of the garages is a museum-quality collection of vintage Soviet automobiles. There are also motorbike collections, sports cars, and a museum of motorboats. A pristine 1963 Chevrolet Impala sits beside a pristine Bentley from 1950. In the oversized main house there is luxury everywhere, from crystal chandeliers to toilets where, indeed, the fixtures are of gold. Perhaps most scandalous are the priceless books and documents that were stolen from Ukraine's history by non-reader Yanukovych, including the original (1654) *Apostolos* by Ivan Fyodorov, the first printed book in Ukrainian. As a result of a hurried and inept attempt to destroy evidence against the fleeing Yanukovych, many recent documents were found floating in the Dnipro near Mezhihirya; they are now being dried and inventoried.

There is more luxury than was imagined in Koncha Zaspa too (Chapter 7), in the lavish mansions of former government officials who also fled when Yanukovych fell. That of ousted Prosecutor General of Ukraine Viktor Pshonka, an especially close associate of Yanukovych, was shown to be extraordinarily extravagant, perhaps even more so than the main house at Mezhihirya. It is a world of priceless antiques and art works, including a large collection of spectacular orthodox religious icons of unknown provenance, as well as of countless modern luxuries and conveniences. Visitors give considerable attention to the irony of an elegant marble bust of Russia's Catherine the Great, under whose reign much of Ukrainian territory was annexed into the Russian Empire, and to the various painted portraits of Pshonka himself in various heroic poses, including as Julius Caesar and as Napoleon. My own favorite is the painting in which Viktor Yanukovych is handing Viktor Pshonka a bouquet of red roses. Art is supposed to make one think; this silly-looking painting makes one wonder about the relationship between the two Viktors.

Like Yanukovych, Pshonka has disappeared. He is also thought to be in Russia. That may be where former Minister of Education and Culture Dmytro Tabachnyk has gone to hide. He might also be in Israel. When Prime Minister Mykola Azarov was forced from office, he fled to Vienna where his family had already evacuated. That was thought to be a curious choice for a man whose party was so unequivocally outspoken against the European Union. All of these and other Party of Regions leaders have had their considerable Western assets frozen and face visa restrictions from the EU and the countries of North America. Yanukovych is wanted by Ukrainian authorities for mass murder of Euromaidan activists. Mass murder warrants have also been drawn up for Pshonka, Andriy Klyuyev, the former chief of staff for Yanukovych, Vitaliy Zakharchenko, the former interior minister, and Olena Lukash, the former justice minister, among others.

Former Prime Minister Yulia Tymoshenko, an arch-enemy of Viktor Yanukovych, has been released from prison, and may or may not decide to run for office. The posts that were vacated by departing Regionnaires are now occupied by luminaries from Euromaidan and politicians from Yanukovych's opposition, at least until the national elections that are scheduled for May 25, 2014. The acting president is Oleksandr Turchynov, a *nardep* from the Batkivschyna Party and ally of Tymoshenko. Arsenyi Yatsenyuk (Chapter 4), the leader of Tymoshenko's Batkivshyna Party, is acting Prime

Minister. From earlier pages in the book, it is worth updating that crusading journalist Tetyana Chornovil has been designated as Ukraine's leading corruption investigator, and that Sergiy Kvit, the President of NaUKMA (see acknowledgements) and frequent foe of Dmytro Tabachnyk about higher education policy for Ukraine, has replaced Tabachnyk as Minister of Education and Culture.

Outside the sphere of politics, we observe that beyond the immediate Euromaidan zone, Kyiv is still abuilding. Renat Akhmetov's developers are making progress with reconstruction of the former TsUM department store (Chapter 6), which promises to be quite attractive, and with the planned new building on St. Andrew's descent (Chapter 6). There are other construction projects moving forward around the city too, reflecting more than a little optimism about the future of Ukraine and Kyiv on the part of investors. Hostynyi Dvir construction is advancing too, even though it was an exceptionally hot flashpoint for historical preservation protestors (Chapter 11).

There is construction coming, too, at the site of the historic Desiatynna Church (Chapter 3). As mentioned before, the site is commonly regarded as especially sacred, and as a foundation point for the glories of ancient Rus and Ukrainian and Russian civilizations. The contest between Russian and Ukrainian churches for access to this ground continues unabated. The Ukrainian Orthodox Church, Moscow Patriarchate, continues to hold the spot adjacent where it had built the log cabin-like Church of the Nativity of the Blessed Virgin. Now, that structure has been substantially enlarged and is of masonry. Meanwhile, the Ukrainian Orthodox Church, Kyiv Patriarchate, is constructing its office headquarters across a short stretch of park nearby, much to the consternation of Save Old Kyiv activists and other historic preservationists who lament the loss of older structures that had been ghosts (Chapter 6) on the site. As seen from a nearby billboard, the office complex looks to be well designed in a style that befits the historic ambience of Kyiv (Chapter 11). Both the new office building and the intrusive Nativity of the Blessed Virgin Church are considered to be examples of "Raiding by Religion" in Kyiv.

Another update from Desiatynna is that the hallowed ground where the ancient church had stood is scheduled to be a museum of that church. It is to be administered by Ukrainian Ministry of Culture. Construction has not started yet, but most of the forbidding green fence that one surrounded the site to keep the competing religious factions away (and to protect archaeological treasures below ground), is now down. That means that equipment for ground breaking and construction is likely to be moved in soon.

Figure 13.1   Honoring the fallen at Maidan Nezalezhnosti after the killings of mid-February, 2014

The "helipad from hell" (Chapter 3) is still in place. It looks finished, but there are no helicopters and, of course, no more chief whirlybirder. The spacious floors below look empty too, but we cannot see what is inside because they are encased with one-way glass. For sure, there are no cars in the parking lot. People gather at the viewpoint above to gawk, and speak about the intrusive monster in tones less hushed than before. The hill slope is denuded and will probably not stay in place during the strong rains of spring.

On a positive note, despite the conflict and worries about war, life goes on as before in the various neighborhoods of Kyiv. More Ukrainian flags hang from residential balconies in reflection of citizens' heightened political awareness, but otherwise the rhythms of local life have not missed many beats. People go to work and school more or less as before, they go shopping, fill their cars with gasoline, and watch over small children as they play in local sand lots. We still see old women vendors wherever there are crossroads of pedestrians, young people enjoying themselves while hanging out after school and on the weekend, blue-collar men looking for work at the morning gatherings at the central train station, and everywhere lots of nicely dressed young Ukrainian women. Quite a few people in all of these categories sport buttons or blue-and-yellow ribbons that identify them as patriots and as supporters of change in Ukraine.

Finally, I can report that for now at least, Kyiv is a city without Bentleys (Chapter 7), Rolls Royces, Lamborghinis, Ferraris, and other extra expensive cars. In a week of touring Kyiv in March, 2014, I saw only one vehicle from this category, a Bentley, and that was on a "safe" Sunday morning. A taxi driver I had hired confirmed that traffic now moves more efficiently and politely, despite the many streets in the center of Kyiv that are blocked with Euromaidan barricades, and that no one misses the cars of the privileged. He and other Kyivans all say that the rich cars have left the country, probably to Russia, along with "the crooks who own them." Likewise, I can say that during that week in March, when I spent almost all of my time in the center of the city, I saw no sex tourists and no sex workers trolling for clients (Chapter 10), and noted that at least some of the city's gaudy striptease clubs seem to be closed. In fact, one establishment that was in the Hotel Dnipro is now occupied as an encampment for a civil defense group in support of Maidan, albeit one about which there is some controversy. Regardless, I expect that Kyiv might indeed be headed for better days.

References

Adams, John S. (2008). "Monumentality in Urban Design: The Case of Russia." *Eurasian Geography and Economics*, 49, 3, pp. 280-303.

Alexander, Catherine, Victor Buchli, and Caroline Humphrey, eds. (2007). *Urban Life in Post-Soviet Asia*. London: University College London Press.

Amchuk, Leonid (2005). "Andriy Yushchenko – Son of God?" *Ukraiyinska Pravda*, July 7, http://eng.maidanua.org/node/356

Archer, Dan, and Olha Trusova (2010). *Na Mezhi*. N.p.: Borderlandcomics.com.

Argenbright, Robert (1999). "Remaking Moscow: New Places, New Selves." *The Geographical Review*, 89, 1, pp. 1-22.

Associated Press (2011). "Yanukovych Accused of Plagiarism in New Book." *Kyiv Post*, October 27. Available at: http://www.kyivpost.com/news/nation/detail/115776/.

Axenov, Konstantin, Isolde Brade, and Evgenij Bondarchuk (2006). *The Transformation of Urban Space in Post-Soviet Russia*. London and New York: Routledge.

Bakanov, Vitalyi (2011). *Zabytie Stranitsi Kievskogo Byta*. Kyiv: Sky Horse.

Baldayeva, Irina (2007). "The Homeless of Ulan-Ude." In Catherine Alexander, Victor Buchli, and Caroline Humphrey, eds., *Urban Life in Post-Soviet Asia*. London: University College London Press, pp. 157-174.

Bartov, Omer (2007). *Erased: Vanishing Traces of Jewish Galicia in Present-Day Ukraine*. Princeton: Princeton University Press.

Barykina, Natalia (2008). "Architecture and Spatial Practices in Post-Communist Minsk: Urban Space under Authoritarian Control." *spacesofidentity.net*, 8, 2. Available at: https://pi.library.yorku.ca/ojs/index.php/soi/article/view/18121.

Basarab, O. (2010). "Tabir ide v nebo." *Ukrainskyi Tyzhden*, 44, 157, pp. 58-59.

Bater, James H. (1980). *The Soviet City: Ideal and Reality*. Beverly Hills, CA: Sage Publications.

Beaumont, Peter (2009). "Anger as Kiev Council Plans to Build Hotel at Biggest Holocaust Shooting Site." *The Guardian*, September 24. Available at: http://www.guardian.co.uk/world/2009/sep/24/hotel-kiev-holocaust-germany-babi-yar.

Belorusets, Evheniya (2010). "Stykhiynyi rynok: Fotoreportazh." *Spilne: Zhurnal Sotsialnoi Krytyky*, 1, pp. 57-78.

Berdahl, D., M. Bunzl and M. Lampland, eds. (2000). *Altering States: Ethnographies of Transition in Eastern Europe from the Former Soviet Union*. Ann Arbor: University of Michigan Press.

Berger, Paul (2012). "Was Kiev Beating Anti-Semitic Act?" *Jewish Daily Forward*, June 3. Available at: http://forward.com/articles/157135/was-kiev-beating-anti-semitic-act/?p=all#ixzz1wjPXF1p5.

Berkhoff, Karel C. (2004). *Harvest of Despair: Life and Death in Ukraine under Nazi Rule*. Cambridge, MA: The Belknap Press of Harvard University Press.

Bilokin, Sergei (n.d.). "1930: The Destruction of Old Kyiv." Sergei Bilokin website. Available at: http://www.s-bilokin.name/Culture/KyivRuined.html.

Boksha, Tetyana, Anna Vaylchenko, Tetyana Ivanova, Dina Kravchuk, and Hanna Nosak (2010). "Kriminalizatsiya mihratsiyi u Kyevi: Pryklad pidpaliv Shulyavskoho sekond hendu." *Spilne: Zhurnal Sotsialnoi Krytyky*, 1, pp. 79-88.

Boltovskaya, Svetlana (2010). "African Communities in Moscow and St. Petersburg: Issues of Inclusion and Exclusion." In Cordula Gdaniec, ed., *Cultural Diversity in Russian Cities: The Urban Landscape in the Post-Soviet Era*. New York: Berghahn Books, chapter 5.

Bouzarovski, Stefan, Joseph Salukvadze, and Michael Gentile (2011). "A Socially Resilient Urban Transition: The Contested Landscapes of Apartment Building Extensions in Two Post-Communist Cities." *Urban Studies*, 48, 13, pp. 2689-2714.

Boychenko, V. O., et al. (1968). *Istoriya Mist i Sil Ukrainiskoi RSR: Kyiv*. Kyiv: Holovna Redaktsiia Ukrainskoi Radianskoi Entsyklopedii.

Brandon, Ray and Wendy Lower, eds. (2010). The Shoah in Ukraine: History, Testimony, Memorialization. Bloomington: Indiana University Press.

Bridger, Sue, Rebecca Kay, and Kathryn Pinnick (1996). *No More Heroines? Russia, Women and the Market*. London: Routledge.

Browne, Michael, ed. (1973). *Ferment in Ukraine*. Woodhaven, NY: Crisis Press.

Brym, Robert J. (1994). *The Jews of Moscow, Kiev and Minsk: Identity, Antisemitism, Emigration*. London: The Macmillan Press and Institute of Jewish Affairs.

Buchli, Victor (2007). "Astana: Materiality and the City." In Catherine Alexander, Victor Buchli, and Caroline Humphrey, eds., *Urban Life in Post-Soviet Asia*. London: University College London Press, pp. 40-69.

Burakovskiy, Aleksandr (2011). "Holocaust in Remembrance in Ukraine: Memorialization of the Jewish Tragedy at Babi Yar." *Nationalities Papers*, 39, 3, pp. 371-389.

Butkevych, Bohdan (2012). "Unwelcome Guests at the Inn." *The Ukrainian Week*, 13, 36, pp. 24-26.

Byelomyesyatsev, A. B., et al. (2012). *Zabudova Kyeva doby klasychnoho kapitalizmu: Abo koly i yak misto stalo evropeiskym*. Kyiv: Varto.

Carynnyk, Marco (2011). "Foes of Our Rebirth: Ukrainian Nationalist Discussions about Jews, 1929-1947." *Nationalities Papers*, 39, 3, pp. 315-352.

Chekmenov, Oleksandr (2011). "Romskyi syndrome: Ukrainski tsyhany pryrecheni na criminal." *Ukrainskyi Tyzhden*, 43, 208, October 20.

Chornovil, Vyacheslav (1968). *The Chornovil Papers*. New York: McGraw-Hill.

Conquest, Robert (2001). *Reflections of a Ravaged Century*. New York: Norton.

Cybriwsky, Roman (2012a). "Kyiv mizh monstramy ta modernizatsiyeyu: Mirkuvannya pro kaptalistychne pereformuvannya postsotsialistychnoho mista." In A. Makarenko et al., eds., *Anatomiya Mista: Kyiv*. Kyiv: Heinrich Böll Stiftung – Smoloskyp, pp. 42-49.

— (2012b). "Feys-kontrol v Arena-Siti: Reportazh iz zolotoi klitky." *Politychna Krytyka*, 3, pp. 207-214.

Czaplicka, John, Nida Gelazis, and Blair Ruble, eds. (2009). *Cities after the Fall of Communism: Reshaping Cultural Landscapes and European Identity*. Washington, DC: Woodrow Wilson Center Press/Baltimore, MD: The Johns Hopkins University Press.

Denisova, Tatyana A. (2001). "Trafficking in Women and Children for Purposes of Sexual Exploitation: The Criminological Aspect." *Trends in Organized Crime*, 6, 3 and 4, pp. 30-36.

Dmytrenko, Ksenia, ed. (2011). *Stratehiyi urbanistychoho maybutnoho Kyeva*. Kyiv: Heinrich Böll Stiftung.

Dmytrieva, Maria (2011). "'FEMEN' na tli hrudey." *Krytyka*, 1-2, 156-160, pp. 20-22.

Drob'yazko, L.Ye. (2009). *Babyn Yar: Shcho? De? Koly?* Kyiv: Kyi Publishing.

Duda, Andriy (2012). "Creeping DeUkrainization." *The Ukrainian Week*, 2, 25, February, pp. 30-31.

Dutchak, Oksana (2009). *Radical Claiming without Radical Claims: Promises and Limits of Transactional Activism in Post-Orange Kyiv*. MA thesis. Social Anthropology. Central European University, Budapest Hungary.

— and Volodymyr Ishchenko (2010). "'Prava na Misto' abo tochkovi protesty proty tochkovykh zabudov? Dylemi miskoho rukhu na prykladi initsiatyvy 'Zberezhy Staryi Kyiv'." *Spilne: Zhurnal Sotsialnoi Krytyky*, 2, pp. 102-117.

Economist, The (2013). "Ukraine and the European Union: Day of the Gangster Pygmy." *The Economist*, November 30 to December 6, pp. 13-14. Available at: http://www.economist.com/news/leaders/21590902-why-despite-appearance-defeat-europe-might-have-won-battle-ukraine-day.

Engel, Barbara (2007). "Public Space in the 'Blue Cities' of Russia." In Kiril Stanilov, ed., *The Post-Socialist City: Urban Form and Space Transformation in Central and Eastern Europe after Socialism*. Dordrecht: Springer, pp. 285-300.

Engel, Barbara Alpern (2004). *Women in Russia, 1700-2000*. Cambridge: Cambridge University Press.

Faryna, Oksana (2012a). "A Landmark since 1939 Closes." *Kyiv Post*, February 2.

— (2012b). "A Sneak Peek at the New TsUM." *Kyiv Post*, March 16.

— (2012c). "Kyiv Forest and Journalist are under Threat," *Kyiv Post*, September 26.

Fonseca, Isabel (1995). *Bury Me Standing: The Gypsies and Their Journey*. New York: Vintage.

French, R. Anthony (1984). "Moscow: The Socialist Metropolis." In A. Sutcliffe, ed., *Metropolis 1890-1940*. London: Mansell, pp. 355-379.

— (1995). *Plans, Pragmatism & People: The Legacy of Soviet Planning for Today's Cities*. Pittsburgh, PA: University of Pittsburgh Press.

Frierson, Cathy A. (2010). "Dilemmas of Post-Soviet Identity in Vologda: A Sacred Landscape in Moscow's Political Shadow." In Mark Bassin, Christopher Ely, and Melissa K. Stockdale, eds., *Space, Place, and Power in Modern Russia: Essays in the New Spatial History*. De Kalb: Northern Illinois University Press, pp. 218-242.

Gdaniec, Cordula, ed. (2010). *Cultural Diversity in Russian Cities: The Urban Landscape in the Post-Soviet Era*. New York: Berghahn Books.

Gnap, Dmitry (2010). "Former MP Hoods Arrested and Judged for the Fight against Illegal Construction" (blog post). *Ukrayinska PravdaUkrayinska Pravda*, 15 March. Available at: http://blogs.pravda.com.ua/authors/gnap/4b9e5e3d85ddd/.

Grava, Sigurd (1993). "The Urban Heritage of the Soviet Regime: The Case of Riga, Latvia."*Journal of the American Planning Association*, 59, 1, pp. 9-30.

Graybill, Jessica K., and Megan Dixon (2012). "Cities of Russia." In Stanley D. Brunn, Maureen Hayes-Mitchell, and Donald Ziegler, eds., *Cities of the World: World Regional Development*. 5th ed. Lanham, MD: Rowman & Littlefield, pp. 237-279.

Griffiths, Mark (2013). "Moscow after the Apocalypse." *Slavic Review*, 72, 3, pp. 481-504.

Gross, Jan T. (2001). *Neighbors: The Destruction of the Jewish Community in Jedwabne, Poland*. New York: Penguin.

Grushenko, Kateryna (2011). "Assaults Revive Fears of Racially Motivated Crime." *Kyiv Post*, April 1, p. 11.

Gubar, Oleg, and Patricia Herlihy (2009). "The Persuasive Power of the Odessa Myth." In John Czaplicka, Nida Gelazis, and Blair Ruble, eds., *Cities after the Fall of Communism: Reshaping Cultural Landscapes and European Identity*. Washington, DC: Woodrow Wilson Center Press/Baltimore, MD: The Johns Hopkins University Press, pp. 137-166.

Hamm, Michael F. (1986). "Continuity and Change in Late Imperial Kyiv." In Michael F. Hamm, ed., *The City in Late Imperial Russia*. Bloomington: Indian University Press, pp. 79-121.

— (1993). *Kiev: A Portrait, 1800-1917*. Princeton: Princeton University Press.

Hancock, Ian F. (2002). *We Are the Romani People*. Hertfordshire, UK: University of Hertfordshire Press.

Harvey, David (2012). *Rebel Cities: From the Right to the City to the Urban Revolution*. New York and London: Verso.

Hentosh, Liliana, and Bohdan Tscherkes (2009). "L'viv in Search of Its Identity: Transformations of the City's Public Space" in John Czaplicka, Nida Gelazis, and Blair Ruble, eds., *Cities after the Fall of Communism: Reshaping Cultural Landscapes and European Identity*. Washington, DC: Woodrow Wilson Center Press/Baltimore, MD: The Johns Hopkins University Press, pp. 255-280.

Hewryk, Titus D. (1982). *The Lost Architecture of Kiev*. New York: Ukrainian National Museum.

Himka, John-Paul (2011). "The Lviv Pogrom of 1941: The Germans, Ukrainian Nationalists, and the Carnival Crowd." *Canadian Slavonic Papers*, 53, 2-4, pp. 209-240.

Hirt, Sonia A. (2006). "Post-Socialist Urban Form: Notes from Sofia." *Urban Geography*, 27, pp. 464-488.

— (2007). "Suburbanizing Sofia: Characteristics of Post-Socialist Peri-Urban Change." *Urban Geography*, 28, pp. 755-780.

— (2010). *Iron Curtains: Gates, Suburbs and Privatization of Space in the Post-socialist City*. Malden, MA: Wiley-Blackwell.

Human Rights Watch (2012). "Ukraine: Investigate Brutal Attack on Gay Activist." Human Rights Watch website, June 26. Available at: http://www.hrw.org/news/2012/06/26/ukraine-investigate-brutal-attack-gay-activist.

Humphrey, Caroline (2002). *The Unmaking of Soviet Life: Everyday Economies after Socialism*. Ithaca, NY: Cornell University Press.

— (2007). "New Subjects and Situated Interdependence: After Privatisation in Ulan-Ude." In Catherine Alexander, Victor Buchli, and Caroline Humphrey, eds., *Urban Life in Post-Soviet Asia*. London: University College London Press, pp. 175-207.

Hürelbaatar, Altanhuu (2007). "The Creation and Revitilization of Ethnic Sacred Sites in Ulan-Ude since the 1990s." In Catherine Alexander, Victor Buchli, and Caroline Humphrey, eds., *Urban Life in Post-Soviet Asia*. London: University College London Press, pp. 136-156.

Interfax-Ukraine (2012a). "Businessmen Inform about Regular Seizure Attempts on Luky-anivsky Market." *Kyiv Post*, March 20. Available at: http://www.kyivpost.com/content/kyiv/businessmen-inform-about-regular-seizure-attempts--124585.html.

— (2012b). "ESTA to Invest over $100 Million in Renovating Kyiv's TsUM Department Store." *Kyiv Post*, February 14. Available at: https://www.kyivpost.com/content/kyiv/esta-to-invest-over-100-million-in-renovating-kyiv-122404.html.

Jerusalem Post (2012). "Hatred in Ukraine." *The Jerusalem Post*, November 3. Available at: http://www.jpost.com/Opinion/Editorials/Article.aspx?id=290350.

Jilge, Wilfried (2010). "Cultural Policy as the Politics of History: Independence Square in Kiev." In Alfrun Kliems and Marina Dmitrieva, eds. *The Post-Socialist City: Continuity and Change in Urban Space and Imagery*. Berlin: Jovis Diskurs, pp. 140-155.

Kalfus, Ken (1996). "Far from Normal: Scenes from the New Moscow." *Harper's Magazine*, December, pp. 53-62.

Kalnytskyi, Mykhailo (2012). "Mynule I Maybutne Kyivskoho Hostynoho Dvoru." Istorychna Pravda, June 4, http://www.istpravda.com.ua/articles/2012/06/1/87831.

Kis, Oksana (2005). "Who Is Protected by Berehynia, or Matriarchy as a Men's Invention." *Zerkalo Nedeli*, April 26 to May 6.

Kliems, Alfrun and Marina Dmitrieva, eds. (2010). *The Post-Socialist City: Continuity and Change in Urban Space and Imagery*. Berlin: Jovis Diskurs.

Kolasky, John, ed. and trans. (1974). *Report from the Beria Reserve: The Protest Writings of Valentyn Moroz*. Chicago: Cataract Press.

Kolin'ko, V. V., and H. K. Kurovskyi (2010). *Kyiv: Sviaschennyi Prostir.* Kyiv: Kyivska Landshaftna Initsiyatyva.

Kolossov, Vladimir, and John O'Loughlin (2004). "How Moscow Is Becoming a Capitalist Mega-City." *International Social Science Journal,* 56, 181, pp. 413-427.

—, Olga Vendina, and John O'Loughlin (2002). "Moscow as an Emergent World City: International Links, Business Developments, and the Entrepreneurial City." *Eurasian Geography & Economics,* 43, 3, pp. 170-197.

Korrespondent (2012). "Regionnaire about High Speed: 'We Were Trying to See How Fast It Was Possible to Travel.'" *Korrespondent,* 23 July. Available at: http://ua.korrespondent.net/ukraine/politics/1375130-regional-pro-veliku-shvidkist-mi-probuvali-naskilki-shvidko-mozhna-rozignatisya.

Kotkin, Stephen (1992). *Steeltown USSR: Soviet Society in the Gorbachev Era.* Berkeley and Los Angeles: University of California Press.

— (1995). *Magnetic Mountain: Stalinism as a Civilization.* Berkeley and Los Angeles: University of California Press.

Kovalinskiy, Vitaliy (2004). *Kyivski Miniatyury, Volume 3.* Kyiv: Kupola.

— (2005). *Kyivski Miniatyury, Volume 4.* Kyiv: Kupola.

Kozmina, Anna (2000). "Of Men and Buildings." *Kyiv Post,* Octpber 26, http://www.kyivpost.com/guide/all/of-men-and-buildings-5539.html?flavour=mobile.

Kramar, Oleksandr (2012). "Russification via Bilingualism." *The Ukrainian Week,* 6, 29, April, pp. 28-29.

Krasnohorodsky, Oleksandr (2012). "A War with Kiosks." *The Ukrainian Week,* 7, 30, May, pp. 16-17.

Kravchenko, Volodymyr (2009). "Kharkiv: A Borderland City." In John Czaplicka, Nida Gelazis, and Blair Ruble, eds., *Cities after the Fall of Communism: Reshaping Cultural Landscapes and European Identity.* Washington, DC: Woodrow Wilson Center Press/Baltimore, MD: The Johns Hopkins University Press, pp. 219-254.

Kravets, Anna, and Nazariy Sovsun (2011). "Pravo na Kontraktovy." In Ksenia Dmytrenko, ed., *Stratehiyi urbanistychoho maybutnoho Kyeva.* Kyiv: Heinrich Böll Stiftung, pp. 79-84.

— (2012). Kultura pobutu v okremomu raioni." In A. Makarenko et al., eds., *Anatomiya Mista: Kyiv.* Kyiv: Heinrich Böll Stiftung – Smoloskyp, pp. 100-107.

Kudrytskyi, A. V., ed. (1982). *Kyiv: Istorychnyi Ohlyad (Karty, Ilyustratsii, Dokumenty).* Kyiv: Holovna Redaktsiya Ukrainskoi Radyanskoi Entsyklopedii.

Kurus, I., et al., eds. (2010). *Putivnyk Kyiv.* Kyiv: Vsia Ukraina.

Kuzio, Taras, and Andrew Wilson (1994). *Ukraine: Perestroika to Independence.* New York: St. Martin's Press.

Kyiv Post (2007). "Surge in Roadway Accidents Detected." *Kyiv Post,* September 19. Available at: http://www.kyivpost.com/content/ukraine/surge-in-roadway-accidents-detected-27393.html.

— (2011). "Ukrainian Weather Woman Creates a storm." *Kyiv Post,* May 18. Available at: http://www.kyivpost.com/content/ukraine/ukrainian-weather-woman-creates-a-storm-104685.html.

Kyiv Urban Design Studio (2006). *Kyiv: Reconsidering the Dnipro.* Cambridge: Massachusetts Institute of Technology Urban Design Studio.

Lazareva, Alla (2010). "Mizh dvokh svitiv." *Ukrainskyi Tyzhden,* 44, 157, pp. 56-57.

Lebedeva, Maria (2012). "A u tsei chas v Hostynomu Dvori." *Ukrayinska Pravda,* June 20. Available at: http://kiev.pravda.com.ua/columns/4fe192be8a7b0/view_print/.

Liégeois, Jean-Pierre (1983). *Gypsies: An Illustrated History.* London: Saqi Books.

Makarenko, A., et al., eds. (2012). *Anatomiya Mista: Kyiv*. Kyiv: Heinrich Böll Stiftung – Smoloskyp.

Makhrova, Alla, and Irina Molodikova (2007). "Land Market, Commercial Real Estate, and the Remolding of Moscow's Urban Fabric." In Kiril Stanilov, ed., *The Post-Socialist City: Urban Form and Space Transformation in Central and Eastern Europe after Socialism*. Dordrecht: Springer, pp. 101-116.

Maksymenko, Olena and Nastia Melnychenko (2012). "Will Andriyivsky Uzviz Disappear?" The Ukrainioan Week, 6 (29), April, pp. 4-5.

Malakov, Dmytro (2009). *Kyiv 1939-1945 Post scriptum: Fotoalbom*. Kyiv: Varto.

— (2010). *Kyiany, Viyna, Nimtsi*. Kyiv: Amadei.

— (2011). *U Kyevi 50-kh*. Kyiv: Varto.

— (2013). *Povoyennya: Spohady Kyyanyna*. Kyiv: Varto.

Males, Lyudmyla, et al., eds. (2010). *Sotsiolohiya Mista: Navchalnyi Posibnyk*. Donetsk: Noulidzh.

Malikenaite, Ruta, ed. (2002). *Touring Kyiv: Guidebook*. Kyiv: Baltija Dryk.

Manzanova, Galina (2007). "City of Migrants: Contemporary Ulan-Ude in the Context of Russian Migration." In Catherine Alexander, Victor Buchli, and Caroline Humphrey, eds., *Urban Life in Post-Soviet Asia*. London: University College London Press, pp. 125-135.

Markulevich, Valeriyi (2010). "Dmitriyi Tabachnik – Korol 'Falshakov'." http://sprotiv. org/2010/02/04/dmitrij-tabachnik-korol-falshakov/#.

Matiukhina, Natalka (2012). "Ukraina homofobska: Mif chy diysnist?" *BBC Ukraine*. Available at: http://www.bbc.co.uk/ukrainian/entertainment/2012/08/120824_ukraine_homopho-bia_it.shtml.

Mayerchyk, Maria, and Olha Plahotnik (2011). "Radykalni 'FEMEN' i novi zhinochyi aktivizm." *Krytyka*, 1-2, 156-160, pp. 7-9.

Medvedkov, Yuri, and Olga Medvedkov (2007). "Upscale Housing in Post-Soviet Moscow and Its Environs." In Kiril Stanilov, ed., *The Post-Socialist City: Urban Form and Space Transformation in Central and Eastern Europe after Socialism*. Dordrecht: Springer, pp. 245-265.

Meir, Natan M. (2010). *Kiev: Jewish Metropolis: A History, 1859-1914*. Bloomington: Indiana University Press.

Michlic, Joanna (2009). "Łódź in the Postcommunist Era: In Search of a New Identity." In John Czaplicka, Nida Gelazis, and Blair Ruble, eds., *Cities after the Fall of Communism: Reshaping Cultural Landscapes and European Identity*. Washington, DC: Woodrow Wilson Center Press/ Baltimore, MD: The Johns Hopkins University Press, pp. 281-304.

Mikheyeva, Oksana (2010). "Derzhavna ideolohiya ta konstruktuyuvannya spilnoi pam'yati pro mynule: orhanizovane zabuttya ta fenomen pryhaduvannya (na prykladi pam'yatnykiv Donetska)." In Lyudmyla

Mirsky, Rudolf (1994). "Antisemitism in Post-Soviet Ukraine." *East European Jewish Affairs*, 34, 2, pp. 141-146.

Molodikova, Irina, and Alla Makhrova (2007). "Urbanization Patterns in Russia in the Post-Soviet Era." In Kiril Stanilov, ed., *The Post-Socialist City: Urban Form and Space Transformation in Central and Eastern Europe after Socialism*. Dordrecht: Springer, pp. 21-34.

Motyl, Alexander J. (2011a). "Finding Ukrainian President Yanukovych's Book." *World Affairs Journal*, 10 November. Available at: http://www.worldaffairsjournal.org/blog/alexander-j-motyl/finding-ukrainian-president-yanukovych%E2%80%99s-book.

— (2011b). "Ukrainians and Jews and Ukrainians and Jews and…" *World Affairs Journal*, 15 April 2011. Available at: http://www.worldaffairsjournal.org/blog/alexander-j-motyl/ukrainians-and-jews-and-ukrainians-and-jews-and-%E2%80%A6.

— (2013). "Misrepresenting History at the Kyiv Museum." *Kyiv Post*, July 30.

Moussienko, Natalia (2009a). "Kyiv u konteksti zabudovnykh viyn XXI stolittia: Case Study –
Metro Teatralna, 2005-2009." In A. O. Puchkov et al., eds., *Suchasni problemy doslidzhennia,
restavratsii ta zberezhennia kulturnoi spadshchyny*. Kyiv: Khimdzhest, pp. 149-162.
— (2009b). "Zabudovni viyny v Kyevi: stanovlennya demokratii chy systemna kryza vlady?"
In Yaroslav Pylynskyi, ed., *Agora: Misto yak chynnyk demokkratychnoho rozvytku Ukrainy,
Vypusk 9*. Kyiv: Stylos, pp. 98-111.
— (2013). *Kyiv Art Space*. Kennan Institute Occasional Paper Series no. 309. Washington, DC:
Woodrow Wilson International Center for Scholars. Available at: http://www.wilsoncenter.
org/publication/kyiv-art-space-2013.
Musekamp, Jan (2009). "Szczecin's Identity after 1989: A Local Turn." In John Czaplicka, Nida
Gelazis, and Blair Ruble, eds., *Cities after the Fall of Communism: Reshaping Cultural Land-
scapes and European Identity*. Washington, DC: Woodrow Wilson Center Press/Baltimore,
MD: The Johns Hopkins University Press, pp. 305-334.
Mykhelson, Oleksandr (2010). "'Yolka' yak instrument rezhymu." *Tyzhden* 50, 163, December
10-16, pp. 10-11.
— and Ruslana Velychko (2013). "Thugs for Hire." *The Ukrainian Week*, 10, 52, pp. 10-11.

Nae, Marina, and David Turnock (2011). "The New Bucharest: Two Decades of Restructuring."
Cities: The International Journal of Urban Policy and Planning, 28, pp. 206-219.
Nasyrova, Olena, Volodymyr Nevzorov, and Volodymyr Kruchynin, eds. (2008). *Kyiv 1943-1970:
Fotoalbom*. Kyiv: Sky Horse.
Naterer, Andrej, and Vesna V. Godina (2011). "*Bomzhi* and Their Subculture: An Anthropological
Study of the Street Children Subculture in Makeevka, Eastern Ukraine." *Childhood*, 18, 1,
pp. 20-38.
Neufeld, Dialika (2012). "The Body Politic: Getting Naked to Change the World." *Der Spiegel*, May
5. Available at: http://www.spiegel.de/international/europe/femen-activists-get-naked-to-
raise-political-awareness-a-832028.html.
Nieczypor, Krzystof (2011). "Ukraine: Did President Yanukovych Threaten a Journalist?" *EastBook.
eu*, December 30, http://eastbook.eu/en/2011/12/uncategorized-en/ukraine-president-
yanukovych-threatened-a-journalist/.
Nigmatullina, Liliya (2010). *Tatar National and Religious Revitalization in Post-Soviet Kazan,
Republic of Tatarstan*, MA thesis, Geography and Urban Studies, Temple University, Philadelphia, PA."No Language – No Ukraine" (2012). *The Ukrainian Week,* 9 (32), June, front cover.

Oleshko, Olesia (2010). "Lenin Stands Tall And Guarded." *Kyiv Post*, June 17. Available at: http://
www.kyivpost.com/content/ukraine/lenin-stands-tall-and-guarded-70078.html.
Oslamovskyi, Yuriy, Tatiana Lytvynenko, and Oleksandr Zayika, eds. (2013). *Kyiv Zhyvopysnyi/
Kyiv Pictorial*. Kyiv: Novyi Druk.
Osmak, Vladyslava (2011). "Andreyevskiyi Spusk: Genius Loci za Zaborom." *Obyekt*, no. 15,
November-December, pp. 94-95.

Pagonis, Thanos, and Andy Thornley (2000). "Urban Development Projects in Moscow: Market/
State Relations in the New Russia." *European Planning Studies*, 8, 6, pp. 751-766.
Panova, Kateryna (2011). "Faking It with Impunity Is Way of Doing Business." *Kyiv Post*, March
11. Available at: https://www.kyivpost.com/content/business/faking-it-with-impunity-is-
way-of-doing-business-99510.html.
Parfan, Nadiya (2010). *Kyiv Graffiti: Production of Space in a Post-Soviet City*. MA thesis, Sociology
and Social Anthropology, Central European University, Budapest, Hungary.

— (2012). "Kraina pryrechenykh narechenykh: Polovi notatky zseredyny sliubnoho biznesu."
    Politychna Krytyka, 3, pp. 102-105.
Pavlychko, Solomea (1992). *Letters from Kiev.* Trans. Myrna Kostash. New York: St. Martin's Press.
Pojani, Dorina (2009). "Urbanization of Post-Communist Albania: Economic, Social, and
    Environmental Challenges." *Journal of Contemporary Eastern Europe*, 17, 1, pp. 85-97.
— (2010). "Tirana." *Cities: The International Journal of Urban Policy and Planning*, 27, pp. 483-495.
Portnov, Andriy (2010). "'Batkivshchyna-maty' versus Stepan Bandera: Ekskursiya vybranymy
    pamyatnykamy druhoi svitovoi viyny." In Lyudmyla Males et al., eds., *Sotsiolohiya Mista:
    Navchalnyi Posibnyk*. Donetsk: Noulidzh, pp. 305-316.
Potichnyj, Peter J., and Howard Aster, eds. (1990). *Ukrainian-Jewish Relations in Historical
    Perspective*. Edmonton: Canadian Institute of Ukrainian Studies Press.
Press Association (2009). "Latvia Runs Out of Patience with Boozy British Tourists." *The Guard-
    ian*, 5 August. Available at: http://www.theguardian.com/world/2009/aug/05/british-tourists-
    riga-latvia.

Radynski, Oleksiy (2010). "Kyivski mistsia transformatsii." *Spilne: Zhurnal Sotsialnoi Krytyky*,
    2, pp. 86-93.
Redlich, Shimon (2002). *Together and Apart in Brzezany: Poles, Jews, and Ukrainians, 1919-1945*.
    Bloomington: Indian University Press.
Reid, Anna (2000). *Borderland: A Journey through the History of Ukraine*. Boulder, CO: Westview
    Press.
Riabchuk, Mykola (2012). "Like Fathers, Like Sons." *The Ukrainian Weekly*, 80, 16, April 15, pp. 1-2.
Riaboshapka, Vitalii (1998). "S segodniashnego dnia Troeshchinskii rynok prekrashchaet rabotu:
    Torgovtsy otkazyvaiutsia pisat' zaiavleniia o poborakh." *Kievskie Vedomosti*, August 13, 1998.
Richardson, Tanya (2008). *Kaleidoscopic Odessa: History and Place in Contemporary Ukraine*.
    Toronto: University of Toronto Press.
RISU (2012). "Gay Pride Parade in Kyiv Cancelled." Religious Information Service of Ukraine web-
    site, 23 May. Available at: http://risu.org.ua/en/index/all_news/community/protests/48204/.
Rossman, Vadim (2013). "In Search of the Fourth Rome: Visions of a New Russian Capital City."
    Slavic Review, 2, 3, pp. 505-527.
Round, John, and Colin Williams (2010). "Coping with the Costs of 'Transition': Everyday Life
    in Post-Soviet Russia and Ukraine." *European Urban and Regional Studies*, 17, 2, pp. 183-196.
Rubchak, Marian J. (2001). "In Search of a Model: Evolution of a Feminist Consciousness in
    Ukraine and Russia," *European Journal of Women's Studies*, 8, 2, pp. 149-160.
—, ed. (2011). *Mapping Difference: The Many Faces of Women in Contemporary Ukraine*. New
    York and Oxford: Berghahn Books.
Ruble, Blair A. (1995). *Money Sings: The Changing Politics of Urban Space in Post-Soviet Yaroslavl*.
    Cambridge: The Press Syndicate of the University of Cambridge.
— (2003). "Kyiv's Troyeshchyna: An Emerging International Migrant Neighborhood." *Nationali-
    ties Papers*, 31, 2, pp. 139-155.
Rudenko, Olga (2012). "Gang Rape, Attempted Murder Outrage Ukraine." *Kyiv Post*, March 16.
    Available at: http://www.kyivpost.com/news/nation/detail/124367/.
Rudling, Per Anders (2006). "Organized Anti-Semitism in Contemporary Ukraine: Structure,
    Influence and Ideology." *Canadian Slavonic Papers*, 48, 1/2, pp. 81-118.
Ryabchuk, Anastasiya (2007). "Work 'in the Shadow': The Experiences of Homelessness among
    Casual Workers in the Construction Industry." *Naukovi Zapysky: Sotsiolohichni Nauky*, 70,
    pp. 72-76.

— (2010). "Ruinuvannya Povsyadennosti: Fotoreportazh z Budynku na Holosivskii." *Spilne: Zhurnal Sotsialnoi Krytyky*, 2, pp. 32-45.

Sarajeva, Katja (2010). "'You Know What Kind of Place This Is, Don't You?' An Exploration of Lesbian Spaces in Moscow." In Cordula Gdaniec, ed., *Cultural Diversity in Russian Cities: The Urban Landscape in the Post-Soviet Era*. New York: Berghahn Books, chapter 7.

Scattone, Maria (2010). "Begging as Economic Practice: Urban Niches in Central St. Petersburg." In Cordula Gdaniec, ed., *Cultural Diversity in Russian Cities: The Urban Landscape in the Post-Soviet Era*. New York: Berghahn Books, chapter 8.

Sereda, Viktoriya (2010). "Analiz protsesiv symvolichnoho markuvannya miskoho prostoru na prykladi polityky pam'yati m. Lvova." In Lyudmyla Males et al., eds., *Sotsiolohiya Mista: Navchalnyi Posibnyk*. Donetsk: Noulidzh, pp. 293-304.

Shcherbak, Iurii (1989). *Chernobyl: A Documentary History*. Trans. Ian Press. Houndmills, UK: Macmillan.

Shevchenko, Daryna (2012). "Ghost Town Revisted." *Kyiv Post*, August 3, http://www.kyivpost. com/multimedia/photo/ghost-town-revisited-2-311003.html.

Shevchenko, Oleksandra (2011). "Na FEMEN zdiysnena reydersa ataka! Klyati Moskali! Pershiy post bez tsytsok" (blog post). *Ukrayinska Pravda*, May 28. Available at: http://blogs.pravda. com.ua/authors/femen/4db9723c85278/.

Shevchenko, Olga (2009). *Crisis and the Everyday in Postsocialist Moscow*. Bloomington: Indiana University Press.

Shlipchenko, Svitlana (2009). "'URBANOPHILIA': Try istorii odnoho mista." In Yaroslav Pylyn-skyi, ed., *Agora: Misto yak chynnyk demokkratychnoho rozvytku Ukrainy, Vypusk 9*. Kyiv: Stylos, pp. 30-43.

— (2011). "Simply Difficult. Kontraktova: 'Ploshcha i misto chy ploshcha u misti?'" In Ksenia Dmytrenko, ed., *Stratehiyi urbanistychoho maybutnoho Kyeva*. Kyiv: Heinrich Böll Stiftung, pp. 57-78.

Shlonskyi, Dmytro, and Oleksiy Braslavets (2008). *Andriyivskyi Uzviz: Yoho Istoriya I Putivnyk po Muzeyu Odnieyi Vulytsi*. Kyiv: Tsentr Evropy.

Shulkevych, M. M., and T. D. Dmytrenko (1982). *Kiev: Arkhitekturno-istoricheskiy ocherk*. Kyiv: Budivelnyk.

Sidorov, Dmitri (2000). "National Monumentalization and the Politics of Scale: The Resurrections of the Cathedral of Christ the Savior in Moscow." *Annals of the Association of American Geographers*, 90, 3, pp. 548-572.

Skibitska, Tetyana (2011). *Kyivskyi arkhitekturnyi modern (1900-1910i roky)*. L'viv and Kyiv: Tsentr Evropy.

Skubytska, Iulia (2012). "Chuzhyi' spal'nyi raion." In A. Makarenko, et al., eds., *Anatomiya Mista: Kyiv*. Kyiv: Heinrich Böll Stiftung – Smoloskyp, pp. 78-88.

Snyder, Timothy (2010). *Bloodlands: Europe between Hitler and Stalin*. New York: Basic Books.

Soroka, Yulia (2010). "Vid Zhdanova do Mariupola" Pytannya pereimenuvannya mista v pub-likatsiyakh mistsevoi presy." In Lyudmyla Males et al., eds., *Sotsiolohiya Mista: Navchalnyi Posibnyk*. Donetsk: Noulidzh, pp. 329-354.

— (2011). "Hola svoboda i tila na drabyni." *Krytyka*, 1-2, 156-160, p. 17.

Stack, Graham (2010). "Ghost Town." *Kyiv Post*, July 9, http://www.kyivpost.com/content/ukraine/ ghost-town-72769.html.

Staddon, Caedmon, and Bellin Molov (2000). "Sofia, Bulgaria." *Cities: The International Journal of Urban Policy and Planning*, 17, 5, pp. 379-387.

Stampfer, Shaul (2003). "What Actually Happened to the Jews of Ukraine in 1648?" *Jewish History*, 17, 2, pp. 207-227.

Stanilov, Kiril, ed. (2007a). *The Post-Socialist City: Urban Form and Space Transformation in Central and Eastern Europe after Socialism*. Dordrecht: Springer.

— (2007b). "The Restructuring of Non-Residential Uses in the Post-Socialist Metropolis." In Kiril Stanilov, ed., *The Post-Socialist City: Urban Form and Space Transformation in Central and Eastern Europe after Socialism*. Dordrecht: Springer, pp. 73-100.

Starr, Terrell (2010). "Blacks in Ukraine." *The Crisis Magazine*, Summer, pp. 21-23.

Stella, Francesca (2013). "Queer Space, Pride, and Shame in Moscow." *Slavic Review*, 72, 3, pp. 458-480.

Subtelny, Orest (1988). *Ukraine: A History*. Toronto: University of Toronto Press.

Suma, Stefania (2010). "Stadio a Dontesk, Ucraina." *Industria delle Costruzioni*, 44, 413 (May), pp. 64-71.

Sýkora, Luděk, and Stefan Bouzarovski (2012). "Multiple Transformations: Conceptualizing the Post-Communist Urban Transition." *Urban Studies*, 49, 1, pp. 43-60.

Sysyn, Frank E. (1988). "The Jewish Factor in the Khmelnytskyi Uprising." In Peter J. Potichnyj and Howard Aster, eds., *Ukrainian-Jewish Relations in Historical Perspective*. Edmonton: Canadian Institute of Ukrainian Studies.

— (2003). "The Khmel'Nyts'kyi Uprising: A Characterization of the Ukrainian Revolt." *Jewish History*, 17, 2, pp. 115-139.

Thum, Gregor (2009). "Wrocław's Search for New Historical Narrative: From Polonocentrism to Postmodernism." In John Czaplicka, Nida Gelazis, and Blair Ruble, eds., *Cities after the Fall of Communism: Reshaping Cultural Landscapes and European Identity*. Washington, DC: Woodrow Wilson Center Press/Baltimore, MD: The Johns Hopkins University Press, pp. 75-101.

Tölle, Alexander (2008). "Gdańsk." *Cities: The International Journal of Urban Policy and Planning*, 25, pp. 107-119.

Tomlinson, Simon, et al. (2012). "Ukrainian Teen Who Posted Harrowing Hospital Bed Video Describing How She Was Gang-Raped and Set on Fire Dies from Her Injuries." *Daily Mail*, 29 March. Available at: http://www.dailymail.co.uk/news/article-2122091/Oksana-Makar-dead-Ukranian-teen-posted-video-describing-gang-rape-dies-injuries.html.

Tret'yakov, Arkadiyi (2013). *Bessarabskaya Ploshchad'*. Kyiv: Imidzh Print.

Tsalyk, Stanislav (2012). *Kiev konspekt 70-kh: Rasskazi o povsednevnoy zhizni goroda i gorozhan*. Kyiv: Varto.

Tsentr Doslidzennya Suspilstva (2011). *Protesty, peremohy I represiyi v Ukraiini: Rezultaty monitoringu, zhovten 2009 – veresen 2010*. Kyiv: Tsentr Doslidzennya Suspilstva.

TSN (2012). http://tsn.ua/ukrayina/u-kiyevi-nevidomi-vlashtuvali-strilyaninu-i-spalili-tabir-cigan.html.

Tuchynska, Svitlana (2010). "Police Hassle Merchants at Troyeshchyna Market; Racism, Corruption Seen." *Kyiv Post*, November 5. Available at: http://www.kyivpost.com/content/ukraine/police-hassle-merchants-at-troyeshchyna-market-rac-88819.html.

— (2012a). "Authorities Demolish Shulayvska Metro Flea Market." *Kyiv Post*, March 16. Available at: http://www.kyivpost.com/content/kyiv/authorities-demolish-shulayvska-metro-flea-market-124396.html.

— (2012b). "Violence against Gays in Ukraine Captured for the Whole World to See." *Kyiv Post*, May 24. Available at: http://www.kyivpost.com/content/ukraine/violence-against-gays-in-ukraine-captured-for-whol-1-128231.html.

— (2012c). "Gays Attacked during Human Rights March, Six Detained." *Kyiv Post*, December 10. Available at: http://www.kyivpost.com/multimedia/photo/gays-attacked-during-human-rights-march-six-detained-2-317426.html.

— (2012d). "'Sabbath of Perverts': Svoboda Boasts of Attacking Gay Demonstration." *Kyiv Post*, December 11. Available at: http://www.kyivpost.com/content/ukraine/sabbath-of-perverts-svoboda-boasts-of-attacking-gay-demonstration-317463.html.

— (2013). "Journalist Goes to European Court to Demand Information on President's Mansion." *Kyiv Post*, February 20. Available at: http://www.kyivpost.com/content/ukraine/journalist-demands-information-on-presidents-mansion-in-european-court-320686.html.

Tyshchenko, Ihor (2012a). "Khronika Andriiyvskoho Uzvozu: istoriya borotby za odnu vulytsyu." In A. Makarenko et al., eds., *Anatomiya Mista: Kyiv*. Kyiv: Heinrich Böll Stiftung – Smoloskyp, pp. 160-184.

— (2012b). "Vynohradar: nezavershenyi ansambl'." In A. Makarenko et al., eds., *Anatomiya Mista: Kyiv*. Kyiv: Heinrich Böll Stiftung – Smoloskyp, pp. 89-99.

Ukrainian Catholic University (2010). "An Appeal by the Ukrainian Catholic University Administration to the Education Community of Ukraine." *Kyiv Post*, March 17. Available at: http://www.kyivpost.com/opinion/op-ed/an-appeal-by-the-ukrainian-catholic-university-adm-61912.html.

Ukrayinska Pravda (2012). "Luk'yanov Drives Again at an illegal Speed, This Time with Journalists." *Ukrayinska Pravda*, July 30. Available at: http://www.pravda.com.ua/photo-video/2012/07/30/6969811/.

Van Assche, Kristof, and Joseph Salukvadze (2012). "Tbilisi Reinvented: Planning, Development, and the Unfinished Project of Democracy in Georgia." *Planning Perspectives*, 27, 1, pp. 1-24.

—, Joseph Salukvadze, and Nick Shavishvili, eds. (2009). *City Culture and City Planning in Tbilisi: Where Europe and Asia Meet*. Lewiston, NY: The Edwin Mellen Press.

Verbov, Oleksiy (2010). "Park konfliktiv: Borotba v lisoparku yak dzerkalo Kharkivskoi hromady." *Spilne: Zhurnal Sotsialnoi Krytyky*, 2, pp. 96-101.

Vernadsky, George (1941). *Bohdan, Hetman of Ukraine*. New Haven, CT: Yale University Press.

Wanner, Catherine (1998). *Burden of Dreams: History and Identity in Post-Soviet Ukraine*. University Park: The Pennsylvania State University Press.

Wilson, Andrew (2000). *The Ukrainians: The Unexpected Nation*. New Haven, CT: Yale University Press.

Yanukovych, Viktor (2011). *Opportunity Ukraine*. Wein: Mandelbaum Verlag.

Yekelchyk, Serhy (2007). *Ukraine: Birth of a Modern Nation*. New York: Oxford University Press.

Yerofalov-Pylypchak, Boris (2010). *Arkhitektura Sovetskogo Kieva*. Kyiv: Izadelskiy Dom A+C.

Yevtushenko, Yevgeny (1998). "Babi Yar." Translated by Ben Okopnik. Available at: http://www.ess.uwe.ac.uk/genocide/yevtushenko.htm.

Zavhorodnya, Inna (2010). "Nezruchni susidy." *Ukrainskyi Tyzhden*, 44, 157, pp. 60-61.

Zawada, Zenon (2013). "Developers Target Historic District in Kyiv, Drawing Public Protests." *The Ukrainian Weekly*, 81, 11, March 17, pp. 1 and 3.

Zychowicz, Jessica (2011). "Two Bad Words: FEMEN and Feminism in Independent Ukraine." *The Anthropology of East Europe Review*, 29, 2, pp. 215-227.

Index

Moskovskyi Bridge 146
Moussienko, Natalia 44, 63, 292, 297
Museum of Corruption (idea) 63
Museum of Soviet Occupation 35
Mykolaiv 215-17

National Art Museum of Ukraine 154
National Museum of Ukrainian History 67
National University of Kyiv Mohyla Acad-
    emy 29, 41, 109, 148, 151, 182, 186, 296, 299,
    306, 317
Nayem, Mustafa 95-97
Nebesna Sotnya 17, 330
"New Jerusalem" 78, 151
Nyzhni Sovky 256-257

Obolon 117, 146, 187, 263, 267-268, 291
    churches in 146
Ocean Plaza Mall 263
Old City *see* Stare Misto
Olympic Stadium 72
Opera Theater 60-61, 152, 189, 198, 325
Orange Revolution 83-84, 90, 106, 111-113, 124,
    167-168, 186, 295
Orobets, Lesya 331
Orlyka (street) 55-56, 64, 102, 152-153
Osmak, Vladislava 180-181, 204, 297
Osokorky 266-267

parking problems 34, 53, 184-187, 210, 260
parks *see* individual parks by name
Park of Glory *see* Park Slavy
Park Slavy 132, 291
Parliament *see* Verkhovna Rada
Party of Regions 17-18, 32, 41, 43, 65, 83, 86, 88,
    90, 92, 105, 168, 173, 212-213, 216, 245, 272, 333
    staged gatherings by 105-109, 110-117,
        118-122, 168, 298
Patriarchal Ukrainian Catholic Cathedral of
    the Resurrection of Christ 51-52, 146
Pecherska Lavra 27, 55, 96, 133, 140, 151, 190, 223
People's Friendship Arch 75-76
People's Movement of Ukraine Party 293
petty traders 171, 220, 223, 228-234, 249
Petrivka Metro Station 235
Peyzazhna Aleya 67, 301, 303-304
Pinchuk Art Center 195
Pinchuk, Viktor 72, 271
place names *see* toponymy
planning *see* city planning
Pochayna River 187
Podil 27, 68-70, 75, 144, 151, 175, 178-179, 182-187,
    237, 282, 297, 300, 305, 307-309, 326
police 47, 62, 74, 81-82, 94-95, 104, 112-113,
    116, 120-121, 125-127, 168, 170, 207, 210, 212,
    229-234, 236-237, 239, 240-243, 246, 250, 283,
    287, 308-309, 313-315, 329-330
Polish population 111
Politkovskaya, Anna 125
Popov, Oleksandr 62, 63, 88-89, 98, 330

population trends 29-30, 31, 33-34
Poshtova Ploshcha 184-185
Post Office Square *see* Poshtova Ploshcha
postsocialist city 50-53
Pozniaky 315-318
Premier Palace Hotel 197
press freedoms *see* journalists
Prospekt Peremohy (street) 132, 291
protests 40-43, 112, 211, 292, 295-298; *see also*
    Euromaidan; Orange Revolution
    anti-development 61-63, 292-293, 298-300,
        301-310, 312
    by FEMEN 37-38, 44, 284-289
    economic issues 105-106, 167-169
    language issues 109-117
Pshonka, Viktor 331, 333
Putin, Vladimir 17, 80, 122, 145, 180, 286

racism 240, 242-243, 296
raiding (the taking-over of real estate or
    institutions) *see Reyderstvo*
reconstruction of Kyiv after World War II 156-
    157, 163
religion 52, 67, 139, 144-149, 179, 334
reyderstvo 58-60, 63, 121, 190, 236, 303, 309,
    324, 334
Roma 137, 171, 200, 221, 247-251
Rukh *see* People's Movement of Ukraine Party
Russian Orthodox Church 80, 83, 130, 164, 289
Rus 28, 64, 78-80, 104, 151, 153, 164, 178-179, 334
Rusnivski Sady 256
Rybalskyi Ostriv 187, 283
Rye Market *see* Zhytnyi Rynok

Sahaidachnoho (street) 185-186
Samson and the Lion statue 306
Savchenko, Lyudmyla 42-43
Save Old Kyiv 162, 297, 301-304, 307-309, 312,
    331, 334
SBU (Security Service of Ukraine) 123, 127
security guards 55, 97, 99, 194, 196-200, 207,
    240, 313
sex tourism 272, 276-279, 285, 296
Shchusev, Alexey 173
Shevchenko, Taras 111, 164, 184, 319, 325
    statue of 169
Sholem Aleichem 192, 195
Sholem Aleichem Museum 192
Sholudenko, Nikifor 157
shopping malls 163-165, 260-264
Shulyavska Market 238-242
Shulyavska Metro Station 238, 242
Sofiivska Ploshcha 118, 175, 198
Soviet city 43, 52-53, 253
Sovsun, Inna 162
Stalin, Joseph 32, 50, 101, 129, 136, 140, 145, 176, 291
Stare Misto 27, 151, 160, 177-178, 306
Stepanenko, Daria 41-42, 111, 272
St. Andrew's Church 67-68, 79-80, 175, 179,
    185, 246